The World-Famous ALASKA HIGHWAY

A GUIDE TO THE ALCAN
& OTHER WILDERNESS ROADS OF THE NORTH

3rd Edition

TRICIA BROWN

Alaska Northwest Books®
Anchorage • Portland

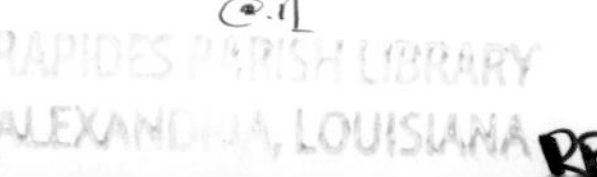

For LWS I, at rest in Fairbanks

The World-Famous Alaska Highway provides many safety tips about weather and travel, but good decision-making and sound judgment are the responsibility of the individual. Neither the publisher nor the author assumes any liability for injury that may arise from the use of this book.

Library of Congress Cataloging-in-Publication Data

Brown, Tricia.
The world-famous Alaska highway : a guide to the Alcan & other wilderness roads of the North / Tricia Brown. — 3rd ed.
p. cm.
Includes bibliographical references and index.
ISBN 978-0-88240-730-2 (softbound : alk. paper) 1. Alaska Highway—Guidebooks. 2. Automobile travel—Northwest, Canadian—Guidebooks. 3. Automobile travel—Alaska—Guidebooks. 4. Wilderness areas—Northwest, Canadian—Guidebooks. 5. Wilderness areas—Alaska—Guidebooks. 6. Northwest, Canadian—Guidebooks. 7. Alaska Guidebooks. I. Title.

F1060.92.B79 2008
917.9804'52—dc22 2007051441

COVER IMAGES—*Front:* Wending through northern B.C. on the Alaska Highway. *Bottom, from left:* Canada's Folded Mountain; Iditarod sled dog hopefuls; Matanuska River, Alaska. *Back cover, from left:* Mile 0 sign, Dawson Creek, B.C.; Interior Alaska gold nuggets; Watson Lake (B.C.) Signpost Forest; Mount McKinley, North America's tallest peak.

Alaska Northwest Books®
An imprint of Graphic Arts Center Publishing Co.
P.O. Box 10306
Portland, OR 97296-0306
(503) 226-2402 * www.gacpc.com

President: Charles M. Hopkins
General Manager: Douglas A. Pfeiffer
Associate Publisher, Alaska Northwest Books: Sara Juday
Editorial Staff: Timothy W. Frew, Kathy Howard, Jean Andrews, Jean Bond-Slaughter
Production Coordinator: Susan Dupèré
Design: Constance Bollen
Maps: Gray Mouse Graphics

Printed in China

Acknowledgments

Thank you, Perry, my wonderful husband, driver, and travel partner. Special thanks to Bob Calderone and the rest of the folks at Cruise America, who helped make our road trips exceptionally comfortable. Thanks also to my friends at Alaska Northwest Books® for agreeing that travelers needed a book like this one, a personal voice with uncomplicated travel directions and friendly advice. And thanks to Marlene Blessing, for getting me started.

Every time I drive the highway, I'm impressed by the people who work in the travel industry throughout western Canada and Alaska. For so many motorists, this trip is a once-in-a-lifetime experience, and your enthusiasm for the place where you live makes the travel experience even better. Thank you, one and all.

On clear days, North America's tallest mountain, Mount McKinley—or Denali, as it's also known—is visible from a paved pullout at Mile 135 on the Parks Highway.

Contents

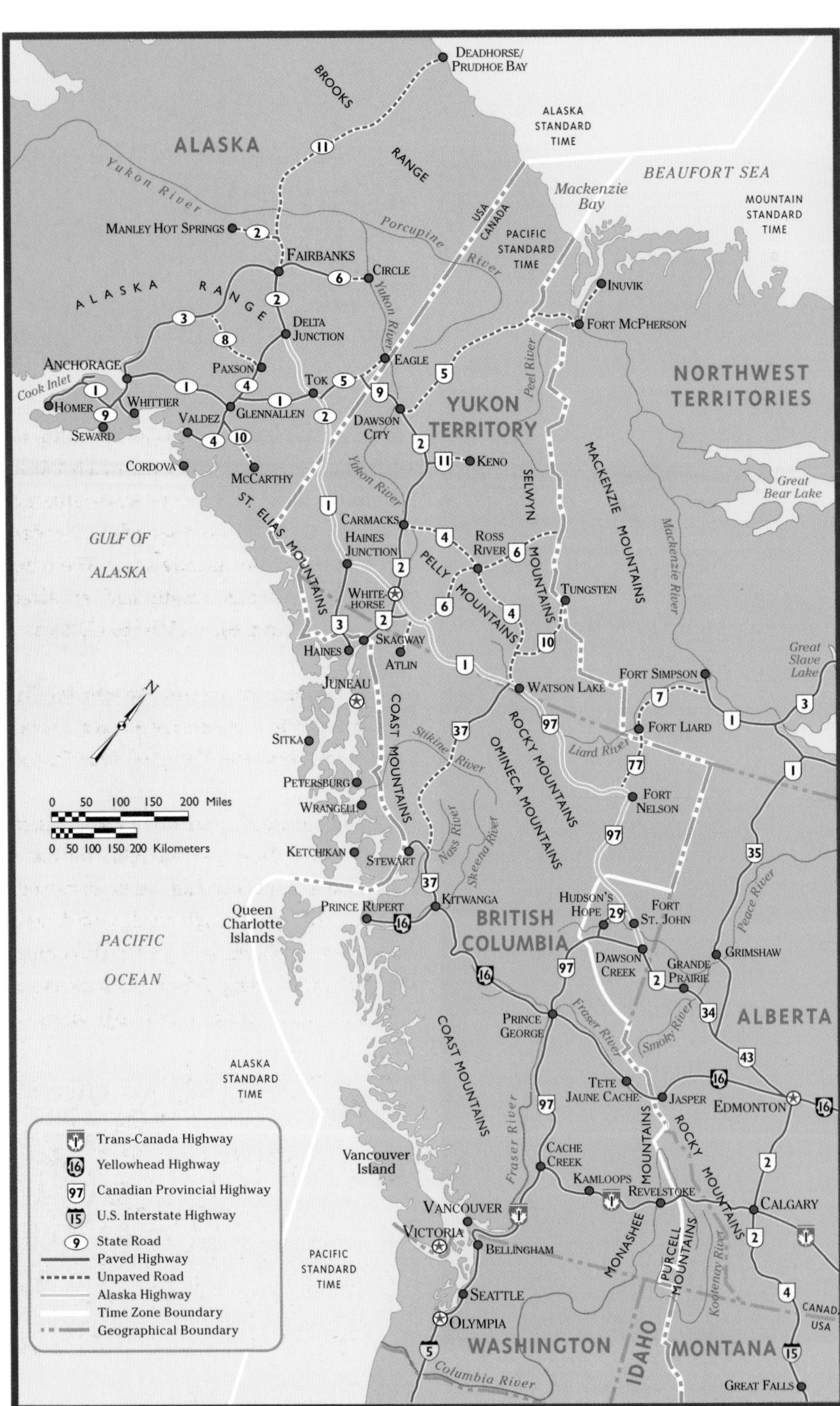

DEADHORSE/
PRUDHOE BAY
BROOKS
RANGE
ALASKA
ALASKA
STANDARD
TIME
BEAUFORT SEA
Yukon River
Mackenzie
Bay
MOUNTAIN
STANDARD
TIME
MANLEY HOT SPRINGS
Porcupine
River
USA
CANADA
PACIFIC
STANDARD
TIME
FAIRBANKS
CIRCLE
INUVIK
ALASKA
RANGE
FORT MCPHERSON
DELTA
JUNCTION
Yukon River
Peel River
NORTHWEST
TERRITORIES
PAXSON
EAGLE
ANCHORAGE
Cook Inlet
TOK
YUKON
TERRITORY
HOMER
WHITTIER
GLENNALLEN
DAWSON
CITY
SEWARD
VALDEZ
CORDOVA
McCARTHY
KENO
MACKENZIE MOUNTAINS
SELWYN
Great
Bear Lake
Yukon River
ST. ELIAS MOUNTAINS
CARMACKS
GULF OF
ALASKA
HAINES
JUNCTION
ROSS
RIVER
MOUNTAINS
Mackenzie River
PELLY
MOUNTAINS
TUNGSTEN
WHITE-
HORSE
HAINES
SKAGWAY
ATLIN
Great
Slave
Lake
JUNEAU
FORT SIMPSON
WATSON LAKE
N
COAST
MOUNTAINS
FORT LIARD
SITKA
Stikine River
ROCKY MOUNTAINS
OMINECA MOUNTAINS
Liard River
PETERSBURG
0 50 100 150 200 Miles
WRANGELL
FORT
NELSON
0 50 100 150 200 Kilometers
KETCHIKAN
Nass River
Skeena River
STEWART
Queen
Charlotte
Islands
PRINCE RUPERT
KITWANGA
BRITISH
COLUMBIA
HUDSON'S
HOPE
FORT
ST. JOHN
Peace River
PACIFIC
OCEAN
DAWSON
CREEK
GRANDE
PRAIRIE
GRIMSHAW
COAST MOUNTAINS
PRINCE
GEORGE
Fraser River
Smoky River
ALBERTA
ALASKA
STANDARD
TIME
TETE
JAUNE CACHE
JASPER
EDMONTON
Trans-Canada Highway
Yellowhead Highway
Canadian Provincial Highway
U.S. Interstate Highway
State Road
Paved Highway
Unpaved Road
Alaska Highway
Time Zone Boundary
Geographical Boundary
Vancouver
Island
Fraser River
CACHE
CREEK
MOUNTAINS
ROCKY
MOUNTAINS
KAMLOOPS
REVELSTOKE
CALGARY
VANCOUVER
VICTORIA
BELLINGHAM
MONASHEE
PURCELL
MOUNTAINS
Kootenay River
PACIFIC
STANDARD
TIME
SEATTLE
OLYMPIA
CANADA
USA
WASHINGTON
IDAHO
MONTANA
Columbia River
GREAT FALLS

INTRODUCTION

North to Alaska

NORTH AMERICA'S FAMOUS WILDERNESS ROAD was coined "the ALCAN" during its construction through Canada and Alaska's backcountry. It began as a rough-and-ready World War II supply line linking the continental United States to its far-off territory, where strategic military posts were poised to fend off enemy aggression. By 1948, however, when the road opened to the public, the civilian world learned what the military already knew: The thing was a beast, known for its twists, miry stretches, and burdensome length, and yet Alcan wound through extraordinary scenery that dared you to take your eyes off the road. It was a love-hate relationship.

The first civilians to tackle the road were true road warriors, driving tanklike vehicles that were burdened with extra tires, gas tanks, provisions, and lots of emergency gear. Many drivers today prepare for the Alaska Highway in much the same way. The good news is, you don't have to anymore.

After decades of improvements, the route has matured into a destination unto itself, and those who travel its length never forget the journey. Now past its 65th birthday, the Alaska Highway has been surveyed, straightened, graded, rerouted, paved, and populated in places, and yet it's still something of a wild thing. Adventure seekers are just as drawn to this route through some of

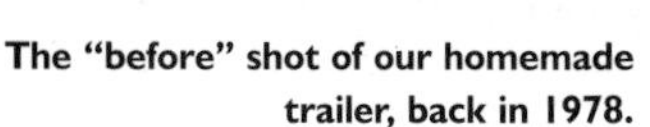

The "before" shot of our homemade trailer, back in 1978.

Yet another stop for more repair work. With all that mud, it was hard to tell there was a trailer under there. We slept in the back of the Blazer.

the most uncivilized parts of the continent. For some, it's not the getting to Alaska that matters anymore—although Alaska is a lifetime dream for many—it's having traveled the road. That's why the souvenirs sell so well—just driving the highway places you in the "I did it!" club.

My first trip up the Alaska Highway was in 1978, when most of the Alcan was still unpaved and unstraightened, and my father's letters beckoned, "Come on up! There's money laying all over the place!" His letters arrived during the years when the trans-Alaska pipeline was under construction and money, indeed, was flowing just as the oil would. I remember a cousin calling from a pipeline construction camp in 1976, his voice echoing in the satellite connection. He told me he was making $1,200 a week picking up garbage. My hourly wage that year was under $2.50. So in July 1978, my young family of four moved from northern Illinois to Fairbanks to join nearly a dozen other family members who had already migrated up, one after another, like caribou crossing a stream. Some had arrived in time for the construction boom. We arrived on its heels, one year to the month after the pipeline first flowed oil. The last to leave Illinois, I was a 23-year-old secretary with a husband and two preschool daughters.

My then-husband and I had gone deep into debt that year and bought a new 1978 Chevy Blazer. He made modifications for our trip, removing the back seats and building a plywood platform. Our little ones just rode back there on the foam bed as we drove (that's right, no seat belts or safety concerns whatsoever). Beneath the platform bed was a storage compartment for our luggage and camp kitchen. On our 4,000-mile trek up the highway, we'd stop to camp, all of us sleeping on the platform after duct-taping mosquito netting to the open windows. In tow was a supremely heavy homemade trailer that held our worldly goods. The tires exploded into thin air regularly; twelve times, in fact. The trailer also suffered a broken tongue and, in a separate, equally inconvenient place, a broken axle.

The road we encountered then seemed to hate us, and bucked like a wild mustang. The surface was either fine dust, squishy mud, or never-ending miles of gravel that made a deafening roar. As we neared a city and crossed onto pavement, the first moments of gravel-free silence were always startling. And oh, the road did wind and rise and fall, yet it had already seen improvements since wartime days when it was hurriedly built around or over every obstacle. Back then, a young man named Troy Hise scrawled a few lines about the Alcan that have since appeared on countless T-shirts, postcards, and placemats, many times offering the only credit to "Anonymous":

Winding in and winding out
Leaves my mind in serious doubt
As to whether the lout who built this route
Was going to hell or coming out.

Now a senior citizen, Hise and his wife can still be found traveling the highway, marketing products that bear his memorable poem.

Going to hell or coming out? Looking back thirty years, I remember asking myself the same question. The answer was several years in coming. Alaska was neither heaven nor hell, but was a rare and beautiful combination, a memorable place to spend most of my adult life.

During my Alaska years, I drove every highway on its limited state road system. I've picnicked above the Arctic Circle, trundled down the sole road into Denali National Park, and often retraced the pioneering route of the Valdez-to-Fairbanks Trail, now the Richardson Highway. In one 10-year span, I put nearly 200,000 miles on my vehicle—all of them Alaska miles. But I never drove the Alaska Highway again. Over the years, friends and relatives made the trip without incident, arriving with glowing reports of moose and bear sightings, serene lakeside campgrounds, and awesome scenery. "The road's great!" they proclaimed. "It's almost completely paved now. You wouldn't recognize it." But I had vowed long ago, when I came off that first killer trip, "I'll never drive that road again!" That's why I laughed when a publisher first asked me to write this book, and found I had to break my self-righteous promise. It was time to get back on the road and see it firsthand once more.

Maybe it's the same urge for you—to see it for yourself. Then it's time to get to it. We drive the highway from the Pacific Northwest every couple of years now. We have a fifth-wheel trailer, but prefer to travel in a one-way RV rental option with Cruise America, driving up and flying back or flying up and driving back. Each time we've enlarged our experiences and watched the road further evolve into the remarkably safe and comfortable route that it is today.

In this book, I'll introduce you to roadside history, geography, Native cultures, and recreational opportunities in Alberta, British Columbia, the Yukon, and Alaska, covering miles well beyond the Alaska Highway itself. I've included details about attractions, restaurants, hotels, and campgrounds. You'll also meet some of the people who make the Northland so memorable. I hope this guide enhances your travels. We've had a great time, and I know you will, too.

Remember this, though: the Alcan, with all of its history, romance, and wonder, is not just about driving. It's a gateway to places you've only seen in pictures: the stomping grounds of the gold-rush stampeders and pioneers. Land that's steeped in centuries of Native culture. Crystalline streams, jade-colored lakes, wild animals, snowy mountain peaks, and spruce forests. You'll meet new friends who are on the same journey, and those who live along the way. Back at home, the images will linger in your mind and you'll wrestle with useless words like "beautiful," "incredible," "big," and "amazing." You'll tell others that until they've experienced the Alaska Highway themselves, words seem inadequate. And you'll know as I do that before long, you'll be talking about the next trip.

Whether you travel by motor home or motorcycle, a successful trip requires careful planning.

CHAPTER 1

Planning and Packing

PLANNING FOR MONTHS, traveling for weeks, remembering for a lifetime. Those are the pleasures of a road trip to the Far North. On the road to Alaska, you'll wend through farms and prairies and vast acres of pristine forest; you'll climb the Canadian Rockies and breach the continental divide. You will head for the Yukon, a place-name that still rings with the promise of gold, as it did more than a century ago during the Klondike gold rush. And you'll get a chance to dip your big toe in the famed Yukon River. The road leads farther north, into Alaska, where you'll explore a state highway system that, measured to scale against this landscape, is nothing more than a dozen pieces of thread thrown against a fabulous, multicolored, king-size quilt.

How to prepare for such an unparalleled adventure? Any experienced traveler knows the importance of researching a place before embarking on a trip. Next in line is packing smart. Not too much, not too little. This chapter outlines in detail how to get ready for weeks on the road.

Your Travel Timeline

Time is the issue that separates the two types of highway travelers: those who just want to get to a place, and those who know that the journey can be as enjoyable as the destination. The first and best rule of thumb is: Take your time. This is not a race. Stop for ice cream. Read the historical signs. Try not to think about making good time. Most of all, be mindful that posted speed limits are not suggestions but law.

The laws of physics aren't flexible either. Some Alaskans (mostly male, for some reason) claim special bragging rights to having made their personal best time in covering the Alaska Highway. "Why, we went from Seattle to Fairbanks in 72 hours. 'Course, we never stopped. We traded off on driving." This is no great achievement, but rather an expression of recklessness, not only for themselves and their passengers, but also for others on the road. The Alaska Highway as yet is no superhighway.

What to Pack

The old joke you've probably heard in your own hometown is true here as well: If you don't like this weather, just wait a few minutes. That's particularly true in the Northland during the summer months. So be ready with a little of everything, and if it turns chilly, put it all on!

The length of the Alaska Highway crosses several climate zones through Canada, with microclimates within them. In Alaska, it's no different. It can be 55°F at Mount McKinley while it's 80°F in Fairbanks, just 2 hours away.

Beauty salons or barbershops are easy to find in most towns. Make an appointment, or walk in. Usually it's not a problem. Pharmacies likewise are not difficult to find.

The benefits of the midnight sun are many, including the growth of unnaturally large cabbages and squash, and excessive energy in human beings. But for those who have trouble getting to sleep in the daylight, bring along a sleep mask.

Following is a packing checklist to help you get started. You decide how many of each item to bring, remembering that there will be no shortage of self-service laundries, so less is better.

Clothing

Several T-shirts
Short-sleeved shirt
Long-sleeved shirt
Lightweight pants or shorts
Pants for chilly weather
Hooded sweatshirt or sweater
Windbreaker
Raincoat
Swimsuit
Knit hat or baseball cap
Jacket with zip-in lining for extra warmth
Comfortable walking shoes (soft soles for grip in slippery places)
Dress clothes (one set, just in case)
Dress shoes
Socks and stockings
Slippers
Lightweight gloves

Other Items

Passport
Toiletries
Hair dryer
Curling iron
Prescription drugs and refill prescriptions
Mosquito repellent
Driver's license
Emergency medical information
Contact numbers
Sunglasses
First-aid kit
Plastic grocery bag
Zip-closure plastic bags
Film, tapes, memory cards, and batteries for your cameras
Bottled water
Your pet's health certificate (for border crossings)
Cash
Bank card/ATM card

What Not to Bring

Although I'm suggesting one set of "nice" clothes might be a good idea—in the "just in case" department—leave your fanciest clothes and jewelry at home. Alaska and the Canadian north are places where informality reigns. Although you can dress up for a night on the town if you like, at any given event or restaurant you'll find people in all kinds of clothes, from cocktail dresses to jeans. Men, pack a jacket and tie if you plan to dine at a four-star restaurant in Calgary, Edmonton, or Anchorage. Ladies, a simple dress will do.

Don't bring guns. Unless you're headed into the backcountry on your own, you won't need one, and unless you know how to use it, you're probably more dangerous to yourself than that charging grizzly bear is. Hire a guide to take you backcountry hiking or fishing; he or she likely will carry a protective weapon. Canada is explicit and firm about the transport of firearms and bear spray across its borders (see the section on Guns/Ammo in Chapter 2, What You Need to Know).

Don't bring extra luggage for bulky or weighty souvenirs. You can have anything shipped home, from a chainsaw carving of a brown bear to a new parka, a hunk of jade, a piece of etched baleen, even your children's book collection—one for every child and grandchild in the family! Don't weigh yourself down. Insure the expensive stuff and ship it. I vote for mailing home all the paper you pick up at visitor centers, too—brochures, travel magazines, postcards, note cards, everything. It's so much better to travel light.

And don't bring your radar detector into Yukon Territory, where it will be confiscated whether or not it's turned on.

Preparing Your Vehicle

Make sure your vehicle is at its best before you leave home. If you're not mechanically oriented, take it to your mechanic for a once-over, or use this checklist to ensure that you don't overlook any of the automotive essentials:

Tires in good condition
Spare tire, fully inflated
Jack, and knowledge of how to use it
Tune-up
Oil change
Fluids
Belts/seals/hoses
Brakes/bearings
Exhaust system
Windshield wipers
Air-conditioning (yes, it may be needed)
Radiator

Also, carry the following emergency equipment:

First-aid kit
Tow cable
Toolbox
Road flares/reflectors
Flashlight and fresh batteries
Jumper cable
Matches in a sealed container, like a film canister
Candles
Pencil and paper
Bottles of drinking water
Paper towels
Nylon rope
Squeegee (for muddy windows)
Spare headlight
Gas can
Cell phone (even though it may not work in some remote regions)

If you're a U.S. resident, check with your insurance company about claims from within Canada and what will be provided for you in case you need assistance. Read your policy and understand it well, then ride on that security. Don't worry. Accidents are not commonplace. If you're a member of an auto club, familiarize yourself with their procedures in case of an emergency. Keep your membership number handy.

Including sections of the route that are under repair or realignment, 99.9 percent of the road is paved. Still, windshields are sometimes nicked or chipped by flying gravel. If you're concerned about your windshield, headlights, or paint job, consider attaching a screen to your vehicle's front end for extra protection.

There was a day when long-distance travelers carried many gallons of extra gas. That's really not necessary anymore, unless you're on Alaska's Dalton Highway or one of Canada's more remote unpaved roads that have not yet developed routine roadside services. (And if you're renting a vehicle, you've probably already agreed, by contract, to stay off certain unpaved highways.) Throughout the length of the Alcan and along most of Alaska's state highways, you'll find gas stations at regular intervals. An informal rule of thumb: Never let the tank get below the halfway mark. Top it off before you leave a community.

Traveling by RV

Everyone who has ever spent a weekend or more in an RV knows the practice of living in a moving motel has its pluses and minuses. It's wonderful to have everything in its place, to unpack only one time, to fix a meal when you're hungry, and to slip between familiar sheets at night. But other matters must be considered, such as: Who is driving and who is navigating? Can he/she be trusted with the task? Did you remember to put the stairs up? Could you at least get your feet out of the way when I'm carrying a hot dish? Like naughty children thrown together in a room to have it out and then get along, traveling companions usually work these things out, and comfortable patterns emerge.

If you're already a regular RV traveler, you'll have shortcuts and camping methods of your own, and likely have traded ideas with others in campgrounds across the country. That's another great thing about RV travel—making new friends and comparing notes about travel experiences and opportunities.

We learned that some people lighten their load by keeping the freshwater tank empty. They bring bottled water for cooking and drinking, and hook up only occasionally for dishwashing and showers (or use the shower house). Others believe that carrying the extra weight is less of a problem than finding a campsite with full hookups.

RV campgrounds with full hookups are not always available without advance reservations, especially in the prime mid-summer travel weeks, so empty your gray water and sewer tanks every day or two, and keep the fresh water topped off in case you decide to switch to the generator and take hot showers. Often, just electricity is available. Hot showers commonly are available at campgrounds that don't offer full hookups. Pull-throughs, those campsites that allow RVers to pull in at one end and go out the other, may be at a premium late in the day, so consider settling in before dinner.

"Dry camping" is a common option, and not a bad one if there's a shortage of space. That can be the case in June, July, and early August. The more spontaneous types don't mind driving into the unknown of "where shall we stay tonight?" Others prefer a smartly choreographed itinerary with reservations in place, from one end of the country to the other,

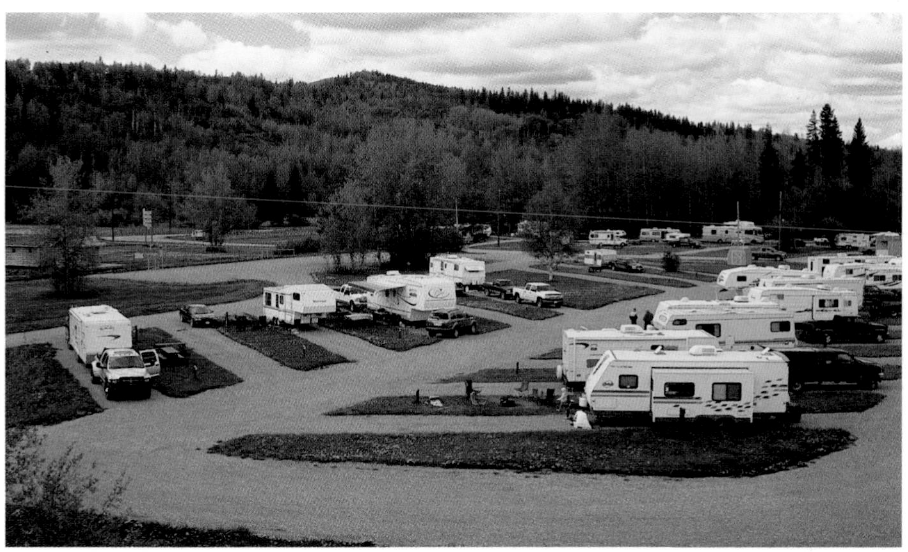

The Peace Island campground lies near a magnificent bridge crossing the Peace River.

before leaving home. That doesn't leave much room for the winds of chance, but offers a lot of security. You'll find lists of campgrounds, some of which accept reservations, in the chapters that follow. And don't forget that, even in Alaska, superstores like Wal-Mart have an open-parking-lot policy for wandering folks like you. This is not recommended for the best camping experience, but it sure works for a middle-of-the-night, sleepy-driver situation—not to mention that you can stock up before you head out again.

One-way or Round-trip?

Driving up then driving back—perhaps you'd rather not put so many miles on your vehicle. You may consider a drive-ship-fly option. You can drive to Anchorage and have your vehicle shipped to Seattle while you rent a car and spend the extra days seeing more of Alaska. On schedule, you fly down and pick up your car or RV from the shipper, usually in the Port of Seattle.

A second option is to drive to Haines or Skagway, where you and your vehicle can board a ferry on the Alaska Marine Highway, sailing southbound on the Inside Passage to Bellingham, Washington. You will not be allowed to sleep in your RV when it is in the ship's hold, but will need to book a stateroom. For more on the Alaska Marine Highway, see Chapter 9.

Own or Rent?

Packing the RV is dependent upon your travel timeline and on whether you own the RV or are renting. Owners normally keep a second set of everything in their campers, road-trip ready. RV renters can arrange one-way or round-trip packages. Towels, bedding, and everything you need for the kitchen are available for an extra fee. Or, one-way travelers can bring along the basics with an eye toward throwing it in an extra suitcase or duffel for the homeward flight.

My husband, Perry, and I chose a rental RV with Cruise America, a company with offices all over the United States and Canada. You can browse their Web site at *www.cruiseamerica.com* for more information on their offerings, or search the Internet or Yellow Pages for other similar options. It's extremely important to pay close attention or even take notes when the rental company representative or dealership is explaining how everything works.

Recommended housekeeping packing for the extra-light, one-way RV traveler: Think paper and plastic. Buy paper plates, but pack a few plastic mugs and glasses, and bring a selection of inexpensive "real" silverware. Personally, I'd rather wash silverware then use the plastic variety. For each person, allow two bath towels, a washcloth, and a hand towel. Other linens for a couple should include one set of sheets, two blankets and pillows, and two dishtowels and dishcloths. For the kitchen, pick up the smallest dish soap size they sell, or just pour some into a small container with a tight lid, rather than carry the full-size bottle.

Buy disposable salt-and-pepper containers and pack minimal other spices. Bring two sizes of cooking pots and lids, one skillet and lid, spatula, large plastic spoon, slotted spoon, ladle, and manual can opener. Bring along a broom and dustpan and, if you can, a small, power vacuum cleaner (especially good for dog fur on upholstery, I found!). I threw in a sample-size piece of leftover carpet as a doormat, which I could toss at the end of our one-way trip—you really do need one, so buy one if you have to. Buy chemicals for the toilet; bring soap, shampoo, and other basic toiletries.

We decided to premeasure laundry soap into sandwich bags so we wouldn't have to deal with a big carton, or coming up short on Canadian coins at a laundry. If you're not picky about your coffee, instant coffee or single-serving coffee bags do the trick, but more and more campgrounds have nice coffee carts. Or bring along a French press.

The RV life really does feel like playing in a dollhouse. Within a day or two, it's easy to make a meal, wash the dishes, sweep up, and be ready to roll in record time. The routine takes on its own familiarity even though you are far from home.

If you're like us, at the end of each day you will be road-weary and yearning for a quiet place, so keep a wary eye out for the location of a busy road or railroad tracks before you choose a campsite. We cruised the campgrounds to check out the party sites before we picked the one farthest away. In most cases, however, people were extremely respectful of each other, and the noise level went down around 10 P.M. Parents with children likewise were understanding of those who are not accustomed to noisy play, and they made sure the kids were in tow by evening.

At the end of the day, we walked, read, and played cards. We visited our neighbors, studied maps, and reviewed all the literature we'd picked up. I created a travel journal and kept track of our daily mileage, too. I encourage you to do the same, for all of those great memories will fade quickly unless you write down impressions and information about the photographs you took that day.

All in all, traveling by RV was extremely satisfying—it allowed the security of familiar surroundings as we entered the larger picture of a world to explore together.

Going by Car

RV life not your cup of tea? Then fear not. When you budget in the cost of gassing up a big rig, you might find hotel-hopping just as affordable, especially for a couple. Sure, there's the ordeal of moving your luggage in and out of the car. Then again, the clean sheets, a "real" mattress, and ease of parking may outweigh the comforts of a home on wheels. Many travelers carry a spacious cooler along and fill it with lunch fixings, snacks, and beverages, then enjoy a nice dinner on the town. Other families fill up the SUV with kids and camping gear, and hit the road. Big-city hotels, in particular, are more family-friendly than ever. In Canada, you'll find indoor water parks under the same roof as the hotel. Check the hotel listings at the end of each section for more details; I've included business Web sites and toll-free numbers to help you plan.

It's all about personal style. You be the judge.

Cameras

Oh, the photos that were never taken because the battery died at that moment! Or you ran out of film. Or the card was full. Alas, it could have been a *National Geographic* cover. So be forewarned and pack plenty of film, and extra camera batteries or the rechargeable kind. Bring along a battery recharger that plugs into your vehicle's cigarette lighter or power outlet.

More and more folks are bringing their laptops and downloading their photos from digital cameras on a daily basis. File management is a job unto itself, isn't it? Just naming and organizing your photos can fill hours. But taking care of it as you go rather than waiting until you get home may prove the smartest, most efficient way to deal with all of those images. Think in terms of the digital slide show—all ready to run—when you get home.

Driving on unpaved roads poses a dust concern, so keep your electronics in their tote bags unless you're shooting pictures.

A few shooting tips: First and foremost, don't harass the wildlife. In most cases, that means "Stay in your vehicle!" Don't creep up too close for their comfort and your safety. The best wildlife photographers choose a spot and wait for their shot. If you don't have time for that, then buy a bigger lens, or risk a ticket from a wildlife protection officer.

Secondly, watch for groups of vehicles that have pulled over. That's a sure sign that something big and hairy, or feathery, or furry, is near the edge of the road and will be the subject of many vacation photographs. Pull off the road completely and stop your vehicle before you begin shooting. Alaskans have seen it a million times—people standing in the middle of the road with their cameras stuck to their faces and no clue that an oncoming Winnebago is about to make a significant impact on their lives.

Videographers, remember to spend a few seconds shooting pictures of identifying signs to help establish where you are. Or while you're taping, have a traveling companion read from a travel guide, brochure, or informational sign as you capture the scene. It's better than relying on memory later.

And one more tip for good measure: Don't forget the people on your trip. Shots of beautiful scenery and wildlife are important vacation remembrances, but 10 or 20 years from now, or more, it will be the photos of the people with you, and the people you meet along the way, that will cause you to ooh and aah.

Strategy for Medical Needs

The greatest disruption on a vacation is getting sick. Worse still is not having the medicine you need to feel better. So bring along the basics, and make sure your prescription

Don't be embarrassed about asking others to assist while you pose for an unforgettable picture.

medications have been filled just before you leave. Ask for a refill slip from your doctor if you expect to be gone for long.

Make a see-through zipper bag your first-aid kit. For its contents, buy travel-size containers to keep it from becoming unwieldy. Drop in your vitamins, adhesive bandages of various sizes, first-aid ointment, aspirin or other pain reliever, alcohol swabs, hydrogen peroxide, an Ace bandage, muscle ache ointment, cotton balls, a few safety pins, hand sanitizer, cold-medicine tablets, chewable tablets for indigestion, and throat lozenges, along with prescription drugs that you don't normally carry on your person. You might keep your written prescriptions for refills in the first-aid kit, too.

In your purse or wallet, along with your identification and insurance card, carry a written statement of any medical conditions, allergies, or other health alerts, and medicines that you're currently taking. List the name and number of your family doctor and of the person to call in case of an emergency.

Driving in Winter

Winter driving is possible, and some people actually prefer it, claiming that the road is better with fewer vehicles in front of them and a good layer of compacted snow under them. But extra care must be taken to pack smart. I remember the winter my father and brother slid off the road on a lonely stretch near the Alaska–Canada border. It was –40°F. They bundled up, then Dad built a fire and climbed back up to the road to flag down help, which happily did arrive before either of them suffered frostbite. They had packed emergency gear such as extra warm clothes, sleeping bags, and matches. Even though the car was totaled, in the end they were merely banged up, but it easily could have gone another way had they not been prepared.

It's a good idea to equip your vehicle with these extras:

- Studded snow tires or chains
- Ice scraper/brush
- Nonperishable snack foods
- Heavy-duty extension cord (see next paragraph)
- Sandbag or kitty litter, for extra traction should you become stuck
- Shovel
- Blanket or sleeping bag
- Extra parka, snow pants, warm boots, mitts
- Chemical-pack hand-warmers
- CB radio (if you want an extra measure of security)

The farther north you drive, the colder it gets. So before you leave home, ask your mechanic to use 5-30W motor oil in your car. And have the shop install an engine-block heater or, at the least, an oil-pan heater, so the oil will not become so thick that you can't turn the engine over. With either heater under the hood, you will end up with a short, three-pronged electric cord sticking out of the grill. Buy a 15- to 20-foot heavy-duty extension cord so you can access power when you turn the car off for two or more hours, or when you park it for the night. Many hard-core northerners loosely loop this extension cord from their side mirrors, so it's always handy.

In the Far North, outdoor electric outlets are common; in Fairbanks or Dawson City, you'll see them at the heads of parking spaces in public lots. Ask about where to plug in when you check in at your motel. If you haven't plugged in all night, do so an hour or so before you plan to leave. Plugging in at 10°F or colder is a good idea. It means less wear and tear on your engine and less drain on your battery, not to mention a reassuring sound when the engine turns over effortlessly. And the sooner the engine heats up, the sooner you'll have warm air coming out of your interior blower.

Another trick among winter drivers of the north has to do with a quick-and-cheap addition to your front end: a large piece of corrugated cardboard. Wedge the flattened piece between your grill and radiator to prevent super-cold air from passing through the radiator. The engine will get warm and stay warm much faster, and in the end, your interior heater will be much more effective.

Remember that winter days in the north are extremely short. You'll be driving in dim light or darkness, even if you limit your driving time to daytime, so working headlights are especially important. Snowstorms can surprise you, too, so check your radio dial and ask the locals about the forecast when you stop, or request a number to call for recorded messages on road conditions.

Sharing the road with tractor-trailers can be a challenge, because they tend to kick up a blinding snow shower, so back off rather than pass them. Vision is critical, so make sure your windshield wipers are in good shape. Use common sense for safe snow driving: Bring down your speed a notch, never jam on the brakes, and as your driver's ed teacher told you, steer in the direction of the slide.

And, at the risk of nagging, we'll say it again: Take your time.

This is a no-no. Don't leave your vehicle and approach a wild animal.
Not only is it stressful for the animal, it could be dangerous for both of you.

CHAPTER 2

What You Need to Know, A to Z

Alaska-speak

English is spoken in Canada and the United States, but occasionally a regional term can trip you up. Here's a quick list of words in the Alaskan vocabulary:

Outside. Anywhere not in Alaska
Lower 48. Refers to the 48 continental states to the south.
Cheechako. A greenhorn, a newcomer
Wanigan. Lean-to, usually in add-a-room style attached to a cabin
Carhartts. Brand of warm, durable clothing commonly worn in winter; the Alaska tuxedo
Bunny boots. Large, usually white, rubber boots with a built-in vapor barrier for extra insulation; boomed in use during construction of the trans-Alaska oil pipeline during the 1970s; still very popular
Breakup. Spring season when ice breaks up and moves out from the rivers
Termination dust. First snow that dusts the mountaintops; signals the termination of summer
Kuspuk. Brightly colored cotton tunic with flounce worn by Native Alaskan women
Alaska Native. Person of ancient heritage—Eskimo, Indian, or Aleut descent
native Alaskan. Person of any race who was born and raised in Alaska
Sourdough. An old-timer, a pioneer Alaskan
Snowmachine. Used in Alaska in reference to a snowmobile
Rondy. Anchorage Fur Rendezvous, the biggest winter carnival in the country
PFD check. Portion of interest dividends and capital gains on state's oil revenues; annual payment mailed by the state to every eligible resident. In 2007, the amount was $1,107.56 per person.

Alaska State Troopers

Not every town on the Alaska road system has its own police force. Alaska State Troopers enforce the law along the miles and miles of highway. Dialing 911 remains the universal call for help throughout the state, and Trooper posts may be found in the following communities along the main highways: Anchorage, Cantwell, Coldfoot, Cordova, Cooper Landing, Delta Junction, Fairbanks, Girdwood, Glennallen, Homer, Nenana, Ninilchik, Northway, Palmer, Seward, Soldotna, Talkeetna, Tok, and Valdez.

The Municipality of Anchorage extends from the Knik River Bridge on the Glenn Highway to the town of Girdwood on the Seward Highway, and a host of police officers patrols the highways in this vast area, with support from the Alaska State Troopers.

Your welcome begins near the border crossing from Washington state into British Columbia.

Other road-system cities with their own police force include Wasilla, Palmer, North Pole, Whittier, Valdez, Homer, Soldotna, Kenai, Seward, and Fairbanks. In the remote, off-road villages, law enforcement often is handled by a VPSO, a Village Public Safety Officer. State Troopers fly into villages when a VPSO needs assistance.

Alaska Wildlife Troopers serve in a special branch of the Department of Public Safety. Even though they focus their efforts on enforcing fish-and-game laws, they can and will issue traffic tickets and pursue other criminal activity.

Alaska has no counties, so there are no sheriffs or deputies.

Alcoholic Beverages

Alcohol is not sold in grocery stores in Alaska, and liquor stores will not sell to individuals younger than 21. Drinking-and-driving laws are tough, so stop for the night before you crack open that beer. Some Alaska villages are dry; some are damp. Just to be sure, don't fly into a village with alcohol in your suitcase.

U.S. citizens who are 19 or older may transport duty-free alcoholic beverages over the U.S.-Canada border in these quantities: 48 ounces (1.4 liters) of liquor or wine, or 24 containers, at 12 ounces (355 milliliters) each, of beer or ale.

Border Crossings

On January 23, 2007, new regulations required valid passports for citizens of the U.S. and Canada who were flying into their neighboring country. However, the mandate did not yet apply for those who were traveling to, or returning to, the U.S. from Canada by land or sea. The U.S. State Department delayed the enforcement date requiring passports to sometime in 2008 or early 2009. Be certain well before you travel: consult *www.visitcanada.com/PassportsAndCustoms.html.* U.S. citizens should apply up to six months in advance, as processing time is much longer than normal due to the overwhelming number of applicants.

Until passports are required, citizens of the U.S. or Canada who do not have a valid passport must instead show photo identification and proof of citizenship—a driver's license with a birth certificate or voter's registration card will work. Have your vehicle registration or rental documents available, too, and your pet's health certificate.

For visitors from the U.S. who were not born in the U.S., Canadian authorities will ask for a Certificate of Naturalization, a "Green Card," and perhaps a visa, depending on one's country of citizenship. No photocopies will be accepted.

Most crossings are fairly routine. You will be asked a dozen questions or more, and allowed to continue on your journey.

Occasionally, officials ask permission to look around inside a car or camper. Every so often, even after answering all questions honestly, a driver may be detained further as officials make a more thorough inspection of the vehicle or its contents. (Also see the following entries in this chapter: Alcoholic Beverages; Duty-free Shopping; Guns/Ammo; Pets; Plants.)

Campgrounds

Among those who love to camp, you'll find the spectrum of tastes and comfort zones. Some folks take their home with them on vacation in the form of a recreational vehicle—and their rolling accommodations include power, water, microwave, stove, refrigerator, toilet, shower, stereo, and VCR. At the other end of the scale are the tent campers, who sleep with a thin layer of waterproof material separating them from raw nature. No matter what the style, great numbers of mobile travelers have discovered the joys of camping.

As you travel throughout the north, you'll find plentiful options among campgrounds, and good signage to help direct you. In the chapters that follow, we've included directions and contact information for campgrounds along the way. Operated privately or by government agencies, campground offerings range from a simple opening in the forest with a picnic table and fire ring, to places equipped with extras such as cable, a swimming pool, golf course, horseshoe pits, playgrounds, swimming beach, boat dock and, almost as important as hot showers to some campers, access to a computer modem or wireless connection.

RV travelers will be most interested in whether a campground offers full hookups, meaning power, water, and sewer service. In a partial hookup, power and water are usually available, but sewer service is not. In most cases, however, a dump station (or sani-station, as it's often called in Canada) is available for emptying gray water and sewerage. Also note that campgrounds in Canada will refer to sites as serviced or unserviced, indicating whether hookups are available.

In Alaska it is legal (but not much fun) to park for the night on a road wayside where the parking area is fully off the road. Nowhere in Alaska or Canada is it legal to dump sewerage or gray water anywhere except in designated dump stations.

For provincial parks, you can pay in person at the campground fee station after you've chosen your site.

For details, contact these sources:

Alaska: State campgrounds do not accept reservations. Charge cards are accepted in most privately owned campgrounds. Checks are rarely accepted. Visit the Alaska Campground Owners Association online at *www.alaskacampgrounds.net*. For more on camping in Alaska's state or national parklands, see *www.travelalaska.com/regions/stateparks.aspx*.

Alberta: For details on provincial or national parks, see *www.travelalberta.com/camping.*

British Columbia: For information or provincial campground reservations, call 1-800-689-9025, or visit *www.discovercamping.ca.*

Yukon Territory: Yukon travelers may prepurchase daily territorial campground permits at retail outlets along the highway, visitor reception centers, lodges, and fuel stations. For more on Yukon Government campgrounds, phone the Department of Environment at 867-667-5658. For other camping information, see *www.environmentyukon.gov.yk.ca/camping.*

Canada-speak

Americans engaged in conversation with a Canadian swear they're from the same country until an unusual treatment of a familiar word pops up: "I'm in the PRO-cess of moving," "Let's check the SHED-yule," or "Tell me a-BOOT your problem." Here are some tips to aid interpretation:

Eh? This nonword peppers the ends of many sentences. It is not a question, but rather a charming way to end a statement with an invitation for the other person to speak next . . . or it's just a regional speech pattern that means nothing whatsoever.

First Nations people. Descendants of the ancient Native groups who first made this region their home

Gold dredges. Floating gold PRO-cessing ships that sorted out nuggets from rock and soil before depositing the tailings back on the ground

Loonie. The $1 coin imprinted with the image of a loon

Mounties. Royal Canadian Mounted Police, or RCMP

Pumpjack. Slow-moving oil pumps that draw oil out of the ground and into a pipeline or storage tank; often seen in rolling fields

Stampede. The "rush" in gold rushes of a century ago, when men and women stampeded from one gold discovery to the next. Or the term for a regional rodeo event, as in the Calgary Stampede.

the Yukon. Use the territory's name without the "the" and you've just revealed that you're not from around these parts. That, and you keep getting your quarters mixed up with Loonies.

Toonie. The $2 coin, worth two Loonies

YOOP. Yukon Order of the Pioneers

Cell Phone Service

As you travel north into mountainous or less-populated regions, you'll likely find gaps in your cell phone service, although areas surrounding major urban centers usually pose no problem. The best advice is to mentally prepare yourself for that reality, and don't let the number of bars on your phone dictate whether you're going to have a good day. You can get yourself a calling card, if you don't already have one, and use a pay phone.

Children

Due to the increase in child abduction by noncustodial parents, travel agencies and airlines are suggesting that you always travel with paperwork that documents your right to travel with

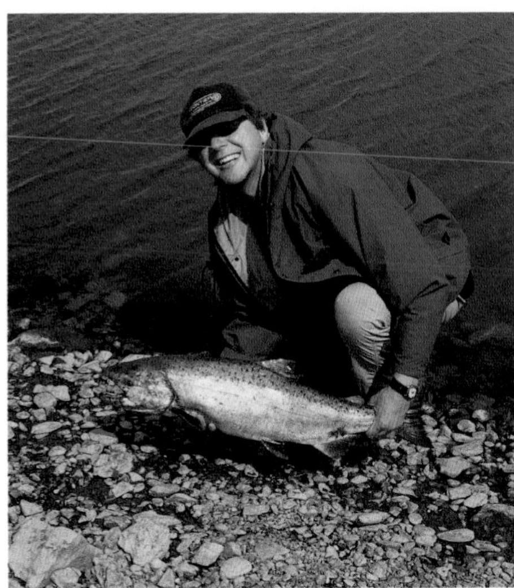

Perry Brown landed this king salmon on the Homer Spit in Alaska, where dozens of other anglers gathered in late summer at a hole called "The Pond."

minor children. The same is true for border crossings between the United States and Canada. Carry birth certificates for the children and, if you're divorced, your proof-of-custody papers. For non-custodial parents or grandparents, ask the child's custodial parent to sign and notarize a permission slip for that child to travel with you, stating where you plan to go and the dates you will be traveling.

Daylight Hours

The farther north you travel in summer, the more daylight you will encounter, especially during the days surrounding June 20 or 21, the summer solstice. Fairbanks basks in 22 hours of daylight during its Solstice Celebration, which includes a Midnight Sun Baseball Game that begins at 10:30 P.M. without artificial lights. Farther south, in Anchorage, the longest day provides a mere 19.5 hours of daylight, enough to make bedtimes a challenge for adults and children alike.

Throughout the Yukon, northern British Columbia, northern Alberta, and Alaska, short growing seasons are supplemented by these long, long hours of sunlight, resulting in exceptional floral displays, grain crops, and certain vegetables that grow to gigantic proportions. Look for giant cabbages mixed in with border plants in many northern gardens.

On the other side of the calendar, December 20 or 21 is winter solstice, when darkness is at its peak after eating away at hours of daylight for months. In Fairbanks, the sun may rise and set before office workers get a chance to look out the window, rising at about 11 A.M. and setting just 3 hours later. In Dawson City, Yukon, daylight on winter solstice is 4.5 hours; in Whitehorse, the shortest day is 5.5 hours.

Duty-free Shopping

If the value of your purchases does not exceed $400, residents of the United States who travel in Canada for more than 48 hours and less than 30 days may bring home personal or household merchandise without paying U.S. duty and tax. The $400 figure applies for each member in your party. To avoid delays at the border crossing, keep receipts and purchases handy.

Fishing

A fishing license is required in all provinces and in Alaska, but it is easy to obtain one through most sporting goods stores or other businesses.

Alberta. Sportfishing licenses are available at Natural Sustainable Resources offices, most tackle shops and sporting goods stores, campgrounds, and many department stores. No license is required for children 15 and younger. You may pick up the current *Alberta Guide to Sportfishing Regulations* when you purchase your license. Fees for anglers who are not residents of Canada are: $23.50 for one day; $41.50 for five days; $61.50 for the year. For more information, contact Alberta Sustainable Resource Development, Fish and Wildlife, at *www.srd.gov.ab.ca* or call 780-944-0313.

British Columbia. You'll have to buy separate licenses for saltwater and freshwater fishing in British Columbia. You can pick them up at government agency offices, sporting goods stores, and many other retailers. Other specific licenses are required in all national parks and may be obtained at park headquarters. For inquiries, call 1-877-855-3222, Monday through Friday, 8:30 a.m. to 4:30 p.m. Pacific Time. Or read the freshwater fishing regulations on the Ministry of Environment Web site at *www.env.gov.bc.ca/fw/wild/hunting/regulations*. For tidal water or saltwater regulations, the federal Web site of Fisheries and Oceans Canada may be found at *www.pac.dfo-mpo.gc.ca.*

Yukon Territory. Licenses are valid from April 1 to March 31 and available at most sporting goods stores, highway lodges, or convenience stories. Barbless hooks are recommended for angling on all Yukon waters, and required in certain waters. Salmon fishing is permitted throughout the territory, with restrictions. Pick up the *Recreational Fishing Regulations Summary* when you obtain your license, but be aware that short-notice closures can occur. Before you go fishing, check with the Environment Yukon office in Whitehorse at 867-667-5652. For salmon fishing, you must have both the Yukon Angling License and a Salmon Conservation Catch Card. As soon as you catch a salmon, record necessary details on your catch card. You will be mailing the card to Fisheries and Oceans Canada no later than November 30, the end of the salmon season. If you are fishing in Kluane, Ivvavik, or Vuntut National Parks, a separate National Park Fishing License is required. For more information about sportfishing regulations and fees, browse *www.environmentyukon.gov.yk.ca/yukonfishing.*

The governments of Alaska and Yukon Territory observe a "good neighbor" policy that's beneficial to their sportfishing citizens. Those residents who are licensed in their home state or province may purchase a resident license should they cross the border to fish.

Alaska. Sportfishing licenses are required for anyone 16 and older in fresh and salt waters. A separate fee will be charged for a king salmon stamp. Licenses and fishing regs are available at most sporting goods stores and grocery stores. To arrange a license by mail, or for more information, write the Alaska Department of Fish & Game, Division of Sport Fish headquarters at P.O. Box 115525, Juneau, AK 99811-5526. Call 907-465-4180 or visit the Web site at *www.adfg.state.ak.us.* To speed up the process, you may apply for your license and purchase your king salmon stamp online at *www.admin.adfg.state.ak.us/license.*.

Fuel

In Canada, gasoline is measured by the liter, which equals about a quarter of a U.S. gallon, so there are roughly 4 liters per gallon. However, to convert exactly, multiply the number of liters by 0.2642 to find the number of U.S. gallons. (See the section on Metric Conversion, in this chapter.)

You may see an unusual fuel pump at some stations: Propane-powered vehicles are becoming more common in western Canada.

Guns/Ammo

Canada has strict regulations regarding entry of firearms into the country. The recently enacted Canadian Firearms Act requires individuals to obtain licenses to possess or purchase either guns or ammo. The law applies equally to residents and aliens on Canadian soil.

At the border, you will be asked to declare any firearms. No joking on this matter. If your memory fails you, your rifle or shotgun will be seized, and you may be fined or worse. Nonresidents who declare their sport or recreational-use firearms will complete a Nonresident Firearms Declaration form for a customs officer and pay $50 in Canadian. The approved form is your temporary license and registration certificate while in Canada. Don't plan to add to your collection while you're on the trip. Only licensed gun dealers may import firearms. When you cross back into the United States, officials will want to ensure that the same guns are in your possession as when you entered Canada.

What is prohibited? Fully automatic rifles and machine guns, handguns with a barrel length of 105 mm (about 4 inches) or less, .25- or .32-caliber handguns, sawed-off shotguns, and converted automatics. Other handguns fall under the category of "restricted." A person who is 18 or older must arrange for an Authorization to Transport, or ATT, from a provincial or territorial Chief Firearms Officer before arriving at the border. If you have questions, call the Canadian Firearms Centre, 1-800-731-4000, or visit their Web site at *www.cfc-cafc.gc.ca.*

Headlights

Law officers suggest that you drive with your headlights on, day or night, and always when their use is posted, as on the Seward Highway in Alaska. Yukon Territory law requires headlights at all times; in British Columbia and Alberta, watch for signs.

Hunting

Licenses and permits are required in individual provinces and in Alaska. No hunting is allowed in national parks.

Alberta. Licensing and permits are dependent upon the species, season, location, and other variables. You must be 12 years old to obtain a license. For more information, contact Alberta Sustainable Resource Development, Fish and Wildlife, at *www.srd.gov.ab.ca/fishwildlife* or call 780-944-0313. Hunting regulations may be found online at *www. albertaoutdoorsmen.ca/huntingregs.*

British Columbia. A hunting license as well as a species license is required for all resident and nonresident hunters. For Ministry of Environment hunting regulations or license information, contact the Fish and Wildlife Recreation Branch in Victoria, B.C., at 250-387-9589. A synopsis of the hunting and trapping regulations is available online at *www.env.gov.bc.ca/fw/wild/hunting/regulations.*

Yukon Territory. To hunt for big game in the Yukon, you are required to arrange for a licensed guide. A waiting period is required for licensing, so plan ahead. For more information on local guides, browse *www.yukonoutfitters.net.* Hunting regulations may be found on that

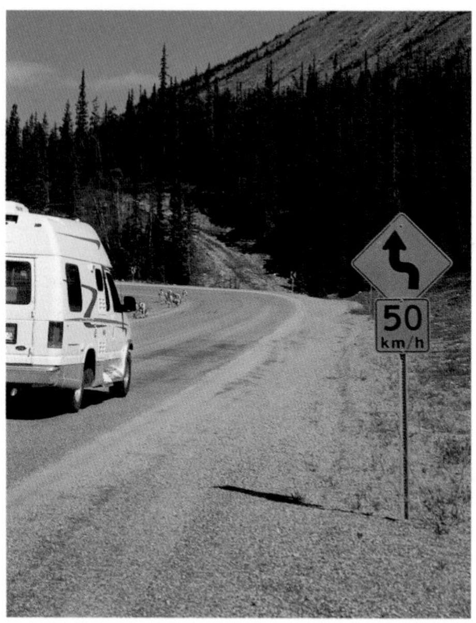

Speed limits in Canada are posted in kilometers. Since most speedometers include miles and kilometers, use yours to make a quick metric conversion for distances, too.

Web site as well, or call the Department of Environment in Whitehorse, Yukon Territory, at 867-667-5652.

Alaska. Licenses for sportfishing or hunting may be purchased online or by mail. U.S. citizens who are not residents of Alaska may obtain a nonresident big-game hunting license for $85 US, or a combination hunting/sportfishing license for $145. Either is good for the calendar year in which it is purchased. Nonresident aliens will pay $300 for a big-game license.

Additional fees will be charged for a tag, dependent upon the species that you're hunting. Licensed, nonresident hunters seeking a brown/grizzly bear, Dall sheep, or mountain goat must hunt with a licensed guide or with a resident family member who is 19 or older. A federal migratory bird-hunting stamp must be obtained for duck hunting. For more details on fees, seasons, and management units, contact the Alaska Department of Fish and Game, P.O. Box 115515, Juneau, AK 99811 or call 907-465-2376. Online hunting information is available at *www.admin.adfg.state.ak.us/license/permit.html.* You pay purchase your license and big-game tags online at *www.admin.adfg.state.ak.us/license.*

Insurance

Health insurance. All legal residents of Canada are part of a national health care system that's paid for through taxes and administered by each province. U.S. citizens who need to see a doctor or visit a clinic while traveling in Canada should expect to pay for services up front. You'll have to file for reimbursement from your insurer later. Check with your insurer regarding extended coverage while you travel, and what kind of help is available in case of an emergency that requires an ambulance or medevac services, which may not be covered on your regular policy.

Vehicle insurance. Check with your insurance agent before you leave home. You may need supplemental insurance for the trip. Make sure you understand how to file a claim if an accident occurs while you are driving in Canada. Carry proof of coverage with you at all times.

Lodging

Noncampers love the daily comfort of a clean, spacious bed, a hot shower, and cable television—and, if they're feeling especially wild, room service. In the following chapters, a list of hotels, motels, and lodges, along with contact information, follows each community profile.

The amenities listed for each property will help you estimate the price range and whether the lodging is suitable for your party. More than ever, people are traveling with pets, and more hotels and motels can accommodate them today, so be sure to ask when making a reservation.

As you travel north, fewer places advertise that they are air-conditioned, and more advertise their "winter plug-ins," parking places where winter travelers can plug in a vehicle that's equipped with an engine-block heater. Contact numbers for local bed-and-breakfast associations also are included in some listings.

Certain hotels in the United States and Canada display their Diamond Rating, awarded by the American Automobile Association or the Canadian Automobile Association. Ratings go from One Diamond for an establishment considered good, to Five Diamonds for a top-ranking luxury property with outstanding amenities. Also look for those businesses that have received a star rating in the Canada Select program, which rates cleanliness and maintenance standards, from one star for "good" to five stars for "exceptional."

Reservations are not always necessary, but it's best to call at least a day or two ahead anyway. Note that in some cases, toll-free numbers are operational only within the province or state, or only within Canada. If you hear that annoying message "Your call cannot be completed as dialed," it means you are outside the toll-free service area that was purchased by that business. Web sites are included where available.

Metric Conversion

Canada uses the metric system of measurement, while the U.S. system prevails on the other side of the border. A Canadian speed limit of 90 kilometers per hour is roughly equivalent to 55 miles per hour. Most speedometers are equipped with a dual scale. After several days in Canada, U.S. residents usually become accustomed to the unfamiliar and make the conversion to kilometers easily.

Here's a tip: Use your speedometer as a scale to translate distances accurately. A kilometer is roughly six-tenths (0.6) of a mile; a mile is roughly 1.6 kilometers. Here are a few sample conversions, all approximate:

To convert precisely between U.S. and metric measurements, use the following chart:

U.S. / Metric Conversion

From	*Multiply by*	*To get*
miles	1.6093	kilometers
kilometers	0.6214	miles
feet	0.3048	meters
meters	3.2808	feet
U.S. gallons	3.7853	liters
liters	0.2642	U.S. gallons
imperial gallons	4.5460	liters
liters	0.2201	imperial gallons
pounds	0.4536	kilograms
kilograms	2.2046	pounds

Kilometers		Miles
1	=	0.6
100	=	60
150	=	90
200	=	120
300	=	180

Money

Visit your bank before you leave home to exchange pocket money into Canadian dollars. Pocket change is handy for snacks, phone calls, souvenirs, etc. Your bank will inform you of the latest exchange rate, which fluctuates almost daily. These days you'll get only slightly more bang for the U.S. buck in Canada. Also, Canadian businesses are savvy about calculating the exchange, and often will do so as a courtesy if you have only U.S. dollars.

Traveler's checks (or *cheques* in Canada) are always a safe way to go, but you'll get the change in Canadian, and may end up with odd dollars and cents in your pocket when you re-enter the United States. If you don't want to carry around large quantities of Canadian cash, use your credit card for purchases and meals. Your bank will make the conversion to U.S. dollars on your billing statement, including a small fee. ATMs, or cash machines, may be found in most towns, and likewise your bank will make the conversion in your account. Be prepared to pay an ATM fee.

Also, get ready to carry your dollars in a coin purse or pocket. Canada's favorite nonpaper currency is the Loonie, a $1 coin imprinted with a loon. The $2 coin, worth two Loonies, is a Toonie. We found it easy to go through them faster than through paper bills, for some reason, and it was harder to keep track of how much change we were carrying, not unlike problems associated with the Susan B. Anthony dollar versus the 25-cent piece in the United States. Just a heads up!

In Alaska most businesses accept Canadian coins, except for the Loonie or Toonie. Visit the bank or currency exchange to trade the Canadian dollar coins and currency.

Mosquitoes

Alaskans like to joke that the mosquito is the Alaska state bird. After you see their unusually large size you may stop laughing and start running. Their cousins in Canada are just as big and persistent. They won't kill you, but they can make your outdoor experience an unhappy one.

Many a sourdough can recount stories of caribou herds incited to stampede because of mosquitoes, or backcountry hikers who jumped in a lake to escape. In fact, the term "gone caribou" often applies to people who, lacking spray-on repellent, begin hollering, waving their arms, and running to get away. Bring mosquito repellent and use it liberally. Anglers should not touch their fishing line with repellent on their hands, however. The chemicals will damage and weaken the line.

Sporting goods stores and catalogs offer hats equipped with mosquito netting to cover your face and neck. Hikers sometimes invest in a full suit of mosquito netting to wear over shorts and a T-shirt, rather than covering up and overheating in long sleeves and pants.

The gnat-size biting insects known as no-see-ums are a greater concern to backcountry travelers, as they can creep under cuffs and into tight places. Sometimes, swarms of no-see-ums can become so thick that, without a headnet, you cannot avoid breathing them in.

Pets

The most important piece of luggage for your dog or cat is a leash. Bring it along and use it. Campgrounds are pet friendly, as are some hotels and motels (call ahead), but

Born to be wild? A cushy ride in a motor home sure beats a hard back porch. Allow plenty of breaks to stretch your pet's legs—and yours.

all of them require pet owners to keep their "fur persons" on a leash when they are outdoors.

Nearly all rest stops have pet areas. Bring a rubber glove or plastic bags and pick up after your pet's daily constitutional. Plastic newspaper wrappers work well.

Take your dog or cat to a licensed veterinarian a week or less before you leave home, and obtain a signed health certificate with the declaration that the animal has received a rabies vaccination within the last 36 months. Keep its health certificate handy for international border crossings. The collar tag will not be enough proof. You may travel with a maximum of two puppies or kittens, along with a veterinarian's certificate stating that they are too young to vaccinate.

Make sure that your pet's prescription drugs are adequate for the number of days you'll be gone. Keep your hometown veterinarian's number close by in case an advisory call is needed.

Plants

If you're an RV traveler who likes the homey look of houseplants, best go with silk or plastic, just to make your crossing at the U.S.-Canada border a breeze. Due to agriculture officials' concerns about native plant health, certain plants may not be allowed entry without an import permit. Fresh fruits or vegetables that cannot be grown in Canada are not problematic, only those that can be grown there. Check with an office of the U.S. Department of Agriculture for more information.

Postage

For those traveling in Canada and sending mail to a U.S. address, expect to pay 93 cents (Canadian) for a stamp on mail weighing up to 30 grams (about an ounce), and $1.10 for postage on 30–50 grams. If your postcard or letter weighs up to 30 grams and is going to an international address, it will need $1.55 (Canadian) in postage.

Restaurants

The restaurant listings in the chapters that follow include a mix of casual family dining establishments, take-out or fast-food restaurants, ethnic dining choices, and fine dining restaurants.

Because chefs of the Northland pride themselves on their regional foods, we suggest you take advantage of northern specialties on the menu. In British Columbia, the Yukon, and Alaska, you may sample seafood entrees such as wild Pacific salmon (far superior in flavor and texture to farmed fish), king crab, shrimp, or scallops. Or try reindeer or buffalo for the first time. You're certain to discover new favorites or find a new spin on an old one.

In Canada, certain ethnic restaurants may also offer what they call a Western menu. You might think of it as an American menu—one for those who are in the mood for chicken or a hamburger.

Road Manners

Good manners know no international boundaries, so when you're driving the Alaska Highway, or any of the highways in this guide, give the other guy the benefit of the doubt, and don't drive like you're on the Beltway. Do not ride his bumper; do not pass in anger, or on a double yellow; and remember that RV drivers go only as fast as safety will allow. They know their vehicle limits.

Especially important for RV drivers: Alaska law states that if you are driving under the speed limit, and there are at least five vehicles behind you, you must pull over at the next available opportunity or you may be ticketed.

Should you pass by a wild animal on or near the road, flash your headlights to warn oncoming drivers to be on alert.

Keep your headlights on. Use your turn signals. Pass on the left. Smile and wave to the flagger. And remember, this is supposed to be a vacation, not a commute.

Royal Canadian Mounted Police

Originally established in 1873 as the North-West Mounted Police, the officers of the RCMP, or Mounties, bear the burden of the romantic image created in movies and books about their daring deeds. During the 1898 gold rush to the Canadian Klondike, the North-West Mounted Police brought order to Dawson City and to the border crossings at the Chilkoot and White Passes, demanding that stampeders carry a year's worth of supplies with them.

The Mounties are easily recognized in their dress uniforms of classic red tunics, sharply creased hats, and leather boots. Their daily work uniforms are much more mundane, as is the nature of most of their work. Like law enforcement everywhere, it's not all that romantic.

While few Mounties conduct their duties on horseback anymore, the image remains. In Whitehorse, you may catch sight of a red-uniformed Mountie and a horse named Chilkoot patrolling the streets and greeting visitors. In Alberta, officers of the K Division, along with other members of the Edmonton community, have formed the nonprofit RCMP Regimental Pipes and Drums corps, with the goal of using Celtic music to promote good relations between the RCMP and the public.

Time Zones

Most of Alaska is in the Alaska Time Zone, one hour behind Yukon Territory and British Columbia (Pacific Time Zone), which is one hour behind Alberta (Mountain Time Zone). So if it is noon in Anchorage, Alaska, it is 1 P.M. in Whitehorse, Yukon; also 1 P.M. in Prince

George, British Columbia; and 2 P.M. in Calgary, Alberta. Daylight saving time applies to all of these time zones. They "spring ahead" one hour in April to daylight saving time, then "fall behind" one hour in October to standard time.

Weather

The following chart provides a range of temperature and precipitation information for Alaska, the Yukon, Alberta, and British Columbia. In Canada, temperature is measured on the Celsius scale, and precipitation is measured in millimeters. Values below have been converted to Fahrenheit and inches.

To convert between U.S. and Canadian measurements, use these formulas:

- *Fahrenheit to Celsius:*
  Subtract 32 from the Fahrenheit temperature. Multiply by 5 and divide by 9.
- *Celsius to Fahrenheit:*
  Multiply Celsius temperature by 9. Divide by 5. Add 32.
  1 mm = .0394 inch 1 inch = 25.38 mm

Weather Chart

	Temperatures °F		
	January	*July*	
Community	*Mean Low*	*Mean High*	*Annual Precip./Inches*
ALASKA			
Anchorage	6	65	15
Denali Park	–8	43	15
Eagle	–13	73	11
Fairbanks	–21	72	10
Haines	18	67	47
Homer	15	61	24
Juneau	16	64	52
Ketchikan	29	65	156
Prudhoe Bay	–22	45	5
Seward	18	63	66
Skagway	19	67	28
YUKON TERRITORY			
Burwash Landing	–9.2	54.5	11
Dawson City	–30.5	72.1	2
Watson Lake	–12.3	58.8	16
Whitehorse	–1.7	57.2	11

(continues)

Community	*January Mean Low*	*July Mean High*	*Annual Precip./Inches*
ALBERTA			
Calgary	14.7	61.5	16
Edmonton	6.4	60.8	18
Grande Prairie	4.3	60.8	18
Lethbridge	16.9	65.1	16
BRITISH COLUMBIA			
Abbotsford	36	62.8	62
Dawson Creek	5.2	59.2	19
Fort Nelson	–7.6	62.1	18
Lytton	27.9	70.5	17
Prince George	14.2	59.5	24

Wheelchair Access

Never before have so many travel opportunities opened for vacationers who rely on wheelchairs for mobility or for seniors who need a little extra help as they travel. Throughout Alaska and western Canada, you will find many hotels and motels equipped with access ramps, nonslip flooring, grab bars in the tub and shower, bath boards, and easy-open doors. Visitors with vision loss will be pleased to find large-print information cards, and phones with extra-large numbers; those with hearing loss may reserve a room with a phone that amplifies sound.

Throughout western Canada, watch for the Access Canada logo in hotel and motel windows. These member businesses have geared a number of their rooms with physical access in mind. For more information on Access Canada and which businesses are participating, contact the following tourism offices.

Alberta: Alberta Hotel & Lodging Association. Call 1-800-252-7852 or visit *www.travelalberta.com.*

British Columbia: Tourism British Columbia. Call 1-800-435-5622 or browse *www.HelloBC.com.*

Yukon: Requests in writing may be mailed to Yukon Tourism and Culture, P.O. Box 2703, Whitehorse, Yukon Y1A 2C6. Call 1-800-661-0494 or visit *www.touryukon.com.*

In Alaska, businesses are tuning in to the needs of visitors who require wheelchair access. State parks and recreation areas are often equipped with wheelchair-accessible restrooms, plus wide, paved surfaces for trails into the woods. Even some of the best fishing holes have been reserved for anglers in wheelchairs. For more details, see *www.travelalaska.com.* Mail correspondents may write Alaska Travel Industry Association, 2600 Cordova Street, Suite 201, Anchorage, AK 99503. Or call the state's Division of Tourism at 907-465-4100.

If you drive north in early spring, you may see black bears feeding on new grasses at the edge of the forest.

Wildlife

You cannot pretend that you are driving on just any road anywhere. Every so often, the path of a plodding moose intersects the highway, and the person in the navigator's seat scrambles to grab the camera as you slow the vehicle and pull over in haste. The panic stop will happen again for a band of Dall sheep, for a caribou, a fox, a ptarmigan. It's hard to think clearly when the adrenalin is rushing through your veins, but stay aware of traffic ahead and behind you, and pull completely onto the shoulder before you stop.

What a rare and thrilling opportunity to observe a world that remains so unchanged in the twenty-first century. But please be mindful of a few basic rules:

Please don't feed the wildlife. Keep a respectful distance, knowing that powerful creatures such as bison or moose may panic and harm you. In the far north, animal life is plentiful, and there are no protective bars between you and the wild things.

Years ago, a Fairbanks woman driving on Chena Hot Springs Road came car hood to kneecaps with a bull moose standing in the middle of the road. She had slowed and stopped, but the moose didn't appear to be in a hurry. He stayed put. She honked her horn. He snorted. She honked again. He lowered his head and did significant damage to her car's front end before he shuffled off in a huff. The moral of the story is: Don't harass the animals. For roadside wildlife sightings—and you're likely to experience several—it's best to stay in the car. But don't creep closer, honk, or yell. From the comfort of your vehicle, enjoy the vision before you, up close and in focus, with your binoculars or camera equipped with a telephoto lens.

If you are involved in an accident with a big animal, immediately contact the local authorities. A charity will be contacted to field-dress the moose, caribou, or bison, and the meat will be donated to needy families.

Full-day or half-day cruises on the ocean afford the opportunity to see marine mammals in spectacular settings. They are well worth the cost, and often include lunch. Several day-cruise operators have ticket offices in downtown Anchorage, and some provide shuttle transportation to their vessels in a community south of the city, such as Seward, Whittier, or Homer. If you spend any time along the Inside Passage, you'll be treated to views of otters, eagles, plentiful bird life, and occasionally a whale.

At Watson Lake, the Alaska Highway Interpretive Centre includes a mini-museum on the building of the highway.

A LONE ROAD THROUGH THE WILDERNESS

Alaska Highway Facts

Length of historic route to Fairbanks: 1,523 miles (2,451 km)
U.S. troops used in construction: 11,000
Civilian workers: 16,000
Pieces of heavy equipment: 7,000
Bridges constructed: 133
Culverts installed: 8,000-plus
Highest mountain pass: Summit, 4,250 feet, at Historic Mile 392
Cost: $140 million (U.S. wartime dollars)
Began: March 1942
Completed: October 1942
Officially opened: November 20, 1942, at Soldiers Summit, Mile 1061
Time of construction: 8 months, 12 days
Opened to the public: 1948
Beginning, Mile 0: Dawson Creek, British Columbia
Official end: Delta Junction, Alaska, Mile 1422
Unofficial end: Fairbanks, Alaska, Historic Mile 1523

During 60 years of road improvements, the road was shortened by 35 miles.

CHAPTER 3

History of the Alcan: The Soldiers' Road

PROTECTING AMERICA'S NORTHERNMOST possession was a matter of national security in the early 1940s, and the task became especially critical after the Japanese bombed Pearl Harbor in December 1941. Alaska then became a potential enemy target. Without a land route between the Lower 48 states and Alaska, the U.S. military outposts in Fairbanks, Anchorage, and elsewhere in the territory were virtually stranded, dependent on supply deliveries by water and air, and vulnerable to attack.

A newer addition to the sights at Mile 0 is this sculpture of a road surveyor.

In 1942, Ladd Air Field in Fairbanks became especially strategic to the Allies' defense plan. Ladd was the final U.S. destination for warplanes that were flown along the Northwest Staging Route from the continental United States to Fairbanks. Small airstrips along the way constituted a dot-to-dot route through the Canadian wilderness. Along this line, Lend-Lease Program pilots—many of them women, who were not allowed to fly in combat—ferried aircraft for delivery to Russian pilots waiting in Fairbanks. These pilots then continued the journey over the Bering Sea to Russia. All told, nearly 8,000 fighters, bombers, and cargo planes were flown along the Northwest Staging Route.

Clearly a road was needed, and in fact it had been considered as early as 1905, when Major Charles Constantine of the North-West Mounted Police was charged to build a road to the Klondike but was later recalled from that effort. In the late 1920s and early 1930s, other proposed routes were examined and discarded. World War II was catalyst enough, and in March 1942, Canada and the United States came to terms on building the military road then known as the Alcan. Canada allowed rights-of-way and provided construction materials, while the U.S. military provided the manpower. It was agreed that the Canadian portion of the road would be turned over to Canada at the war's end.

When troop trains began pulling into Dawson Creek, B.C., a quiet hamlet boomed from a population of 600 to more than 10,000 by late March 1942.

Diaries recorded by the men who built the road portray an existence just as life-threatening as it might have been in battle. In the preliminary stage, workers felled trees to create a corduroy road, and the first bridges floated on pontoons. At Charlie Lake, three American soldiers drowned while crossing the lake on a pontoon barge.

That winter, the piercing cold was the enemy, along with the crude, temporary accommodations, bad food, and backbreaking, seven-days-a-week labor. Heavy equipment was sucked into the miry shoulders and sometimes abandoned. In below-zero temperatures, the big machines were kept running 24 hours a day, as they might not start again if allowed to cool. Trucks and bulldozers were pulled out of seemingly bottomless mud holes, and troop morale sagged with little contact from the outside world. In the summer, mosquitoes, no-see-ums, and black flies tortured the work crews.

Just as the American military had feared, Japan attacked and landed troops on U.S. soil in June 1942, briefly invading Alaska's Aleutian Islands at Kiska and Attu, and further heightening the sense of need for the road's completion. An ensuing battle at Kiska killed soldiers on both sides before Japanese troops retreated under cover of fog. Several Native Alaskans were taken from Attu to Japan as prisoners of war.

On September 25, 1942, the 35th Regiment of the U.S. Army Corps of Engineers, working from the south, met the soldiers of the 340th Regiment, working from the north, at a place named by the soldiers themselves: Contact Creek. The final link occurred a month later in Beaver Creek, Yukon Territory, when members of the 97th Engineers met the 18th Engineers and opened the road for military convoys to pass.

A photograph from that day shows two nose-to-nose bulldozers and two weary soldiers—one African-American, one Caucasian—shaking hands and smiling broadly for the camera. The official opening, along with a formal ribbon-cutting ceremony, came on a bitterly cold day—November 20, 1942—at what is now called Soldiers Summit at Kluane Lake, Mile 1061. Members of the Royal Canadian Mounted Police suffered in their dress uniforms at –35°F.

The Alcan would not be opened to civilian traffic until 1948, well after the war, and it remained a difficult journey suitable only for jeeps and specially equipped vehicles for many years.

The Canadian Army took over jurisdiction of the Canadian portion of the road in 1946 and continued maintenance until 1964, when that responsibility was handed to the Federal Department of Public Works. Since 1971 the Yukon Department of Highways and Public Works has been in charge of the portion that passes through the Yukon Territory.

With the 50th anniversary celebration of the Alaska Highway in 1992, commemorative license plates were issued for those who drove the route. In preparation for the anniversary year, paved but damaged sections of the highway were repaired, and unpaved stretches were widened and improved. In the following 15-plus years, road crews have continued to work at upgrades in targeted sections, and today the only unpaved stretches are those that are undergoing a second round of stripping and repaving or widening. Vestiges of the old road are occasionally visible, especially where engineers have abandoned the wildly curvy route and blasted a straighter line through rocky barriers that confounded the hurried road builders of the 1940s.

Tourism associations on both sides of the border joined forces to erect "historic mileposts"—which in most cases do not match current milepost or kilometer-post numbers. That's because the highway is now shorter than it used to be, thanks to all of the straightening and rerouting improvements of the last six decades.

Significant historic sites include construction camps, airstrips of the Northwest Staging Route, the memorably steep Suicide Hill, memorial sites for those who lost their lives, and boundary lines marking responsibility of various contractors. At Mile 0 of the Alaska Highway, the Dawson Creek Station Museum within the visitor center offers an hour-long video on the road's construction that's well worth the $2 admission fee. Also, the Alaska Highway Interpretive Centre at Watson Lake, Yukon Territory, at Mile 613, invites visitors to view its free exhibits on the building of the Alcan, which include historic documents, photos, and displays of life in the work camps.

On September 28, 1996, the American Society of Civil Engineers recognized the wartime road that was built with remarkable speed. Meeting in Dawson Creek, the organization announced that the Alaska Highway had been designated the 16th International Historic Civil Engineering Landmark. The Alcan joined the Eiffel Tower and the Panama Canal as rare examples of the world's construction marvels.

Alcan road builders battled deep mud that mired bulldozers as well as supply trucks. (Photo courtesy U.S. Army Corps of Engineers.)

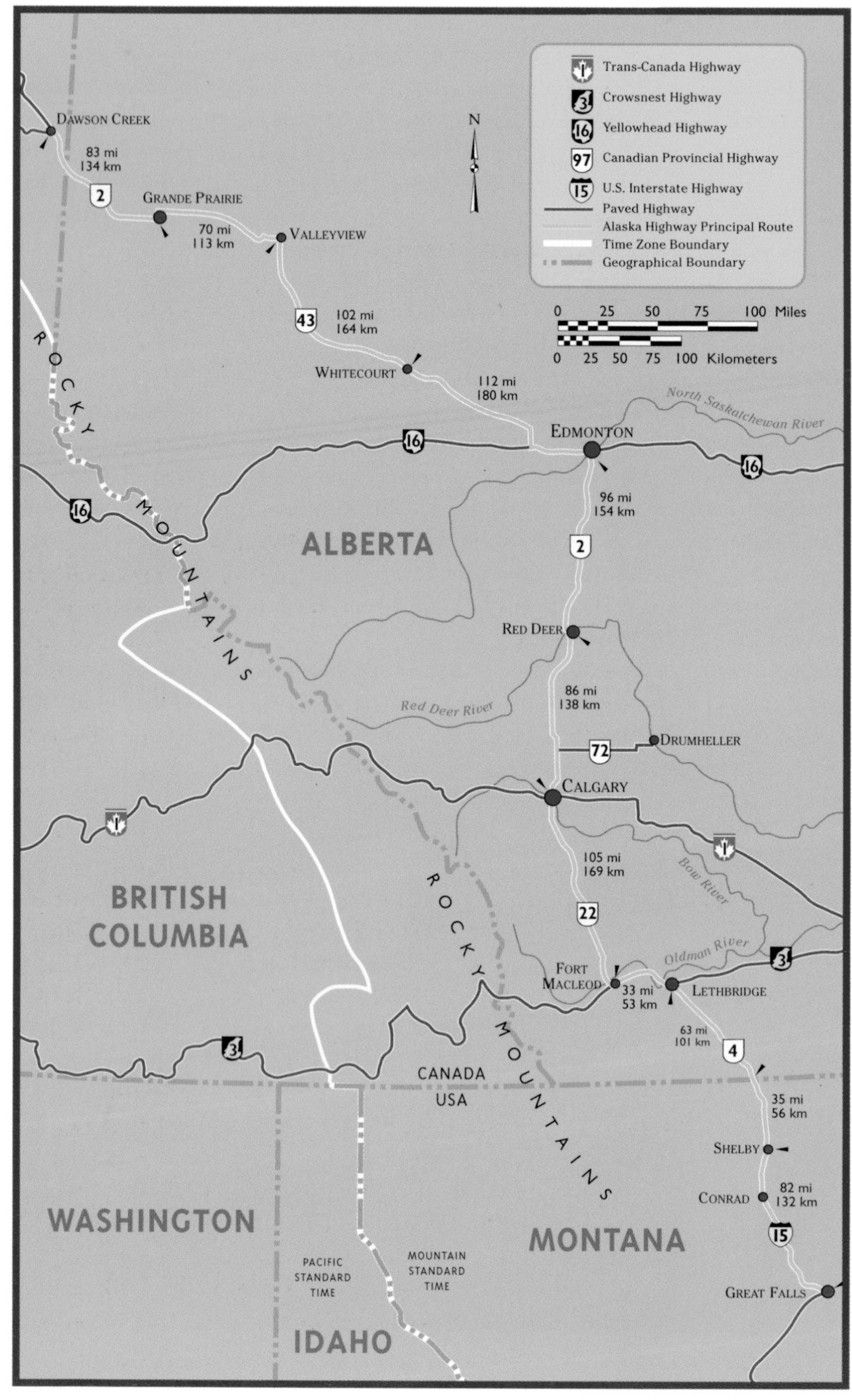
Trans-Canada Highway
Crowsnest Highway
Yellowhead Highway
Canadian Provincial Highway
U.S. Interstate Highway
Paved Highway
Alaska Highway Principal Route
Time Zone Boundary
Geographical Boundary
0 25 50 75 100 Miles
0 25 50 75 100 Kilometers
N
DAWSON CREEK
83 mi
134 km
GRANDE PRAIRIE
70 mi
113 km
VALLEYVIEW
102 mi
164 km
WHITECOURT
112 mi
180 km
EDMONTON
North Saskatchewan River
96 mi
154 km
ALBERTA
RED DEER
Red Deer River
86 mi
138 km
DRUMHELLER
CALGARY
105 mi
169 km
Bow River
Oldman River
FORT MACLEOD
33 mi
53 km
LETHBRIDGE
63 mi
101 km
35 mi
56 km
SHELBY
CONRAD
82 mi
132 km
GREAT FALLS
ROCKY MOUNTAINS
BRITISH COLUMBIA
CANADA
USA
WASHINGTON
MONTANA
IDAHO
PACIFIC STANDARD TIME
MOUNTAIN STANDARD TIME

CHAPTER 4

The Eastern Route: Through Alberta to Dawson Creek, B.C., and Mile 0

DRIVERS HEADED FOR ALASKA from the Midwest, Deep South, and East Coast often make a land cruise across many states on a trek that leads through Great Falls, Montana, and north into Alberta. The passage through northern Montana and into southern Alberta is settling to the soul—farms and fields, horses and cattle, and hard-working barns. Look out the side window, and your gaze may be met by a cow looking back. Fertile farmland rolls away in gentle, undulating waves beneath a bright sky. In late August, farmers may be seen baling hay, and huge, golden rolls are strewn about the fields in broad symmetry. In small towns, grain elevators are clustered next to the railroad tracks. The pace is nice and easy.

And yet this corridor into Alberta no more represents the entire province than the Inside Passage represents all of Alaska. Depending on where you spend most of your time, your definition of Alberta may be drawn from the stark badlands surrounding Drumheller, from the stunning mountain vistas of Waterton Lakes National Park, from the cityscapes of Edmonton and Calgary, or from the raw, mountainous wilderness of the northern regions of the province.

Within the past 200 years, across the desertlike landscape of southern Alberta, the Plains Indians once roamed freely and hunted wild game such as buffalo, pronghorn antelope, and coyotes. Here and farther north, these people of the First Nations lived an untrammeled existence until the arrival of explorers, traders, cowboys, law officers, and government representatives bearing treaties. The stories of the Natives—or at least a portion of them—are told today in culturally important places such as Head-Smashed-In Buffalo Jump, Fort Whoop-Up, Indian Battle Park, and Calgary's Heritage Park, and in smaller interpretive sites throughout the province. In western Canada, as in other regions of North America, aboriginal people are reawakening to some of their lost practices, and celebrating with dance, song, storytelling, and art.

More recent settlers of southern and central Alberta came to farm, work in the forests, or draw oil and natural gas from beneath the ground. Today farming is flourishing with the aid of modern irrigation practices, and oil, timber, and tourism also feed the province's healthy economy. As you motor through, you'll see livestock sharing some fields with working oil pumpjacks. In "fields" of their own, dense forests are grown for the purpose of cutting, just like wheat and hay—but harvest seasons are decades, not months, apart. Roadside signs show the date when a particular forest was last logged and replanted. In mill towns, visitors are invited in to see the latest manufacturing processes.

Tourism is a burgeoning industry as well, growing in leaps after the Alaska Highway was opened, when travelers were more apt to discover the attractions of Alberta during their long-distance journey. Its diverse wildlife, topography, and climate make this province more than just a place to pass through, but rather a place to count among your travel destinations.

For raw backcountry experiences, go northeast to the northern woods surrounding Lesser Slave Lake, or to the top of the province, where much of the wilderness remains untouched. To thrill to the province's prehistory, go east to Drumheller, where the onetime presence of dinosaurs is now a tourist attraction. If outdoor recreation is part of your vacation, throughout Alberta you'll find plenty of opportunity for camping, fishing, boating, swimming, and the like.

To learn more about what to see and do in Alberta, travel information is available at 1-800-ALBERTA (within North America) or at *www.travelalberta.com.* And if you're interested in staying in bed-and-breakfast accommodations, visit the Alberta Bed & Breakfast Association online at *www.bbalberta.com.* Those traveling with a pet should inquire if the B&B or hotel is "pet friendly." Many operations do allow pets for a small additional fee.

MONTANA–ALBERTA BORDER

To Lethbridge, Alberta: 63 miles (101 km)
To Dawson Creek, B.C.: 750 miles (1,200 km)

Interstate Highway 15 is the northbound road from Great Falls, Montana, to the Canada border. Little more than an hour north of Great Falls, stop at the little town of Shelby to top

ALBERTA AT A GLANCE

Size: 255,287 square miles or 661,142 square km
Population in 2006: 3,375,800
Capital: Edmonton
Tourism and Lodging: Travel Alberta, 1-800-252-3782 or *www.travelalberta.com*
Fishing and Hunting: Alberta Sustainable Resources, 780-944-0313 or *www.srd.gov.ab.ca*
Canada Border Information: 204-983-3500 (outside Canada) or *www.cbsa-asfc.gc.ca*

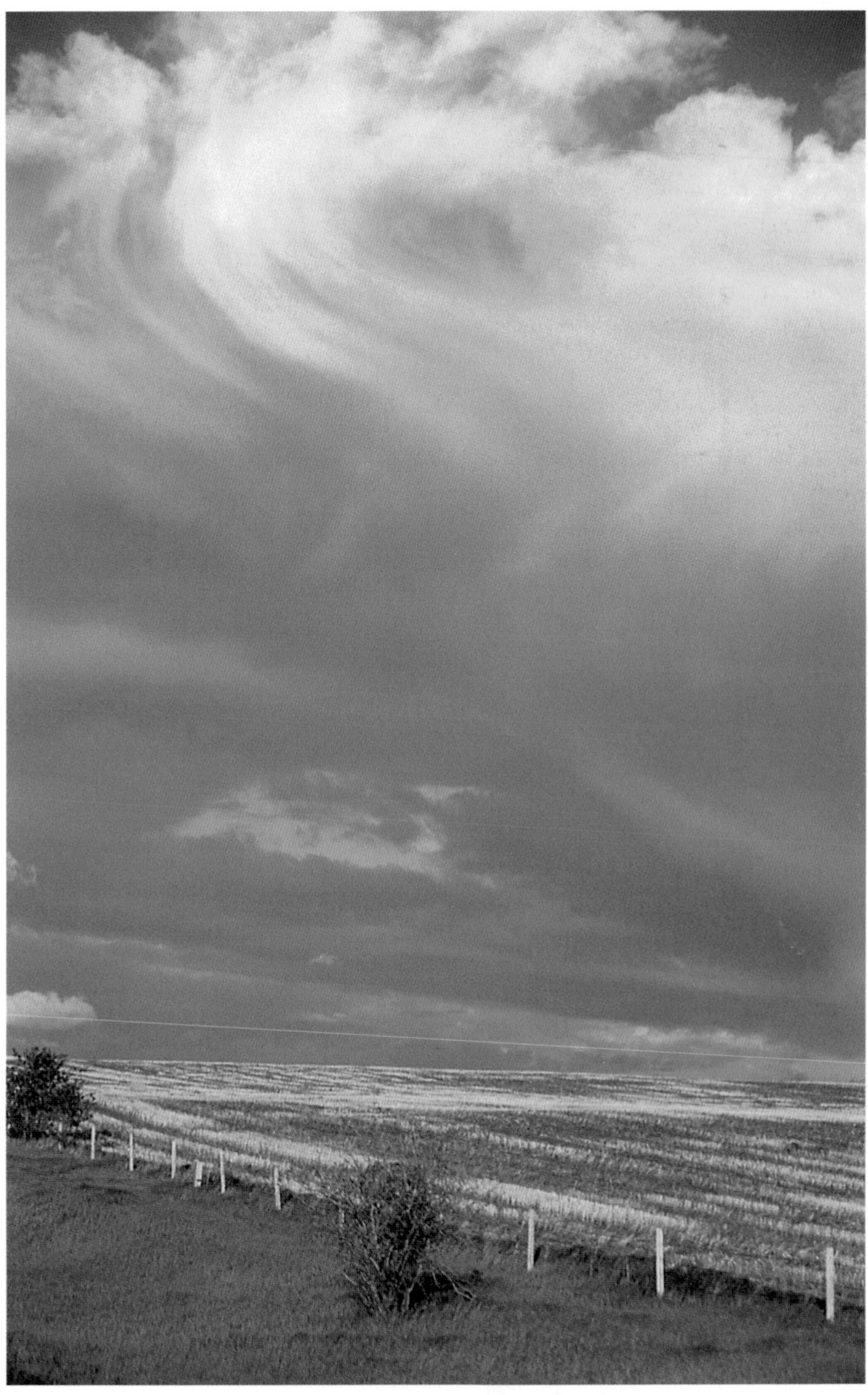

Southern Alberta is a mix of farmlands and badlands.

The border crossing at Coutts.

off the fuel tank. The price there will be lower than any other you'll encounter throughout western Canada. Driving north, the terrain will be familiar in Alberta. Like northern Montana, it is virtually treeless, with grain fields sweeping away from the roadsides. The road is generally straight and wide, with little changing except the occasional rise and fall. Oil pumpjacks are sometimes visible here, too, where a minor oil field lies beneath the farmland.

On the Montana side of the international border, the speed limit is 75 mph (110 kmh). Once you cross the border and start up Alberta Highway 4, no place will be higher than 110 kmh—more often it's 100. If you encounter a stretch of road construction, the speed limit may drop to between 30 and 50 mph (50 to 80 kmh).

The border crossing is a cluster of buildings in the middle of nowhere, and open 24 hours a day. On the Montana side, the place-name is Sweetgrass, a name it shares with the Sweetgrass Hills, a low mountain range on the eastern horizon. Coutts is the Canadian border town. Northbound travelers will stop at U.S. Customs and Immigration to answer a few questions, then continue to Canadian Customs and Immigration. Between them, you'll see a duty-free shop. The shop may be more attractive to southbound U.S. citizens as the place for "last chance" shopping. Here you can purchase Canadian goods with Canadian funds on Canadian soil, with savings on liquor, tobacco, perfume, souvenirs, toys, T-shirts, and caps. (See the section on Border Crossings in Chapter 2, What You Need to Know.)

Road Notes

Like northern Montana, southern Alberta enjoys a semiarid climate, with so much sunshine that farmers rely heavily on irrigation. Above the more level farms, the foothills are wrinkled and dimpled, treeless except for occasional clusters in the distance.

At the Milk River Travel Information Centre, 12 miles (19 km) north of the border, you'll find clean bathrooms, a picnic area, and information about the area's attractions, its history, and prehistory. A dinosaur model is there to greet the public just outside the facility. Nearby is a small, reasonably priced public campground with 34 sites, about half of which have full and partial hookup. Dry camping is available.

Farther up the road in the heart of town, multiple grain elevators alongside the railroad tracks are cleverly painted to look like milk cartons. Expect to see little else but farm country on both sides of the road all the way to Lethbridge—irrigated fields and grain elevators, ranging from the classic wooden buildings to shiny new metal structures.

Just past Milk River, you can take a tour of ancient petroglyphs by turning east for 26 miles (42 km) on Route 501 and following the signs to Writing-on-Stone Provincial Park, which was declared a national historic site in 2005. This archaeological preserve features huge sandstone outcrops with petroglyphs and pictographs inscribed by the Shoshoni and Blackfoot Indians. A camping area includes sites with or without electricity, coin-operated showers, and sani-dump. For more information, call 403-647-2364.

Devil's Coulee Dinosaur Heritage Museum is located in Warner, about 12 miles (19 km) north of Milk River. In the early 1990s, scientists discovered the world's largest dinosaur nesting site in this incredible land formation. Guided site tours twice daily at 10 A.M. and 1 P.M. allow visitors to view the excavation site, including intact embryos and eggs of Hadrosaur (duckbill) dinosaurs. Work continues here as paleontologists search for more clues to this area's prehistory, dating from 230 to 65 million years ago. Admission is charged. For more information, call 403-642-2118 or see *www.devilscoulee.com*.

LETHBRIDGE

From the border: 63 miles (101 km)
To Fort Macleod: 33 miles (53 km)

A lovely settlement along the Oldman River, Lethbridge offers the attractions of a big city in a little package. All services and facilities are available in this city of 82,692, from top-rated golfing to a natural history center, art galleries, a theater, beautifully landscaped gardens, and a university and archives. Shopping malls, vast retail outlets, and little shops provide plenty of shopping opportunities. Dine in style or eat on the run, choosing from among dozens of cafés, restaurants, and fast-food establishments. In 2006, Lethbridge celebrated its 100th birthday with a year of special events.

The Chinook Country Tourist Association operates a visitor center year-round near the junction of Scenic Drive (Highway 4) and Mayor Magrath Drive (Highway 5). Call 1-800-661-1222 or see *www.lethbridge.ca* for information. A second center, open March through October, is located on Scenic Drive off Highway 3, near Indian Battle Park.

Among the premier attractions in Lethbridge is its beautiful High Level Bridge, the longest and highest steel viaduct railroad bridge in the world. It spans the Oldman River Valley and soars above the site of a historic trading post. At Indian Battle Park, the last of the intertribal battles of North America took place, between the Cree and Blackfoot Indians. Besides picnic areas and playgrounds, the park features walking trails.

Beneath the High Level Bridge is Fort Whoop-Up Interpretive Centre, a great place to learn about the city's beginnings. With its log construction, old-time displays, and friendly gift shop, historic Fort Whoop-Up today seems like a tame tourism stop. Although this is a replica of the original, don't forget that log walls such as these have seen passion, fury, and acts of utter lawlessness.

Established in 1869 by two American fur traders, Fort Whoop-Up was once a critical post for whiskey runners. At that time, trade in buffalo robes flourished between Montana and Alberta. Payment with guns or illegal alcohol was commonplace, and powerful men took advantage of those who were addicted to the drink—trappers and pioneers, as well as members of local tribes.

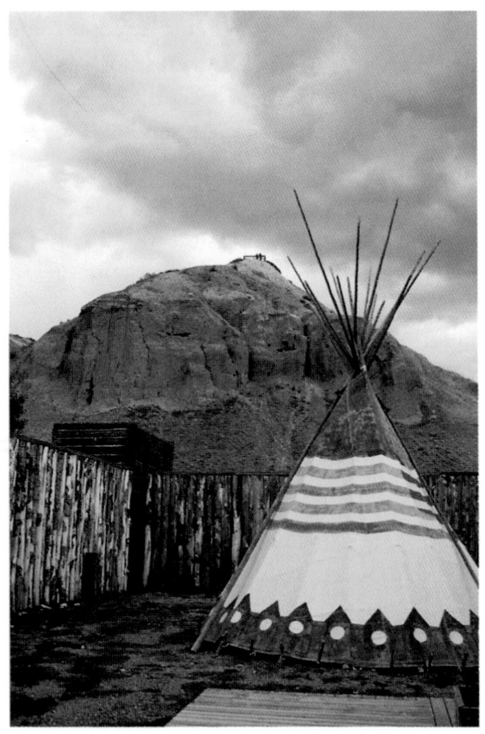

Fort Whoop-Up in Lethbridge flourished as a whiskey-running stop until the North-West Mounted Police arrived to stop the illegal activity.

With the arrival of the North-West Mounted Police in 1874, the lawlessness was contained, but the name stuck. A sign in northern Montana—the southern end of the whiskey trail—offered this explanation for the unusual name: "Origin of the name Whoop-Up is possibly from a conversation by a trader on the whiskey-for-furs trade route. Upon his return to Fort Benton, Johny LaMotte was asked 'How's business?' His reply, 'Aw, they're just whoopin' 'er up!'" Call about the historical reenactments at the present-day fort: 403-329-0444. See more at *www.fortwhoopup.com.*

For outdoor enthusiasts, the Helen Schuler Coulee Centre is an urban nature retreat that includes interpretive programs and touchable displays, as well as self-guided trails through the coulees and cottonwood forests on a 200-acre reserve. Watch for great horned owls, deer, and porcupines that make their homes in the reserve. The city offers numerous other hiking and biking opportunities, too, especially around Henderson Lake Park.

Events that draw big crowds are hosted at the Lethbridge Exhibition Park at 3401 Parkside Drive, east of Henderson Lake. More than a million visitors will roam the 67-acre grounds during events such as the Spring Rodeo and, in December, the Country Christmas Craft Show. The big daddy of them all, Whoop-Up Days, is held in early August, with a parade, chuckwagon races, midway rides, and a professional rodeo. The event line at the Exhibition Park is 403-317-3222, or browse *www.exhibitionpark.ca.*

The Galt Museum & Archives is located in what was once the Galt Hospital, overlooking the Oldman River Valley at the west end of 5th Street off Scenic Drive. Sir Alexander Galt was the founder of North Western Coal and Navigation Co. Displays and interactive programs teach about the history of Lethbridge, the settling of southern Alberta, and the area's first people. Some claim the museum is haunted. Call 403-320-GALT for recorded information or browse *www.galtmuseum.com.*

Golfers will be thrilled to play at the championship course of Paradise Canyon Golf Resort, once rated among Alberta's top seven golf courses by Canada's Golf Course Ranking Magazine and one of the best in North America by Golf Digest. Located at 107 Canyon Boulevard West. Call 403-381-4653 or see *www.paradisegolfresort.com*. Another option is a round at the Henderson Lake Golf Course at 2721 South Parkside Drive South, in the heart of the city. Call 403-329-6767 or see *www.hendersonlakegolfclub.com*.

The annual Alberta International Airshow is one of western Canada's best, according to Canadian Aviation News. Scheduled for early August at the Lethbridge Airport, south on Highway 5 from Lethbridge. The show features military and civilian aircraft in flying demonstrations, while ground displays invite visitors for a closer look. Admission is charged. For details, call 403-380-1222. Browse *www.albertaairshow.com.*

For more information about Lethbridge, call the Chinook Country Tourist Association at 1-800-661-1222, browse *www.lethbridge.ca.*

A GARDEN OF INTERNATIONAL FRIENDSHIP

The walkway to the entrance of Nikka Yuko Japanese Garden offers a clue to the visual treat on the other side of the gates. With a name that translates to "Japan–Canada Friendship," the garden is located on the corner of 9th Avenue South and Mayor Magrath Drive. On either side of the entry path, pink and white impatiens have been planted to create a specific, rigid pattern. But that is the last of the brash color. Don't enter this garden expecting a rush of floral sights and scents. A true Japanese garden offers quietude and the opportunity for meditation, not overstimulation of the senses. In these 4 acres, you will appreciate the beauty in simplicity, in a garden designed by respected landscape architect Tadashi Kubo, assisted by Masami Sugimoto.

At the center, an authentically built Japanese teahouse—shoes off at the door, please—is surrounded by carefully groomed walkways, pruned trees, and paths that have been meticulously landscaped. Nothing is out of place, not even the rocks in the pond, or the pebbles along its shore specially chosen for their size and shape, then laid in an overlapping design. Everything about this controlled landscape reflects the Japanese desire to express an understanding of humanity's place in the environment.

In the distance, you'll occasionally hear the low, muffled toll of a huge bell. You will find it at eye level near the end of a path, and you may move the clapper if you like. The weight of the bell hanging inside a unique gazebo-like structure actually keeps the walls and beams together. Like the Japanese house, this perfectly engineered and fitted structure contains no manufactured nails.

Kimono-clad women of Japanese heritage guide the way and explain cultural practices as well as relate how this lovely place came to be. Admission is charged. For more information, call 403-328-3511.

Other attractions within Henderson Lake Park include a picnic area, bowling green, golf course, swimming pool, and rose gardens.

TABER: WHERE CORN IS KING

One of the pleasures of road travel is stopping at a roadside stand and picking up fresh fruits or vegetables for the evening meal. Or you may choose to just eat a sweet, juicy peach right there over the grass and let the juice drip off your chin and fingers. I quickly became obsessed with finding the best sweet corn.

Driving through this part of western Alberta, or west in British Columbia, you'll see many fruit and vegetable stands with crudely made signs declaring TABER CORN! "What in the world is Taber corn," we wondered, "and what makes it better than any other?" We got our answers when we stopped where a woman was selling several corn varieties from the back of her truck—and was giving out corn recipes and information with each purchase. She knew a lot about flavor differences among varieties, and she solved for us the mystery of Taber corn.

It seems that the Taber area, east of Lethbridge on Highway 3, has become known far and wide for its sweet corn: delicate and white, or bulky yellow, or multicolored beauties. The Taber Cornfest in early August includes corn-tasting, fireworks, midway rides, car show, entertainment, and beer garden. With an average of more than 2,300 hours of sunshine a year and up to 120 frost-free days, the Taber area grows much more than just corn. It is known as the Market Garden of Canada, with crops that include beets, potatoes, grains, and many types of vegetables.

"The area has near-perfect growing conditions," says farmer Carl Valgardson, "with sandy loam soil, long warm summers, and irrigated fields." We picked up half a dozen ears and immediately learned why Taber is the corn capital. The kernels fairly exploded with sweetness. If you appreciate a good ear of corn or other fresh vegetables and fruits, make road-stand shopping part of your drive.

If you're traveling through the area in late August, make a point of joining the end-of-season harvest celebration at the Taber Cornfest. For more information, call 403-223-2265.

LODGING

Best Western Heidelberg Inn
1303 Mayor Magrath Drive
1-800-791-8488 or 403-329-0555
66 air-conditioned rooms with cable TV and Internet. Fitness room, sauna. Three-Diamond rating, AAA/CAA. Pub, liquor store, restaurant.

Canada's Best Value Inn Lethbridge
1030 Mayor Magrath Drive
403-328-6636
56 air-conditioned units, Internet, cable TV with free movies. Family rates. Discount at adjacent restaurant.

Chinook Motel
1245 Mayor Magrath Drive
1-800-791-8488 or 403-329-0555
20 air-conditioned rooms, telephones, cable TV, Internet. Vehicle plug-ins.

Comfort Inn
3226 Fairway Plaza Road South
1-866-554-4110 or 403-320-8874
58 units, cable TV, Internet, fridge/microwave. Pool, hot tub, exercise room. Free continental breakfast, coffee. Family rates.

Days Inn Lethbridge
100 3rd Avenue South
1-800-DAYS INN or 403-327-6000
www.daysinn.ca
91 units including nonsmoking rooms. Cable TV, movies, exercise room, whirlpool. Free continental breakfast, coffee. Winter plug-ins, coin laundry. Senior discount.

Econo Lodge and Suites
1124 Mayor Magrath Drive
403-328-5591 / *www.choicehotels.ca*
44 air-conditioned units with fridges, cable TV. Vehicle plug-ins. Adjacent to restaurant/lounge.

Holiday Inn Express Hotel & Suites
120 Stafford Drive South
1-877-508-1762 or 403-394-9292
102 air-conditioned units with fridges, high-speed Internet, cable TV. Exercise room. Family rates, vehicle plug-ins.

Howard Johnson Express Inn
1026 Mayor Magrath Drive
1-800-597-1114 or 403-327-4576 / *www.hojo.com*
37 air-conditioned units with fridges, hair dryers, iron and board, Internet, cable TV. Bridal suites available. Pool, vehicle plug-ins, free continental breakfast.

Lethbridge Lodge Hotel
320 Scenic Drive
1-800-661-1232 or 403-328-1123
www.lethbridgelodge.com
Full-service hotel with 190 rooms around tropical courtyard, indoor pool, hot tub, fitness facility. Two restaurants, lounge, downtown location. Free shuttle service.

Lethbridge Village Inn
207 Fourth Avenue South
1-800-416-0305 or 403-327-2104
32 units with fridges, hair dryers, Internet, cable TV. Park Café, lounge and night club. Vehicle plug-ins. Family rates.

Parkside Inn Lethbridge
1009 Mayor Magrath Drive South
1-800-240-1471 or 403-328-2366
65 air-conditioned rooms. Cable TV, room service, laundry service, whirlpool, exercise room, sundeck. Lounge with live entertainment. Adjacent to Henderson Lake Golf Course and Nikka Yuko Japanese Garden.

Peppertree Inn Lethbridge
1142 Mayor Magrath Drive
1-800-708-8638 or 403-328-4436
56 air-conditioned rooms, with refrigerators, fax jacks, VCRs, cable TV, and movies. Nonsmoking available.

Premier Inn & Suites Lethbridge
2225 Mayor Magrath Drive South
403-380-6677
50 rooms, business center, free continental breakfast. Fitness room, shuttle, laundry facilities.

Ramada Hotel & Suites Lethbridge
2375 Mayor Magrath Drive South
403-380-5050
Well-appointed rooms, full business and fitness facilities. Close to attractions. Two waterslides, kiddie pool, wave pool.

Sandman Hotel Lethbridge
421 Mayor Magrath Drive
1-800-266-4660 or 403-328-1111
www.sandmanhotels.com
139 air-conditioned rooms, with nonsmoking available. Cable TV and movies. Executive floors, exercise room. Restaurant, room service, lounge, hair salon, vehicle plug-ins.

CAMPGROUNDS

Bridgeview RV Resort
1501 2nd Avenue West (just west of Oldman River)
403-381-2357
163 sites, 30- to 50-amp service, 70 pull-throughs, full and partial hookups, Internet. Laundry, heated pool. Restaurant.

Henderson Lake Campground
3419 Parkside Drive South (next to Henderson Lake Park)
403-328-5452
100 sites with full or partial hookups. Showers, laundry, restrooms. Grocery store, canoeing. Shopping and dining nearby. Next to golf course.

RESTAURANTS

Also note in the Lodging list that most major hotels include restaurants and lounges.

Bottomley's Fish & Chips
425 13th Street North
403-317-3007
Traditional, authentic English fish-and-chips shop.

Casa Mayas Mexican Eatery
1020 Mayor Magrath Drive South
403-327-5660
Full menu in Mexican-themed setting.

Cheesecake Café
904 2nd Avenue South
403-394-2253
Full menu, family dining, fireplaces, outdoor seating, lounge. Sunday brunch.

Dionysios Restaurant
635 13th Street North
403-320-6554 / *www.dionysios.ca*
Greek food, East Indian, pastas, steaks, ribs, etc.

Earl's Restaurant
203 13th Street South
403-320-7677
Family dining, indoor and outdoor seating.

East Side Mario's
3720 Mayor Magrath Drive South
403-331-0123
American-Italian food in a fun eatery.

Georgio's Contemporary Dining
1520 3rd Avenue South
403-328-0676
Modern and traditional cuisine.

Keg Steakhouse & Bar
1717 Mayor Magrath Drive
403-327-2727
Steaks and more on upscale menu, lounge.

La Bella Notte
402 2nd Avenue South (in Old Firehall No. 1)
403-320-0533
Italian dining in the historic Old Firehall No. 1, downtown.

Lethbridge Lodge
320 Scenic Drive South
1-800-661-1232 or 403-328-1123
Four dining and entertainment choices including Botanica's Restaurant, Anton's Restaurant, Cotton Blossom lounge, and Esmeralda's (Essie's) Bar.

Luigi's Pizza & Steak House
1119 Mayor Magrath Drive South
403-329-8322
Casual atmosphere with meat and pasta dishes; close to hotels.

Never on Sunday Authentic Greek Restaurant
365 Stafford Drive North
403-327-5413
Authentic Greek dishes, appetizers to desserts.

O-Sho Japanese Restaurant
311 4th Street South
403-327-8382
Extensive menu for diners at tables, booths, tatami rooms, or sushi bar.

Penny Coffee House
331 5th Street South
403-320-5282
Coffee and other beverages, sandwiches, baked goods.

Ric's Grill
103 Mayor Magrath Drive South
403-317-7427
Stunning views from the top of the old Lethbridge Water Tower. Award-winning cuisine. Lounge.

Streetside Eatery
317 8th Street South
403-328-8085
Salads, burgers, steaks, Greek food, pasta in relaxed, downtown setting.

Top Pizza & Spaghetti House
11th Street and 4th Avenue South
403-327-1952
Pizza and pasta in a casual setting.

Road Notes

You won't see a lot of rest stops as you drive west from Lethbridge on Highway 3, then north from Fort Macleod on Highway 2. So plan your stops around these bigger towns instead.

The prairies of southern Alberta are windy. The prevailing wind ruffles through the crops on either side of the road, and it takes only a little imagination to see the surface of the grain fields as sea waves or a living thing that ripples with movement. Lift your eyes and enjoy the prairies and badlands beneath this big sky.

About 18 miles (29 km) west of Lethbridge, you'll enter the Oldman River Valley. Note where, over time, the river has created coulees: treeless valleys beneath high ridges. To the west, the Canadian Rockies are visible.

WEST TO A NATIONAL TREASURE

Consider a side trip to **Waterton Lakes National Park**, which lies about 75 miles (120 km) south and west of Lethbridge on Route 5, or the same distance traveling due west from Milk River on Highways 501 and 5. This area is rich in biological diversity and is extraordinarily beautiful, marked by vast lakes, waterfalls cascading from dramatic mountain peaks, and streams full of fish. The park's southern boundary lies adjacent to Glacier National Park in Montana. Like Waterton Lakes, **Glacier National Park** is a natural beauty worthy of exploration. Of course the two national parks are part of a single landscape onto which political boundaries have been drawn—and that was only yesterday in geologic time. Indeed, billion-year-old rocks have been identified in this glacier-carved region.

In 1932, Waterton Lakes National Park and Glacier National Park were together designated as the first International Peace Park, commemorating the friendship between the countries and their commitment to shared resource management. The combined national parks are included on a list of modern-day wonders of the world as a UNESCO World Heritage Site. Both parks offer backcountry hiking, camping, horseback riding, rafting, biking, and other recreation. For more information on Waterton Lakes National Park, call 403-859-2224; *www.pc.gc.ca./pn-np/ab/waterton*. For more on Glacier National Park: 406-888-7800 or *www.nps.gov/glac*.

FORT MACLEOD

From Lethbridge: 33 miles (53 km)
To Calgary: 105 miles (169 km)

This charming city of nearly 3,000 people is centrally located on the crossroads of Highways 2 and 3. One of Alberta's oldest communities, Fort Macleod (muh-CLOUD) was founded in 1874 by the North-West Mounted Police when the patrol established a post on the Oldman River. Today the downtown historic district includes more than 30 historic and architecturally significant buildings dating from 1880 to 1920. Guided or self-guided walking tours are fun, and shopping is plentiful.

Stay on Highway 3 West and it will become a one-way street through the downtown core. At 219 25th Street, you'll find the Visitor Information Centre, located in the Fort Museum of the North West Mounted Police. This is a replica of the original fort that depicts pioneer and Native life in the late 1800s, and a highly recommended stop for history buffs. Mid-August brings the Annual Heritage and Quilt Show. Check for details at *www.nwmpmuseum.com*.

Other historic buildings include the Fort Macleod Empress Theatre on Main Street (Red Coat Trail), which opened in 1912 and is still in operation. The Empress is Canada's oldest continually operating theater west of Winnipeg. Ask about Eddy, the resident ghost.

HEAD-SMASHED-IN BUFFALO JUMP

For centuries, the buffalo hunters of the Plains Indians counted on this region's topography to help them kill their prey. Incited to stampede, a portion of the herd would follow the natural contours of the land along a route that gradually narrowed until the animals encountered an escarpment, 37 feet high and 1,000 feet (305 m) long. The buffalo would fall headlong to their deaths, and the waiting party at the bottom of the cliff would immediately set to work on the meat and hides. Only the bones were left behind to disintegrate with time.

The Plains Indians hunted buffalo this way for more than 6,000 years. At the first arrival of Europeans, there were an estimated 16 million bison on the North American plains. By 1879 they were virtually extinct due to hunting by non-Natives.

Head-Smashed-In, a UNESCO World Heritage Site, is one of the largest and best-preserved buffalo jumps on the continent. Most jumps were disturbed prior to World War II because they held centuries of bones, which are high in phosphorous, a necessary ingredient for munitions, explosives, and gunpowder. Through these hurried and haphazard excavations, most archaeological sites of the Plains Indians were destroyed.

To reach Head-Smashed-In, turn off from Highway 2 about 4.5 miles (7 km) north of Fort Macleod. Then take Route 785 west for 10 miles (16 km) to the RV parking area.

A five-level interpretive center built into the cliffside is open year-round. Displays include a diorama with full-size mounted buffalo, films explaining the traditional hunt, a restaurant, and a gift store. Visitors can handle objects such as a stone club, an arrow, a buffalo robe, tools made from bone, a hide scraper, and a flint knife. Native interpreters are on duty to add to the store of information. A wheelchair-accessible trail leads to the buffalo jump along the edge of the escarpment.

In the museum, the treatment of Natives at the hands of non-Natives is presented without anger: The objects and documents themselves tell the tragic stories. Artifacts include a payment book from 1890 listing names of reservation residents and what they were paid annually. Men, women, boys, and girls were paid differently, amounts ranging from $1 to $7. Also on display is a book of passes to leave the reservation, which required the signature of a Department of Indian Affairs agent. Each person's name seems to hold a story: One Owl; Rises with the Sun; No Account Woman.

The name Head-Smashed-In comes from the story of a young man, many years ago, who hid beneath the escarpment during a buffalo hunt and died from a skull fracture.

Westerly winds are nearly constant at Head-Smashed-In, blowing 314 days of the year, sometimes with almost hurricane force. Wear a scarf or a secure hat and clothes that you can button up or zip shut. Bring your sunglasses, too.

Every Wednesday in July and August, First Nations people gather on the plaza for dancing and drumming. The public is invited to the celebration at 11 A.M. and 1:30 P.M.

For more information, call 403-553-2731, or visit the center's Web site at *www.head-smashed-in.com*.

Even the local golf course is rooted in history. This is western Canada's oldest course, having been established in 1890. For more on this and other area attractions, check *www.fortmacleod.com.*

The provincial government operates a recreation area on the Oldman River, north of town on Highway 2 near the bridge (see list of campgrounds), and a wildlife reserve adjacent to the Oldman River offers hiking, biking, birding, and fishing. The reserve habitat supports deer, many species of birds, and beavers. Spend a few hours berry picking for local varieties such as Saskatoon, chokecherry, and buffalo.

A side trip to the municipality of Crowsnest Pass—56 miles (91 km) west of Fort Macleod on Highway 3—has much to offer. A nearby interpretive center provides a slide show, self-guided walks, and programs that recall the Frank Slide, the 1903 disaster that wiped out half the town of Frank as it dumped 90 million tons of rock. Nearby Leitch Collieries features the ruins of a powerhouse, mine manager's residence, coke ovens, and other signs of earlier life in this coal-mining valley. An admission fee is charged. For more information: 403-562-7388 or *www.frankslide.com.*

Elsewhere in Crowsnest Pass, you may go underground for a tour of the Bellevue Mine. Throughout the guided tour, each visitor wears a hard hat equipped with a miner's lamp. You will descend through about 330 feet (100 m) of the main rock tunnel and into 660 feet (200 m) of the coal seam. Admission is charged. Call 403-564-4700 or see *www.bellevuemine.ca.*

Head-Smashed-In Buffalo Jump is an architectural beauty set into the side of a bluff.

LODGING

FORT MACLEOD:

Century II Motel
462 Main Street East
403-553-3331
14 air-conditioned units, cable TV, coffee, modem jacks. Pets upon approval.

DJ Motel
416 Main Street
403-553-4011 / *www.djmotel.com*
15 air-conditioned units, some nonsmoking. Cable TV and movies, data ports, barbecue area.

Fort Motel
451 24th Street
403-553-3115
14 air-conditioned units, with cable and satellite TV. Nonsmoking, kitchenettes, rooms with data ports available. Free coffee, free local calls.

Heritage House Motel
140 Col. Macleod Trail (West End)
403-553-2777
12 units, some with air-conditioning. Cable TV, coffee, family plan. No phones in room. Senior rates. Pets upon approval.

Red Coat Inn
359 Main Street
403-553-4434
www.redcoatinn.com
28 air-conditioned units, fridges, microwaves. Cable TV, free movies, barbecue area, senior and family rates. Pets upon approval.

Sunset Motel
104 Highway 3 West
1-888-554-2784 or 403-553-4448
22 air-conditioned units. Refrigerators, free coffee. Fax-ready telephones, cable TV and movies, winter plug-ins. Gift shop, free continental breakfast. Adjacent to self-service laundry. Two-Diamond rating, AAA.

CAMPGROUNDS

Buffalo Plains RV Park & Campground
7.5 miles (12 km) west of Fort Macleod, via Route 785
403-553-2592
www.buffaloplains.com
23 sites with views of foothills and mountains, partial hookups. Tenting area, firewood, community fire pit. Showers, laundry, restrooms, sani-station. Playground. Open May-early October. Near Head-Smashed-In Buffalo Jump.

Daisy May Campground
249 Lyndon Road
403-553-2455
www.daisymaycampground.com
120 sites, with full and partial hookups. Laundry, camp kitchen. Heated pool, game room, mini-golf. Across from golf course. Open May–October.

Oldman River Provincial Recreation Area
0.3 miles (.5 km) northwest of Fort Macleod on Highway 2
403-627-3765
40 sites on Pincher Creek. Sheltered picnic areas, dump station, fishing, canoe access.

River's Edge RV Park & Campground
Near junction of Highways 2 and 3 on the Oldman River
403-553-0334
Partial hookups or dry camping. Open mid-April to mid-October.

RESTAURANTS

Aunty Lynda's Dining Room
170 24th Street, No. 2
One-half block from Fort Museum
403-553-2655
Family dining featuring steaks, seafood, pasta, soups, salad.

Crossroads Café
813 11th Street
In the Fort Macleod Auction Market Building
403-553-4040

Head-Smashed-In Buffalo Jump Restaurant
11 miles (18 km) northwest of Fort Macleod at Buffalo Jump
403-553-2731
Cafeteria-style dining at interpretive center for Buffalo Jump.

Luigi's Pizza & Steak House
537 24th Street
403-553-4555
Pasta and steak, lounge.

Macleod's Restaurant & Lounge
271 23rd Street
403-553-8841
Full menu for family dining.

New Hong Kong Restaurant
520 25th Street
403-553-3838
Family dining for Chinese and Western-style meals.

Silver Grill
246 24th Street
403-553-3888
Chinese and Western-style dining in family atmosphere.

Westerner Family Restaurant
404 24th Street
403-553-4066
Restaurant, ice cream. Lounge.

Road Notes

This semiarid region seems like a Hollywood Western backlot. There is little shade from the sun, the soil is dry and rocky, and hot wind snaps your clothing when you step outside. It's easy to imagine that this place was once thick with buffalo, and you can picture nomadic Indian tribes setting up seasonal hunting camps as they traveled and hunted.

Just ahead is a UNESCO World Heritage Site called Head-Smashed-In Buffalo Jump, where the hunting practices of the Plains Indians, as well as their cultural history, are presented in a beautiful interpretive center.

As you continue driving north, the road divides Claresholm, a town of over 3,600 people at the edge of beautiful foothills. The townspeople call their place, "Where the wheatlands meet the range." The Claresholm Museum and visitor information is found in an elegant old sandstone railroad station at 5126 Railway Avenue. You can also visit the town's original 1903 schoolhouse and a nearby log cabin dating from 1902. Other local offerings include bowling, billiards, motels, auto repair, a car dealer, and a grocery store. Camping with a dump station and playground is available in the town's Centennial Park. A new full service, 18-hole golf course called The Bridges of Claresholm rounds out the recreational offerings, along with the town's swimming pool, and curling and skating rinks. It's a lovely little town. For more details, call 403-625-3381 or see *www.townofclaresholm.com.*

About 25 miles (40 km) beyond Claresholm, you'll enter the historic village of Nanton, where antiques are taken seriously. Downtown Nanton shops hold uncountable treasures, crafts, and collectibles, plus the town's old blacksmith shop, the Willow Creek Forge. Also downtown: a tearoom, restaurants, and auto repair and gas services. Aircraft buffs will enjoy a stop at the Lancaster Air Museum on Highway 2 South. Open daily May to October. Weekends in off-season. The visitor center is in the little yellow MacEwan School House on Highway 2 north near Main Street. Built in 1906, it was relocated here and lovingly restored. Call 403-646-6228 for more information on Nanton happenings.

Driving north of Nanton, we encountered our first roadside wildlife: a buffalo herd grazing in the roadside grass. Numbering about a dozen, they didn't seem to mind the traffic or the idea of having their picture taken by a woman hanging out of an RV window. Remember, that's the best advice—stay in your vehicle, and if you want close-ups, get a longer lens. But don't risk your safety or harass the wildlife by approaching on foot.

Alberta's open skies are spectacular in this region, with shades of blue from delicate to rich, velvety hues—and the natural artistry in the clouds, in their streaks, layers, balls, and fingers in tones from gray to bleach white. It's a pleasure to just gaze at the heavens.

About 163 miles (262 km) north of the Canadian border, you'll see the turn onto Highway 23 West for High River, population 9,500. Architects, geologists, and historians alike will enjoy touring High River's sandstone buildings. You can also take a guided tour of local murals. Each summer the city hosts championship chuckwagon racing and a favorite local event, the Little Britches Rodeo. For more information, call the Chamber of Commerce at 403-652-3336. This is the last stop before Calgary, 37 miles (59 km) to the north. However, if your family likes to track down natural wonders and oddities, there's one more place to see: the Okotoks Erratic, the largest known glacial erratic in the world. Basically it's a gigantic boulder that was kicked out as glaciers retreated from this region. Look for the exit to Okotoks via Highways 7 and 547.

CALGARY

From Fort Macleod: 105 miles (169 km)
To Red Deer: 86 miles (138 km)
To Edmonton: 181 miles (291 km)

At the confluence of the Bow and Elbow Rivers, with the purple Rocky Mountains to the west, Calgary is a marvelous place to work and play. And judging from the city's calendar of events, it seems that there's plenty of both here.

With a population of nearly 1,038,000, this town is experiencing a growth spurt, but it hasn't forgotten its roots in the Wild West. It is that usual contrast of wilderness and metropolis, cowboys and businessmen, a rodeo among the skyscrapers, that makes Calgary such a popular destination. Throughout western Canada, this city has gained a winning reputation for its restaurants, shopping, museums, festivals, art, music, and flowers. And in the world of professional rodeo throughout North America, it is famed for its main event, the Calgary Stampede.

In the summer of 1875, when an expedition of North-West Mounted Police arrived to establish a fort here, the place very nearly was named Fort Brisebois. Inspector Ephraim Brisebois, an unpopular leader of the troop, intended to name the new fort for himself. Instead, Col. James Macleod, a Scotsman, suggested the name Fort Calgary in remembrance of his ancestral castle on the island of Skye. His choice prevailed.

The presence of white settlers was troubling and unwelcome to the local Niitsitapi, which means "real people" in the Blackfoot language. More than a century of resistance had already passed in bloody and destructive warfare. In 1877 the tribes of the Blackfoot Confederacy signed an important peace agreement, called Treaty 7, which designated boundaries for Native land reserves. Representing the North-West Mounted Police for the Queen of Great Britain and Ireland was James Macleod. Timing was important to the government, which planned to build a railway across aboriginal land by 1881.

Alberta's Blackfoot Confederacy tribes—Kainai (Blood), Pekani (Peigan), Siksika (Blackfoot), and Tsuu T'ina (Sarcee)—continue to practice traditions handed down from generation to generation. Learn more about the First Nations people at the Tsuu T'ina Culture Museum, 3700 Anderson Road. The museum features artifacts from Edmonton's Provincial Museum and from area residents whose ancestors traded with aboriginal people.

For more information, call 403-238-2677. Explore *www.treaty7.org* to gain insight on this Calgary-area Nation, its history, customs, and spiritual life.

The Calgary Exhibition and Stampede, held in mid-July each year, has earned the name "Greatest Outdoor Show on Earth," filling the town with rodeo fans, cowboys, and cowgirls who come for some of the hottest competition in North America. Events include saddle bronco-riding, bull-riding, chuckwagon races, bareback riding, wild cow–milking events, and wild horse races. Rodeo clowns, parades, agriculture exhibitions, square dancing, a midway, and lots of food fill out the 10-day celebration. For more information, call 1-800-551-1767 or 403-269-9822. See more at *www.calgarystampede.com.*

Calgary was the host city for the 1988 Winter Olympic Games, and the ski jump, bobsled run, and slopes became familiar sites to television viewers, who can now ski the same slopes at Canada Olympic Park. In fact, you may even meet one of tomorrow's Olympic champions among the many skiers who train here year-round. You can share the slopes, the 295-foot ski jump, and the bobsled run from November through March. In summer, you'll spy young, daring mountain bikers who ride the ski lift with their bikes hooked on the side of their chairs. They virtually fly back down on two wheels. Admission into the park is free, but activities within the park charge fees.

Calgary's Olympic Park continues to draw athletes and fans from all over the world.

TAKE A WALK THROUGH HISTORY

Canada's largest living-history village, Heritage Park, is strewn among 66 acres with an entrance at 1900 Heritage Drive SW. One section features an 1860s fur-trading post; another is reminiscent of an 1880s pre-railway pioneer settlement; another is a street of businesses and residences set in about 1910. You are free to mill in and out of the buildings, relax in the grassy areas, or travel on a steam railway, a riverboat, or an antique carnival ride.

Antique machinery is well oiled and working at the old wooden oil rig. Elsewhere, the village blacksmith is hard at work, but willing to share his knowledge with visitors. A schoolmarm invites you into the old one-room school. Other costumed interpreters reenact a suffragette march, a wedding, a shootout. Children play on the antique carnival rides while parents read about how these attractions were the hit of their day.

Take a ride on the riverboat SS *Moxie* as it cruises the adjacent reservoir. Peek into every room in the circa-1904 Burnside Ranch House, and wander through the Hudson's Bay Company fort and Indian village across the way. Buy goodies at the bakery, see how a printing press worked, step inside the historic church, savor an ice cream cone in the heat of the day.

It's a lot of walking, but you can pick up a ride on the train or a horse-drawn buggy. Plan your time well and make a day of it. If you arrive between 9 A.M. and 10 A.M. and pay full admission price, you are entitled to the free Western buffet-style breakfast served in the Wainwright Hotel.

The entire park is a simple pleasure. Follow suggested walking trails if you want to soak it all in. Parking may be some distance from the park entrance, but you can hop on an antique trolley to shorten the ride. For more information, contact 403-268-8500 or browse *www.heritagepark.ca*.

Throughout Heritage Park, costumed interpreters are on hand to answer any questions about the history of Calgary and its people.

The Olympic Hall of Fame and Museum in the park honors the stars of Olympic history. Bobsled and ski jump simulators make the experience real, and exhibits teach about developments in snow sports through decades. For more information, call 403-247-5452 or visit *www.canadaolympicpark.com.*

Wondering where to take the kiddies? Let 'em run wild at Calaway Park, the largest outdoor amusement park in Western Canada, with rides, mini-golf, and live musical productions for the whole family. It's located 6 miles (10 km) west of Calgary on Trans-Canada Highway 1. Call 403-240-3822 or browse *www.calawaypark.com.*

Fort Calgary Historic Park, at 950 9th Avenue SE, is a reconstruction of the original 1875 fort and 1888 barracks on a 40-acre site at the confluence of the Bow and Elbow Rivers. Interpreters share the stories of the early settlers and of this site. For information, call 403-290-1875 or see *www.fortcalgary.com.*

Even if you were just an average student in science, you'll reawaken a sense of discovery during a visit to the Calgary Science Centre. Hands-on, discovery-oriented exhibits make science fun again. Enter a world of adventure in the Discovery Dome theater, a surround-your-senses journey. The center is found at 701 11th Street SW. Call 403-268-8300 for more information or see *www.calgaryscience.ca.*

Glenbow Museum, Art Gallery, Library and Archives, at 130 9th Avenue SE, has something of interest for everyone, from excellent displays on cultural and military history to a mineralogy exhibit that includes one of the oldest rocks on the planet. The art gallery shows off its collection of block prints, early watercolors, and Inuit sculpture. For information, call 403-268-4100 or visit *www.glenbow.org.*

Calgary Zoo, Botanical Garden & Prehistoric Park is not just for the kids. This world-class zoo features more than 1,000 animals, including some rare and endangered species, and a tropical aviary. Walk among spectacular, life-size replicas of dinosaurs in a vast park that's a re-creation of their surroundings. It's all found on St. George's Island in the middle of the Bow River. Open year-round. Call the zoo at 1-800-588-9993 or visit *www.calgaryzoo.com.*

Bird-lovers can explore the Inglewood Bird Sanctuary, at 2425 9th Avenue SE, an attraction that features more than 250 species of birds and some mammals. Natural history programs for families introduce children to these natural wonders. Admission is free and they're open year-round. Call 403-269-6688. Another free-of-charge, family-oriented natural wonder is Devonian Gardens, with waterfalls, flowers, walkways, fountains, artwork, and playground, all located downtown in TD Square. Call 403-221-4274 or go to *www.calgary.ca/parks.*

Just twenty-five minutes from downtown Calgary, golfers will want to find The Links of GlenEagles at 100 GlenEagles Drive, in Cochrane. This 18-hole course is the "Home of the PGA Tour," and a challenge for any level. Call 403-932-1100 or go to *www.gleneaglesgolf.com.* In Calgary itself, stop by the McKenzie Meadows Golf Club, a championship, 18-hole public course in Fish Creek Provincial Park, offering power- and pull-carts, pro shop, restaurant, lounge, and patio. Call 403-257-2255 for tee times or visit *www.mckenziemeadows.com.*

If you're up for outdoor adventure, there are plenty of options: motor sports, world-class fly-fishing, photo safaris, hunting, horseback riding, rafting, hiking, and mountain biking.

For more details on anything Calgary has to offer, call 1-800-661-1678 or 403-263-8510. Visit their Web site at *www.tourismcalgary.com.*

LODGING

For information on local bed-and-breakfasts, contact the B&B Association of Calgary at www.bbcalgary.com.

Ambassador Motor Inn Calgary
802 16th Avenue NE
403-276-2271
Rooms with high-speed Internet, pool, on-site restaurant.

Best Western Calgary Centre Inn
3630 Macleod Trail South
1-877-287-3900 or 403-287-3900
www.bwcalgarycentre.com
Air-conditioned units in full-service hotel. Cable TV, hair dryers, business center, indoor heated pool, kiddie pool, deluxe continental breakfast. High-speed Internet access.

Best Western Port O' Call Inn
1935 McKnight Boulevard NE
1-800-661-1161 or 403-291-4600
www.bestwesternportocall.com
201 rooms, nonsmoking floors, movies, laundry service. Indoor pool, whirlpool, fitness center. Restaurant and two lounges. 15 minutes from downtown. Free shuttle service.

Best Western Suites Downtown
1330 8th Street SW
1-800-981-2555 or 403-228-6900
www.bestwesternsuitescalgary.com
123 suites with kitchens, cable TV, laundry, fitness center, sauna. Three-Diamond rating, AAA. Close to downtown attractions and Stampede Grounds.

Blackfoot Inn Calgary
5940 Blackfoot Trail SE
403-252-2253
Elegant accommodations minutes from Stampede Grounds, close to downtown. Restaurants, lounges, fitness facilities, whirlpool, sauna, seasonal pool.

Calgary Marriott Hotel
110 9th Avenue SE
1-800-896-6878 or 403-266-7331
www.calgarymariott.com
384 air-conditioned rooms, nonsmoking floors, cable TV, valet parking, gift shop. Room service, roll-in showers, Internet.

Coast Plaza Hotel
1316 33rd Street NE
Off Highway 1 at 36th Street
1-800-661-1464 or 403-248-8888
www.calgaryplaza.com
248 rooms, cable TV, movies, voice mail, Internet, coffee. Indoor pool, sauna, whirlpool. Restaurant, lounge, gift shop. Free shuttle.

Comfort Inn & Suites—Calgary South
4611 Macleod Trail SW
403-287-7070
Air-conditioned rooms, suites. Fitness facility, swimming pool, whirlpool. Coffee, free continental breakfast.

Comfort Inn & Suites—Motel Village
2369 Banff Trail NW
403-284-3897
www.comfortinncalgary.com
82 units, nonsmoking floors available, cable TV, hair dryers, high-speed Internet. Two-story waterslide. Free continental breakfast.

Days Inn Calgary South
3828 Macleod Trail
403-243-5531
Air-conditioned rooms, suites, kitchenettes. Exercise facility, pool, whirlpool. Restaurant, lounge.

Deerfoot Inn & Casino Calgary
11500 35th Street SE
403-236-7529
Rooms, suites. Exercise facility, pool. Lounge, dining, entertainment.

Delta Bow Valley Calgary
209 4th Avenue SE
403-205-5459
www.deltabowvalley.com
398 rooms in landmark facility, nonsmoking floors. Cable TV, exercise facilities, gift shop.

Econo Lodge Inn & Suites—University
2231 Banff Trail NW
1-800-55-ECONO or 403-289-1921
www.econolodgecalgary.com
62 rooms, cable TV, free movies, hair dryers, irons and boards, high-speed Internet access. Swimming pool, whirlpool, hot tub.

Econo Lodge—Motel Village
2440 16th Avenue NW
1-800-55-ECONO or 403-289-2561
56 rooms and kitchenettes, hair dryers, Internet access, laundry. Fitness center, pool, free movies. Restaurant, free continental breakfast.

Executive Royal Inn North Calgary
2828 23rd Street NE
403-291-2003
Air-conditioned rooms, coffee, dining, lounge.

Fairmont Palliser
133 9th Avenue SW
1-800-441-1414 or 403-262-1234
www.fairmont.com
405 rooms in historic downtown landmark, full-service hotel, cable TV, health club, hot tub, modem jacks, covered parking. Room, service, saltwater pool.

Four Points Sheraton Calgary West
8220 Bow Ridge Crescent NW
1-877-288-4441 or 403-288-4441
www.fourpointscalgarywest.com
118 units, suites with fireplaces and Jacuzzis available, cable TV, fridges, hair dryers, high-speed Internet service, microwaves. Gift shop, covered parking, room service. Indoor pool and waterslide.

Glenmore Inn & Convention Centre
2720 Glenmore Trail
403-279-8611
www.glenmoreinn.com
Well-appointed guest rooms, business suites, laundry, exercise facility. Dining, lounge, room service. Downtown location.

Greenwood Inn & Suites
3515 26th Street NE
1-888-233-6730 or 403-250-8855
www.greenwoodcalgary.com
213 units, full-service hotel. Cable TV, nonsmoking floors, laundry and room service. Indoor pool, whirlpool, steam room, gift shop. Restaurant, lounge. Rated Three Diamond, AAA. Close to airport.

Hampton Inn & Suites—Calgary
2231 Banff Trail NW
1-888-432-6777 or 403-289-9800
www.hamptoncalgary.com
96 units, cable TV, free movies, fridges, microwaves, hair dryers, free high-speed/wireless Internet access. Exercise facility, hot tub, gift shop. Waterslide, deluxe continental breakfast, free shuttle service.

Holiday Inn Express Hotel & Suites
1020 8th Avenue SW
403-508-1762
56 rooms in downtown location, some nonsmoking units. Refrigerators, cable TV, Internet access, heated parking.

Hotel Arts Calgary
119 12th Avenue SW
403-266-4611
Air-conditioned rooms, high-speed Internet, coffee, laundry, exercise facility. Restaurant, lounge, room service.

Inn on Crowchild
5353 Crowchild Trail NW
1-800-735-7502 or 403-288-5353
www.innoncrowchild.com
58 units, cable TV, hair dryers, irons and boards, Internet access. Exercise room, hot tub, room service. ATM, sports bar, vehicle plug-ins.

International Hotel of Calgary
220 4th Avenue SW
403-265-9600
Air-conditioned rooms and suites, kitchenettes. Hot tub, swimming pool, dining.

The Pointe Inn
1808 19th Street NE
1-800-661-8164 or 403-291-4681
www.pointeinn.com
151 units, cable TV, fridges, high-speed Internet service, laundry. Room service, vehicle plug-ins.

Quality Inn University
2359 Banff Trail NW, off Highway 1
1-800-661-4667 or 403-289-1973
105 rooms. Indoor heated pool, whirlpool, sauna, steam room. Lounge, poolside restaurant. High-speed wireless and 24-hour business center. Free continental breakfast.

Ramada Limited
2363 Banff Trail NW
1-800-272-6232 or 403-289-5571
www.ramada.com
70 units, close to university, cable TV, free movies, hair dryers, irons and boards, laundry, Internet access. Hot tub. Free continental breakfast.

Sandman Hotel & Suites—Calgary West
125 Bowridge Drive NW
403-288-6033
www.sandmanhotels.com
121 deluxe rooms, indoor pool, whirlpool, fitness center, high-speed Internet, lounge, Denny's 24-hour restaurant.

Sandman Hotel Downtown
888 7th Avenue SW
1-800-726-3626 or 403-237-8626
www.sandmanhotels.com
301 rooms, cable TV, movies, voice mail. Indoor pool, whirlpool, sauna, fitness center. Moxie's Grill & M Bar Lounge, room service.

Sheraton Cavalier Hotel
2620 32nd Avenue SE
1-800-325-3535 or 403-291-0107
www.sheraton–calgary.com
306 units in full-service hotel. Cable TV, hair dryers, hot tub, high-speed Internet service, concierge, room service, sports bar. Indoor water park. Shuttle service.

Sheraton Suites Calgary Eau Claire
255 Barclay Parade SW
403-266-7200
325 all-suite rooms, high-speed Internet, exercise facility, pool, whirlpool. Restaurant and lounge on site. Close to shopping and attractions.

Super8 Motel Village Calgary
1904 Crowchild Trail NW
403-289-9211
Air-conditioned rooms, suites, kitchenettes, free coffee. Swimming pool.

Travelodge Calgary South
7012 Macleod Trail South
403-253-1111
Air-conditioned rooms, nonsmoking available, coffee, pool.

The Westin Calgary
320 4th Avenue SW
1-800-937-8461 or 403-266-1611
525 deluxe air-conditioned rooms in full-service hotel. Cable TV, high-speed Internet, business center, gift shop. Pool, whirlpool, exercise facility. Senior discount. Downtown location.

Wingate Inn Calgary
400 Midpark Way SE / 866-875-7666
Well-appointed, air-conditioned rooms, suites. Exercise facility, pool, whirlpool. Coffee, laundry, high-speed Internet, nonsmoking rooms available. Business center.

CAMPGROUNDS

Calaway RV Park and Campground
6 miles (10 km) west of Calgary on Highway 1
403-249-7372 / *www.calawaypark.com*
84 sites in country setting, full and partial hookups. Showers, laundry, dump station. Grocery store. Walking distance to amusement park. Shuttle service to Stampede Grounds.

Calgary West Campground
On western city limits, Highway 1 southside near Olympic Park
1-800-562-0842 or 403-288-0411
More than 300 sites, with and without hookup. Showers, laundry, flush toilets, dump station. Picnic grounds, outdoor pool, mini-golf, store. Wheelchair access. Downtown shuttle.

Camp 'N Water Park
Near Chestermere Lake
1-888-899-2267 or 403-273-5122
180 sites with full and partial hookups, tenting. Fire pits, picnic tables, Internet access. Lake nearby. Waterslide. Adults-only section. Shuttle during Calgary Stampede.

Mountainview Camping
2 miles (3 km) east of Calgary on Highway 1
403-293-6640
www.calgarycamping.com
160 sites with and without hookup. 15- and 30-amp service. Propane, showers, restroom, campfire pits, shelter. Mini-mart. Playground, petting zoo, fish pond, mini-golf. Tours available by coach or van. Open year-round. Reservations recommended.

Symon's Valley RV Park
26001 Symons Valley Road
403-274-4574
www.symonsvalleyranch.com
140 campsites, open year-round. General store, showers, 15 minutes from downtown.

SOUTH OF CALGARY:
Country Lane RV Park
On Highway 2, 4 miles (6.5 km) east of Okotoks
403-995-2330
www.countrylanerv.com
300 treed sites, paved roads, gated security. Clubhouse, showers, store, lounge, kitchen, library, Internet. Fitness area, games room. Newer playground. Wheelchair access. Reservations recommended.

Nature's Hideaway Campground
DeWinton, on Highwood River
403-938-8185
www.natureshideaway.com
Tent and RV campsites. Fishing, swimming, playground, free showers. 15 minutes from Calgary.

Pine Creek RV Campground
DeWinton, south of Calgary
403-256-3002
99 sites with 30- and 50-amp service in country setting, picnic tables, showers, lounge, billiards, covered pavilion, laundry, wheelchair access, store. Reservations recommended.

RESTAURANTS

1410 World Bier Haus
1410 17th Avenue SW
403-229-1410
Beers from around the world, lively menu.

Bear's Den
254028 Bearspaw Road NW
403-241-7611
Upscale dining, service in sophisticated setting. Live entertainment, parking, licensed.

The Belvedere
107 8th Avenue SW
403-265-9595
Reviewers' choice for continental fine dining and service. *Wine Spectator* citing as in top 500 wine lists worldwide.

Blink Restaurant and Supper Club
111 8th Street SW
403-263-5330
Fine dining, service, wine list.

DINO DELIGHTS

If you have an extra day in your travel schedule, by all means take a side trip to Alberta's Badlands and the city of Drumheller, 83 miles (134 km) east of Crossfield and the Queen Elizabeth II Highway (Highway 2), via Highway 72. Experience a dramatic change in scenery, as the land around you changes from farms and field to canyonlands, rock walls, and hoodoos. You can't miss the dinosaur sculptures on nearly every corner of the town, and a true giant presides over the grounds of the visitor center. He's many stories high, and after climbing many stairs inside, visitors can peek out through his dino-teeth. Tourism information can be found at *www.traveldrumheller.com* or call 403-823-8100.

Billed as the world's largest dinosaur, this monster towers over the Drumheller visitor information center. Climb the stairs inside and grab the view from its open jaws.

The town is named for American businessman Sam Drumheller, who in 1911 launched the area's first coal-mining operation. Now his name is synonymous not with coal, but with dinosaurs. Just outside town, follow the Dinosaur Trail on a 33-mile (53-km) loop from the north side of the river off Highway 9 into the Valley of the Dinosaurs.

Along the way, in Midland Provincial Park, you'll find the Royal Tyrell Museum of Paleontology. In 1884 Joseph Burr Tyrrell found a fossil of a dinosaur nearly as large as the famed tyrannosaur; he named the find Albertosaurus. His discovery launched even more digging as other paleontologists arrived to launch their own excavations. The museum features more than two dozen complete dinosaur skeletons, along with finds of other prehistoric creatures. Little is left to the imagination in the walk-through diorama-style exhibits and Cretaceous Garden. It's as if you were entering the days of the dinosaurs. Admission is charged. Call 403-823-7707 or browse *www.tyrrellmuseum.com*.

Brava Bistro
723 17th Avenue SW
403-228-1854 / *www.bravabistro.com*
Modern Mediterranean. Honored in *Calgary Magazine.*

Brewsters Brewing Company & Restaurant
101 Barclay Parade SW (Eau Claire Festival Market)
403-225-1767 / *www.brewsters.ca*
Pizza, burgers, entrees, premium beers brewed on site. Three other locations in Calgary.

Broken Plate Kitchen & Bar
302 10th Street NW
403-283-6300
Contemporary Greek cuisine.

Buchanan's
738 3rd Avenue SW
403-261-4646 / *www.buchanans.ca*
Steaks, chops, seafood, burgers. Wine and broad choice of single-malt whiskeys.

Buon Giorno Ristorante Italiano
823 17th Avenue SW
403-244-5522
Northern Italian cuisine. Fireplace, private dining area.

Buzzards Cowboy Cuisine
140 10th Avenue SW
403-264-6959 / *www.cowboycuisine.com*
Cowboy restaurant featuring steaks, burgers, pub fare.

Cadence
6407 Bowness Road NW
403-247-9955
Breakfast and lunch specialties; great coffee.

Calgary Tower Panorama Dining Room
101 9th Avenue
403-508-5822 / *www.calgarytower.com*
Above downtown Calgary, a revolving restaurant with a 360-degree view of city and mountains; breakfast, lunch, and dinner.

Catch Oyster Bar & Seafood Restaurant
100 8th Avenue SE (Stephen Avenue Walk)
403-206-0000
www.catchrestaurant.ca
Oyster bar, dining room, Calgary skyline view.

Ceili's on 7th Irish Pub & Restaurant
803 8th Avenue SW
503-265-1200 / *www.ceilis.com*
Irish pub sprawling over four floors with theme décor. Rooftop and street patios. Lunch and dinner.

Centini Restaurant & Lounge
160 8th Avenue
403-269-1600
Italian/Continental cuisine, extensive wine selection.

Conga Room
109 8th Avenue SW
403-262-7248
Traditional Latin cuisine served in historic 1888 building on Stephen Avenue Walk.

Dakota
310 8th Avenue SW
403-262-4967
Cuisine inspired by American Southwest. Pub atmosphere, patio, pool table.

Eat! Eat!
1325 9th Avenue SE
403-532-1933
Family dining in bright atmosphere.

Ed's Restaurant
202 17th Avenue
403-262-3500 / *www.edsrestaurant.com*
Traditional steakhouse menu featuring Alberta beef, pasta, seafood. Six dining rooms in 1911 house.

Divino Wine & Cheese Bistro
113 8th Avenue SW
403-410-5555
Seasonal menu, pizza, pasta, entrees, lounge/entertainment.

The Elephant & Castle Restaurant & Pub
751 3rd Street SW, No. 100
403-265-3555 / *www.elephantcastle.com*
British fare, fish and chips a specialty.

Fionn MacCool's Irish Pub
255 Barclay Parade SW
403-517-6699
Traditional Irish and Canadian cuisine. Steak, seafood, sandwiches. Live Celtic entertainment.

Glory of India
515 4th Avenue SW
403-263-8804 / *www.gloryofindia.com*
Fine dining in downtown location. Authentic East Indian and Pakistani cuisine.

Il Giardino Ristorante
344 17th Avenue SW
403-541-0088
Traditional Italian cuisine. Pasta, veal, seafood, chicken, beef, lamb. Near Stampede Park.

Il Sogno
4 24th Street NE
403-232-8901
www.ilsogno.org
Upscale dining, fine wines, Italian cuisine. Features Alberta beef, house-made pasta. Reservations recommended.

Japanese Village Restaurant
317 10th Avenue SW
403-262-2738
Teppan-grill dining, tableside cooking. Steak, chicken, seafood.

La Caille on the Bow
100 LaCaille Place, 7th Street and 1st Avenue SW
403-262-5554
Casual eatery, two floors, view of Bow River, more than 250 wines.

La Chaumiere Restaurant
139 17th Avenue SW
403-228-5690
French cuisine featuring rack of lamb, grand marnier souffle, grilled tuna, extensive wine list.

The Living Room
514 17th Avenue SW
403-228-9830
Oysters, seafood, Alberta beef, cheese and chocolate fondues.

The Metropolitan Grill
880 16th Avenue SW
403-802-2393
Steaks and other daily features, upscale casual. Sunday brunch, dancing and DJ weekend eves.

Mescalero's Restaurant
1315 1st Street SW
403-266-3339
Southwestern cuisine, New Mexican and Latin American with South American influence.

Mother Tucker's Food Experience
345 10th Avenue SW
403-262-5541
Famed salad bar. Prime rib, steaks, ribs, children's menu. Expansive Sunday brunch.

Murrieta's Westcoast Bar & Grill
200—808 1st Street SW
In historic Alberta Hotel Building
403-269-7707
www.murrietas.ca
Pacific crab cakes and other seafood, pastas, steaks. Comprehensive wine list.

Oh! Canada Restaurant & Bar
815 7th Avenue SW, Nexen Tower
403-266-1551
www.ohcanadarestaurant.com
Seasonal and regional features, food and drink from across Canada. Downtown location. Closed on weekends.

Oriental Phoenix
401 9th Avenue SW
403-262-3633
One of three locations, this one in Gulf Canada Square downtown. Features Vietnamese cuisine. Reservations recommended.

The Ranche
15979 Bow Bottom Trail SE
403-225-3939
www.theranche.com
Located in Fish Creek Provincial Park. Rocky Mountain cuisine served in historic mansion built in 1896. Seafood, game specialties.

River Café
Prince's Island Park
403-261-7670 / *www.river–café.com*
Canadian fare, wood-fired cuisine. Organic, locally grown ingredients. Park setting. Casual fine dining.

Rouge
1240 8th Avenue SE
403-531-2767
www.rougecalgary.com
French cuisine in former home of A. E. Cross. Seafood, game, beef, lamb. Private rooms, garden patio.

Sushi Ginza
276-10816 Macleod Trail S
403-271-9642
Sushi, sashimi, teriyaki dishes, and more.

Teatro
200 8th Avenue SE
403-290-1012
Italian-inspired regional cuisine. Wood-burning oven, extensive wine selection.

The Tribune Restaurant
118 8th Avenue SW
403-269-3160
www.thetribunerestaurant.ca
Elegant surroundings; continental dining in historic Tribune Block of Stephen Avenue.

Road Notes

The Queen Elizabeth II Highway (or Highway 2) between Calgary and Edmonton follows the route of a century-old trail. In the mid-1880s, entrepreneur John Dickson established several "stopping houses" along this rude trail. When he abandoned the southernmost stopping house, a neighboring homesteader, Johnston Stevenson, claimed the site and building and reopened it. Their names were merged as "Dickson-Stevenson Stopping House" for the roadhouse that served travelers during the decades that followed.

Although that building no longer stands, southbound motorists can still pull over near its original site for rest and refreshment at the modern Dickson-Stevenson Stopping House, located about 24 miles (38 km) north of Calgary on the QEII Highway. The rest stop offers snacks, fast food, visitor information, and historical plaques about the Old Calgary Trail. The first automobile journey over the decaying trail between Calgary and Edmonton took place in 1906.

A distinct line exists between city and farmland as you travel north out of Calgary. Clearly, controlled growth is under way as subdivision homes are tightly clustered in the middle distance, while cows graze alongside the road. The speed limit is 68 mph (110 kmh) on this six-lane highway. It's easy driving on a flat landscape. You can see a rain shower coming for miles before the first drop hits the windshield.

As you continue north, dairy cattle become more and more a part of the landscape, and the road is no longer a superhighway. The land begins to roll in low hills, and more sections are wooded. Here and there, you'll see evidence of the oil industry with solitary pumpjacks at work in fields and pastures.

As we entered Red Deer, we spied a hawk perched on the sign that gave the name of the town. We laughed because he looked like a stuffed bird in a museum exhibit that was grossly mislabeled. He just glared into space as we drove by, obviously not getting the joke.

RED DEER

From Calgary: 86 miles (138 km)
To Edmonton: 96 miles (154 km)

Roughly halfway between Calgary and Edmonton, Red Deer is the government seat for a county of the same name. A city of more than 83,000, it offers full services for travelers, from automotive repair to major shopping areas, entertainment, lodging, campgrounds, and an abundance of restaurants. And it's a golf enthusiast's dream—no fewer than 10 courses with beautiful settings and challenging greens dot the region.

In 2003, Red Deer was honored by the Minister of Canadian Heritage when it was named a "Cultural Capital of Canada." With the award comes a grant that the city tagged for expanding its already abundant arts and culture programs and celebrations.

Red Deer also takes pride in its area parklands, which range from swimming beaches and wooded trails to an equestrian facility, golf courses, and (surprisingly) a ski area amid these low, rolling hills. The Red Deer River cuts a canyon through the fertile farms and parklands, and flows through the center of town.

The Visitor Center exit for northbound travelers is north of 32nd Street. The staff is friendly and knowledgeable, and you'll find a gift shop and café. The adjacent Heritage Square is a gateway to the Waskasoo Park system, which lies at the heart of Red Deer. From here, you can walk, skate, or cycle the vast corridor of river valley nature trails. Within the park you'll find picnic areas, playgrounds, and fishing ponds. To find out more on the Red Deer & District Museum and Heritage Square historic site, call 403-309-8405.

The Kerry Wood Nature Centre hosts nature walks and canoe tours, as well as presentations for children. An exhibit gallery, theater, and bookstore are on site at 6300 45th Avenue. Admission is free. Call 403-346-2010.

You can wander through the original James Bower homestead on a lovely 10-acre site bordering Piper Creek. The homestead is at the Sunnybrook Farm Museum and Agriculture Interpretive Centre, 4701 30th Street, and offers a relaxing as well as informative tour and a look back at the pioneering ways of running a farm. Donations are welcome. Call 403-340-3511.

Another county jewel is Sylvan Lake, 10 miles (16 km) west of Red Deer on Highway 11, which has been a holiday destination since 1901. Each summer the lake is dotted with fishermen and water-skiers, boaters, and windsurfers. Even parasailers can be seen flying overhead. Its sandy beaches are perfect for family fun, and playing on the Wild Rapids water-slides will consume a whole day before you know it. Nearby are several private campgrounds and the Sylvan Lake Provincial Park.

Red Deer is proud of its Collicutt Centre, billed as a "state-of-the-art leisure and wellness centre." The Collicutt houses the ENMAX Water Park, with a wave pool, water park, waterslide, lazy river, and water playground. The facility also includes an ice arena, climbing walls, and much more. Located south of 32nd Street on 30th Avenue, it's a terrific place for families. Other indoor and outdoor pools can be found throughout town. And be sure to investigate Red Deer's historical treasures as well. For more information about Red Deer events and attractions, call 1-800-215-8946 or 403-346-0180, or visit the city's Web site at *www.tourismreddeer.net.*

LODGING

Aladdin Motor Inn
7444 Gaetz Avenue
403-343-2711 / *www.aladdinmotorinn.com*
80 air-conditioned units, some family suites and kitchenettes. Refrigerators, laundry, cable TV, modem jacks. Dining and sports bar. Family rates.

Best Western Red Deer Inn
6839 66th Street
403-346-3555
www.bestwesternreddeer.com
Comfortable rooms with free high-speed Internet, fridges and microwaves, cable TV, free local calls. Indoor pool, whirlpool, exercise facility, deluxe continental breakfast. Near shopping and parks.

Black Night Inn
2929 Gaetz Avenue
1-800-661-8793 or 403-343-6666
www.blackknight inn.ca
98 deluxe rooms, suites, cable TV, high-speed Internet, fridges, ATM. Whirlpool, indoor/outdoor pool, spa. Restaurant, lounge.

Capri Hotel & Convention Centre
3310 50th Avenue
1-800-662-7197 or 403-346-2091
www.capricentre.com
219 air-conditioned luxury rooms in full-service hotel. Cable TV, movies, Internet access, hair dryers, irons and boards. Exercise room, hair salon, gift shop, business center. Winter plug-ins.

Comfort Inn & Suites Red Deer
6846 66th Street
403-348-0025
www.comfortinnreddeer.com
Spacious accommodations, free high-speed Internet access, deluxe continental breakfast. Indoor pool, waterslide, fitness room. Near restaurants. Ask about pets.

Days Inn Red Deer
1000,5001 19th Street, Southpointe Common
1-800-DAYS INN or 403-340-3297
www.daysinnreddeer.ca
Zoned areas of newer hotel invite families as well as business clientele. Some wheelchair accessible rooms. High-speed Internet, corporate gym, pool, two-story waterslide, free continental breakfast. Restaurant on site.

Econo Lodge Inn & Suites
37433 Highway 2 South
403-346-4188
21 units with fridges, coin-op laundry, cable TV. Vehicle plug-ins, gas bar, RV dump.

Holiday Inn 67 Street
6500 67th Street
1-800-661-4961 or 403-342-6567
www.hi67.com
97 units in full-service hotel. Cable TV, games, fridges, modem jacks, hair dryers, high-speed Internet. Roll-in shower, health spa, room service. Sports bar, business center. Kids eat and stay free with some restrictions.

Holiday Inn Express—Red Deer
2803 50th Avenue
1-800-223-1993 or 403-343-2112
92 air-conditioned rooms, family suites, hair dryers, microwaves, irons. Cable TV, laundry, high-speed Internet, coffee. Indoor atrium with saltwater pool. Free continental breakfast.

North Hill Inn
7150 Gaetz Avenue
1-800-662-7152 or 403-343-8800
www.northhillinn.com
117 rooms, including 40 executive rooms. Cable TV, hair dryers, irons, modem jacks. Hot tub, sports bar with nightly entertainment.

Red Deer Lodge
4311 49th Avenue
1-800-661-1657 or 403-346-8841
www.reddeerlodge.net
233 deluxe rooms, air-conditioning, phones, coffee. Hair salon, exercise room, indoor pool, whirlpool, restaurants.

Red Deer Travellers Inn
4124 Gaetz Avenue
1-866-343-0771 or 403-342-6969
48 air-conditioned rooms, kitchenettes and nonsmoking available. Cable TV, laundry, free local calls, Internet access. Restaurants nearby.

Sandman Hotel Red Deer
2818 Gaetz Avenue
1-800-SANDMAN or 403-343-7400
www.sandmanhotels.com
142 rooms, cable TV, hair dryers, irons, Internet access. Exercise rooms, restaurant, bar, room service.

Service Plus Inns & Suites
6853 66th Street
1-888-875-4667 or 403-342-4445
www.serviceplusinns.com
92 units, fridges, hair dryers, modem jacks, free local calls. Small pets okay in smoking rooms. Exercise room.

Stanford Inn—Red Deer
4707 50th Street
1-877-347-5551 or 403-347-5551
www.stanfordinn.net
62 air-conditioned rooms, hair dryers, irons and boards, cable TV, ATM. Family restaurant, bar and grill. Downtown location.

Super 8 Motel Red Deer
7474 50th Avenue
1-877-488-2288 / *www.super8.com*
72 units, cable TV, Internet access. Free local calls, winter plug-ins.

Travelodge
2807 50th Avenue
1-800-578-7878 or 403-346-2011
www.travelodge.com
136 air-conditioned rooms, kitchenettes and nonsmoking available, cable TV. Internet access, self-service laundry. Indoor pool, whirlpool. Restaurant, room service.

Western Budget Motel
37468 Highway 2 South
403-358-5755
www.westernbudgetmotel.com
58 units, all with fireplaces, fridges, hair dryers, modem jacks. Cable TV, laundry.

AREA CAMPGROUNDS

RED DEER:
Lions Campground
4723 Riverside Drive, east of 49th Avenue
403-342-8183
89 sites with full hookups, 38 with partial. Dump station, wheelchair access, showers. Playground, bike trails to Waskasoo Park.

Westerner Campground
4847D 19th Street, from Highway 2, take 2A exit
403-352-8801
www.westernercampground.com
99 sites with full or partial hookups, 41 pull-throughs. Pool, biking and hiking trails. 30- and 50-amp service, laundry, showers. Close to shopping and dining, and RV dealerships.

RED DEER AREA:
Aspen Beach Provincial Park
On Gull Lake, 10.5 miles (17 km) west of Lacombe on Highway 12
403-784-4066
www.campingaspenbeach.com
600 private, treed sites for dry-camping or tents; some pull-throughs, full and partial hookups. Playgrounds, washrooms, showers, trails, beaches within walking distance.

Crooked Tree RV Park & Campground
Highway 2 to 11A West, to 275 North
403-314-9577
46 sites with power, water, showers, play area, dump station, wood. Near Spirit Lake Golf & Country Club.

DeGraff's Camp Resort
On Gull Lake, 5.8 miles (9.4 km) north of Highway 12, or 6.8 miles (11 km) south of Highway 53 on Sec. Road 792
403-782-2193
98 sites with full and partial hookups. Family fun: fishing, swimming, horse rides, wading pools, trampolines, mini-golf, games. Boat launch, laundry, showers, wheelchair accessible.

Fawn Meadows Lodge & RV Park
Village of Delburne, 31 miles (50 km) east of Red Deer
www.fawnmeadowslodge.com
32 fully serviced RV sites, open year-round, adjacent to Fawn Meadows Golf Course. Golf carts are welcome in the RV park.

Green Acres
On Pine Lake, east on Highway 42, then south to #816
1-888-999-4833 or 403-886-4833
450 sites with full or partial hookups. 15-, 30-, and 50-amp sites. Heated swimming pool, playgrounds, boat rentals, marina, coffee shop, store, near golf. Security patrols.

Leisure Campgrounds & Cabins
Highway 42, north end of Pine Lake
403-886-4705
www.leisurecampgrounds.com
200 hookup sites and 10 cabins. Sandy beaches, fishing boats and watercraft rentals, arcade, café, groceries, liquor store, fishing tackle. Security.

Michener Park Campground
5429 53rd Street, Highway 12 on west end of Lacombe
403-782-1250 / *www.town.lacombe.ab.ca*
37 sites, pull-throughs available. Showers, fire pits, free firewood, picnic tables, day use area. Across from Lacombe Golf & Country Club.

RESTAURANTS

Albert's Family Restaurant & Lounge
5020 47th Avenue, # 9
403-341-5397
Full menu for family dining.

Botanica
4311 49th Avenue
403-346-8841
Fine dining inside the Reed Deer Lodge.

Café Tiffany's
3515 Gaetz Avenue
403-341-3366
Casual dining, steak, chicken, seafood. Patio seating, lounge.

Caper's Pasta & Ribs
3301 50th Avenue, #4
403-347-1184
Family dining, specializing in ribs and pasta.

Dino's Family Restaurant
4617 Gaetz Avenue
403-347-5585
Italian and Western cuisine, pizza, pasta.

Dragon City Café
22325 50th Avenue, #157
403-340-3388
Weekday lunch buffet, weekend brunch and evening buffet.

East Side Mario's
2004 50th Avenue
403-342-2279
A taste of New York's "Little Italy," pasta, pizza, salad, New York sandwiches.

The Keg Steakhouse & Bar
6365 50th Avenue
403-309-5499
www.kegsteakhouse.com
Steak, prime rib, seafood, pasta.

Kelsey's Restaurant
1935 50th Avenue
403-346-7565
Neighborhood bar and grill.

Mohave Grill
6608 Orr Drive
403-340-3453
Southwest cuisine and steaks, located on Red Deer's west side.

Montana's Cookhouse
195, 2004 50th Avenue
403-352-0030
Country cooking.

Red Deer Chinese Buffet Restaurant
5320 50th Avenue, #35 in Village Mall
403-342-5555
Szechwan and Cantonese cuisine.

Ricky's All-Day Grill
10,7110 50th Avenue
403-340-3288
Family-style dining; breakfast, lunch, dinner. Former location of Humpty's.

Ricky's All-Day Grill
37452 Highway 2 South
403-348-5522
Family-style dining; three meals a day.

Rusty Pelican
2079 50th Avenue
403-347-1414
Oyster bar and more.

Sylvan Lake Golf & Country Club
5331 Lakeshore Drive, 12 miles (18 km) west of Red Deer
403-887-6695
Bogie's Restaurant features casual dining; Eagle's Nest for fine dining. Sunday Brunch.

Tony Roma's
5250 22nd Street
403-358-3223
Ribs, chicken, pasta, seafood entrees.

White Spot
6701 Gaetz Avenue
403-358-6092
Breakfast, lunch, dinner.

Road Notes

North of Red Deer, a display well-rig stands on the left amid more fields. During late summer, farmers bale the hay into huge, golden rolls that remain in the fields.

As you travel, you'll decide where to spend your nights—in the dazzling excitement of the big city, off the highway in a provincial park, or maybe in a private campground.

During our trip, the day was winding down as we approached Edmonton. Rather than push hard and navigate a strange city in the dark (in an RV), we chose to spend the night in Ponoka, the Cattle Capital of Canada, 35 miles (56 km) north of Red Deer. A bucking-horse bronze in the town's Centennial Park says it all about this cowboy town.

This sleepy little western community of 6,576 people explodes into life each summer when the Ponoka Stampede picks up speed. In late June and early July, the city hosts a six-day rodeo extravaganza—second only to the Calgary event in all of Canada. Highlights include professional rodeo, chuckwagon races, midway rides, entertainment, fireworks, a beer garden, and a dance. RV parking on site is free during the Stampede, but it's a first-come, first-served opportunity. For tickets or information, call 403-783-0100. (Other times of the year, the campground rates run from $15 to $20 per night.)

Ponoka ("elk" in the Blackfoot language) lies on the Battle River, site of a major clash in the early 1880s between two local Native peoples, the Blackfoot and the Cree.

To soak up some local history, visit Fort Ostell Museum in Centennial Park, at 5320 54th Street (*www.fortostellmuseum.com*). Open only in summers; call 403-783-5224 for details. An interesting slice of history can be seen at the Cowboy Museum at the Stampede grounds.

You'll find two top-notch golf courses in this area, too. For more on accommodations or other visitor information, contact 403-783-4431 or *www.ponoka.org*.

Back on the road to Edmonton, just north of Ponoka you'll find a roadside turnout with a litter barrel and pay phone. Along here the trees have thinned out again. It's mostly farms and fields, and many local drivers sport cowboy hats. Fifteen miles (24 km) from Ponoka is a major rest stop for northbound travelers.

We recommend a side trip through Devon on your way to Edmonton. Just past the town of Leduc, take Exit 525 and turn west on Highway 39 (or 50th Avenue), then north on Highway 60 to visit the Leduc No. 1 Historic Site, birthplace of Alberta's oil industry. Here the first major oil find was made on February 13, 1947. A 174-foot (53-meter) replica of the original oil derrick stands beside an information center. Other tools of the trade and interpretive signs may be viewed in outdoor and indoor exhibits.

Visit the Devonian Botanic Garden, operated by the University of Alberta, on Highway 60 about 3 miles (5 km) north of Devon. Various gardens roll over its 190 acres, including the popular Kurimoto Japanese Garden. Another 110 acres is in its natural state. You can walk among the butterflies in the Butterfly House and on trails through forest and wetlands. Orchid lovers will find their own house of orchids. There's a gift shop, plant sales, tours, and picnic area, too. Plenty of parking for RV travelers.

Another worthwhile stop is Wetaskiwin, a town that truly values history. Back on Highway 2, about 40 miles (67 km) before Edmonton, turn east on Highway 13. Collectors will enjoy exploring the many antique shops and restored historical buildings, while the motorheads in the family will linger with the historical cars, tractors, and airplanes in the Reynolds-Alberta Museum collection. This is not your average museum approach to gazing at displays. Visitors may ride in the cockpit of a plane, or go for a joy ride in an antique car. The museum celebrating the "Spirit of the Machine" also houses a café and gift shop. Call 1-800-661-4726 or 780-361-1351. Browse their Web site at *www.reynoldsalbertamuseum.com*.

EDMONTON

From Calgary: 181 miles (291 km)
To Whitecourt: 112 miles (180 km)

Edmonton is an old city by western standards. It dates back to 1795, when the Hudson's Bay Company established Edmonton House, a trading post along the mighty North Saskatchewan River. Here, local Cree and Blackfoot Indians traded furs for goods. After a century of growth, it was an incorporated city of 700 people. Another century passed to find Edmonton a city of polish and sophistication sprouting in the midst of fields, reminiscent of the Emerald City in *The Wizard of Oz*. The city's population today: 666,000. And in 2004, Edmonton celebrated a century as an incorporated city.

This is Alberta's capital city, Canada's second-largest metropolitan area west of Toronto, and the fifth-largest city in Canada. Edmonton also is home to West Edmonton Mall, the largest shopping mall in the world (see accompanying sidebar).

Edmonton is known as the Oil Capital of Canada. Edmonton Tourism cites this amazing statistic: The amount of crude oil processed in metropolitan Edmonton each day is enough to change the oil of every car in Canada.

The dollars from oil have been poured into the culture and comfort of the citizenry. The city has two dozen art and history museums and more than a dozen theater companies (more per capita than any other city in Canada). Rain or shine, downtown pedestrians can freely move about in elevated, enclosed walkways or through underground and street-level "pedways."

There are 84 golf courses in the Edmonton area, hundreds of shops, dozens of hotels, and more than 2,000 dining establishments. If you want to spend money and feel like you're getting something for it, this is the place to visit. And by the way, Alberta has no provincial sales tax.

Edmonton is a city that loves to play—every month, it seems, the city hosts a festival, rodeo, carnival, anniversary, or other celebration, earning it yet another title: Canada's

A popular shopping and entertainment attraction for more than 25 years, the West Edmonton Mall receives nearly 30 million visitors a year.

Festival City (see *www.festivalcity.ca)*. These celebrations of music, theater, history, horsemanship, and home can be found in every season, among them: Silver Skate Festival (mid-February); Canadian National Competition Powwow (late May); Canada Day Celebrations (July 1); International Street Performers Festival (early July); A Taste of Edmonton (late July); Canada Klondike Days (late July); Edmonton Heritage Festival (early August); Folk Music Festival (late August); Poetry Festival (mid-September) and North of Nowhere Expo (late September); Edmonton International Film Festival (early October); Canadian Finals Rodeo (mid-November); and Festival of Trees (last weekend in November).

For stunning beauty, albeit manmade, visit the Great Divide Waterfall on the High Level Bridge. Built to honor Alberta's 75th anniversary, the waterfall is 24 feet higher than Niagara Falls.

The Royal Museum of Alberta is one of Canada's most popular museums, at 12845 102nd Avenue, featuring exhibits on a broad range of subjects, from the province's aboriginal people to dinosaurs, geology, insects, Ice Age mammals, and more. Admission is charged. Call 780-453-9100 or visit *www.royalalbertamuseum.ca.*

Fort Edmonton Park, at Fox and Whitemud Drives, is a 158-acre living-history park, the country's largest, with 60 period buildings to explore. Walk through time at the 1846 Hudson's Bay Trading Post, or down streets from 1885, 1905, and 1920. Watch a blacksmith

SHOPPING WITH A MAP

The West Edmonton Mall is billed as "Alberta's No. 1 Attraction." Sprawling over a 110-acre site, this remarkable indoor megamall features 800 stores and services, an ice arena, thrill rides, kiddie rides, a water park, and aquariums. Located at 87th Avenue and 107th Street, it's not hard to find. Roadside signs will lead the way, especially as you travel north on Highway 2—it rounds the city limits and practically lands you in the parking lot. And once you're inside, you'll pick up a map to figure your way from there. Wear your walking shoes, and be sure to bring your swimsuit, ice skates, and maybe your bowling ball.

Chose among more than 110 restaurants, not to mention each of the attractions that could serve as parks all by themselves. Kids in Edmonton have no excuse for saying, "There's nothing to do!" More likely it's, "There's too much to do!"

The mall includes Galaxyland Amusement Park, with 24 rides and attractions, including the new spinning rollercoaster called the Orbiter; World Waterpark, with slides, a wave pool, and kiddie water play; the Deep Sea Adventure, with submarine rides; Sea Life Caverns; Professor Wem's Adventure Golf, a miniature course; and the Ice Palace, an ice rink that's occasionally used by the Edmonton Oilers hockey team. Dining and entertainment options include Planet Hollywood, Red's, Space Race, Lazer Extreme, Wild West Shooting Theatre, and Jubilations Live Dinner Theatre. Not to mention the shopping.

For more information, call 780-444-5200 or visit *www.westedmontonmall.com*. And remember, this is the only province with no provincial sales tax, so shop to your heart's delight!

or an old-fashioned rope-maker at work. Catch a ride on a stagecoach or the steam train. This is a great place to teach kids about history while they're having fun. You'll find plenty of gift shops and restaurants. For more information: 780-496-8787 or visit the Web site *www.edmonton.ca/fort.*

A futuristic building at 142nd and 112th Avenues houses the TELUS World of Science, Edmonton's space and science museum with exciting, interactive galleries. Inside, kids and adults alike will enjoy observation and hands-on science—from learning more about wildfires and the weather, to other wonders of space. Features include a planetarium—the largest in North America—laser shows, mock Challenger missions, and an IMAX theater. Call 780-451-3344 or visit *www.odyssium.com.*

Church Street (officially 96th Street) is listed in *Ripley's Believe It or Not* for the 16 churches you'll find in one small section. Another local "oddity," although it's not listed in Ripley's, is Edmonton's prized four-story-high cowboy boot at a now-closed boot factory, 10007 167th Street. This city also claims the distinction of having the longest stretch of urban park in Canada: the North Saskatchewan River Valley park system.

The Alberta Legislature Building, at 10820 98th Avenue, is an architectural beauty built in 1912 on the site of Fort Edmonton. An interpretive center follows the building's history and provincial politics. Guided tours are available daily. Call for scheduled times at 780-427-7362 or visit the Web site at *www.assembly.ab.ca.*

Take a cruise on the *Edmonton Queen* riverboat, which offers daily cruises through the river valley. Dinner cruises with Dixieland entertainment are available, too. Call 780-424-2628 or see *www.edmontonqueen.com.*

For more information on local events and attractions, call Edmonton Tourism at 1-800-463-4667 or 780-496-8400 or visit their Web site: *www.edmonton.com.*

LODGING

Aladdin Motel
15425 111th Avenue
1-866-484-3348 or 780-484-0071
37 units, free movies, microwaves, fridges, free local calls. Small dogs accepted.

Alberta Place Suite Hotel
10049 103rd Street
1-800-661-3982 or 780-423-1565
www.albertaplace.com
85 units, all with kitchens, cable TV, high-speed Internet, free local calls, laundry. Exercise room, indoor pool. Pets welcome. Discounts to West Edmonton Mall attractions.

Algonquin Motor Lodge
10401 Mayfield Road
780-489-4001
64 units, some with air-conditioning. Cable TV, free coffee, hot tub. Vehicle plug-ins. Close to restaurants, tourist attractions.

Argyll Plaza Hotel
9933 63rd Avenue
1-800-737-3783 or 780-438-5876
48 rooms, kitchenettes, suites, cable TV, movies. Whirlpool, sauna, lounge, restaurant. Free continental breakfast.

Aurora Motel
15145 111th Avenue
780-489-1581
Amenities include air-conditioning and whirlpool.

Best Western City Centre
11310 109th Street
1-800-666-5026 or 780-479-2042
www.bestwestern.com
109 air-conditioned rooms, indoor pool, whirlpool, laundry, data ports. ATM, restaurant, lounge. Close to shopping. Children under 18 stay free.

Best Western Westwood Inn
18035 Stony Plain Road
1-800-557-4767 or 780-483-7770
169 air-conditioned rooms, cable TV, movies, laundry service. Indoor pool, sauna, whirlpool, steam room, squash court. Restaurant, lounge.

Campus Tower Suites Hotel
11145 87th Avenue
780-439-6060
Located near university, fine dining, entertainment, park system. On-site restaurant and lounge.

Canterra Suites Executive Hotel
11010 Jasper Avenue
1-877-421-1212 or 780-421-1212
www.canterrasuites.com
44 apartments, 1–3 bedrooms, cable TV, free movies. Fridges, microwaves, washer/dryer, free Internet, hair dryers, irons and boards. Close to food and shopping.

Century Casino and Hotel Edmonton
13103 Fort Road
780-643-4000
26-room hotel in facility with casino, two fine dining rooms, and a deli. Waterfalls and stone fireplaces in casino.

Chateau Louis Hotel
11727 Kingsway
1-800-661-9843 or 780-452-7770
140 rooms, suites, family rooms in European-style boutique hotel. Cable TV, hair dryers, irons, data ports, roll-in shower. Business center, 24-hour room service, restaurant, piano bar, gaming room. Outdoor courtyard and gazebo.

Coast Edmonton Plaza Hotel
10155 105th Street
780-423-4811
www.coasthotels.com
299 deluxe rooms, suites, cable TV, laundry service. Exercise room, indoor pool. Lounge, family restaurant. Downtown, close to business and government.

Coast Terrace Inn Edmonton South
4440 Gateway Blvd.
1-888-837-7223 or 780-437-6010
www.coastterraceinn.com
234 spacious rooms with amenities. Fitness and racquet club, indoor saltwater pool, sauna, steam rooms. Restaurant, lounge, pub. Located between airport and downtown.

Crowne Plaza—Chateau Lacombe
10111 Bellamy Hill NW
780-428-6611
307 rooms, downtown upscale hotel overlooking river valley. All amenities included. Revolving restaurant.

Coliseum Inn
11845 Wayne Gretzky Drive South
1-877-471-1231 or 780-471-1231
98 units with cable TV, high-speed Internet, laundry. ATM, exercise room, sports bar, room service.

Comfort Inn (West Edmonton)
17610 100th Avenue West
1-800-228-5150 or 780-484-4415
100 rooms, cable TV, movies, PC friendly, hair dryers, irons, restaurant. Close to West Edmonton Mall.

Continental Inn & Suites
16625 Stony Plain Road
1-888-484-9660 or 780-484-7751
www.continentalinn.ca
100 units with amenities, cable TV, free movies, data ports, laundry. Dining, lounge, coffee shop, room service. Vehicle plug-ins.

Courtyard by Marriott
99th Street and Jasper Avenue
780-423-9999
Comfortable, air-conditioned rooms with coffee, mini-bar, room service, free continental breakfast, high-speed Internet. Fitness facility, restaurant, lounge on site.

Days Inn & Suites West Edmonton
10010 179A Street
84 guest rooms and 24 suites, some with kitchenettes. Three-minute drive to West Edmonton Mall. Business center, free high-speed Internet, laundry. Restaurant and fitness center.

Days Inn Downtown Edmonton
10041 106th Street
1-800-267-2191 or 780-423-1925
www.daysinn.com
71 units, cable TV, hair dryers, data ports, ATM. Covered parking, room service. Airport shuttle.

Delta Edmonton Centre Suite Hotel
10222 102nd Street
1-800-268-1133 or 780-429-3900
www.deltaedmontoncentre.com
169 deluxe suites and rooms. High-speed Internet, business center, babysitting. Whirlpool, sauna, restaurant, lounge. In City Centre Shopping Complex.

EastGlen Inn Edmonton
6918 118th Avenue
1-888-411-2610 or 780-471-2610
www.eastglennmotorinn.com
47 units with cable TV, fridges, data ports. Vehicle plug-ins. Some pets accepted.

Edmonton Inn
11830 Kingsway Avenue
1-800-661-7264 or 780-454-9521
www.edmontoninn.com
115 units, cable TV, games, laundry, data ports. ATM, business center. Exercise room, gift shop, hair salon, hot tub. Sports bar. Close to airport, mall.

Executive Royal Inn West Edmonton
10010 178th Street
1-800-661-4879 or 780-484-6000
www.executivehotels.net
236 units, cable TV, games, high-speed Internet. ATM, business center, executive wing. Room service. Gift shop.

Fairmont Hotel Macdonald
10065 100th Street
1-800-441-1414 or 780-424-5181
www.fairmont.com
198 units in downtown four-Diamond hotel. Cable TV, modem jacks, minibars, hair dryers, high-speed Internet. Exercise room, hot tub, business center, ATM. Saltwater pool.

Fantasyland Hotel at West Edmonton Mall
17700 87th Avenue
1-800-737-3783 or 780-444-3000
www.fantasylandhotel.com
355 units with 11 theme rooms, cable TV, games, high-speed Internet, fridges, hair dryers. Health club/spa, hair salon, vehicle plug-ins. Adjacent to World Waterpark.

Four Points by Sheraton Edmonton South
7230 Argyll Road
780-465-7931
Grand waterfall and pond greets guests entering 139-room deluxe hotel. Business center, free wireless high-speed Internet, pool, whirlpool, fitness center. Restaurant and pub.

Glenora Bed & Breakfast Inn
12327 102nd Avenue
780-4888-6766
Historic 1912 hotel with 21 rooms and suites, each decorated with antiques. In Art Gallery District of West Edmonton.

Grand Hotel
10266 103rd Street
1-888-422-6365 or 780-422-6365
71 units, cable TV, data ports. Liquor store, vehicle plug-ins. Free breakfast.

Greenwood Inn
4485 Gateway Blvd. (Highway 2)
1-888-233-6730 or 780-431-1100
224 rooms in southside hotel. Cable TV, movies, laundry service. Indoor pool, whirlpool, steam room, exercise room. Gift shop, restaurant.

Hilton Garden Inn West Edmonton
17610 Stony Plain Road
780-443-2233
www.hiltongardeninn.com
160 units, cable TV, free movies, high-speed Internet, fridges, hair dryers, irons and boards. Exercise room, hot tub, sports bar, room service.

Holiday Inn Express Downtown
10010 104th Street
1-800-877-4656 or 780-2450
140 air-conditioned rooms, cable TV, balconies. Laundry facilities, room service. Indoor pool, whirlpool, sauna, hair salon. Restaurant, lounge.

Holiday Inn Hotel & Suites West Edmonton
11330 170th Street
780-484-1515
Comfortable, air-conditioned rooms with coffee, laundry, high-speed Internet. Pool, fitness room, whirlpool.

Hotel Selkirk
1920s Street, Fort Edmonton Park
Deluxe hotel furnished in 1920s style, with air-conditioning, echoes an earlier building which stood from 1903 to 1962. Now fully restored to its grand days. Restaurant and lounge on site.

Howard Johnson Hotel
15540 Stony Plain Road
1-800-556-4156 or 780-484-3333
www.hojoedmonton.com
60 air-conditioned rooms, nonsmoking floor, high-speed Internet, cable TV, free movies. Family restaurant, lounge, room service. Free parking.

Inn on 7th
10001 107th Street
1-800-661-7327 or 780-429-2861
www.innon7th.com
172 units, cable TV, wireless high-speed Internet, data ports. Free local calls. Room service.

Jockey Motel
3604 118th Avenue
1-800-843-7703 or 780-479-5981
52 units, cable TV, free movies, free local calls. Family rates.

Lodge Motor Inn
18125 Stony Plain Road
1-877-489-3321 or 780-489-3321
54 units, cable TV, free movies, modem jacks, free local calls. Family rates. Close to West Edmonton Mall.

Mayfield Hotel & Suites
16615 109th Avenue
1-800-661-9804 or 780-423-1650
www.mayfieldinnedmonton.com
327 units, cable TV, games, high-speed Internet. ATM, health club/spa, lounge with live music/entertainment, saltwater pool, room service. Shuttle to West Edmonton Mall.

Ramada Hotel & Conference Centre
11834 Kingsway Avenue
1-888-747-4114 or 780-454-5454
www.ramadaedmonton.com
316 units, cable TV, games, hair dryers, irons, laundry, high-speed Internet. Hair salon, gift shop, sports bar, room service.

Ramada Inn & Waterpark
5359 Calgary Trail
1-800-661-9030 or 780-434-3431
www.the.ramada.com/edmonton07838
123 rooms, nonsmoking floor, cable TV, movies, laundry service. Two giant waterslides, pool, exercise room, hot tub. Restaurant, lounge.

Rest E-Z Inn
21640 Stony Plain Road
780-447-4455
40 units, most with air-conditioning. Cable TV, free movies, data ports. Next door to waterslide and restaurant.

Rosslyn Inn & Suites
13620 97th Street
1-877-785-7005 or 780-476-6241
www.albertadirectory.com/edmonton/rosslyn
92 units, some wheelchair accessible, cable TV, free movies, high-speed Internet, hair dryers, irons, laundry. ATM, exercise room, roll-in shower. Restaurant, close to shopping.

Sandman Hotel West Edmonton
17635 Stony Plain Road
780-483-1385
Air-conditioned rooms with coffee, pool, whirlpool. Wheelchair access. Restaurant on site.

Sands Motor Hotel
12340 Fort Road
1-888-444-3402 or 780-474-5476
54 units with cable TV, free local calls, hair dryers, modem jacks. ATM, family restaurant, room service.

The Sutton Place Hotel Edmonton
10235 101st Street
1-866-378-8866 or 780-428-7111
www.suttonplace.com
313 deluxe units, cable TV. ATM, hair salon, health club, spa, pool, hot tub. Restaurant and lounge.

Travelodge East
3414 118th Avenue
1-800-665-0456 or 780-474-0456
85 rooms, cable TV, adjoining units. Barber shop, restaurant, lounge. Cold-weather hookups.

Travelodge Edmonton South
10320 45th Avenue South
1-800-578-7878 or 780-436-9770
www.the.travelodge.com/edmonton09761
219 rooms with cable TV, movies, hair dryers, room service. Indoor pool, whirlpool. Restaurant. Close to shopping, dining, nightclubs.

Union Bank Inn
10053 Jasper Avenue
1-888-423-3601 or 780-423-3600
www.unionbankinn.com
34 units in full-service hotel. Cable TV, free movies, PC friendly, fireplaces and goose-down bedding in all rooms. Exercise room, free full breakfast.

West Edmonton Mall Inn
17504 90th Avenue
780-444-9378
In the great West Edmonton Mall; features 88 well-appointed rooms with voice mail, modem services, cable, coffee, hair dryers.

West Harvest Inn Edmonton
17803 Stony Plain Road
780-484-8000
160 guest rooms, with air-conditioning, free high-speed Internet in some rooms, coffee, wheelchair access. Restaurant and lounge on site.

Westin Edmonton
10135 100th Street
1-800-228-3000 or 780-426-3636
www.westin.com/edmonton
413 deluxe units, cable TV, free movies, fridges, hair dryers, irons and boards, PC friendly. Exercise room, hot tub. Business center, babysitting. Downtown location.

AREA CAMPGROUNDS

EDMONTON:

Glowing Embers Travel Centre & RV Park
2 miles (3.2 km) west of Edmonton on Highways 16A and 60
780-962-8100
268 full-service sites. Internet access, RV wash, laundry, washrooms, store. Close to West Edmonton Mall. Reservations accepted.

Rainbow Valley Campground
Whitemud Park off 122nd Street, south of Whitemud Freeway
1-888-434-3991 or 780-434-5531
88 sites, with and without power; tent camping. Showers, washrooms, laundry, dump station. Store, playground, nature trails.

Shakers Acres
21530 103rd Avenue (off Highway 16A)
780-447-3564
165 sites with full or partial hookups, showers, laundry, groceries, public phone.

Whitemud Creek Golf & RV Park Resort
3428 156th Street
780-988-6800
125 sites. Access to course makes this a golfer's delight. Boat launch, store, pit toilets and water pump.

LEDUC:

Lions Campground
20 miles (32 km) south of Edmonton
50th Street South, then east on Rollyview Road
780-986-1882
69 sites with full hookups, tent area. Washroom, phone, dump station. Heated picnic shelter. Open in summers. Reservations accepted.

DEVON:

Lions Campground
20 miles (32 km) southwest of Edmonton
520 Haven Avenue
780-987-4777
200 sites with and without full hookups; tent camping. restrooms, fire pits. Playgrounds, baseball diamond, gold panning, horseshoe pits. Adjacent to Devon Golf & Country Club.

SHERWOOD PARK:

Half Moon Lake Resort
16 miles (25.5 km) east of Edmonton via 23rd Avenue
780-922-3045
www.halfmoonlakeresort.com
196 sites, with and without power. Hayrides, ponies, horseback rides, petting zoo, wading pool, lake, playground, trout pond, mini-golf, boat rentals. Reservations accepted.

Sherwood Forest Campground & RV Park
23242 Highway 14
780-467-3329
40 sites, with and without power. Café. Adjacent to golf course and bird sanctuary.

SPRING LAKE:

Spring Lake Resort & RV Park
499 Lakeside Drive, 30 minutes west of Edmonton off Highway 16A
780-963-3993
160 sites with full and partial hookups or dry-camping. No tenting sites available. Dump station, swimming, trout fishing, concession, picnic area. Boat and log cabin rentals.

STONY PLAIN:

Allan Beach Resort Campground & RV Park
20 miles (31 km) west of Edmonton, Highway 43 to Range Road 13
780-963-6362
174 sites with full and partial hookups, showers, playground, laundry.

RESTAURANTS

4th & Vine Wine Bar
11358 104th Avenue
780-497-7858
Food and wine in a friendly atmosphere.

ABC Country Restaurant
10804 170th Street
780-484-2600
Homemade is the watchword on full menu, including baked goods.

Barb & Ernie's Restaurant
9906 72nd Avenue
780-433-3242
German restaurant famed for its extensive selection of omelettes and varieties of Eggs Benedict. There's always a line, so come early.

Brits Fish & Chips
6940 77th Street
780-485-1797
Classic British-style fish and chips.

Café Lacombe
10111 Bellamy Hill
780-428-6611
Open daily with full menu and gorgeous view. Brunch on weekends.

Characters
10257 105th Street
780-421-4100 / *www.characters.ca*
Elegant dining, seasonal menu items.

Chili's Texas Grill
9315 137th Avenue
780-478-0606
Casual dining with fajitas, burgers, steaks, chicken. Southwest cooking.

The Copper Pot Restaurant
9707 110th Street, #101
780-452-7800 / *www.copperpot.ca*
Specializing in Canadian fare.

The Creperie
10220 103rd Street
780-420-6656
French country cuisine, crêpes. Award-winning restaurant in downtown location.

Da-De-O New Orleans Diner & Bar
10548A 82nd Avenue
780-433-0930
Favorites from New Orleans in 1950s-style setting. Fried chicken, ribs, po' boys.

Delux Burger Bar
9682 142nd Street
780-420-0101
Gourmet burgers coupled with premium wine, beer, and spirits. Other inventive menu items. Eat indoors or on the heated patio.

Doan's Restaurant
Downtown: 10130 107th Street
780-424-3034
Southside: 7909 104th Street
780-434-4448
Vietnamese cuisine.

Famoso Neapolitan Pizzeria
11750 Jasper Avenue
780-732-0700 / *www.famoso.ca*
Casual restaurant, wood-fired pizzas, salads, and desserts imported from Italy.

Hardware Grill
9698 Jasper Avenue
780-423-0969
Upscale restaurant features award-winning cuisine and impressive wine list. Reservations recommended.

Haweli Restaurant & Lounge
10220 103rd Street
780-421-8100
Authentic East Indian cuisine.

Highlevel Diner
10912 88th Avenue
780-433-1317
Local favorite for lovers of cinnamon buns. Full menu, three meals a day. Located at the foot of the High Level Bridge.

Japanese Village
10126 100th Street
780-422-6083
Sushi, steak, seafood.

The King and I
8208 107th Street
780-433-2222
Thai cuisine with vegetarian, meat, seafood, and poultry selections.

La Spiga Ristorante Italiano
10133 125th Street
780-482-3100
Fine Italian dining in 1913 mansion. Award-winning menu.

Lumber Jack's Pancake & Steak House
8170 50th Street, #145
780-469-6702
Hearty meals, family dining and comfortable setting.

Montana's Cookhouse Saloon
10330 G. A. MacDonald Avenue
780-434-2886
Casual restaurant with cabin décor, extensive menu.

New Asian Village
10143 Saskatchewan Drive
780-434-38303
www.newasianvillage.com
East Indian dining. Top honors among Canada's ethnic restaurants.

Pepper 'n' Chili
10406 Mayfield Road
780-487-6688
Szechuan and Cantonese selections in large, modern restaurant.

Ruth's Chris Steak House
9990 Jasper Avenue, #100
780-990-0123
Top-of-the-line steaks, seafood, award-winning wine list. Reservation recommended.

Smokey Joe's Hickory Smoke House
15135 Stony Plain Road
780-413-3379
Hickory-smoked beef, chicken, and pork, and side dishes.

Tom Goodchild's Moose Factory
4810 Calgary Trail South
780-437-5616
Alberta beef plays a central role in the menu, along with seafood, alligator, even sushi.

Road Notes

To leave Edmonton, take 16A West toward Spruce Grove and Stony Plain and connect with Highway 43 north. You'll stay on Route 43 all the way across northern Alberta as it wends north and west.

A series of small towns along Route 43 forms a dot-to-dot line between Edmonton and Whitecourt. Services and facilities such as gas stations, self-service laundries, restaurants, motels, and campgrounds are available all along this stretch.

(A few miles past Stony Plain is the junction for the westbound Yellowhead Highway 16A. For more information, see the section on the Yellowhead-Cassiar Highways in Chapter 7, Western Canada's Northbound Byways.)

WHITECOURT

From Edmonton: 112 miles (180 km)
To Valleyview: 102 miles (164 km)
To Grande Prairie: 175 miles (282 km)

The confluence of the Athabasca and McLeod Rivers, two major transportation routes, seemed a natural place for a settlement to spring up in rich, forested land. A family-operated sawmill was established here in 1922 and has since grown into a major employer, along with two other timber-related companies. Forestry, oil and gas, sand and gravel, and tourism keep Whitecourt's 8,800 people happy and hard at work. Nearly half of all adults are involved in some form of volunteerism.

The Whitecourt Tourist Information Centre off Highway 43, at the east end of town, is open 7 days a week in summer. The staffers offer directions and advice as well as plenty of printed material. Choices for local recreation include horseback riding, boating, fishing, shopping, or visiting a guest ranch. Watch for moose, deer, and elk in this area. Less visible are black and brown bears.

Golfers are invited to try their hand at the par-72 Graham Acres Golf Club. There's something to satisfy every level of expertise, from practice on the putting green and driving range to the challenging 18-hole course, which parallels the Athabasca River.

To prepare for a fishing adventure, call the Fish and Wildlife office in downtown Whitecourt at 780-778-7112 for license and season information. Go after walleye, northern pike, rainbows, and grayling. Another option is to hire a guiding service, such as Eagle River Wilderness Adventures (780-778-3251), which offers half-day and full-day services or drop-off fishing, wilderness camping, and float fishing trips over several days.

The forest products industry has a standing invitation for visitors to tour local state-of-the-art sawmills and fiberboard and pulp plants. For a program of industrial tours, contact the Chamber of Commerce. Call 708-778-5363 or visit their office on Highway 43 by the traffic lights.

Just northwest of town on Highway 32, you'll find the Eric S. Heustis Demonstration Forest, with 4 miles (6.5 km) of self-guided trails and interpretive sites about forest management and the forest industry. Near the entrance, a variety of trees are identified on interpretive plaques.

For more information on Whitecourt, visit *www.whitecourtweb.com.*

LODGING

Alaska Highway Motel
3511 Highway Street
1-800-778-4156 or 780-778-4156
36 units with balconies, cable TV, fridges, data ports, free coffee.

Green Gables Inn
3527 Highway Street
1-800-779-4537 or 780-778-4537
www.telusplanet.net/public/ggables
49 units, kitchenettes, some nonsmoking. Cable TV with movie channel, free continental breakfast. Restaurant.

Lakeview Inn & Suites Whitecourt
3325 Caxton Street
780-706-3349
50 rooms, some deluxe suites. Coffee, hair dryers, cable TV, free continental breakfast.

Quality Inn Whitecourt
5420 47th Avenue, just off Highway 43 North
1-800-265-9660 or 780-778-5477
74 air-conditioned rooms, suites. Executive rooms with high-speed Internet, modem ports. Cable TV, sauna, hot tub, exercise facility. 24-hour café, restaurant; dining overlooks McLeod River. Children under 18 stay free.

The Ritz Café & Motor Inn
Highway 43 North
1-800-639-6765 / *www.ritzmotorinn.com*
63 units, cable TV, free movies, fridges, free coffee, modem jacks. Winter plug-ins, restaurant.

Royal Oak Inn
3305 Highway Street
780-778-4004 / *www.theroyaloakinn.com*
38 rooms, some nonsmoking. Cable TV, ATM, fridges, data ports. Free full breakfast at The Oak Restaurant.

Super 8 Motel Whitecourt
4121 Kepler Street
1-877-778-8940 or 780-778-8908
59 air-conditioned rooms, king and queen suites with whirlpool. Continental breakfast, voice mail, data ports, laundry service, 24-hour fitness room.

Western Budget Motel
3405 Kepler Street
780-706-2030 / *www.westernbudgetmotel.com*
58 units, cable TV, free movies, fireplaces, fridges, VCRs, hair dryers, high-speed Internet service, laundry. Free continental breakfast, wheelchair access rooms.

Whitecourt Inn
3415 Caxton Street
1-888-416-4844 or 780-778-4844
62 air-conditioned rooms, cable TV, fridges, free coffee. Pool, restaurant, laundry.

CAMPGROUNDS

Alaska Highway Motel & RV Park
3511 Highway Street
780-778-4156
22 campsites. Showers, restrooms, dump station. Sheltered picnic sites.

Camp in Town RV Park
Downtown Whitecourt
780-706-5050
70 sites, 35 with all services. Year-round camping, pull-throughs. Washrooms, showers, laundry.

Carson-Pegasus Provincial Park
14.5 miles (23 km) north of Whitecourt on Highway 43; follow signs
780-778-2664
182 sites (41 with power); group camping, firewood. Showers, laundry, tap water, dump station. Store. Beach, swimming, fishing, wheelchair-accessible fishing area, horseshoe pits. Boat rentals, snack bar.

Eagle River Outfitters
10 minutes south of Whitecourt on Highway 32
780-778-3251
27 sites with 15-amp service, pull-throughs, cabins. Fishing, tubing, canoe rentals, fire pits, swimming area.

Sagitawah RV Park
Just northwest of town on Highway 43
780-778-3734
88 sites, some with full hookups, pull-throughs. Free showers; laundry, fire pits. Store, propane sales, RV parts and service. Playground, mini-golf, movie rentals. Senior discount.

Whitecourt Lions Club Campground
1 mile (1.5 km) east of Whitecourt on Highway 43
780-778-5363
60 stalls (30 with power). Some pull-throughs, water, firewood, showers, laundry facility, dump station. Lots of trees, playground, horseshoe pits. Senior discount.

RESTAURANTS

Boston Pizza
3836 Kepler Street
780-778-2500
Family dining, pizza, pasta, sandwiches.

Crown & Anchor Pub
4802 51st Street
780-776-1900
Pizza, sandwiches, beer and wine.

Ernie O's Restaurant & Pub
Next to the Guest House Inn
780-778-8600
Steaks, seafood.

Humpty's Family Restaurant
5123A Kepler Street West
780-778-8703
Full menu in family dining room.

Joey's Only Seafood Restaurants
3722 Kepler Street
780-779-9988
Fish and chips.

KG's Sandwich Bar
4912 50th Avenue
780-778-5286
Fresh-baked cinnamon buns, homemade soups.

Mountain Pizza & Steakhouse
3823 Highway Street
780-778-3600
Pizza, steaks, Italian food, ribs, chicken, soups, salad.

My Little Saigon Restaurant
4812 50th Street
780-778-1911
Vietnamese cuisine.

Pizza Shack
5115 50th Avenue
780-778-5151
Pizza, sandwiches, and more.

Rainbow Restaurant
4904 51st Avenue
780-778-6333
Chinese menu.

Road Notes

Between Whitecourt and Grande Prairie are 172 miles (277 km) of increasingly striking vistas as the route leads toward the foothills of the Canadian Rockies and away from populated areas. The Athabasca River, then the Little Smoky River, may be seen along the road as you continue north and west on Highway 43.

Fifty miles (80.5 km) past Whitecourt is Fox Creek, the seat of the area's oil-and-gas exploration efforts. Lodging, meals, laundry facilities, and gas stations may be found in this community. A few miles farther still is the tiny town of Little Smoky.

Just before you enter Valleyview, a roadside visitor information center and rest stop offers picnic tables, water, and a dump station for RV travelers. You can make a phone call, mail a letter, and buy souvenirs here, too.

Valleyview calls itself the Portal to the Peace Country, a region through which the mighty Peace River flows. Originally a transportation route for trappers, explorers, and traders, the river today is famed for its outdoor recreation opportunities and oil, ever since discovery in the 1950s. When you reach Valleyview, you have traveled 214 miles (344.5 km) from Edmonton. Grande Prairie, the next large community on the Alaska Highway, lies 70 miles (112.5 km) ahead, via Highway 43.

Eleven miles (17.5 km) past Valleyview, we followed the signs to Williamson Provincial Park for our next overnight stay. Located on Sturgeon Lake, Williamson Park is a forested campground, which lends a sense of privacy to each campsite. The park offers 67 sites, with full or partial hookups, or tent camping. There are showers, a dump station, and a public phone. The nearby lake is an easy place to launch a boat to fish for perch, pickerel, northern pike, or whitefish.

Other camping also is available on this stretch of Highway 43 that leads to Grande Prairie. Watch for private and provincial campground signs.

GRANDE PRAIRIE

From Whitecourt: 175 miles (282 km)
To Dawson Creek: 83 miles (134 km)

Grande Prairie, at the junction of Highways 43 and 40, is the regional center for northwest Alberta and northeast British Columbia, with an economy that's based on agriculture, forestry, oil, and gas. The city symbol is the trumpeter swan, and these elegant white birds are frequently seen on local lakes. A portion of the city's Web site focuses on the swans, with interesting natural history facts and lovely photographs from throughout the year. See *www.cityofgp.com/swans.*

As you enter the city, stay on the Highway 43 bypass and watch for the blue-and-white question-mark signs that lead the way to the impressive cedar-and-pine Visitor Information Centre 2000, with restrooms, free literature about Grand Prairie and other towns in the region, and helpful travel counselors at the counter.

Centre 2000 overlooks Muskoseepi Park and the Bear Creek Reservoir. Nearby is the Rotary Park Campground along the reservoir (see list of campgrounds). The fraternal organization also offers free bus tours of the city and county every Monday, Tuesday, and Thursday evening during summer months, leaving Centre 2000 at 7 P.M.

RV travelers will appreciate the city's free sani-dump and fresh water at the old visitor information log cabin, located about five minutes south of Centre 2000 on 106th Street. And a fully accredited medical facility, the Queen Elizabeth II Hospital, is located at 98th Street and 105th Avenue.

This region was home to First Nations people for centuries. The first white arrivals were fur traders, who came on the scene in 1771. The town's name is credited to Father Emile Grouard, who first viewed this vast, treeless area around Lake Saskatoon in the mid-1800s and called it *la grande prairie.* The first settlement here was established in 1911 and the city has prospered ever since. In August 2007, Grand Prairie passed the 50,000 population mark. Another 300,000 live in the surrounding region, with Grande Prairie as a hub.

At the information center, ask for directions to Kleskun Hills, east of town, where you can view fossilized marine life and dinosaur remains in an area that was once a river delta. Or visit the Crystal Lake Waterfowl Refuge for birding, walking along nature trails, or just soaking up the sunshine. Call 780-538-0451 for details.

Another local natural treasure is Muskoseepi Park, which covers about 1,100 acres in Bear Creek Valley. *(Muskoseepi* is the Cree word for "bear creek.") The park pavilion is the stage for outdoor concerts and festivals. Recreation includes camping, golf, hiking, wildlife-watching, and lawn bowling. The park also invites swimming, boating, fishing, and other water sports.

The city symbol of Grand Prairie, the swan, is sometimes visible on local lakes.

In this wonderful park you'll find the Grande Prairie Museum and Heritage Village, with exhibits on dinosaurs, aboriginal tribes, explorers, trappers, traders, missionaries, and pioneer families. Early-day buildings, churches, and bridges moved here from their original sites tell the story of the city's beginnings. The museum is wheelchair accessible and open year-round. Another place to enjoy a portion of the museum's collection is at the Heritage Discovery Centre, on the lower level of Centre 2000 on the Highway 43 bypass. Call 780-532-5482.

And don't miss the Grand Prairie Stompede, featuring broncos, bulls, ponies, and professional chuckwagon races, a town tradition since 1977. Festivities include a giant midway, entertainment, and all the professional rodeo you can handle. Call 780-532-4646 or browse *www.gpstompede.com.*

Also browse the Grand Prairie Region Tourism Web site at *www.northernvisitor.com.*

LODGING

For bed-and-breakfast accommodations in Grande Prairie, phone 1-800-661-8888 or 780-427-4321.

Best Western Grande Prairie Hotel & Suites
10745 117th Avenue
1-866-852-2378 or 780-402-2378
www.bestwestern.com
100 units, some theme rooms. Cable TV, high-speed Internet, fridges, microwaves, hair dryers, free newspaper, data ports. Roll-in shower, swimming pool, tanning salon, room service. Free shuttle.

Canadian Motor Inn
10901 100th Avenue
1-800-291-7893 or 780-532-1680
www.canadianmotorinn.com
64 air-conditioned rooms, kitchenettes and nonsmoking available. Cable TV, in-room coffee, high-speed Internet, laundry, whirlpools, winter plug-ins. Restaurant, pub, free continental breakfast.

Grande Prairie Inn
11633 Clairmont Road
1-800-661-6529 or 780-532-5221
206 deluxe air-conditioned rooms in full-service hotel. Whirlpool, sauna, indoor pool. Gift shop, restaurant, piano bar lounge, night club. Three-Diamond rating, AAA. Next to major shopping mall.

Holiday Inn Grande Prairie Hotel & Suites
9816 107th Street
1-888-307-5529 or 780-402-6886
www.pomeroygroup.ca
146 units in large convention facility, cable TV, high-speed Internet, free local calls. Health club/spa, hair salon, room service, free shuttle service.

The Lodge Motor Inn
10909 100th Avenue (Highway 2 West)
1-800-661-7874 or 780-539-4700
www.lodgemotorinn.com
53 air-conditioned rooms with cable TV, free movies, fridges. Heated outdoor pool in summer. Restaurant, close to shopping. Vehicle plug-ins.

Pomeroy Inn & Suites
11710 102nd Street
1-877-977-9678 or 780-831-2999
Extra-large rooms, suites, deluxe continental breakfast, indoor pool, waterslide and hot tub. Free Internet access, shuttle service.

Prairie Haven Motel
12002 100th Street
780-539-5500
Rooms with satellite TV and Superchannel. Free local calls. Laundry. Restaurant on site. Across from Prairie Mall.

Quality Hotel & Conference Centre Grand Prairie
11201 100th Avenue
1-800-661-7954 or 780-539-6000
www.qualityhotelgrandprairie.com
102 air-conditioned rooms, executive suites, kitchenettes, nonsmoking rooms available. Cable TV, free breakfast, exercise room, gift shop. Shuttle service.

Sandman Hotel Grande Prairie
9805 100th Street
1-800-726-3626 or 780-513-5555
www.sandmanhotels.com
136 air-conditioned rooms, executive suites, nonsmoking available. Cable TV, fax/modem outlets, in-room movies and games. Fitness facilities, swimming pool, hot tub, whirlpools. Vehicle plug-ins. 24-hour Denny's restaurant adjacent.

Service Plus Inns & Suites
10810 107A Avenue
1-888-875-4667 or 780-538-3900
www.serviceplusinns.com
123 deluxe air-conditioned rooms. Cable TV, movies, laundry service, continental breakfast. Indoor pool, waterslide, hot tub. Exercise room, restaurant, lounge. Shuttle service.

Silver Crest Lodge
11902 100th Street
1-800-422-7791 or 780-532-1040
95 units with cable TV, movies, copy/fax services, fridges, microwaves, PC workstations. Plug-ins.

Stanford Inn
11401 100th Avenue
1-800-661-8160 or 780-539-5678
www.stanfordinn.net
206 units, nonsmoking available. In-room movies and coffee, modem jacks, high-speed Internet. Family restaurant, pub.

Super 8 Motel
10050 116th Avenue
1-888-888-9488 or 780-532-8288
www.super8.com
103 air-conditioned rooms, suites, kitchenettes; nonsmoking floors available. Laundry, free continental breakfast and newspaper. Indoor heated pool with waterslide, exercise room, barbecue area with playground.

Trumpeter Hotel & Meeting Centre
12102 100th Avenue
1-800-661-9435 or 780-539-5561
www.trumpeterhotel.com
118 air-conditioned rooms, suites, nonsmoking available. High-speed Internet, in-room coffee, cable TV. Exercise room, hot tub. Sports bar. Vehicle plug-ins.

CAMPGROUNDS

Camp Tamarack RV Park
5 miles (8.5 km) south of Grande Prairie on Highway 40
1-877-532-9998 or 780-532-9998
www.camptamarackrv.com
89 sites with power and water, most with pull-throughs, plentiful trees. Private showers, laundry, restrooms, dump station. Satellite and cable hookups, fax machine, Internet access. Store, RV supplies, RV pressure-wash, recreation room.

Country Roads RV Park
2.5 miles (4 km) west of Highways 43 and 2 junction
780-532-6323
www.countryroadsrvpark.com
115 sites with power, some pull-throughs; tent sites. 15-, 30-, and 50-amp sites. Showers, laundry, washrooms, fire pits, lots of trees. Fish pond, playgrounds. Open year-round. Close to golf.

Grande Prairie Rotary Park
108th Street and Highway 43 Bypass
780-532-1137
59 sites with full and partial hookups. Firewood, shelter, laundry, phone. No reservations.

Saskatoon Island Provincial Park
13 miles (21 km) west of Grande Prairie and 2.5 miles (4 km) north of Highway 43
780-766-3485
103 sites with partial hookups; group camping and day-use area. Dump station, store. Beach, swimming, playground, wheelchair access.

Stompede Campground & RV Park
4.0 miles (6.5 km) south of Holiday Inn on Highway 407, 2.8 miles (4.5 km) east to Evergreen Park
780-532-4568
80 sites with full and partial hookups. 15- and 30-amp service. Equestrian trails, stabling. Archery range, batting cage, close to golf. Laundry, free firewood, phone, fire pits. Open May through September.

Wee Links Golf & Campground
9209 95th Avenue, south end of city
780-538-4501
23 sites with 30-amp service. Water, phone, fire pits, concession. 9-hole par 3 golf course and driving range.

RESTAURANTS

Acropolis
10011 101st Avenue
780-538-4424
Family restaurant, local favorite for food, service, and cleanliness.

BJ's Q Club
10013 97th Avenue
780-539-6576
www.bjsqclub.com
Pizza and live entertainment in a locally owned pub.

Badass Jack's Subs & Wraps Co.
9606 100th Street, #105
780-814-7942
Sandwiches, Asian soup bowls and boxes.

Cherry Lounge
10833 100th Street
780-832-0494
Appetizers, soups, salads, inventive dinner entrees.

Crown 'n'Anchor
8024 100th Street
780-532-5444
Family meals, pizza, sandwiches, burgers.

Cygnet
12102 100th Street, at the Trumpeter Hotel
1-800-661-9435 or 780-539-5561
Casual fine dining, featuring Alberta beef.

Earl's
9825 100th Street, downtown
780-538-3275
Canadian-certified Angus steaks.

East Side Mario's
10622 99th Avenue
780-513-8900
New-York-style Italian food, pizza, pasta, sandwiches.

Golden Star Restaurant
101112 101st Avenue
780-532-7546
Chinese specialties, eat in or take-out. Lounge.

Gulliver's
10829 104A Avenue
780-513-8328
Chicken, beef, daily specials. Located across from college.

Jake's Down South
10702 108A Street
780-532-5667
Specializing in Texas-style, bayou, and Mexican fare.

Joey's Only Seafood
10420 116th Avenue
780-538-2722
Shrimp, fish and chips, ribs, chicken. Eat in or take-out.

Pita Pit
10061 108A Street
780-532-7215
Meat, seafood, vegetarian pitas.

Ramona Pizza
10120 100th Avenue
780-532-1534
Pizza, souvlaki, fish and chips, ribs.

Sarpino's Pizzeria
11030 100th Street
780-538-1700
Pizza to go or dine in.

Smitty's
11070 100th Avenue
780-513-1223
Breakfast specialties, burgers, all-day selections.

Tony Roma's
102, 10745 177th Avenue, next to Best Western
780-538-4546
Ribs, steak, chicken.

Wok 'n' Grill Restaurant & Lounge
12335 99 th Street
780-402-8787
Seafood, chicken, beef, combination Chinese dinners.

Road Notes

Eighty-three miles (134 km) ahead is Dawson Creek. Don't let a finish-line mentality stop you from enjoying the hospitality offered by small towns between Grande Prairie and Dawson Creek, however. Wembley, Beaverlodge, Tupper, and Pouce Coupe are towns of varying size and distinct personalities. This region is steeped in pioneering history, so be sure to take in small-town attractions such as the South Peace Centennial Museum, just east of Beaverlodge, where antique farm equipment has been restored to working order. Also, Pouce Coupe is proud of its museum in the old railroad station, which houses artifacts tracing this community's beginnings as a trading post in 1908.

These roadside communities also offer fuel, meals, and lodging. Multiple camping opportunities lie along this stretch of the road, from small municipal campgrounds to provincial parks. Watch for the signs.

As you near Dawson Creek and enter British Columbia, be sure to set your clocks back one hour to reflect the Pacific Time Zone. If you follow the Alaska Highway through British Columbia and the Yukon Territory, you won't have to change the time again until you cross the Alaska–Yukon border.

DAWSON CREEK, British Columbia

From Grande Prairie: 83 miles (134 km)
From the Montana border: 750 miles (1,200 km)
To the Alaska border: 1,190 miles (1,915 km)
To Fairbanks: 1,488 miles (2,395 km)

Symbolically, Dawson Creek is the end of this road, and the beginning of another. You have arrived at Mile 0 of the famed Alaska Highway, and a new leg of your adventure is about to begin. For a complete description of Dawson Creek and its services, facilities, and attractions, see Chapter 6, The Alaska Highway.

YOU ARE NOW ENTERING THE
WORLD FAMOUS
ALASKA HIGHWAY
DAWSON CREEK B.C.
ALBERTA POOL ELEVATORS LTD. DAWSON CREEK
ART GALLERY

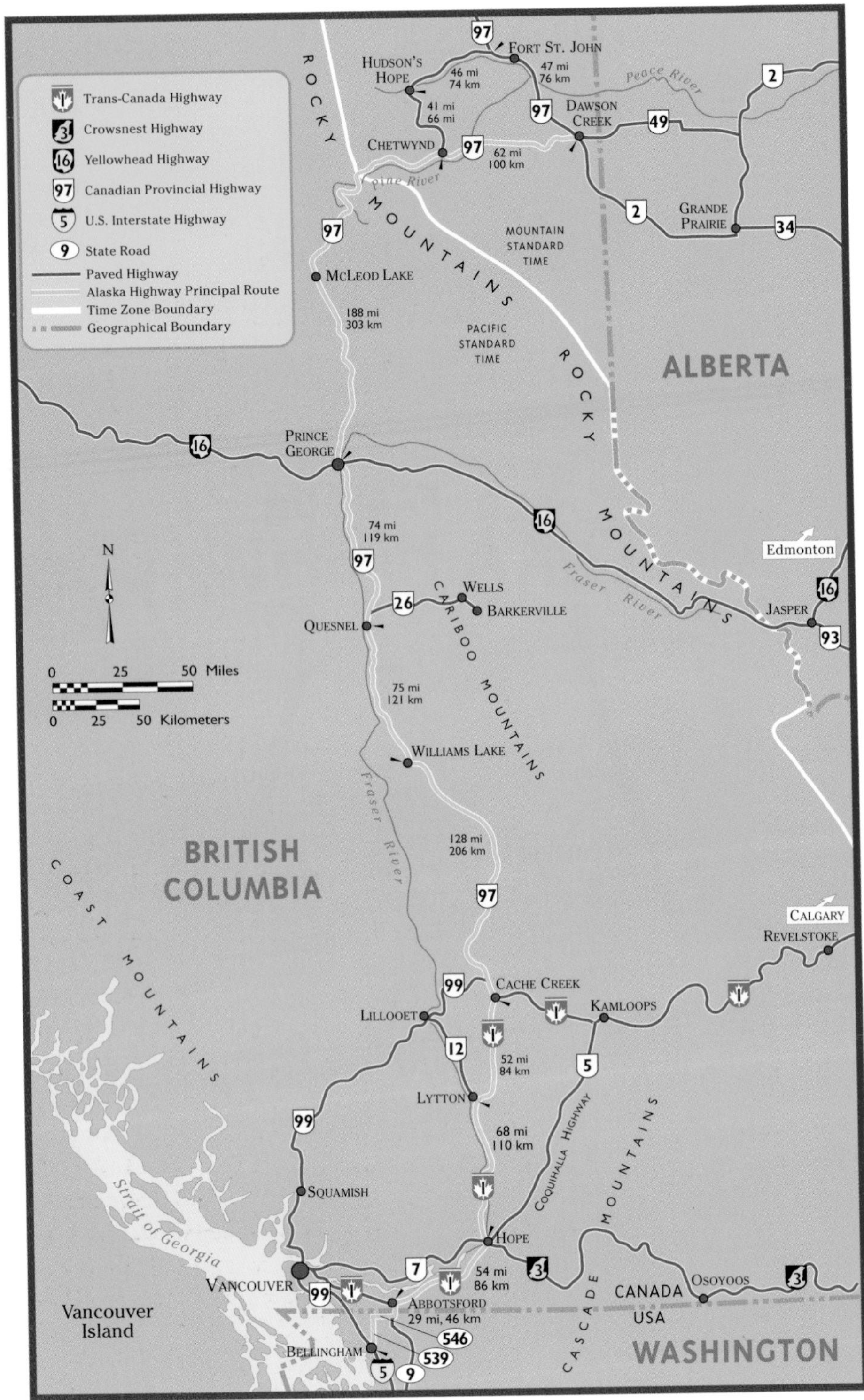

Trans-Canada Highway
Crowsnest Highway
Yellowhead Highway
Canadian Provincial Highway
U.S. Interstate Highway
State Road
Paved Highway
Alaska Highway Principal Route
Time Zone Boundary
Geographical Boundary
Fort St. John
Hudson's Hope
46 mi 74 km
47 mi 76 km
Peace River
41 mi 66 mi
Dawson Creek
Chetwynd
62 mi 100 km
Pine River
Grande Prairie
Mountain Standard Time
Pacific Standard Time
McLeod Lake
188 mi 303 km
Rocky Mountains
Alberta
Prince George
74 mi 119 km
Edmonton
Wells
Barkerville
Quesnel
Fraser River
Jasper
Cariboo Mountains
75 mi 121 km
N
0 25 50 Miles
0 25 50 Kilometers
Williams Lake
128 mi 206 km
British Columbia
Coast Mountains
Calgary
Revelstoke
Cache Creek
Kamloops
Lillooet
52 mi 84 km
Lytton
68 mi 110 km
Coquihalla Highway
Cascade Mountains
Squamish
Strait of Georgia
Hope
54 mi 86 km
Vancouver
Abbotsford
29 mi, 46 km
Osoyoos
Canada
USA
Vancouver Island
Bellingham
Washington

CHAPTER 5

The Western Route: Through British Columbia to Dawson Creek, B.C., and Mile 0

IF NATURAL BEAUTY WERE MEASURED on a scale of 1 to 10, British Columbia would easily break out the top, like an overheated thermometer. Canada's westernmost province is flat-out gorgeous from south to north, west to east.

Motoring along the northbound highways that lead to Dawson Creek, you will see for yourself the fascinating juxtaposition of the cultivated and uncivilized: orderly farms and untamed rivers, formal street grids beneath a tumble of mountains, logging trucks rumbling by tearooms.

Evidence of British, French, and American influence is visible in this province; the region also is rich in ancient culture that should not be overlooked in your travels. In museum exhibits and in daily practice, the First Nations people demonstrate the continuation of centuries-old traditions. Be sure to stop at the exciting culture-based attractions offered by members of various Native American groups. Learn about life in this country before contact with Europeans, along with customs and traditions in dance, art, and storytelling that continue today.

This traditional homeland of Canada's first people remains rich in resources such as big game, fish, birds, and small furbearers. As you drive, take care to watch for wildlife-viewing opportunities. We saw caribou, stone sheep, bison, eagles, hawks and other birds, plus numerous species of fish during our trip. In the case of big game on the road, keep your eyes open for safety's sake, as well as for photographic opportunities.

B.C. also can boast of its magnificent coastline and islands, the Fraser and other wild rivers, fruitful farmlands, mountain lakes, glaciers and ice fields, and the longest stretch of the Canadian Rockies. Victoria and Vancouver, its major cities in the southwestern part of the province, rival many in Europe for cultural attraction and architectural wonder. Fertile farms in the south feed British Columbia and contribute to the province's export economy. Inland, the historic Cariboo Country holds stories of a gold rush that lingered well past that of the Klondike.

As you travel toward Cache Creek, the landscape turns drier and rockier, and the scent of sagebrush and juniper lingers in the air, bringing with it a sense of the Old West. Indeed, Canada's Old West holds as much wonderful and bizarre history as that of the United States, with ranchers, cowboys, miners, outlaws, and the women who loved them. You can visit historic Hat Creek Ranch or Barkerville to learn more about the Cariboo Wagon Road and the stagecoach line that once connected the western towns.

Like elsewhere in western Canada, the northernmost reaches are the rough-and-ready regions, where timber, oil, and natural gas take economic precedence over farming. This is not surprising, considering that the number of frost-free days shrinks with every northbound step in latitude, and the soil tends toward spotty sections of permafrost. As you drive, you'll also see incredible evidence of mankind's ability to harness energy through building dams and extracting oil and gas.

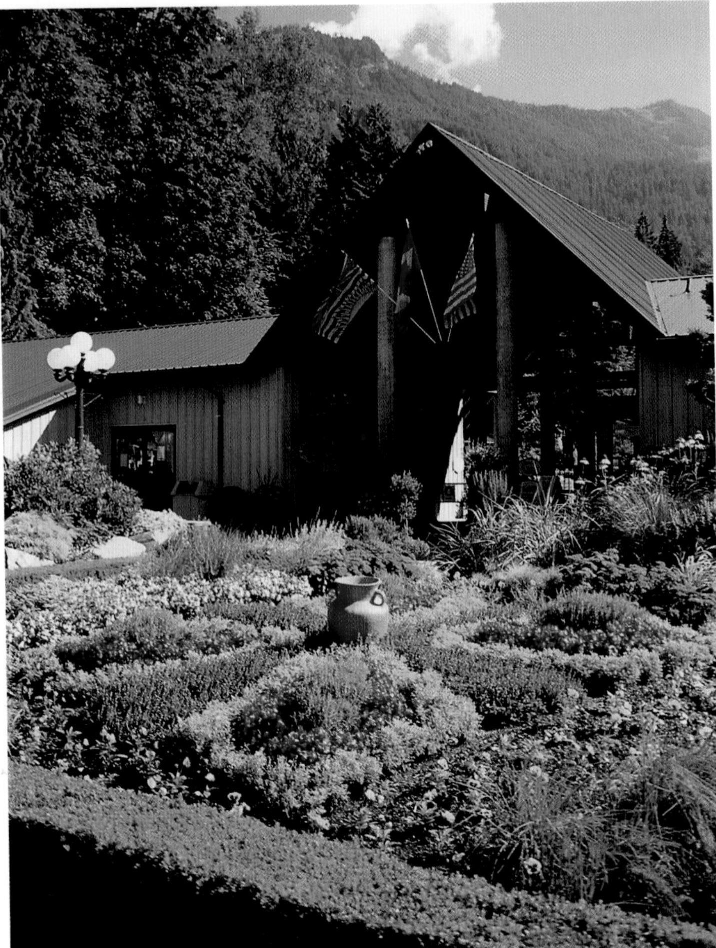

Minter Gardens in Chilliwack features 32 acres of themed gardens, topiary, water gardens, and rest stops.

BRITISH COLUMBIA AT A GLANCE

Size: 365,948 square miles or 947,800 square km
Population in 2006: 4,310,452
Capital: Victoria
Tourism, Lodging: 1-800-435-5622 or *www.hellobc.com*
Provincial and National Park Camping: 1-800-689-9025 or *www.discovercamping.ca*
Sport Fishing: *www.env.gov.bc.ca/fw/fish*
Hunting: *www.env.gov.bc.ca/fw/wildlife*
Canada Border Information: 204-983-3500 (outside Canada) or *www.cbsa-asfc.gc.ca*
Road conditions: 1-800-550-4997 (anywhere in North American) or *www.drivebc.ca*

WASHINGTON–BRITISH COLUMBIA BORDER

To Chilliwack, B.C.: 27 miles (43 km)
To Dawson Creek, B.C.: 705 miles (1,128 km)

To begin your northward journey through British Columbia, you will likely be starting out on north-south U.S. Interstate 5 in western Washington. Take I-5 north from Seattle to Bellingham, the southernmost port city on the Alaska Marine Highway System. (See Chapter 9 for more information on ferry routes.)

At Bellingham, I-5 connects with northbound Route 539. Take Exit 256A and stay on this road to the junction with Highway 546 to Sumas. From the I-5 turn-off to the international border it's about 25 miles (40 km). (See the section on Border Crossings in Chapter 2, What You Need to Know.)

On the U.S. side, the border town is Sumas, Washington; on the Canada side, it's Huntington, B.C. The border crossing is open 24 hours a day.

Road Notes

Heading north from the border, stay on Highway 11 for 4.5 miles (7 km) to Abbotsford, a community that's booming—so much, in fact, that in 2004, it was named Canada's fastest-growing economy. Abbotsford's also famous for its temperate climate, which allows golfers to stay in the game 12 months of the year, and feeds the region's abundant crops of raspberries, blueberries, and strawberries. You can pick your own at area farms, and join the Berry Festival in early July for a taste of desserts and berry entrees. A month later, cowboys and farmers congregate for the Agrifair, what local folks call "The Best Little Country Fair."

In mid-August, the Abbotsford International Airshow features flying stunts by Canadian and international pilots, plus ground displays of fixed-wing, military, warbird, homebuilt, and civilian planes. It's been drawing fans since 1962. For information, call 604-852-8511 or see *www.abbotsfordairshow.com*.

Unleash your daring side—give skydiving a try in the safest possible way. The Abbotsford Skydive Centre can arrange for a tandem jump, so you're "attached" to an experienced diver, making that first jump virtually danger-free, if not fright-free. And they'll take pictures of you while you're airborne. Call 1-888-738-5867 or 604-854-3255, or browse *www.vancouver-skydiving.bc.ca.*

Grab a taste of cultural history at The Xa:ytem Longhouse Interpretive Centre in Mission, an important archeological site that revealed evidence of its occupation thousands of years ago. The Sto:lo Nation erected a longhouse at the site and offers First Nations' culture and history tours. From Abbotsford, turn north on the Trans-Canada Highway 1 and cross the Fraser River to reach Mission via Highway 11.

The mechanically oriented member of the family will enjoy a tour of the Barrowtown Pump Station, 10 miles (16 km) east of Abbotsford off Trans-Canada Highway 1, where since 1923 pumps have drained what once was Sumas Lake, opening up 30,000 acres of land for farming. There's a picnic area here.

To learn more about area attractions, events, lodging, and dining, visit the Tourism Abbotsford Society at 2478 McCallum Road or call 604-859-1721. Another tourism information Web site is *www.tourismabbotsford.ca.*

From Abbotsford, follow Highway 1 east for 17 miles (27 km) to Chilliwack.

CHILLIWACK

From the border: 27 miles (43 km)
To Hope: 22 miles (36 km)

The Fraser River Valley is a suitable setting for a painting, with snowcapped peaks as a backdrop to widespread farms and a pretty city. This is a place for folks who appreciate life in a rural setting with the convenience of a nearby metropolis. Vancouver is just an hour's travel to the west.

Home to about 76,000 people, Chilliwack prides itself on its recreational opportunities as well as its agriculture-based economy. Water is the tie that binds—the Fraser River, Chilliwack River, and Cultus, Chilliwack, and Harrison Lakes are playgrounds for locals and visitors.

Generous water sources, along with southern B.C.'s climate and good soil, have made agriculture king here. In local fields, you'll find flowers, grain, corn and other vegetables, herbs, pumpkins and, like the northwest United States, apples. Among growers with an open-door policy is The Apple Farm & Country Store at 4490 Boundary Road in Yarrow. The farm produces 25 varieties of apples, and offers tastings, tours, and school visits, as well as dinner on the farm. The Apple Farm suffered greatly in 2007 due to severe windstorms, and had to close to U-pick visitors and tours, but they were busily preparing for a better 2008. Phone 604-823-4311 or see *www.applesandstuff.com.*

If golf is your game, you'll find more than 10 courses within a half-hour from downtown Chilliwack. Among them is a full range of challenge up to world-championship level, and in southern B.C.'s mild temperatures, you can easily golf into late autumn.

At the Chilliwack Museum, objects and artifacts help tell the story of this community's beginnings and the diverse people who have lived in this valley. Rated one of the top 10 museums in British Columbia by *Westworld Magazine*, the Chilliwack Museum is located at 45820 Spadina Avenue, in a 1912 structure that was the former city hall. Call 604-795-5210.

In late August, Chilliwack hosts an annual Bluegrass Festival at the Chilliwack Heritage Park, Highway 1 at Lickman Road (Exit 116). It's a popular weekend, full of music, crafts, and free nightly corn roasts. There's even bluegrass church on Sunday morning. Check *www.chilliwackartscouncil.com* for dates and the list of performers.

For family fun, look just east of Chillwack, where Bridal Falls offers a dinosaur theme park, golfing, waterslides, and bumper boats. Campsites for tents or RVs are nearby. To reach the Trans-Canada Water Slides and these other neighboring attractions, take Exit 135 on Highway 1 east. Call 1-888-883-8852 or 604-794-7455.

Or check out the Cultus Lake area, where either the provincial park or resort accommodations offer more fun for all members of the family. On the water: canoeing, kayaking, and fishing. On land: hiking, horseback riding, biking, and walking trails. Or in the resort park, enjoy the waterslides and go-carts, come rain or shine. Access to Cultus Lake is via Exit 119B south. Call 604-858-7241 or browse *www.cultus.com*.

For more on local heritage, events, and activities, visit the Chilliwack Visitor Information Centre, 44150 Luckakuck Way, or call 1-800-567-9535 or 604-858-8121. Visit *www.tourismchilliwack.com*.

COLORFUL MINTER GARDENS

Minter Gardens bills itself as a "world-class garden attraction," and now that I've seen it in person, I second the vote. Paths wend through, under, and around 32 acres of perfectly groomed hillsides that look as if an artist has applied color to the foliage in sweeps of paint, not plantings. Eleven themed gardens feature creative topiary, water gardens, and serene rest stops. Allow at least 2 hours to walk the paths among the gardens, aviary, and bonsai displays.

With 7,000-foot Mount Cheam as a backdrop, skilled gardeners show off their talents in artfully pruned shrubbery, an archway of trained boughs, and topiary sculptures. My favorites included a shrub woman whose Southern belle hoopskirt was a blaze of flowers; another was a peacock whose body was a piece of topiary art and his tail feathers swept across a downward slope in a rush of color.

One of the most photographed gardens is a tidy hillside with the words "Minter Gardens" snipped with sharp-edged precision in letters so large, you have to stand a half a football field away just to get your picture. Which reminds me, bring plenty of film or space on your digital camera. On the grounds, you'll also find a gift shop and snack and coffee bar. During the busy visitor months, mid-May to late September, the Trillium Restaurant offers a gourmet buffet lunch from 11 A.M. to 2 P.M. Call 604-794-7044 for reservations. Minter Gardens is off Highway 1 at Exit 135. Call 1-888-MINTERS or visit *www.mintergardens.com*.

LODGING

Best Western Rainbow Country Inn
43971 Industrial Way
1-800-665-1030 or 604-795-3828
www.rainbowcountryinn.com
74 air-conditioned rooms. Laundry, coffee, sauna, whirlpool. Indoor pool, family restaurant, coffee shop, lounge. Golf packages available.

Comfort Inn
45405 Luckakuck Way
1-800-228-5150 or 604-858-0636
www.choicehotels.ca/cn235
83 air-conditioned rooms, nonsmoking available. Cable TV, data ports, hair dryers, irons and boards. Continental breakfast available. Restaurants, shopping, golf nearby. Kids 18 and younger stay free with parent or grandparent.

Days Inn—Chilliwack
8583 Young Road S.
1-800-329-7466 or 604-792-1955
www.daysinn.ca
29 air-conditioned units. Cable TV, fridges, microwaves, data port. Continental breakfast, newspaper. Free local calls; near attractions.

Parkwood Lodge
8600 Young Street
1-877-793-1234 or 604-795-9155
30 deluxe air-conditioned rooms, some kitchenettes, cable TV, coffee. Heated outdoor swimming pool, playground. Close to restaurants, shopping, attractions.

Rainbow Motor Inn
45620 Yale Road
1-800-834-5547 or 604-792-6412
www.rainbowmotorinn.com
40 air-conditioned rooms, efficiencies, free local calls, movies, laundry. Adjacent to restaurants, garden. Senior discount.

Rhombus Hotels & Resorts—Downtown Chilliwack
45920 1st Avenue
1-800-520-7555 or 604-795-4788
www.rhombushotels.com
110 air-conditioned rooms with mountain views. Coffee, sauna, whirlpool, restaurant, lounge, fitness center, pool, hot tub. Downtown location.

Royal Hotel
45886 Wellington Avenue
1-888-434-3388 or 604-792-1210
www.valleyimall.com/royal
30 units in circa 1908 inn, private baths, cable, air conditioning. Honeymoon suite with Jacuzzi. Full breakfast included. Restaurant.

Traders Inn Motor Hotel
45944 Yale Road
1-888-792-9839 or 604-792-0661
www.tradersinn.bc.ca
32 air-conditioned rooms, cable TV, movies. Internet access. Whirlpool, sauna, exercise room. Near shopping, restaurants, library. Senior discount.

Travelodge Chilliwack
45466 Yale Road
1-800-566-2511 or 604-792-4240
www.travelodgechilliwack.com
82 air-conditioned units, some kitchenettes. Cable TV, in-room coffee. Indoor pool, Jacuzzi, laundry, arcade, restaurant.

CAMPGROUNDS

Camperland RV Resort
53730 Bridal Falls Road; Highway 1, Exit 135
604-794-7361
www.holidaytrailsresorts.com
180 sites for high-quality resort camping with amenities: pool, hot tubs, clubhouse, restaurant. Near dining, attractions, golf, entertainment.

Chilliwack Campsite & RV Park
50850 Hack Brown Road; Highway 1, Exit 129
604-794-7800
51 sites with full hookups, some pull-throughs. Treed wilderness setting. Showers, cable, laundry, store. Near golf course.

Cottonwood Meadows RV Country Club
44280 Luckakuck Way
604-824-7275
109 level sites with full hookups, pull-throughs, cable hookup, security gate. Free showers, clubhouse, steam room. Close to services.

Cultus Lake Provincial Park
Columbia Valley Highway; Highway 1 to Cultus Lake Road
604-795-6169
281 sites, flush and pit toilets, fire pits, hiking, swimming, sani-station.

Orchard Trailer Park
46289 Yale Road East; Highway 1, Exit 119A
604-795-7634
20 sites three blocks east of downtown, off highway, treed sites, full hookups, pull-throughs, showers, cable, laundry.

Sunnyside Campground
3405 Columbia Valley Highway; Highway 1, Exit 119.
604-858-5253 / *www.cultuslake.bc.ca*
245 campsites. Showers, restrooms, firewood. Boat launch, fishing, canoeing, hiking, go-karts, waterslide, beaches. Restaurants.

Vetter River Campground
5215 Giesbrecht Road; West from Hope, Exit 119A
604-823-6012 / *www.cultuslake.bc.ca*
196 sites, full hookups, pull-throughs, showers, sani-station, laundry. Group sites, playground, horseshoe pits.

RESTAURANTS

Bellamy's Fish & Chips
46170 Yale Road
604-792-3655
Breakfast, lunch and dinner, specializing in English-style fish and chips; locally owned. Across from Paramount Theatre.

Bravo Restaurant & Lounge
46224 Yale Road
604-792-7221
Casual fine dining with Pacific Northwest fare. Reservations accepted.

Dakota's Restaurant
45850 Yale Road, #200
604-795-2215
Angus Beef, prime rib, ribs, seafood. Bar, two patios, private dining room.

Garden Court Atrium Dining Room
43971 Industrial Way, in Best Western Rainbow Country Inn
1-800-665-1030 or 604-795-3828
Continental menu featuring aged steaks, seafood. Live entertainment on weekends. Sunday brunch buffet.

La Mansione Ristorante
46290 Yale Road East
604-792-8910
Steak and seafood; historic setting in nearly century-old mansion decorated with collectibles and fine art.

Mill Street Café
9381 Mill Street
604-795-4640
Casual fine dining. Organic and whole foods, Old World wines.

The Pantry
45610 Yale Road West
604-792-2110
Family dining, breakfast all day. Seniors' and children's menus.

Wellington Cottage Tearoom
45775 Wellington Avenue
604-795-4848
Reservations recommended for tea in a 1927 Victorian cottage. Light lunch, home baking, gift shop.

White Spot Restaurant
45373 Luckakuck Way
604-858-0602
Well-known B.C. restaurant serves breakfast, lunch, dinner. Burgers, pasta, steak, chicken.

Road Notes

Wouldn't a nice soak in a mineral hot springs do the trick right now? If you're willing to follow that urge, just past Chilliwack take Exit 135 to Highway 9 and east to Highway 7.

Harrison Hot Springs is a lovely resort village in the mountains, and only about a half-hour away from Chilliwack. The city bills itself as the "Sand Sculpture Capital of the World." Little more than 1,000 people live here on the shores of Harrison Lake, but water enthusiasts come from miles around for boating, windsurfing, swimming, or camping. At 37 miles (60 km) long, this is the largest body of fresh water in southwestern British Columbia. Each September, sand sculptors and their fans arrive for the World Championship Sand Sculpture Competition on the beaches of the lake. Their amazing creations remain on display for a full month.

The hot springs itself is a rare treat, with water coming out of the ground so hot that it must be cooled to 85°F to 104°F (30°C to 40°C). The public pool is open year-round. For more information, call 1-866-638-5075 or see *www.harrisonresort.com.*

If you go, retrace your route back to Highway 1 for the best, fastest access to Hope.

HOPE

From Chilliwack: 22 miles (36 km)
To Lytton: 68 miles (110 km)

This charming community at the confluence of the Fraser and Coquihalla Rivers is home to about 7,000 people. Hope seems surrounded by mountains as well as by rivers, and its beautiful natural setting has made it a vacation destination as well as the site for two major motion picture productions: *First Blood,* starring Sylvester Stallone as John Rambo, and *Shoot to Kill,* starring Sidney Poitier and Kirstie Alley. The area and its temperate climate attract a unique variety of coastal and interior birds, so birders often arrive hoping to add to their life lists.

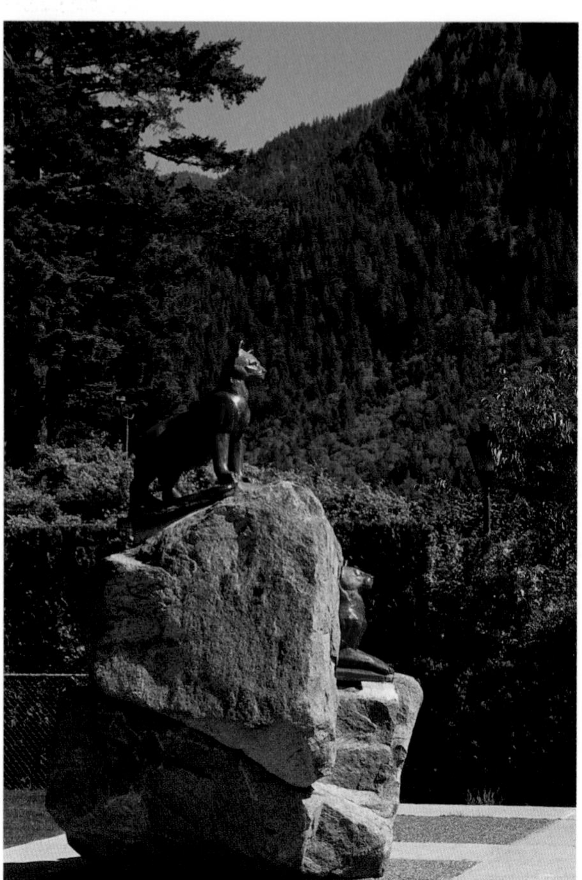

Chainsaw sculptures throughout Hope make a stroll through the downtown area something of an art walk.

For all the possibilities of how Hope was named, there is no agreement. One of our favorites was attributed to old-time gold miners who wintered here between lousy mining seasons: "They lived in Hope and finally died in despair."

This little city vies with Chetwynd, B.C., as Chainsaw Sculpture Capital of British Columbia. Hope's grassy, treed downtown park features the chainsaw artistry of a local sculptor named Pete Ryan. In 1991, when a few of the giant old trees in Memorial Park began to die, Ryan made a proposal. Rather than raze the

A Shakespeare fan and railroad builder blasted five tunnels through solid rock near Hope. Today the route is a hiking path through what are collectively known as the Othello-Quinette Tunnels.

trees, he asked the city to leave 12-foot stumps. From them he has carved detailed works of art depicting miners, burros, rams, and, best of all, bears. Today you can see two dozen or more of his works in the park and in other venues around town.

In 1981 Hollywood transformed Hope into a movie set for its filming of *First Blood* at sites all over town. A hundred locals were cast as extras, and for a while, actors Sylvester Stallone and Brian Dennehy were small-town regulars. Just outside the visitor center, a full-size wooden cutout of Stallone (minus the face), in warfare gear and muscles, allows visitors to photograph each other in good humor.

East of town, in the Coquihalla Canyon Provincial Recreation Area, five tunnels were cut through solid granite for the long-abandoned Kettle Valley Railway, built from 1911 to 1916. Because the chief engineer was a Shakespeare fan, he used Shakespearean names on railroad bridges, waysides, and this grouping of five tunnels: the Othello-Quintette Tunnels.

Hiking trails for all levels of fitness can be found throughout the area, and the Hope Visitor Information Centre has detailed maps of local trails, plus maps of nearby Manning and Skagit Valley Provincial Parks. Members of the Hope Volunteer Search & Rescue have prepared trip itineraries for you to fill out and leave at the visitor center, in case of an emergency. Visitor center maps include walking tours to Pete Ryan's sculptures and to locations where *First Blood* was filmed.

The helpful people at the center will tell you about local activities and attractions and answer questions about highway conditions and weather, as well as direct you to lodging and restaurants. The center is at 919 Water Avenue, along Highway 1. Call 604-869-2021, or browse *www.destinationhopeandbeyond.com*.

LODGING

Alpine Motel
505 Old Hope–Princeton Way
1-877-869-9931 or 604-869-9931
14 air-conditioned, ground-level rooms, kitchenettes. Free coffee, fridges. At-door parking.

Beautiful Lake of the Woods Resort
22805 Trans Canada Highway 1
1-888-508-2211 or 604-869-9211
www.lakewoods–resortmotel.com
9 units, 2 and 3 bedrooms, lake views, cable TV, fridges, free coffee. Canoe rental, fishing, swimming, hiking, playground. Senior discount.

Best Continental Motel
860 Fraser Avenue
604-869-9726
13 air-conditioned units, cable TV, free movies, fridges, free coffee, Internet access. Near shopping, bus depot. Senior discount.

City Centre Motel
455 Wallace Street
604-869-5411
16 air-conditioned rooms, cable TV, fridges, in-room coffee/tea, movies. Senior discount. Close to park, grocery. Small pets okay.

Colonial "900" Motel
900 Old Hope–Princeton Way
604-869-5223 / *www.colonial900motel.com*
16 air-conditioned, nonsmoking rooms with mountain views. Cable TV, fridges, free coffee, landscaped grounds. Adjacent to restaurant.

Coquihalla Motel
724 Hope Princeton Highway
604-869-3572
18 recently renovated units in quiet setting, air-conditioned 1-, 2-, or 3-bedroom suites, some with kitchens. Cable TV, movies, free coffee.

Holiday Motel & RV Resort
63950 Old Yale Road
604-869-5352 / *www.holiday–motel.com*
20 cabins and kitchenettes with 1 or 2 bedrooms in quiet neighborhood. Outdoor heated pool, playground. Near restaurant, pub.

Inn Towne Motel
510 Trans Canada Highway 1
1-800-663-2612 or 604-869-7276
www.inntowne–motel.com
26 air-conditioned rooms, deluxe suites, kitchenettes, nonsmoking available. Laundry, indoor pool, whirlpool, sauna, garden patio. Close to attractions.

Lucky Strike Motel
504 Old Hope–Princeton Way
604-869-5715 / *www.luckystrikemotel.com*
14 air-conditioned units, cable TV, movies, mountain views, landscaped grounds. Near restaurant, shopping. Senior discount.

The Maple Leaf Motor Inn
377 Old Hope–Princeton Way
1-888-530-1995 or 604-869-7107
38 quiet, air-conditioned rooms, kitchenettes, cable TV, movies. Indoor pool, whirlpool, sauna. Dining, coffee shop.

Park Motel
823 4th Avenue
1-888-531-9933 or 604-869-5891
19 air-conditioned units with fridges, cable TV, free Internet, coffee. Nice landscaping in downtown location.

Quality Inn
350 Old Hope–Princeton Way
1-800-424-6423 or 604-869-9951
25 air-conditioned rooms, 24-hour movies, sports, news. Free continental breakfast. Indoor hot tub, pool, sauna. Three-Diamond rating, AAA. Walk to downtown.

Red Roof Inn
477 Trans Canada Highway 1
604-869-2446
27 air-conditioned units, some nonsmoking. Cable TV, indoor spa, whirlpool. Mountain views, restaurant, indoor swim spa, whirlpool.

Royal Lodge Motel
580 Old Hope–Princeton Way
604-869-5358
www.royallodgemotel.ca
20 air-conditioned units, some connecting. Movie and sports channels, in-room coffee, wireless Internet, continental breakfast, ATM.

Skagit Motor Inn
655 3rd Avenue
1-888-869-5228 or 604-869-5220
www.skagit–motor–inn.com
30 air-conditioned rooms at ground floor in wooded setting. Cable TV, free movies, Continental breakfast, pool, whirlpool, spa. Mountain views, close to downtown. Near restaurants. Senior discount.

Slumber Lodge
250 Fort Street
1-800-757-7766 or 604-869-5666
34 air-conditioned rooms, suites. Downtown location. Indoor swimming pool, sauna, restaurant.

Swiss Chalets Motel
456 Trans Canada Highway 1
1-800-663-4673 or 604-869-9020
www.swisschaletsmotel.com
26 air-conditioned rooms, family chalets, kitchenettes, fireplaces. Cable TV, in-room coffee. Near Fraser River.

Windsor Motel
778 3rd Avenue
1-888-588-9944 or 604-869-9944
www.bcwindsormotel.com
24 air-conditioned rooms in downtown setting. Family units, kitchenettes, nonsmoking available. Cable TV, in-room coffee, senior discount.

CAMPGROUNDS

Coquihalla Campsite Hope
800 Kawkawa Lake Road
1-888-869-7118 or 604-869-7119
Full or partial hookups, riverfront sites, 24-hour security. Laundry, dump station, store. Recreation area, playground. Video games, covered picnic area. Senior discount. Pets allowed.

Holiday Motel & RV Resort
63950 Old Yale Road
604-869-5352
www.holiday-motel.com
20 sites with full hookups, cable, heated outdoor pool. Near restaurant, pub.

Hope Valley Campground
62280 Flood Hope Road; Highway 1, Exit 168
604-869-9857
130 sites with full or partial hookups, pull-throughs, tent sites. Showers, laundry, restrooms. Store, ice, gift shop. Game room, swimming pool, playground.

Kawkawa Lake Resort
55427 Kawkawa Lake Road
604-869-9930
Full hookups, fire rings, picnic area, swimming, store. No dogs, no boats.

Othello Tunnels Campground & RV Park
67851 Othello Road; Highway 5, Exit 183
604-869-9448
www.othellotunnels.com
40 sites with full and partial hookups, tent sites, fire pits. Laundry, free showers, barbecue area, rainbow trout fishing pond. Store, playground. Near Othello-Quinette Tunnels.

Telte Yet Campsite
600 Water Avenue
604-869-9481
29 full hookup sites, tent camping. Showers, laundry, dump station. Group rates. Acres of trees along Fraser River. Walking distance to Hope.

Whistlestop RV Park
59440 St. Elmo Road; Highway 1, Exit 160
1-877-869-5132 or 604-869-5132
39 sites, full and partial hookups, tent sites, fire pits. Wheelchair access. Free showers; laundry, dump station. Store, playground, grass and shade.

Wild Rose Campground & RV Park
62030 Flood Hope Road; Highway 1, Exit 165 or 168
604-869-9842
www.wildrosecamp.com
68 sites with full and partial hookups. 15- and 30-amp service. Cable TV, Internet, showers, laundry, dump station. Discount for Good Sam, KOA, CAA/AAA, seniors.

RESTAURANTS

Blue Moose Coffee House
322 Wallace Street
604-869-0729
Sandwiches, soups, espresso, desserts, high-speed wireless Internet.

Darrell's Place Family Restaurant
241 Wallace Street
604-869-3708
Hearty breakfasts, old-fashioned burgers, fries, homemade pies.

Home Restaurant
665 Old Hope-Princeton Highway
604-869-5558
Home-cooked burgers, ribs, baked goods, family dining.

Hope Drive-in & Restaurant
590 Hope Princeton Highway
604-869-5380
Family owned since 1962, seating for 100.

Kibo Japanese Restaurant
267 King Street
604-869-7317
Teriyaki, ribs, tempura, and more.

Kim Chi Japanese & Korean Restaurant
821A 6th Avenue
604-869-0070

Little Tokyo Japanese Restaurant
259 Wallace Street
604-869-5628
Sushi, sashimi, teriyaki, tempura, Canadian cuisine.

New Golden Star Restaurant
377 Old Hope-Princeton Way
604-869-9588
Chinese and Western cuisine with no MSG. Lunch and dinner buffets.

Papandreas Greek Taverna
904 Old Hope-Princeton Way
604-869-7218
Family-owned restaurant serving Greek cuisine.

Rolly's Restaurant
888 Fraser Avenue
604-869-7448
Breakfast all day, casual dining.

Sharon's Deli & Lunch Bar
340A Wallace Street
604-869-3354
Daily luncheon menus, sandwiches, salads, hard ice cream.

Road Notes

Fourteen miles (23 km) north of Hope, you'll come upon Yale, a historic village site along the gold-rush trail. In its advantageous position at the southern entrance of the Fraser Canyon, Yale was the site for paddle wheelers to unload cargo that would continue its journey on the Cariboo Wagon Road, more commonly known as the Cariboo Trail. The Cariboo gold rush was still going strong by 1863, when the Church of St. John the Divine was constructed. It is now the oldest church on the B.C. mainland, and designated a B.C. Heritage Site. As you take a tour of the town, peek inside the church and get an eyeful of its magnificently carved pump organ. Visit the pioneer cemetery with its unique grave markers.

Arrange a rafting trip on the mighty Fraser or other area rivers. Call Fraser River Raft Expeditions in Yale at 604-863-2355 or see *www.fraserraft.com.*

The Fraser Canyon is postcard beautiful from one end to the other. Just past the first of several tunnels in this section of road, note the historical marker at a pullout to the east. This explains more about the Cariboo Trail and the difficulty of transportation during that mid-1800s gold rush.

Some 35 minutes east of Hope on Highway 1, you will encounter the natural wonder called Hell's Gate, a tight narrowing in the canyon through which the Fraser River pours at

The Cariboo gold rush shaped the history of this region. You'll find this mural in downtown Lytton, B.C.

For a fee, you can ride the Hell's Gate Airtram over Fraser Canyon.

great speed. In 1808 explorer Simon Fraser wrote, "We had to travel where no human being should venture for surely we have seen the gates of hell." Look down from the edge, watch 200 million of gallons of water per minute thunder past, and you'll know why the name stuck. Hell's Gate Airtram offers a thrilling look at the river from above. For a fee, you can ride the tram across the canyon while descending 502 feet. On the opposite side, explore the family-oriented boardwalk village that's built into the cliff. And for the intrepid, a suspension bridge lets you walk back over the river and enjoy an unadulterated view of the swirling current beneath your feet. Enjoy a meal at a family restaurant, or buy some food and eat at a picnic table in the sun. Watch a film about the salmon and their upriver trek, buy books and souvenirs in the themed gift shops, and load up on fudge at the candy store. Pan for gold! Informative signs add to the enjoyment. We were amazed to learn that nearly 2 million salmon swim up the Fraser River each summer. For more information, call 604-867-9277 or visit *www.hellsgatetram.com.*

Two campgrounds operate within the 10 miles (16 km) north of Hell's Gate. Canyon Alpine RV Park & Campground offers 31 sites, with full hookups and pull-throughs, fire pits, washrooms, and showers. The facility is close to a restaurant, store, phone, and self-service laundry. For information, call 604-867-9734. Anderson Creek Campground is alongside the Fraser and Anderson Rivers in a 30-acre setting with lots of trees. They offer full and partial hookups, showers, and a sani-dump. Call 1-604-867-9089.

LYTTON

From Hope: 68 miles (110 km)
To Cache Creek: 52 miles (84 km)

Situated at the confluence of the Thompson River and the powerful Fraser River (Canada's third largest), Lytton is the place to park and play—a river-rafter's dream. Looking down at the rivers' confluence from above, you can see a distinct edge where the clear, blue Thompson blends into the cloudy gray of the Fraser. A third, the Nahatlatch River, is smaller and steeper, offering dramatic class 4 and class 5 rafting.

As the whitewater rafting capital of British Columbia, Lytton offers plentiful choices for outfitters. You can go with a group, hire a guide for your own group, or rent what you need to go on your own. You can't miss rafting company signs all along this stretch of road. Among them is Kumsheen Raft Adventures, which has been leading power and paddle rafting trips on area rivers for more than 30 years. The business also offers other adventures such as rock climbing, kayaking, and bike touring, along with comfortable or rustic overnight accommodations. Call 250-455-2296 or visit the Web site at *www.kumsheen.com*. The Reo Rafting Resort specializes in tips on the Nahatlatch. Call 1-800-736-7238 or see *www.reorafting.com*.

This meeting place of the rivers has been a gathering spot for centuries, as evidenced in ancient pictographs and rock paintings. First Nations people chose the spot for its abundance of wildlife, water, and trees for food and building material. The Lytton Museum & Archives is located at 425 Fraser Street. Phone 250-455-2254 for details. A walking tour of the community is a good way to learn more about the people and their special place. Ask at the visitor information center, or go online and take a virtual walking tour at *www.lytton.ca*. During the annual Lytton Days, you can learn more about First Nations culture through art, dance, and storytelling. Native arts and crafts, including soapstone carvings, baskets, and beaded leather, can be purchased in Lytton. Call 250-455-2523 for more information.

After prospector Billy Barker discovered gold in 1862, more than 100,000 people joined the ensuing rush and swarmed into British Columbia to mine for gold, traveling the famed Cariboo Wagon Road to reach the goldfields. As a stop along the way, Lytton thrived as a place for the stampeders to outfit themselves.

In 1881 intrepid railway builders arrived to cut a rail bed into the sides of this canyon. The Canadian Pacific Railway and the Canadian National Railway continue to move freight and passengers on this route that parallels the river and the road through Fraser Canyon.

ROCK-HARD JELLYROLL

Sedimentary geologists and other earth scientists will appreciate an unusual attraction in the heart of downtown Lytton. Across from Lytton's Visitor Information Centre, at 400 Fraser Avenue, is the tiny Caboose Park, where a retired Canadian National Railway caboose is parked alongside a picnic table and grassy area. But it's the thing on the exterior wall of an adjacent building that makes scientists and curiosity seekers walk closer and squint. The "thing" is called the Lytton Jellyroll, a cast of a geological formation that was discovered south of the village. The unusual structure is a rolled layer of silt encased in coarse sands and gravel. Scientists believe it was created from 11,000 to 25,000 years ago during an event in the last glaciation period. That makes it very young by geological standards. But it is the size of the formation that makes it special. Normally a find such as this would be measured in inches, not feet. Erected by the Lytton and District Chamber of Commerce, this detailed replication of the real thing could fool an amateur.

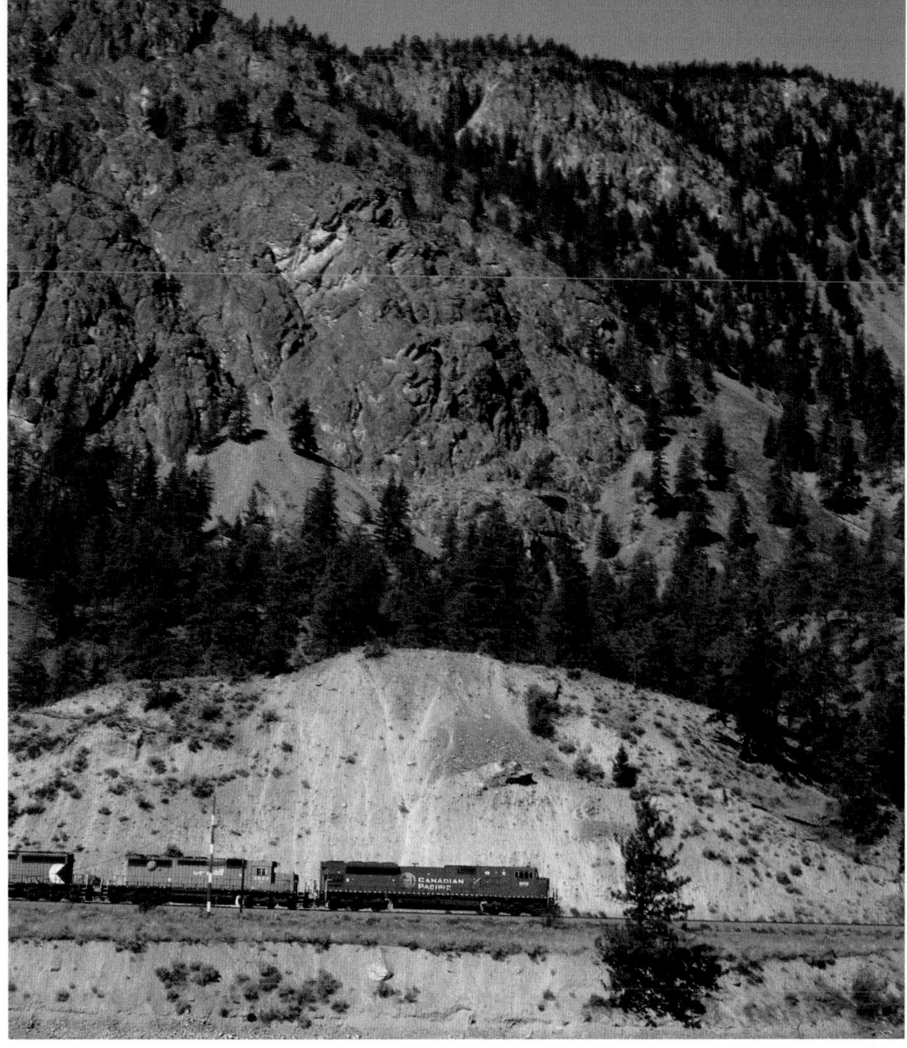

Laying rail through Fraser Canyon proved a challenge for the railroad builders of the 19th century.

This area is still rich with wildlife. Along the back roads and hiking trails, you may see elk, bighorn sheep, deer, eagles, and ospreys. Hidden from sight are the more human-shy animals: coyotes, bears, cougars, bobcats, and lynx.

The city was named for Sir Edward Bulwer-Lytton, whose writing is familiar to almost everybody. Drawing a blank? He's the one who penned the famous introductory phrase, "It was a dark and stormy night."

Lytton is also Canada's "hot spot" with a recorded high of 111 °F.

For more information on the area, stop by the Lytton Visitor Information Centre, open year-round at 420 Fraser Street. Call 250-455-2523 or visit *www.lytton.ca.*

Road Notes

In the 52 scenic miles (84 km) between Lytton and Cache Creek, you'll find two provincial parks and several private campgrounds.

Just 5 miles (8 km) beyond Lytton is Skihist Provincial Park, with 56 campsites, a picnic area, restrooms, and an RV dump station. Another 12 miles (19 km) later, the less-developed Goldpan Provincial Park lies to the west, with 14 sites along the river. You can go fishing or put your canoe in the water here.

Along the way, pay attention to the historic buildings and opportunities to stop for coffee, pie, or a meal, and learn more about the area's gold-rush history. Less than 10 miles (16 km) south of Cache Creek, the oldest roadhouse in British Columbia is still in business, as it has been since 1862. The Ashcroft Manor & Tea House offers rooms, meals, campground (with pull-through sites for RVers), jade gifts, and an invitation to walk the grounds and visit the historic outbuildings. For more information, call 250-453-9983.

Seven miles (11 km) south of Cache Creek is the Eagle Motorplex, a drag-racing facility sanctioned by the National Hot Rod Association. Racers come from around the world to race and show their cars. Check *www.eaglemotorplex.com* for details.

During Cache Creek's mid-June Graffiti Days, restored vehicles are paraded and parked for a Show-and-Shine celebration. Festivities include a dance, barbecue, and racing at the motorplex.

CACHE CREEK

From Lytton: 52 miles (84 km)
From Hope: 120 miles (193 km)
To Williams Lake: 128 miles (206 km)

Set in a semiarid region of low, rolling hills, Cache Creek is home to a scant 1,115 people who live at the confluence of the Bonaparte River and Cache Creek. Here, too, is the junction of Trans-Canada Highway 1 with Highway 97.

The scent of sage wafts through the air on hot, summer days, and at the town's main intersection, a wooden gold miner stands, arms extended, to welcome you to this frontier town that was built on the backs of gold miners.

These days there's less gold mining than there is cattle ranching and the latest gold-rush crop: ginseng. The regional boom began in 1982 with one growth on five acres near Lytton. By 2003, there were about 30 growers in this part of B.C., members of the Associated Ginseng Growers of British Columbia. Farmers also grow wheat in irrigated fields.

Cache Creek services include lodging, restaurants, grocery stores, a post office, and a golf course. Most visitors are passing through on their vacations. But 150 years ago, this town was overrun with miners and people who wanted to trade gold for goods and services.

As a major point on the Cariboo Wagon Road, Cache Creek grew quickly. After the rush, some mining continued, along with farming, logging, and cattle ranching. Tourism helps keep Cache Creek cooking, too.

Just north of town, an 1860 landmark along the Cariboo Wagon Road is the Historic Hat Creek Ranch, at the intersection of Highways 97 and 99. This 320-acre ranch was once an important roadhouse stop for horse-drawn wagons along the B.C. Express Stage line (also known as the BX) that led to Barkerville and beyond. More than 20 buildings dating

The world's longest cross-country skis are on display outside the visitor center at 100 Mile House, a town named for a roadhouse on the old Cariboo wagon road.

from 1863 to 1915 may be found on the grounds. Step back in time and explore the Victorian-style rooms of the main house, visit the BX Barn, watch the blacksmith at work, and view a First Nations pit house. You can also take a horse-drawn ride on the famous Cariboo Wagon Road and follow the footsteps of the gold miners. For more information, contact the Cache Creek Tourist/Visitor Information folks. Their booth at the junction of Highways 97 and 99 is open May 15 through Sept. 30. Phone 1-800-782-0922 or 250-457-9722, or browse their Web site at *www.hatcreekranch.com.*

Road Notes

From Cache Creek to the towns of 100 Mile House and 150 Mile House, the highway continues to follow the historic route of the Cariboo Wagon Road. The numbers used in the names of these towns and of other sites along this way are a measurement of their distance from Lillooet, which was Mile 0 on the mid-1880s Cariboo route. 100 Mile House today is a lumber town that also claims the title of Handcrafted Log Home Capital of North America and International Nordic Ski Capital. It hosts the Cariboo Marathon each February, attracting skiers from around the world. Outside the town's information center, you can see the world's longest cross-country skis, 39-foot-long Karhu racers. Learn more about this

LODGING

Best Value Inn Desert Motel
1069 Trans-Canada Highway South
1-800-663-0212 or 250-457-6226
43 air-conditioned units, kitchenettes. Cable TV and in-room coffee. Grass courtyard with outdoor pool. Winter plug-ins. In town center, close to shops and restaurants.

Bonaparte Motel
1395 Cariboo Highway 97 North
1-888-922-1333 or 250-457-9693
24 air-conditioned rooms and kitchenettes with refrigerators, cable TV, fax service. Outdoor pool, indoor whirlpool. Close to restaurants and golf.

The Good Knight Inn
827 South Trans-Canada Highway
1-800-736-5588 or 250-457-9500
20 deluxe rooms with cable TV and movies, data phones, e-mail. Whirlpools, continental breakfast, picnic area.

The Oasis Hotel
1064 South Trans-Canada Highway
(250) 457-6232
Full hotel facilities, banquet room, lounge, restaurant.

Robbie's Motel
1067 Todd Road
1-866-327-6221 or 250-457-6221
18 air-conditioned units at ground level, cable TV, movies, fridges, microwaves, free coffee. Near restaurants, shopping, golf.

Sage Hills Motel
1379 Cariboo Highway 97 North
1-888-794-9494 or 250-457-6451
www.bcinfonet.com
18 air-conditioned units, cable TV, in-room coffee. Pool with slide and shower, grassy courtyard. Senior discount.

Sandman Inn Cache Creek
Intersection of Highways 1 and 97
1-800-726-3626 or 250-457-6284
www.sandmanhotels.com
35 air-conditioned units, cable TV, in-room coffee. Restaurant. Senior discount.

Sundowner Motel
1085 Trans-Canada Highway
1-877-507-2887 or 250-457-6216
18 air-conditioned units, cable TV, movies, kitchens, fridges, microwaves. Near restaurants, golf.

Tumbleweed Motel
1221 Quartz Road
1-800-667-1501 or 250-457-6522
25 deluxe air-conditioned rooms in parklike setting, cable TV, free movies, picnic area. Near restaurants, golf.

CAMPGROUNDS

Brookside Campsite
0.6 miles (1 km) east of Cache Creek on Highway 1
250-457-6633
Pull-through sites, tent sites, free showers, heated pool. Washroom, sani-dump. Playground, arcade, store. Adjacent to golf course.

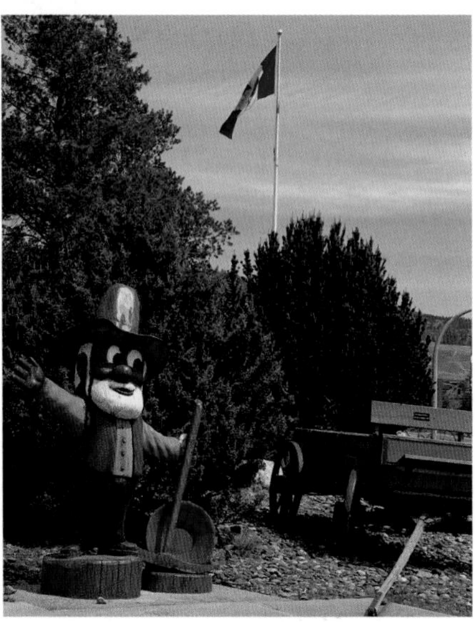

Evergreen Fishing Resort
1820 Loon lake Road
250-459-2372 / *www.evergreenfishingresort.ca*
Furnished lakeside log cabins, tenting campsites, full and partial hookups, store, laundry. Boat rentals, moorage.

Historic Hat Creek Ranch
Junction of Highways 99 and 97
1-800-782-0922 or 250-457-9722
www.hatcreekranch.com
8 campsites with electrical hookups only. Flush toilets, hot showers. Near historical roadhouse, Native interpretation site, restaurant, gift shop. Also available are 2 sleeping units.

RESTAURANTS

BB's Bar & Grill
In the Oasis Hotel
1064 South Trans-Canada Highway
250-457-6232
Canadian fare, entertainment.

Chum's Restaurant
1108 East Trans-Canada Highway
250-457-6735 / Family dining.

Horsting's Farm
2 km north of town on Highway 97
250-457-6546 / *www.horstingfarms.com*
Farm market, bakery, with sandwiches, ice cream, long list of fresh-baked pies.

Hungry Herbie's Drive-In
Highway 97 North
250-457-6644
Burgers, fries, and more.

North End Restaurant
Cariboo Highway 97
250-457-6261

Sandman Inn Family Restaurant
Junction of Highways 1 and 97
250-457-9330
Pasta, steaks, Greek dishes, coffee shop, dining room, cocktail lounge.

Wander Inn Restaurant
Junction of Highways 1 and 97
250-457-6511
Sterling Silver AAA Steaks, Cantonese food, coffee shop, dining room, cocktail lounge.

A sculpture of a miner and his tools welcomes visitors to Cache Creek at the junction of Highway 97 and the Trans-Canada Highway 1.

GREEN AND GOLD

Outside Cariboo Jade & Gifts in Cache Creek, B.C., at 1093 Todd Road, you'll see a massive boulder made of jade, an obviously valuable piece of inventory that just sits out on the sidewalk, day and night. Managers Ben Roy and Bill Elliott don't worry too much about shoplifting. It would take a D-9 Caterpillar to get away with that boulder.

Inside, these two brothers-in-law manage the business traffic that the boulder generates, like a billboard that says, "Come inside." Routinely, busloads of tourists offload into the store to shop for quality Canadian gifts and Native crafts in a wide price range.

A jade boulder appropriately rests outside Cariboo Jade & Gifts, in Cache Creek.

In the back of the shop, behind a glass partition, Ben cuts British Columbia jade on a special rock saw to accommodate its extreme hardness. Bill's specialty is working in gold. Together they create jewelry and other specialty pieces.

British Columbia jade is nearly as prized as gold and known throughout the world. Four times harder than marble, this jade is difficult to cut and finish into sculpture and jewelry. For more information on B.C. jade, call 250-457-9566.

district, its history, natural history, as well as local dining and lodging at the South Cariboo Visitor Info Centre, 422 Highway 97 in 100 Mile House. Call 1-877-511-5353 or 250-395-5353 or see *www.southcaribootourism.com.*

WILLIAMS LAKE

From Cache Creek: 128 miles (206 km)
To Quesnel: 75 miles (121 km)
To Prince George: 149 miles (240 km)

During construction of the Cariboo Wagon Road, a Williams Lake landowner would not lend money to road builders, so the trail bypassed the town, instead routing through 150 Mile House. That decision nearly killed the town's economy, putting it off the major transportation route for the thousands of people moving in and out of the goldfields.

Williams Lake was nearly abandoned, except for two business partners, William Pinchbeck and William Lyne, who built a lumber mill, grist mill, and a farm. But their real income earner was the sale of home-brewed whiskey. You might assume that this town took its name from the two Williams, but it is attributed to the local Shuswap Chief William.

By the 1940s, twenty years after the railway arrived, this was a ranching town that had grown into the largest cattle-shipping center in British Columbia. Today about 12,000 people call Williams Lake home and more than 25,000 live in the area, called "The Hub of the Cariboo." Ranching remains an important part of the economy.

Williams Lake is the Old West in action, and at no time of the year is there more action than during the Williams Lake Stampede. Counting the spectators, the town's population doubles for the Stampede, held during the early July long holiday weekend (Canada Day is July 1). This family event includes chuckwagon races, barn dances, a rodeo, and mountain horse races. A parade and midway are part of the fun, too. Camping is available right next to the Stampede grounds. For more information, call 1-800-71RODEO or 250-392-6585. The Museum of the Cariboo Chilcotin is a full-fledged ranching and rodeo museum that is entrusted with the story of the Williams Lake Stampede, which dates back to 1919, and the history of this region, the Cariboo Chilcotin. It's also home to the B.C. Cowboy Hall of Fame, and located on the corner of Fourth and Borland Street (250-392-7404).

The Xats'ull Heritage Village at 3405 Mountain House Road is an excellent place to learn about the region's first people. Hear the stories and view the village site, artifacts, petroglyphs, and a sweat lodge. For more information browse *www.xatsull.com.*

Williams Lake—the actual lake itself—lies along a major flyway for migrating waterfowl. Scout Island Nature Centre, at the west end of the lake, offers bird-watching opportunities along a corridor of trails, open from 8 A.M. to dusk. Between the Fraser River and the lake, you can see sandstone hoodoos—mushroom-shaped formations still standing after the forces of erosion removed the rock all around them.

The Williams Lake Visitor Information Centre, at 1148 Broadway South, is open year-round, and they can help you with such things as lining up a stay at a guest ranch or arranging for some horseback riding. Golfers can choose between two courses, and there's mini-golf for the kids. For more information on Williams Lake and the surrounding district, call 1-877-967-5253 or 250-392-5025. Check the Web site at *www.williamslakechamber.com.*

LODGING

Drummond Lodge & Motel
1405 Highway 98 South
1-800-667-4555 or 250-392-5334
www.drummondlodge.com
24 air-conditioned units, kitchenettes, nonsmoking units available. Movie and sports channels, high-speed Internet, in-room coffee, continental breakfast, laundry facilities. Overlooking lake.

Fraser Inn Hotel
285 Donald Road
1-800-452-6789 or 250-398-7055
www.fraserinn.com
75 air-conditioned units, cable TV, movies, room service. Gift shop, whirlpool, sauna, free passes to Gold's Gym. Restaurant, lounge, patio.

Lakeside Motel
1505 Highway 97 South
1-800-663-4938 or 250-392-4181
32 units overlooking Williams Lake and Scout Island Nature Centre. Free coffee/tea, local calls, barbecues for family picnics. Small pets welcome.

Overlander Hotel
1118 Lakeview Crescent
1-800-663-6898 or 250-392-3321
www.overlanderhotel.com
57 air-conditioned units in full-service hotel. Fitness facilities, tour packages. Restaurant, pub. Downtown location, near shopping. Senior discount.

Sandman Inn Williams Lake
664 Oliver Street
1-800-726-3626 or 250-392-6557
www.sandmanhotels.com
96 air-conditioned units, executive suites, kitchenettes. Cable TV, laundry, room service, sauna, pub. Near shopping, adjacent to 24-hour restaurant.

Springhouse Trails Ranch
3061 Dog Creek Road
250-392-4780
www.springhousetrails.com
22 units available May–September. Kitchenettes, some with fireplaces. Meals, lounge. Horseback riding.

Super 8 Motel (Williams Lake)
1712 Broadway Avenue South
1-800-800-8000 or 250-398-8884
www.super8williamslake.com
53 air-conditioned units, nonsmoking available. Cable TV, whirlpool, complimentary breakfast, free high-speed Internet.

Valleyview Motel
1523 Highway 97 South
250-392-4655
18 sleeping and housekeeping units with mountain and lake views. Cable TV, free coffee, near restaurant. Senior discount. Pets welcome.

CAMPGROUNDS

Big Bar Provincial Park
26.5 miles (42 km) northwest of Clinton off Highway 97
1-800-689-9025
www.britishcolumbia.com/parks
46 sites in two campgrounds: Lakeside Campground and Upper Campground. Full and partial hookups, pull-throughs.

Springhouse Trails Ranch
3061 Dog Creek Road
250-392-4780
www.springhousetrails.com
12 RV full-hookup sites, showers, washrooms. Horseback riding.

Williams Lake Stampede Campground
850 South Mackenzie Street
250-398-6718
www.williamslakestampede.com
74 sites with full or partial hookups, phone, cable hookup. Tent sites, free firewood. Showers, restrooms. Four blocks to downtown.

RESTAURANTS

Alley Katz Bistro
27 Seventh Avenue South
250-398-8700

Great Cariboo Steak Company
285 Donald Road, inside the Fraser Inn
1-800-452-6789 or 250-398-7055
Breakfast, all-you-can-eat lunch buffets, steak, chicken, seafood, pasta. Outdoor seating available, lounge.

The Hearth Restaurant
99 Third Avenue South
250-398-6831
Sandwiches, soups, salads.

Joey's Grill
177 Yorston Street
250-398-8727
Pasta, steak, chicken.

Laughing Loon Neighbourhood Pub
1730 South Broadway
250-398-5666
Beef, chicken, pork dishes.

Leones Pizza & Steak House
36 Third Avenue North
250-398-8299
Family-style dining.

The Overlander
1118 Lakeview Crescent
1-800-663-6898 or 250-392-3321
Downtown restaurant, adjacent to hotel.

Stockmen's Café
4665 North Mackenzie
250-398-5366

Trattoria Pasta Shop
23A South 1st Avenue
250-398-7170

THE GHOSTS OF BARKERVILLE

For a worthwhile side trip, take the Highway 26 turnoff just beyond Quesnel and follow it north and east for 51 miles (82 km) to Barkerville, where the gold-rush past comes alive again.

Founded in 1862, Barkerville first sprang to life when Billy Barker discovered gold in Williams Creek. Now more than 120 heritage buildings and displays on the original town site celebrate the past. Costumed interpreters remains in character as they answer questions and carry on conversation, moving about the streets of the mining town.

Actors in costume introduce visitors to life in the 1860s.

Museum displays about mining and about Barkerville and its namesake are in the main building through which you access Barkerville—which is kind of like a Hollywood back-lot, except that this town was and is for real. And at each house or business, you learn about its former owner. Street performances add to the feeling that this was once a busy town of miners, Chinese immigrants, churchmen, and partygoers. Two cemeteries hold the remains of former residents. A stagecoach driver invites passengers to ride to the other end of the town. Guided tours begin at regular intervals, and musical comedy is on the bill for evenings in the Theatre Royal. There's a new show each year.

Restaurants, snack shops, gift stores, an old-time photo studio—the shopkeepers and wait staff are dressed in gold rush–era clothing, all lending to the sense of stepping back in time. There's even a judge on the bench in the courthouse, pontificating about justice in his wild-and-wooly town.

We were pelted by a hailstorm while visiting Barkerville, and people rushed into the saloon, candy store, general store, or museum building. Others huddled beneath building overhangs until the storm passed. This was in August—an indicator of this place's elevation of about 4,200 feet (1,280 m) above sea level. Museum docents explained that snow comes early in these mountains. The mining was hard work; the living was just as hard.

Two bed-and-breakfast businesses operate in the town: Kelly House (250-994-3312) and the St. George Hotel (250-994-0008). Tent or RV campers will find space at Barkerville as well. For more information, call BC Heritage at 250-994-3302 or visit the agency's Web site at *www.heritage.gov.bc.ca.*

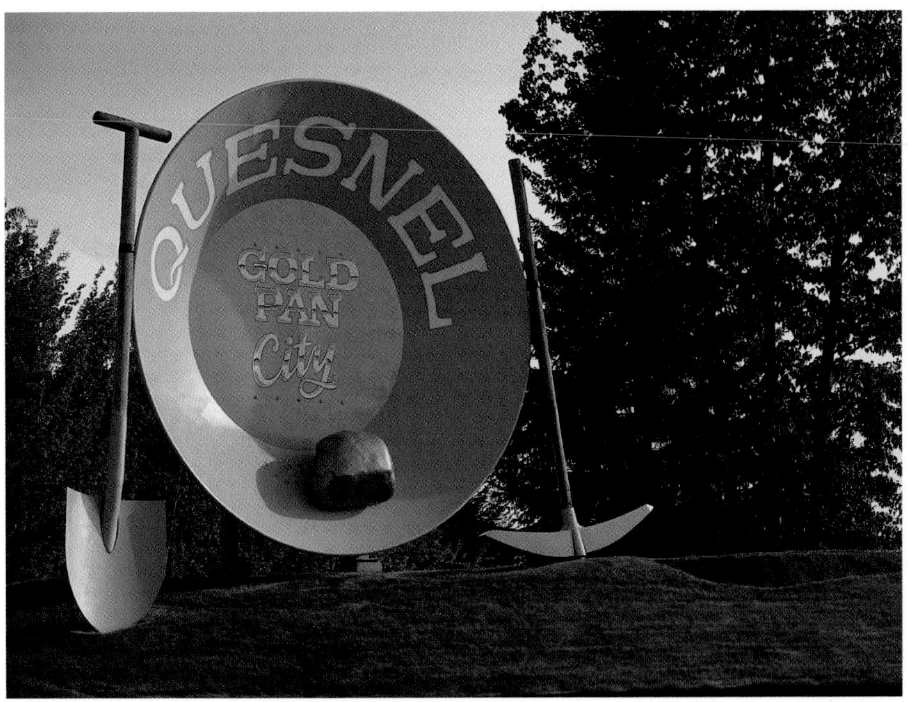

The city of Quesnel is proud of its mining roots.

Road Notes

Seventy-five miles (121 km) north of Williams Lake is Quesnel, which, like many area towns, boomed during the Cariboo gold rush of the early 1860s. Today this town of more than 11,000 people is supported by lumber, pulp and plywood manufacturing, cattle ranching, mining, and, of course, tourism. All travelers' services may be found here, from shopping, lodging, and dining to assistance in planning your trip. Learn more about Quesnel's history, which really began long before the gold rush, at the Quesnel Museum in the Visitor Info Centre, at the south entrance to the city center on Highway 97. You can go on a self-guided walking tour of historic Quesnel. Or take in the city's illustrated history of more than a century in photos, and see Mandy, the famed "haunted doll" in their collection.

If you're feeling hot and dusty, you'll find two swimming pools at the Quesnel Arts and Recreation Center, 500 North Star Road. A weight room, saunas, and whirlpool are here, too.

In mid-July, Quesnel celebrates Billy Barker's discovery of gold with Barker Days, four days of river races, dances, games, concerts, and contests for pie eaters and watermelon-seed spitters. Snowmobile races—without the snow—are a kick. A midway multiplies the family fun. An amateur rodeo draws big crowds to Alex Fraser Park. Learn more at *www.quesnelbc.com/billybarkerdays* or call 250-992-1234.

West of Quesnel the Blackwater River flows almost 200 miles (322 km) from the Coast Mountains to the Fraser River. Its pristine waters attract fly fishers, canoeists, and kayakers.

The Alexander Mackenzie Heritage Trail parallels the river; in 1793, Mackenzie followed this Native trading trail to the Pacific Ocean.

Heading north toward Prince George, you will be within range of some excellent lake fishing for rainbow and brook trout, char, burbot, and more. There are about 1,600 lakes within a 100-mile radius of Prince George. Contact Tourism Prince George at 1-800-668-7646 or 250-562-3700 for a free fishing guide and info on licensing.

Ten Mile Lake Provincial Park, 7 miles (11 km) north of Quesnel, offers two campgrounds with a total of 142 campsites, including 22 pull-throughs. There's water, showers, restrooms, and an RV dump station. You'll find a playground, a swimming beach on the lake, and a boat launch, as well as nature trails for walking and wildlife viewing. Watch for several private campgrounds just south of Prince George, too.

PRINCE GEORGE

From Quesnel: 74 miles (119 km)
To Chetwynd: 188 miles (303 km)
To Dawson Creek: 250 miles (402 km)

Here in what is known as the Lakes and Rivers District, Prince George is looked on as the capital of northern British Columbia. It is home to about 80,000 people who understand and enjoy the natural treasure that's around them and the city they helped to create.

Prince George's history is played out in mosaics at the Centennial Fountain.

Just minutes from downtown in any direction, you'll find some form of outdoor recreation: walking, fishing, swimming, boating, backpacking. The local lakes and streams are thick with trout, salmon, burbot, Dolly Varden, char—for a fly fisher, this is world-class water. And there's no shortage of campgrounds, provincial and private. Hunkering in the distance is Mount Robson, highest peak in the Canadian Rockies, inviting those who prefer a lot of challenge in their outdoor adventure.

In winter, visitors and residents head out for downhill skiing, cross-

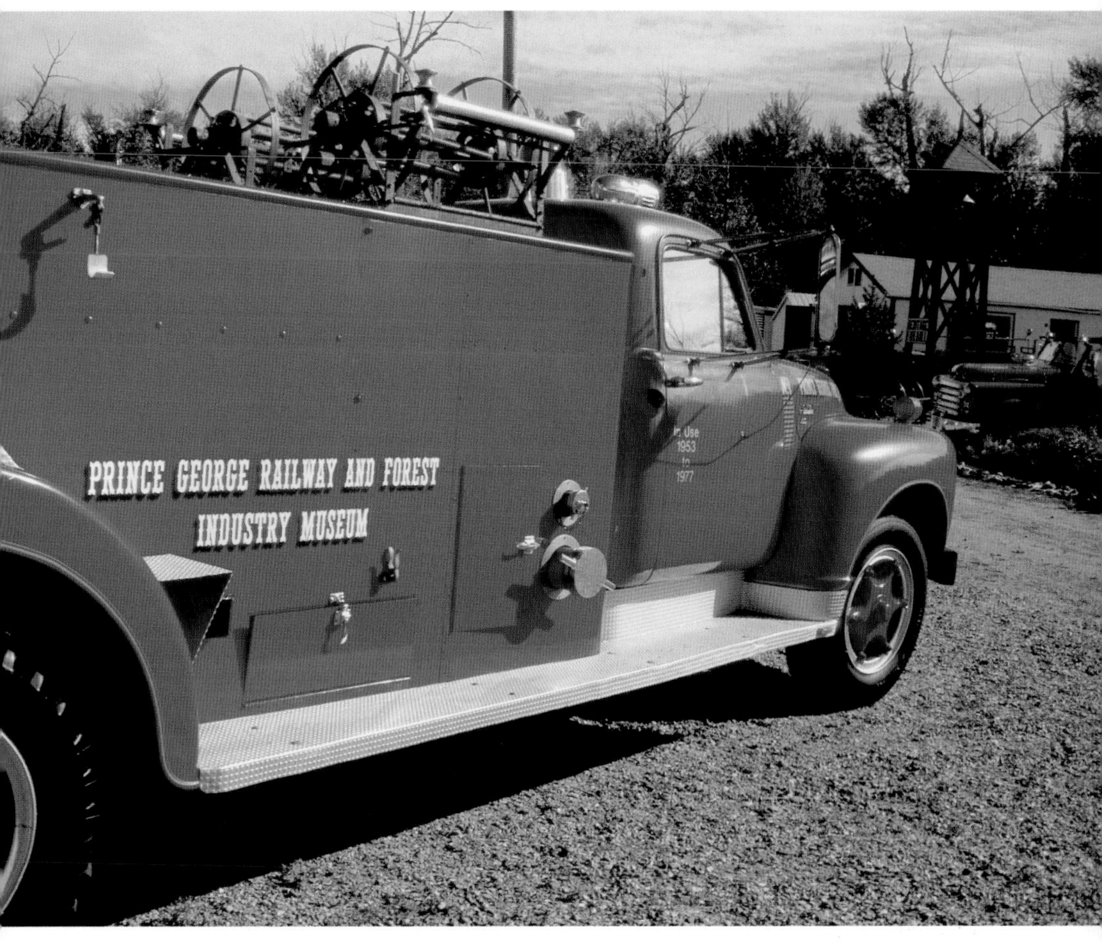

The Prince George Railway and Forestry Museum features retired vehicles, railway cars, cabooses, and track.

country skiing, hockey, ice skating, even dogsledding. Snow typically begins in November and stays on the ground into late March.

A big piece of the Prince George economy is the pulp and forest industry. One leading company, Canfor, offers scheduled tours of its pulp mill, sawmill, and plywood mills. Call Tourism Prince George to arrange a tour: 1-800-668-7646 or 250-649-3202. Also see *www.tourismpg.com.*

This is a frontier city at its roots, yet it "cleans up real nice" with its own brand of polish. Just as you finish a half-day trail ride, Prince George's nightlife offerings will revitalize you with concerts, art galleries, theater openings, or an evening of jazz. The city claims several resident theater groups, a symphony orchestra, and many dance troupes. The Two Rivers Art Gallery, with pieces by local, regional, and national artists, can be found in the downtown Civic Complex; in summers, the gallery organizes its "Artists in the Garden" annual event, combining a tour of the city's most beautiful gardens with art and musical performances.

Also downtown, the Centennial Fountain at 7th Avenue and Dominion Street depicts the early history of Prince George in mosaic tile, from life among the First Nations people to the arrival of explorers, settlers, the railway, and forward into 20th-century life.

Along the banks of the Fraser River, at the end of 20th Avenue, Fort George Park is the place that locals bring their visiting friends and relatives, so you should see it, too! Come down to the river to picnic, and follow the Heritage Trail that links this park with several others. Inside the park, you'll find The Exploration Place Science Centre and Museum, which accelerates learning by linking it with entertainment. Their Sim-Ex Theatre is one of the biggest draws in Prince George, creating a you-are-there experience as you travel around Earth and into the galaxy. Explore prehistory and human history as the family scrambles around dinosaurs or on the decks of a replica paddlewheel. For more details, call 250-562-1612 or see *www.theexplorationplace.com.*

Nearby, stop by the Prince George Railway and Forestry Museum, an 8-acre park that's an outdoor repository for antique or merely retired railcars, engines, and more. Ride the miniature train, the Cottonwood Railway. There's even a full-size train depot here, faithfully moved piece by piece from a spot along the British Columbia Railway between Quesnel and Prince George. Steam locomotives, cranes, sleeping cars, cabooses, snow plows, even logging and agricultural machinery are part of the walk-about display. Located at 850 River Road, the museum is open from mid-May to October. Call 250-563-7351 or visit *www.pgrfm.bc.ca.*

If you're in Prince George on Canada Day, July 1, you'll be in for a real treat. Join nearly 10,000 residents in Fort George Park, where they gather to celebrate the city's multicultural makeup with music, dance, and food in the colors and flavors of countries throughout the world.

For a special remembrance of this rare and wonderful place, stop at the Prince George Native Art Gallery & Gift Shop at 1600 Third Avenue (250-614-7726). Another unique shop is the Chinese Store, at 1193 Fifth Avenue (250-562-3498), in Prince George's Chinatown, where you'll find Asian groceries, medicines, jewelry, and other keepsakes.

The city and its people are busy year-round. Almost like a city unto itself, the Treasure Cove Casino & Hotel can be found at the junction of Yellowhead Highway 16 and Highway 97. It boasts Las Vegas-style entertainment, spas, shopping, water park, restaurants, and, of course, a gaming area.

One of Prince George's two visitor centers is located near the casino at the intersection of Highways 16 and 97. Though open in summer months only, it is a popular stop for photographs with the three-story "log man" whose friendly wave welcomes you to town. A second visitor center, open year-round, is located at 1300 First Avenue. Call 1-800-668-7646 or 250-562-3700. Browse their Web site at *www.tourismpg.com.*

(For more on Yellowhead Highway 16, see Chapter 7, Western Canada's Northbound Byways. If you're heading to Dawson Creek, however, you will continue your journey north on Highway 97.)

LODGING

For information on Prince George bed-and-breakfast accommodations, call 1-877-562-2626 or browse www.princegeorgebnb.com.

97 Motor Inn
2713 Spruce Street
250-452-6010
17 air-conditioned rooms, suites, and kitchenettes in downtown location. Cable, movies. Close to restaurants, shopping.

Anco Motel
1630 East Central Street
1-800-553-3290 or 250-563-3671
www.ancomotel.ca
63 extra-large rooms, 4 one-bedroom, kitchenettes. Free local calls, free wireless Internet. Restaurant. Fee for pets.

Best Western City Centre
910 Victoria Street
1-888-679-6699 or 250-563-1267
www.bwcitycentre.com
53 air-conditioned units in downtown location. Free local calls, cable TV, indoor pool, sauna, fitness room, laundry. Restaurant. Next to Civic Centre. Senior discount.

Bon Voyage Motor Inn
4222 Highway 16 West
1-888-611-3872 or 250-964-2333
96 air-conditioned units, kitchenettes, suites. Cable TV, free coffee. Gift shop, restaurant, RV parking, winter plug-ins. Adjacent to gas, diesel station, car wash. Winter plug-ins.

Carmel Motor Inn
1502 Highway 97
1-800-665-4484 or 250-564-6339
90 air-conditioned sleeping and kitchen units. Cable TV, movies, restaurant, RV parking. Gift shop, adjacent to diesel station, carwash.

Coast Inn of the North
770 Brunswick Street
1-800-663-1144 or 250-563-0121
www.coasthotels.com
153 air-conditioned deluxe units. Three restaurants, pool, sauna, gym, hair salon, free high-speed wireless, lounge. Senior discount.

Downtown Motel
650 Dominion Street
250-563-9241 / *www.downtownmotel.ca*
43 air-conditioned rooms, cable TV, movies. Winter plug-ins. Close to Civic Centre and pool. Senior discount.

Economy Inn
1915 3rd Avenue
1-888-566-6333 or 250-563-7106
www.economyinn.ca
30 air-conditioned rooms, kitchenettes. Cable TV, in-room coffee, data ports. Whirlpool, exercise room. Winter plug-ins. Near restaurants, shopping.

Esther's Inn
1151 Commercial
1-800-663-6844 or 250-562-4131
www.esthersinn.com
122 air-conditioned rooms. Whirlpools, sauna, exercise club, pool with waterslides. Dining room, lounge. Close to attractions, shopping.

Grama's Inn
901 Central Street
1-877-563-7174 or 250-563-7174
www.esthersinn.com/gramas
60 air-conditioned rooms, hospitality room. Guests may use facilities of sister hotel, Esther's Inn: pool, whirlpool, exercise club.

PG Hi-Way Motel
1737 20th Avenue
1-888-557-4557
www.princegeorge.com/pghiway
45 budget and deluxe rooms, kitchenettes. Winter plug-ins. Near restaurants, laundry, shopping.

Ramada Hotel Downtown Prince George
444 George Street
1-800-830-8833 or 250-563-0055
www.ramadaprincegeorge.com
193 air-conditioned units and executive suites in downtown location. Cable TV, movies, indoor pool, sauna, whirlpool. Dining, pub, casino, gift shop. Airport shuttle.

Sandman Inn
1650 Central Street
1-800-726-3626 or 250-563-8131
www.sandmanhotels.com
144 units, from 1- and 2-bedroom suites to kitchenettes. Free in-room coffee, indoor pool, sauna, 24-hour restaurant, room service. Senior discount.

Travelodge Goldcap
1458 7th Avenue
1-800-663-8239 or 250-563-0666
www.travelodgeprincegeorge.com
77 air-conditioned units in downtown location. Cable TV and movie channel. Laundry, beauty salon, sauna. Family restaurant, lounge. Close to Civic Centre.

Treasure Cove Hotel & Casino
2005 Highway 97 South
1-877-614-9111 or 250-615-9111
www.treasurecovehotel.com
Well-appointed rooms, suites. Exercise facility, day spa, restaurants, casino, entertainment.

Southpark RV Park
9180 Highway 97 South
1-877-963-7275 or 250-963-7577
www.southparkrv.com
Extra-long pull-throughs, free hot showers, Internet access, wireless, satellite TV, golf nearby.

CAMPGROUNDS

Bednesti Lake Resort
Mile 33 Highway 16 West
250-441-3500
7 sleeping units and 40 campsites with full or partial hookups, some pull-throughs, satellite TV, flush toilets, showers, laundry, picnic area, playground. Dining, café, lounge. Swimming, boating, boat launch, convenience store. Fuel, propane.

Bee Lazee RV Park and Campground
15910 Highway 97, 9 miles (15 km) south of Prince George
250-963-7263
49 sites with full hookups, pull-throughs, tent camping. Free showers; laundry, washrooms, car and RV wash. Playground, heated pool.

Blue Spruce RV Park and Campground
3 miles (5 km) west on Highway 16 from intersection with Highway 97
250-964-7272
128 sites with full hookups, pull-throughs, cable TV, tent camping, cabins. Showers, laundry, store. Heated pool, mini-golf, playground, sani-station. Near golf, gas, shopping.

Hartway RV Park
7729 Kelly Road South, 6 miles (9 km) north of Prince George on Highway 97
250-962-8848
40 landscaped sites with full and partial hookups, pull-throughs, free cable TV. Free showers, self-service laundry, gift shop, near restaurants and shopping.

The Loghouse Restaurant and RV Park
11075 Hedlund Road
250-963-9515

Sintich RV Park
7817 Highway 97 South, 3 miles (5 km) south of Prince George on Highway 97
250-963-9862
www.sintich.bc.ca
50 spacious landscaped lots for adult campers, pull-throughs, power, cable TV. Free showers; laundry. Near store and gas station.

RESTAURANTS

Bonnet Hill Pub & Grill
6957 Giscome Road
250-963-8134
Pub grub and libations, minutes from downtown.

Cariboo Steakhouse
1165 5th Avenue
250-564-1220
Steaks, seafood, salad bar.

Cimo Mediterranean Grill
601 Victoria Street
250-564-7975
Pasta, grill, seafood, wine.

De Dutch Pannekoek House
101-910 Victoria Street
250-563-2946
www.dedutch.com
Continental dining, breakfast, burgers and more.

Earl's Place
1440 Central Street East
250-562-1527
Family dining, appetizers, desserts. Licensed.

The Keg
582 George Street
250-563-1768
Steak, prime rib, other favorites.

The Loghouse Restaurant and RV Park
11075 Hedlund Road
250-963-9515

Mai Thai
484 Douglas Street
250-563-7779
Thai cuisine. Seafood, appetizers, curries.

Moxie's Classic Grill
1804 Central Street East.
250-564-4700
Burgers, pasta, daily entrees. Mixed drinks.

Noodles
395 Quebec Street
250-564-6767
Eat in or take-out menu, pasta of all varieties. Pizza, sandwiches. Downtown.

Ric's Grill
547 George Street
250-614-9096
Steak, chicken, seafood.

Sgt. O'Flaherty's Pub
770 Brunswick Street
250-563-0078
Pizza and other pub grub, beer and wine. Entertainment.

Temptations Restaurant
409 George Street
250-563-7109
Nouveau French cuisine.

Waddling Duck Restaurant
1157 5th Avenue
250-561-1167
www.waddlingduck.ca
Ribs, steaks, seafood, fish 'n' chips. Beer and wine. Seating indoors or out.

Winston's
770 Brunswick Street, inside the Coast Inn
250-563-0121
Quality dining in well-appointed restaurant.

Road Notes

In the 188 miles (303 km) between Prince George and Chetwynd, you'll follow the John Hart Highway, which is Highway 97. The Rocky Mountain Trench, 95 miles (153 km) north of Prince George, marks the western boundary of the Rocky Mountains. This land of lakes, rivers, and fertile valleys beneath snowcapped peaks will have you shooting pictures in every direction. There are plenty of pullouts for a short rest, most with garbage cans, some with picnic tables or toilets.

CHETWYND

From Prince George: 188 miles (303 km)
To Dawson Creek: 62 miles (100 km)

Whereas the town of Hope seems content with claiming the title of Chainsaw Sculpture Capital of British Columbia, Chetwynd is more ambitious—seeing itself as the Chainsaw Sculpture Capital of the World. Chetwynd is proud of the dozens of sculptures you'll see around town—mostly wildlife—beginning with the welcome sign that features a family of curious bears. Stop at the Chetwynd Visitor Information Centre along Highway 97 to pick up a driving map that shows where the sculptures are on display: at the Chainsaw Sculpture Park and at businesses around town.

And for lovers of chainsaw sculpture, you can't do better than watching the artists at work. Come and observe during the annual Chetwynd International Chainsaw Carving Championship Invitational, held in early June.

Chetwynd lies in coal and timber country in Little Prairie Valley. In fact, the early-day fur traders originally called it Little Prairie. The name Chetwynd honors Ralph Chetwynd, a government minister who helped bring the Pacific Great Eastern Railway to town. Many of Chetwynd's 3,100 people are employed at the sawmill, the coal mine, or the two dams up

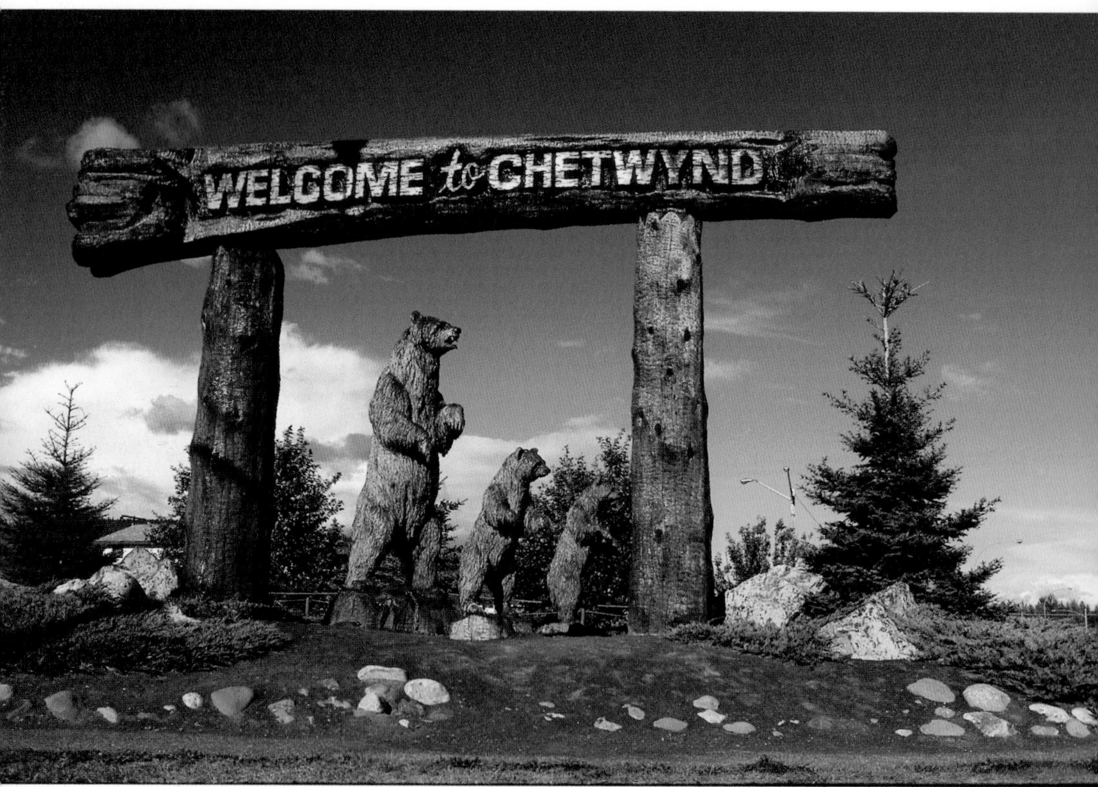

Chetwynd has so many chainsaw sculptures around town that it claims the title of "Chainsaw Sculpture Capital of the World."

Hudson's Hope Loop. If you want to learn more about mining and forestry, industrial tours are available. Check at the visitor center for reservations.

Take a walk along any of the extensive trails in the Chetwynd Greenspace Trail System. They range from a 5-minute walk to an hour or more on trails varying from rustic to improved. A popular route is the Old Baldy Hiking Trail, which offers excellent views of the valley, along with plenty of places to rest. The Community Forest features interpretive walking and hiking trails, a tree registry, and a demonstration forest, along with picnic areas in forested settings.

Take the kids for a few hours of water fun at the Chetwynd Leisure Pool, one of the best in the area, located at 46th Street and the North Access Road off Highway 97. Other local recreation includes golfing, mountain biking, and terrific fishing. You can obtain your mandatory fishing license and all the tackle you need at Lonestar Sporting Goods. Call 250-788-1850.

For more information on the chainsaw-carving competition or any Chetwynd activities and events, call the Chetwynd Visitor Information Centre at 250-788-1943 or browse their Web site at *www.gochetwynd.com.*

DINOSAURS AND DAMS

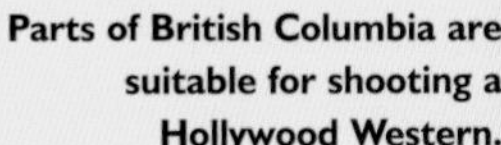

Parts of British Columbia are suitable for shooting a Hollywood Western.

On the map, the Hudson's Hope Loop road—Highway 29 running north from Chetwynd—looks like a great way to shave off time and miles from your Alaska Highway trip. Don't be fooled by the two-dimensional aspects of the map. The 87-mile route will lead you through some beautiful country, but it is a narrow, winding affair that's best left to the sports-car set. And besides, if you take this cutoff, you'll miss Dawson Creek completely, along with the fun of seeing your way around the Mile 0 City.

But do make a side trip along Hudson's Hope Loop to enjoy the countryside and visit two massive dams across the Peace River: the Peace River Dam and the W.A.C. Bennett Dam. See the dams, and then come back to Chetwynd so you can launch your Alaska Highway adventure at Dawson Creek.

Along Hudson's Hope Loop, the landscape changes from pasture to aspen forest to wheat fields in a broad river valley. The narrow road is patchy at times, and elevation changes can be rather steep, so you may just decide to pass on this side trip if you're driving a big rig.

Dinosaur footprints are part of an outside display at the W.A.C. Bennett Dam. The dam itself is 600 feet (183 m) tall and 1.25 miles (2 km) long, creating Williston Lake, a 230-mile-long (370-km) reservoir that's the 10th largest in the world. In the modern visitor center theater, a film shows historical footage of the river before the dam's construction, explains why it was built here, and how it all came together. Hands-on science experiments demonstrate how much energy is needed to light a bulb. Take a tour of the underground powerhouse. Parking is plentiful, and there are excellent views and photo opportunities. For information on tours of the Bennett Dam, call 1-888-333-6667.

Farther along the loop road is Peace Canyon Dam. While this is the more modest of the two dams, the visitor center here includes museum dioramas that depict early life for settlers in this area. Just inside the front door are full-size replicas of dinosaurs that once roamed the region. An upper deck allows a generous view of the dam and the valley. For information on tours of the Peace River Dam, call 250-783-9154.

LODGING

Chetwynd Court Motel
5104 North Access Road
250-788-2271
17 rooms, kitchenettes, cable TV, laundry facilities, wheelchair access, pets allowed. Restaurant.

Country Squire Motor Inn Chetwynd
5317 South Access Road
250-788-2276
51 deluxe units with wireless Internet, air-conditioning, kitchenettes. Fitness center.

High Country Inn
5000 North Access Road
250-788-9980
32 air-conditioned rooms, pets allowed, coach parking. Dining. Cold beer and wine store.

Lakeview Inns & Suites
4820 North Access Road
250-788-3000
Full kitchen units, wheelchair-accessible rooms. Business center, free continental breakfast, laundry.

Pine Cone Motor Inn
5224 53rd Avenue
1-800-663-8082 or 250-788-3311
54 air-conditioned units, including kitchenettes. Cable TV. Pets allowed. Coffee shop, dining room.

Stagecoach Inn
5413 South Access Road
1-800-663-2744 or 250-788-9666
55 air-conditioned rooms, kitchenettes, nonsmoking available, wheelchair access. Cable TV, sauna, whirlpool, laundry. Winter plug-ins. Pets on approval. Restaurant.

The Swiss Inn
4812 North Access Road
(250) 788-2566
Quality, comfortable accommodations. CAA Diamond rated. On-site restaurant.

CAMPGROUNDS

Caron Creek RV Park
On Highway 97, 10 miles (16 km) west of Chetwynd
250-788-2522
40 sites with full and partial hookups, pull-throughs on gravel and grass. Free showers; washrooms. Pay phone. Senior discount.

Westwind RV Park
4401 53rd Avenue, 2 miles (3 km) north past junction of Highways 97 and 29
250-788-2190
50 pull-through sites with full hookups. Showers, laundry, restrooms, dump station. Grassy sites, tent sites, picnic tables, fire pit area, playground.

RESTAURANTS

Dee's Diner
4741 52st Street
250-788-3778
Home-style cooking.

Dragon Place
5317 South Access Road
250-788-3700
Chinese cuisine. Eat in or take-out.

High Country Inn
5000 North Access Road
Adjacent to Chetwynd Court Motel
250-788-2271
Dining, cocktails.

Kentucky Fried Chicken
4800 North Access Road
250-788-9866
The fast-food favorite in chicken.

Murray's Pub and Kitchen
4613 47th Avenue
250-788-9594
Appetizers, meals, cocktails.

New Blue Sky Restaurant
5217 South Access Road
250-788-2777
Full menu, family dining.

Stagecoach Restaurant
5413 South Access Road
250-788-9665
Dining with views of Sunkunka Valley.

The Swiss Inn Restaurant
4812 North Access Road
250-788-2566
Steaks, pizza, European cuisine.

DAWSON CREEK, British Columbia

From Chetwynd: 62 miles (100 km)
From the Washington border: 705 miles (1,128 km)
To the Alaska border: 1,190 miles (1,915 km)
To Fairbanks: 1,488 miles (2,395 km)

Symbolically, Dawson Creek is the end of this road, and the beginning of another. You have arrived at Mile 0 of the famed Alaska Highway, and a new leg of your adventure is about to begin.

For a complete description of Dawson Creek and its services, facilities, and attractions, see Chapter 6, The Alaska Highway.

We made out the "Alaska or Bust" message on the back of this vehicle during a construction stop. Later, we met the young driver, a wrangler who was on his way to a summer job in Alaska's Denali National Park and Preserve.

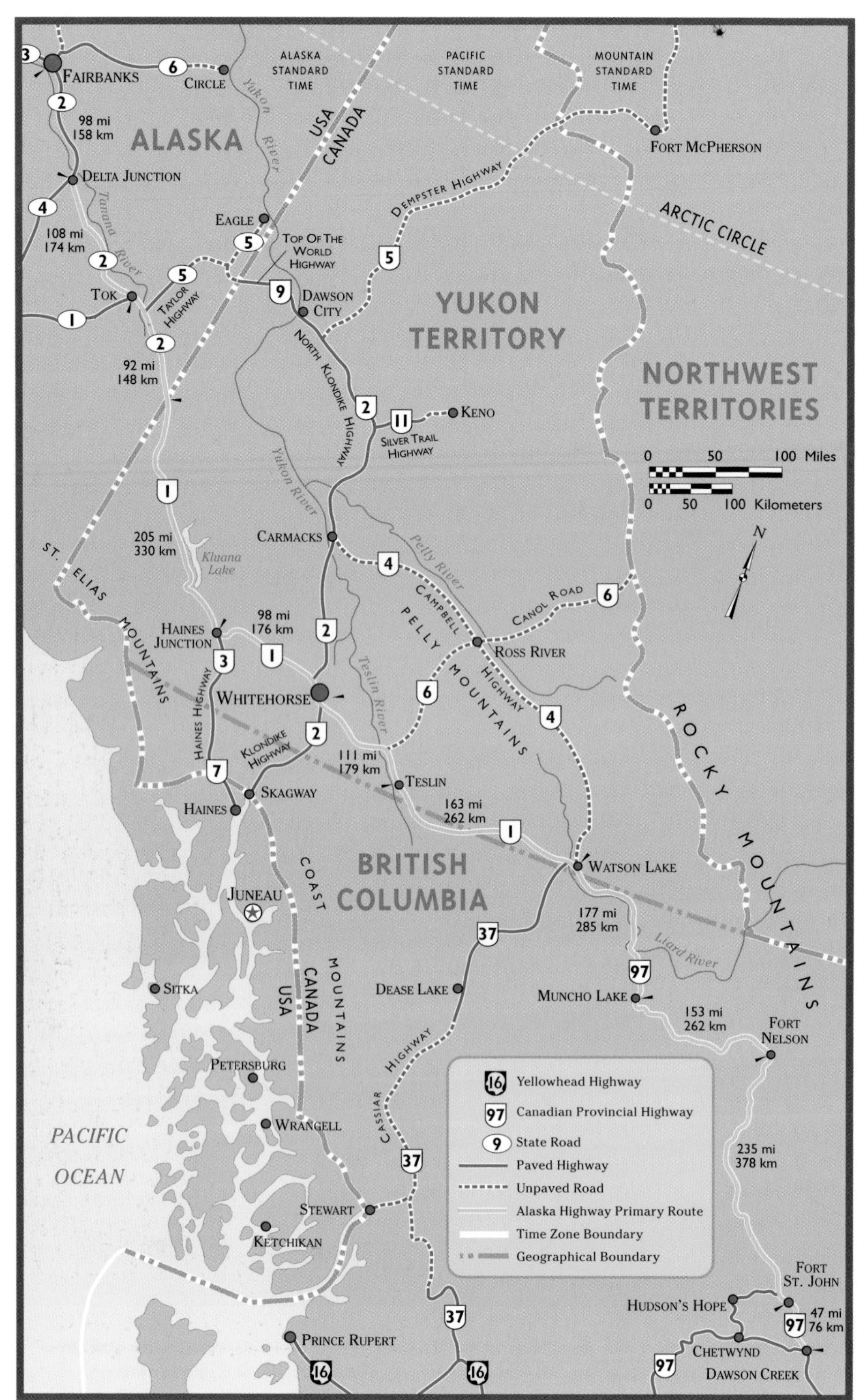

ALASKA
YUKON TERRITORY
NORTHWEST TERRITORIES
BRITISH COLUMBIA
USA CANADA
ALASKA STANDARD TIME
PACIFIC STANDARD TIME
MOUNTAIN STANDARD TIME
ARCTIC CIRCLE
FAIRBANKS
CIRCLE
DELTA JUNCTION
EAGLE
TOK
DAWSON CITY
KENO
FORT MCPHERSON
CARMACKS
ROSS RIVER
HAINES JUNCTION
WHITEHORSE
TESLIN
SKAGWAY
HAINES
WATSON LAKE
JUNEAU
SITKA
DEASE LAKE
MUNCHO LAKE
FORT NELSON
PETERSBURG
WRANGELL
STEWART
KETCHIKAN
PRINCE RUPERT
FORT ST. JOHN
HUDSON'S HOPE
CHETWYND
DAWSON CREEK
PACIFIC OCEAN
TOP OF THE WORLD HIGHWAY
TAYLOR HIGHWAY
NORTH KLONDIKE HIGHWAY
SILVER TRAIL HIGHWAY
DEMPSTER HIGHWAY
CAMPBELL HIGHWAY
CANOL ROAD
HAINES HIGHWAY
KLONDIKE HIGHWAY
CASSIAR HIGHWAY
ST. ELIAS MOUNTAINS
PELLY MOUNTAINS
COAST MOUNTAINS
ROCKY MOUNTAINS
Yukon River
Tanana River
Kluana Lake
Pelly River
Teslin River
Liard River
98 mi 158 km
108 mi 174 km
92 mi 148 km
205 mi 330 km
98 mi 176 km
111 mi 179 km
163 mi 262 km
177 mi 285 km
153 mi 262 km
235 mi 378 km
47 mi 76 km
0 50 100 Miles
0 50 100 Kilometers
N
Yellowhead Highway
Canadian Provincial Highway
State Road
Paved Highway
Unpaved Road
Alaska Highway Primary Route
Time Zone Boundary
Geographical Boundary

CHAPTER 6

The Alaska Highway

YOU MAY HAVE ARRIVED in Dawson Creek, B.C., via the Alberta route or the British Columbia route. Either way, about now you're probably thinking, "I thought we'd never get here!" It's true that the starting line of the Alaska Highway, or Mile 0, is more than 800 miles from the Canada border on either access route. So if you're saying "Finally!" join the crowd. But if you're like most people, here you'll shed any lingering road weariness and find revival in a sense of excitement and anticipation.

I'll warn you, don't expect the "wilderness adventure" part to begin immediately, for the road really doesn't change for many more miles. It's still paved and easy to navigate and is basically a continuation of what you've been seeing for a long distance already—farmlands—for some travelers, not too different from the place they started.

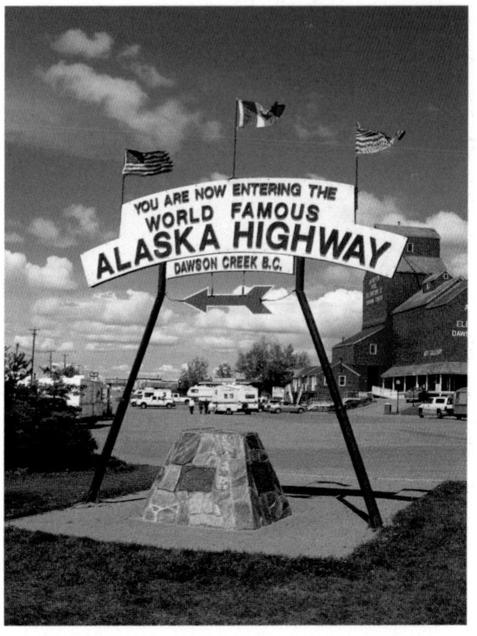

No trip up the Alaska Highway can begin without a photo of the sign that marks the starting line.

Yet as you visit the historic sites of Dawson Creek and make final preparations, you realize that you'll be following the footsteps of those intrepid workers who laid the groundwork for this highway more than six decades ago—and endured a frigid winter, no less—pushing a route through forests and over mountains, skirting jewel-colored lakes, and battling the quagmire of newly exposed permafrost, to complete one of the world's greatest road-building projects. Carry those images with you as you travel, and be sure to stop at the historic signposts and pullouts to learn more about this incredible road north.

DAWSON CREEK, British Columbia

Mile 0 of the Alaska Highway
To Fort St. John: 47 miles (76 km)
To the Alaska border: 1,190 miles (1,915 km)
To Fairbanks: 1,488 miles (2,395 km)

Tucked into the far northeast corner of British Columbia, little Dawson Creek gained international attention in March 1942 when thousands of U.S. troops "invaded" to begin construction of the Alaska Highway from the south end of the route. For a brief time, Dawson Creek's population of 850 was overrun with 10,000 GIs, straining local accommodations and food services, filling its sidewalks, and clogging the only movie theater in town. The boom was short-lived, however, as most of the men and equipment trailed northwest in the months to come.

Dawson Creek, B.C., and Dawson City, Yukon, farther north, were both named for George Mercer Dawson, a geologist who surveyed these parts of Canada in 1879. His work paved the way for settlement and development in both Dawsons. Incorporated as a city in 1958, Dawson Creek remains a small town with fewer than 12,000 residents.

At the city limits, near Dawson Creek Airport, stands a welcome sign declaring *Mile Zero City, Where the Adventure Begins!* And at the traffic circle in Dawson Creek that connects Highway 2 to Highway 97, you'll spot the oft-photographed sign proclaiming: *You Are Now Entering the World Famous Alaska Highway.*

Another not-to-be-missed landmark, the Mile 0 Milepost, erected in 1946, is in an unfortunate place—dead center in the busy intersection of 10th Street and 102nd Avenue—making posed photos a dangerous proposition. We saw others like us, passing off their cameras to friendly strangers and dodging traffic, trying to keep an eye on the crossing signals as well as vehicles that might ruin the photo shoot.

Atop the monument, sign-makers have painted the number of miles from Dawson

Frans and Paula, a couple from Rotterdam, Holland, paused for a photo by the Milepost 0 monument in downtown Dawson Creek, B.C. Taking pictures at the obelisk is a tradition among Alaska Highway travelers, yet it does pose some health hazards: the monument was erected in the center of a busy intersection. Locals have become accustomed to the sight of tourists trotting across the street or waiting for cars to pass.

Creek to Fort St. John (48), Fort Nelson (300), Whitehorse (918), and Fairbanks (1,523). The numbers no longer match the actual driving distances, because the road has been straightened (and shortened) since it was first constructed. At that time, Canada used miles to measure distance. The country has since switched to the metric system, and kilometerposts have replaced mileposts along the highway.

Just inside the roundabout connecting Highways 2 and 97, a metal sculpture by Carl Mattson points the way to Alaska and honors the surveyors of the historic Alcan. This is such a busy, dangerous traffic area, visitors are well-advised to stay on the safe side of the street and forego posing by the sculpture. It's not worth the risk.

Better, get your picture taken nearby at the "World Famous" sign over the Mile 0 cairn. It's a must, and if you time it right, you can pose with a Mountie. Check the photo schedule at *www.dawsoncreek.com.*

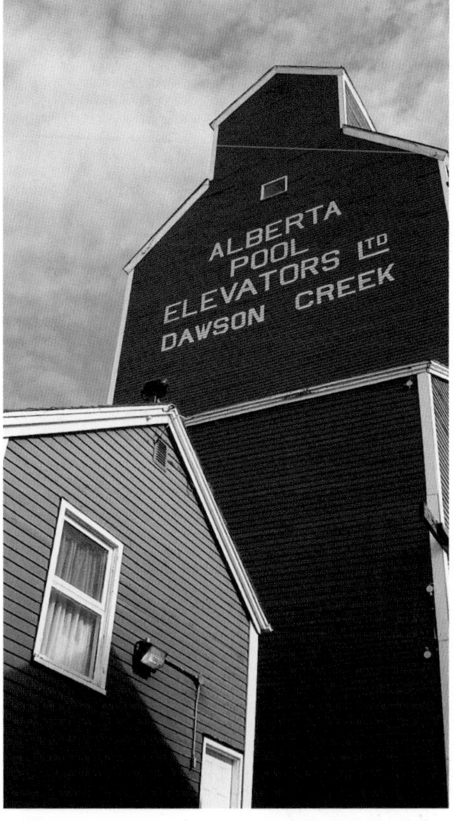

Restored grain elevators in the Northern Alberta Railways Park are home to the Dawson Creek Art Gallery and feature traveling art collections and an excellent photo exhibit of the Alaska Highway construction.

Behind you towers another Dawson Creek classic dressed in red: a historic wooden grain elevator that was relocated to this place in the Northern Alberta Railway Park (NAR Park). Today it houses a gift shop and art gallery, and features a spiral ramp, making access to the exhibits easy for everybody. The building of the Alaska Highway is portrayed in historical photos.

On any given summer day, the NAR Park lot is filled with RVs from all over the United States and Canada—a true cross-section of the North American camping world. These are people who are always ready for conversation and to compare travel notes, and new friendships have been forged here.

From the parking area of the NAR Park, it's an easy stroll to the Dawson Creek Visitor Information Centre at 900 Alaska Avenue. Just follow the brick footpath past the railcar to the renovated 1931 railway station that's now a combination visitor center/museum. Tens of thousands visit the center each year to get answers, pick up free brochures, freshen up in the public restrooms, and buy books and souvenirs that mark this memorable trip. Access to the museum is at a nominal fee. Browse their site at *www.calverley.ca*. With a free copy of the self-guided Historic Walking Tour, you'll stroll by the buildings that were standing when the

American soldiers began arriving in March of 1942. A mural project enhances the beauty and history of the downtown core.

You'll also find that the downtown core is a free wireless hotspot for your laptop or PDA, courtesy of Tourism Dawson Creek and the Peace Region Internet Society

The town supports a wide-ranging community of farming families. Agriculture and tourism are the leading economic drivers. If you're visiting during early August, be sure to make it to the Dawson Creek Fall Fair, Exhibition & Pro Rodeo, which includes farming exhibits, horse shows, handicrafts, a food fair, and rodeo events. And for the fright of your life, watch the professional chuckwagon drivers' race. The Mile Zero Park (oddly enough, located at Mile 1 of the Alaska Highway) includes the Walter Wright Pioneer Village and some beautiful botanical treats, shops, and a restaurant. A picnic area, swimming lake, and adjacent RV park and campground round out the attraction.

Golfers can test their skills on two courses. In town is the 18-hole, par-70 Dawson Creek Golf & Country Club. Cart and equipment rentals are available, and tee-time reservations are recommended. Call 250-782-7882. Just 10 miles along the Alaska Highway in Farmington is a 12-hole, well-treed course that's a 3,228-yard par 36. Farmington Fairways also offers an on-site campground with pull-throughs and tent sites so you can stick around if the clubs are hot. Cart and club rentals, driving range, pro shop, and clubhouse round out your holiday. For tee-times, call 250-843-7774.

Dawson Creek has many restaurants, hotels, campgrounds, bakeries, car and RV washes—anything you need for resting up or stocking up before beginning your journey up the Alaska Highway. For more information on the area's attractions and services, call 1-866-645-3022 or 250-782-9595. View the Web site at *www.tourismdawsoncreek.com.*

LODGING

Please browse www.bbcanada.com to locate a bed-and-breakfast.

Airport Inn
800 120th Avenue
1-800-555-2809 or 250-782-9404
www.airportinn.ca
40 air-conditioned rooms, suites, cable TV, laundry.

The Alaska Hotel
10213 10th Street
250-782-7998
www.alaskahotel.com
12 units, old-world decor. Restaurant, entertainment.

Aurora Park Inn & Suites
12004 8th Street
1-877-782-8006 or 250-782-8006
45 deluxe rooms, suites. Free breakfast. Near airport and highway.

Best Western Dawson Creek
500 Highway 2
1-800-528-1234 or 250-782-6226
www.pomeroygroup.ca
100 deluxe, air-conditioned rooms, cable TV, Internet. Laundry service, exercise facility, whirlpool/sauna. Pet friendly. Free breakfast.

Cedar Lodge Motel
801 110th Avenue
250-782-8531
41 units, with kitchenettes, refrigerators, cable TV, laundry. Pet friendly. Across from mall.

Central Motel
1301 Alaska Avenue
250-782-8525
15 air-conditioned units, cable TV, Internet.

Dawson Creek Super 8 Motel
1440 Alaska Avenue
1-888-482-8884 or 250-782-8899
66 business suites and kitchenettes. Free Internet, microwaves, refrigerators, irons, cable TV. Fitness center. Pet friendly. Free breakfast.

The George Dawson Inn
11705 8th Street
1-800-663-2745 or 250-782-9151
www.georgedawsoninn.com
80 well-appointed, air-conditioned rooms, executive suites, cable TV. Coffee shop, lounge, dining room, fitness center. Small pets. Senior rates.

Inn on the Creek
10600 8th Street
1-888-782-8136 or 250-782-8136
www.innonthecreek.bc.ca
48 deluxe air-conditioned rooms and kitchenettes. Fridges, microwaves, family restaurant. Adjacent to mall, close to attractions.

The Lodge Motor Inn & Café
1317 Alaska Avenue
1-800-935-3336 or 250-782-4837
www.lodgemotorinn.com
40 modern, air-conditioned rooms, cable TV, free local calls. Dining. Centrally located, near mall.

Northwinds Lodge
623 103rd Avenue
www.northwindslodge.com
1-800-665-1759 or 250-782-9181
20 air-conditioned units; kitchenettes. Cable TV, fridges, free Internet, winter plug-ins.

Peace Villa Motel
1641 Alaska Avenue
1-877-782-8175 or 250-782-8175
48 air-conditioned rooms, movies, laundry, office services, sauna. Senior discount. Near golf course and restaurants.

Ramada Limited Dawson Creek
1748 Alaska Avenue
1-800-663-2749 or 250-782-8595
www.ramada.ca
41 units on one level, fridges, coffee, irons and boards, cable TV, high-speed wireless Internet. Free deluxe continental breakfast. Close to restaurants, downtown, and tourist information.

Travellers Inn
800 112th Avenue
250-782-5333
36 air-conditioned rooms, kitchenettes, cable TV, Internet. Pet friendly. Free breakfast.

Voyageur Motor Inn
801 111th Avenue
1-877-782-8006 or 250-782-1020
19 air-conditioned rooms, cable TV. Pet friendly. Restaurant.

CAMPGROUNDS

Alahart RV Park
Junction of Highway 97 and Alaska Highway
250-782-4702 / *www.alahartrvpark.com*
Full hookups, pull-throughs, tent camping. Free showers, self-service laundry, cable TV, dump station, free ice. Windshield repair. Close to downtown, next to restaurant.

Mile 0 RV & Campground
Mile 1.5, next to Rotary Lake and Walter Wright Pioneer Village
250-782-2590
Partial hookups, pull-throughs, shady sites. Free showers; laundry, dump station, Mile 1 Café.

Northern Lights RV Park
On Highway 97 South, just west of junction with Highway 97 North
1-888-414-9433 or 250-782-9433
55 sites, spacious pull-throughs, full and partial hookups. Free satellite TV and wireless Internet, modem hookup, free showers, self-service laundry, washrooms. RV wash; full service for Alaska Highway preparation. Gift shop, trout-fishing pond. Large groups welcome.

Tubby's RV Park
1913 Hart Highway (Highway 97 South)
250-782-2584
97 full-hookup sites, pull-throughs, tenting. Free showers, self-service laundry, restrooms, dump station. Car and RV wash, auto services. Internet access. Near swimming pool and Pioneer Village.

RESTAURANTS

The Alaska Café & Pub
Near Mile 0 milepost
10209 10th Street
250-782-7040
www.alaskahotel.com
Full menu. Private dining and meeting rooms. Caravans welcome.

Caruso's
1025 Alaska Avenue
250-782-4938
Steak, seafood, pasta. Licensed. Reservations.

China Kitchen
10600 8th Avenue
250-782-1596
Chinese favorites, full menu or take-out.

Dawson Co-Op Cafeteria
11300 8th Street
250-782-4858
Full menu and take-out.

Dawson Creek Diner & Deli
10221 10th Street
250-782-1182
Burgers, sandwiches, pizza.

Dawson Creek Golf & Country Club
Highway 97 North
250-782-5156
Breakfast, lunch, dinner, views. Reservations.

Fireside Steakhouse & Lounge
1029 102nd Avenue
250-782-4881
Full menu for lunch and dinner. Licensed. Reservations accepted.

Fly North Café
Dawson Creek Airport
250-782-8822
Breakfast, lunch, dinner. Reservations accepted.

Lily's Dining Room
11705 8th Street, in the George Dawson Inn
250-782-9151
Full menu, fine dining.

Lodge Café
1317 Alaska Avenue
250-782-4837
Full menu, breakfast specials. Licensed.

Ma's Stopping Place
11705 8th Street, in the George Dawson Inn
250-782-9151
Coffee shop featuring down-home breakfasts, lunches, dinners.

Mr. Mike's West Coast Grill
1501 Alaska Avenue
250-782-1577
Full menu or take-out. Patio seating. Reservations accepted.

Panago Pizza
10508 8th Street
250-310-0001
Pizza, wings, salads. Eat in or take-out.

Rockwell's Bar & Grill
1440 Alaska Avenue
250-782-8890
Full menu for lunch and dinner. Licensed. Reservations accepted.

Road Notes

The price of gas in Dawson Creek is typically higher than in the smaller towns to the south. Generally, the farther north you go in Canada, the more you pay. In the summer of 2007, we paid the most per gallon up ahead at Fort Nelson, where after converting Canadian dollars to U.S., and liters to gallons, we were paying $4.57 US per gallon. Ouch!

As you drive north toward Fort St. John, notice the pumpjacks in the fields. These mechanisms draw the oil out of the ground and into a pipeline or a storage tank. Most of the oil and gas is sold to markets in Canada and the United States.

Get sweeter than honey just south of Fort St. John at The Honey Place, which boasts the world's largest glass beehive. You can learn about bee behavior and what makes quality honey. Get your honey here, or pollen, or other souvenirs. It's on the west side of the road, about 5 miles (8 km) before Fort St. John. Call 250-785-4808 or see *www.honeyplace.com.*

FORT ST. JOHN

From Dawson Creek: 47 miles (76 km)
To Fort Nelson: 235 miles (378 km)

Fort St. John calls itself The Energetic City and the Energy Capital of British Columbia, with a nod to the industries that power the city's economy: natural gas and oil extraction, hydroelectric power, forestry, agriculture, and tourism. This city of nearly 19,000 people is the oldest non-Native settlement on the British Columbia mainland. Another 30,000 people live throughout the North Peace region, where the Peace River snakes through a broad, green valley. These rural residents and First Nations communities look to Fort St. John as a regional hub for business and services. The city offers shopping, dining, and cultural attractions such as live theater, dance, and music at the North Peace Culture Centre, 10015 100th Avenue. Call 250-785-1992. And it's a pet-friendly town—your traveling pets are welcome in nearly every hotel, motel, or lodge in Fort St. John.

If you make it to a grocery store, you may see a clever way to keep carts from going off the premises. The carts are attached to a locking device—you pay a deposit, pull one out, and get your money back when you return it.

As the main town of the North Peace region, Fort St. John lies within a diverse landscape, from rolling farmlands and valleys to canyons carved by rivers. The staff at the Visitor Information Centre, open year-round at 9923 100th Street, will help you plan an outdoor adventure. Call 250-785-3033 or browse the Web site at *www.fortstjohn.ca*. The center offers a list of local guides and outfitters and their specialties. Think about a day of hiking on Fish Creek Community Forest trails, golfing on one of the three nearby courses, swimming, horseback riding, or fishing for walleye or northern pike in Charlie Lake.

Check with the folks at Backcountry, 10040 100th Avenue, for mandatory fishing licensing as well as outdoor clothing and gear. The folks there can book a guide for you, too. Call 250-785-1461. In Charlie Lake, stop by the General Store at Mile 52 Alaska Highway, or call 250-787-0655.

The North Peace Leisure Pool complex, at 9505 100th Street, is a modern addition to the recreational possibilities in Fort St. John. Outside is a free splash park, perfect for kids on hot, sunny days. Inside you'll find a six-lane lap pool, wave pool, rapids channel, waterslide, and a kiddie pool. Relax in the steam room or sauna and the road-miles will melt away. Call 250-785-8178.

Exhibits at the North Peace Museum reflect on the area's First Nations roots, its settlement by fur traders, and its development into the regional power that it is today. Back in 1942, Fort St. John was the unofficial starting line for the builders of the Alaska Highway. A gravel road already existed between Dawson Creek and this outlying community, and that road was incorporated into the route. Six thousand troops descended on what was then a town of 200 people. You'll find the museum at the foot of the landmark oil derrick at 9323 100th Street. Call 250-787-0430.

Golf enthusiasts can play a 9-hole course with bent-grass greens at Fort St. John Golf Course, 12707 86th Street. You'll find cart rentals, club repairs, and lessons from a CGPA pro on staff. For information, call 250-285-9995. North of town is Lakepoint Golf & Country Club at Mile 54 Alaska Highway, offering an 18-hole championship course, pro shop, rentals, and restaurant. Call for tee-times at 250-785-5566.

Just north of town, you can turn west to access Highway 29, Hudson's Hope Loop, from the north end. This road leads to some beautiful driving country, but the road does get narrow and patchy in places. Steep grades and switchbacks are not advisable for oversize RVs. Two dams along this loop road are major area attractions, as is Hudson's Hope Museum. For more information, see the section on the town of Chetwynd in Chapter 5, The Western Route.

LODGING

Please browse www.bbcanada.com to locate a bed-and-breakfast.

Alexander Mackenzie Inn
9223 100th Street
1-800-663-8313 or 250-785-8364
www.mackenzieinn.com
126 air-conditioned rooms, kitchenettes. Cable TV, ATM, laundry, wheelchair access. Restaurant, lounge, night club. Close to shopping.

Best Western Coachman Inn
8540 Alaska Road
1-888-388-9408 or 250-787-0651
70 deluxe rooms, nonsmoking and pet rooms available. Cable TV, sauna, whirlpool, fitness room.

Blue Belle Motel
9705 Alaska Road, Mile 47 of the Alaska Highway
1-866-833-2121 or 250-785-2613
40 air-conditioned units in newer motel, kitchenettes, fridges, microwaves, cable TV. Free coffee, laundry, barbecues.

Caravan Motel
9711 Alaska Road
1-888-663-2552 or 250-787-1191
28 air-conditioned suites; some kitchenettes. Cable TV, free coffee, laundry, wheelchair access.

Cedar Lodge Motor Inn
9824 99th Avenue
1-800-661-2210 or 250-785-8107
47 air-conditioned units, some kitchenettes. Fridges, microwaves, cable TV. Winter plug-ins.

Econo Lodge
10419 Alaska Road
250-787-8475
42 air-conditioned units, coffee, fridges. Cable TV, laundry services, health club, swimming pool. Free hot breakfast. Winter plug-ins. Restaurant, coffee shop, pub.

Four Seasons Motor Inn
9810 100th Street
1-800-523-6677 or 250-785-6647
www.fourseasons.wo.to
60 air-conditioned rooms, kitchenettes, cable TV, high-speed Internet, winter plug-ins. Close to shopping, restaurants. Senior discount.

Good Host Inns & Suites
Fort St. John Motor Inn
10707 102nd Street
1-888-988-8846 or 250-787-0411
www.fortstjohnmotorinn.com
96 air-conditioned rooms, cable TV, free local calls, fridges, laundry, winter plug-ins. Quiet surroundings.

Lakeview Inns & Suites
10103 98th Avenue
1-888-346-7711 or 250-787-0779
73 deluxe rooms, suites, kitchenettes, fridges, microwaves, irons and boards. Cable TV, high-speed Internet, guest laundry. Fitness facility, winter plug-ins. Free airport shuttle. Free light breakfast.

Northwoods Inn
10627 Alaska Road
250-787-1616
Comfortable air-conditioned rooms, cable TV. Dining, coffee shop, lounge, pub, entertainment.

Nova Star
9603 Alaska Road
250-785-6777
Air-conditioned rooms and kitchenettes, cable TV, microwaves, fridges, free coffee. Plug-ins. No pets.

Quality Inn Northern Grand
9830 100th Avenue
1-888-663-8312 or 250-787-0521
www.qualityinnnortherngrand.com
125 units in full-service hotel, suites, cable TV. Fitness facility, swimming pool, sauna, whirlpool. Restaurant, lounge, pub. Downtown location.

Roost Motel
9207 Alaska Road
250-785-2906

Super 8 Motel
9500 Alaska Way
1-866-828-8885 or 250-785-7588
www.super8.com

CAMPGROUNDS

Ariana Gardens & RV Park
8428 Alaska Road
250-785-4218

Charlie Lake RV & Leisure
Mile 52 Alaska Highway
250-787-1569
Campsites among shade trees, minutes north of Fort St. John. Some pull-throughs, coin-op shower, laundry, phone, fire pits. Boat rentals on Charlie Lake.

Rotary RV Park
6 miles (9.5 km) north of Fort St. John
250-785-1700
40 sites with full or partial hookup, pull-throughs. 30-amp service, showers, laundry, dump station. Boat dock on Charlie Lake. Next to nature reserve.

Sourdough Pete's RV Park
7704 Alaska Road, Mile 45 Alaska Highway
250-785-9255
94 sites, full and partial hookups, long pull-throughs. Tent camping, flush toilets, laundry, showers, sani-dump. Next to family amusement park.

The province manages two easy-access parks north of Fort St. John. For more information, contact the Parks District Office in Fort St. John at 250–787–3407. Also stop by major local hotels, which feature full lunch and dinner menus in their dining rooms. The parks are:

Beatton Lake Provincial Park
1-800-689-9025
2 miles (3 km) north, then 5 miles (8 km) east of Fort St. John
37 RV and tent sites, with Charlie Lake access. Swimming, playground, fishing, boat launch.

Charlie Lake Provincial Park
1-800-689-9025
7 miles (11 km) north of Fort St. John
58 treed sites with picnic tables, outhouses, dump station. Playground, short hiking trail to Charlie Lake.

RESTAURANTS

Also stop by major local hotels, which feature full lunch and dinner menus in their dining rooms.

Apple Betty's
10108 101st Avenue
250-787-2585
Lunch and early buffet for families.

Buster's—The Steak Place
9720 100th Street
250-785-0770
Beef is king; choose your cut and extras.

Centre Dining
10228 100th Street
250-785-2812
Cantonese dishes with eat in, take-out, delivery.

Charlie Lake General Store
Mile 50.6 Alaska Highway
Charlie Lake
250-787-0655
Take-out chicken and ribs.

Chatter's Restaurant
10440 100th Street, #5
250-785-1117
Greek dishes, pasta, steak, and regional Canadian.

Egan's
9404 Alaska Road
250-263-9992
Appetizers, soups, salads, burgers, sandwiches.

Forty-Niner Steak House
8111 100th Avenue
250-787-9292
Steak and more on the Western-style menu.

Irene's Tiny Café
10608 100th Avenue
250-787-7147
Breakfast and lunch specialties.

Jackfish Dundees
Mile 52 Alaska Highway
Charlie Lake
250-785-3233
Seafood, sirloin burgers, prime rib.

Mings Kitchen
9005 100th Avenue
250-787-1177
Lunch, dinner buffet, eat in or take-out.

North Star Restaurant
8540 Alaska Road
250-787-1454
Western-style cuisine. On-site lounge.

Northern Lights Restaurant
9823 100th Avenue
250-787-9085
Greek and Western cuisine.

Silver Creek Cookhouse
10104 Alaska Road
250-785-4888
Lunch restaurant with sandwiches and meals.

Yoko Beef
In the Totem Mall
250-787-8778
Chinese take-out and delivery. No MSG.

Road Notes

Certain mileposts you may see at roadside represent the distance from Dawson Creek on the original Alaska Highway—they show the Historical Miles. Many were erected in 1992, the road's 50th-anniversary year, as a way to provide markers with historical information about the significance of various places. These mileposts do not take into account the road improvements and shortening that have taken place over the years. Many towns and businesses have refused to give up their former addresses when the road was shortened, so they now refer to themselves as being at Historic Milepost such-and-such, further muddying the question of just exactly where you are. And as British Columbia and the Yukon work on the road, milepost markers are often missing. So if you are following the numbers closely and your math is coming out funny—it's not you.

The next major city, Fort Nelson, is 235 miles (378 km) down the road. That's the longest segment of the Alaska Highway without a town of 1,000 residents or more. Nonetheless, on this wilderness drive you'll find the occasional roadhouse, gas station, restaurant, or campground tucked in quaint little places along the way, so don't worry about heading into the unknown. You won't starve and you will find a safe place to camp or lay your head. Services are available at these locations with their Historic Milepost addresses: Shepherd's Inn (Mile 72), Wonowon (Mile 101–102), Pink Mountain (Mile 143–147), Sasquatch Crossing (Mile 147), Sikanni Chief (Mile 162), Buckinghorse (Mile 175), and Prophet River (Mile 233). Plus, there's so much beauty to behold: This country is crisscrossed with rivers, and the Rocky Mountains to the west will keep you company.

Use extra caution as you approach Sikanni Chief, as there's a 9 percent grade with a 50-km/hr speed corner as you descend this dangerous hill—really tough if you're pulling a big rig. Note the remains of the original wooden bridge crossing this stream. During road construction, as temporary bridges were replaced with permanent spans in 1943, this was the first bridge to be replaced. The historic structure was burned by an arsonist in 1992.

Workers in 1942 construct a makeshift log bridge, one of 133 that were eventually built on the road.

Also through this stretch, you'll come across a couple of historical stops on the Northwest Staging Route, the series of airstrips that were used during World War II to deliver supplies and Lend-Lease Program airplanes to Fairbanks. From there, Russian pilots ferried the planes over the Bering Sea. One such historical site is at Mile 146 (236.5 km), the Sikanni Chief flight strip on the east side of the road. This was the southernmost end of the Northwest Staging Route. Another abandoned airstrip can be seen near Mile 217 (349 km), where a side road crosses the old airstrip. As you drive, you'll notice segments of the original road that have been abandoned to the weeds through the years as the route has been straightened (and shortened).

The Muskwa Bridge at Mile 281 (452 km), just a couple of miles before Fort Nelson, is the lowest point on the Alaska Highway, at an elevation of only 1,000 feet (305 m).

While driving the road for the third edition of this book, we traveled in early June and saw single black bears on several occasions before we reached Fort Nelson. The bears were feeding at the forest edge, well away from the roadside, but clearly visible. They were intently munching on the new grasses of spring, and while they kept a wary eye on slow-moving vehicles with cameras, they didn't instantly scramble away. Again, we stayed in the camper and took pictures from a distance.

FORT NELSON

From Fort St. John: 235 miles (378 km)
To Muncho Lake: 153 miles (246 km)
To Watson Lake: 330 miles (531 km)

Fort Nelson boasts that it has the longest main street in the world: the Alaska Highway. And the city's address is Historical Mile 300 (483 km)—a reference to the town's distance from

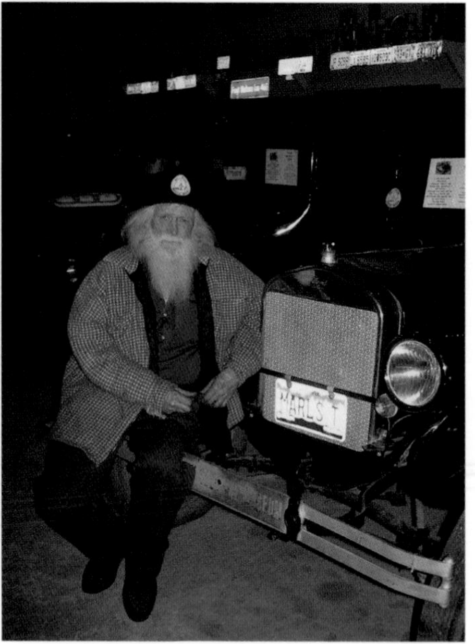

Marl Brown is the Fort Nelson man whose love for local history (and mechanical things) has resulted in the incredible collection at the Fort Nelson Heritage Museum.

Dawson Creek on the original Alaska Highway. (Road realignment now puts Fort Nelson just 282 miles from Dawson Creek.)

Established in 1805 as a fur trading post, this community in the northeast corner of British Columbia was named for Admiral Horatio Nelson, famed for the Battle of Trafalgar. About 5,000 people live in this town near the convergence of four rivers: the Muskwa, Prophet, Sikanni, and Fort Nelson. The extraction of natural resources fuels the local economy, with diverse industries represented on the city's snowflake-shaped emblem: gas and oil, mining, lumber, wildlife, agriculture, tourism, and trapping.

Like other small towns of the north, the emphasis is on opportunity and friendliness. Each Monday through Thursday in June and July, travelers are invited to stop by the Phoenix Theatre in the town square for a free welcome-visitor slide show presentation at 6:45 P.M. For information: 250-774-2956. This town is a good place to restock the RV with groceries and other necessities.

At the Fort Nelson information center, located inside the recreation center at Mile 284 Alaska Highway, help yourself to a free cup of coffee and browse through the printed materials about things to see and do in the Northern Rockies. The center's number is 250-774-6400; check out their Web site at *www.northernrockies.org*. Cash machines and U.S. currency exchanges are available at banks located along the frontage road of the highway.

For the flavor of the past, visit the Fort Nelson Heritage Museum, in a log cabin across from the information center. The museum features a mounted white moose in its display of local wildlife, and film footage taken during the building of the Alaska Highway can be seen in the museum's Muskwa Theatre. On the grounds are several historical buildings that have been recovered and moved here, as well as a vintage car collection. Browse through the trapper's log cabin, gift shop, and an old-time general store. Call 250-774-3536.

Golfers can play a 9-hole, par-35 course with grass greens at Poplar Hills Golf and Country Club, just outside town. Take advantage of the midnight sun and play from 8 A.M. to dusk in summers. Call 250-774-3862.

Winter visitors will marvel at the northern lights in these parts. Aurora borealis displays above Fort Nelson draw scientists who observe and record the events. The northern lights can occur year-round, but are easiest to see during the winter months.

LODGING

Please browse www.bbcanada.com to locate a bed–and–breakfast.

The BlueBell Inn
4203 50th Avenue South, Mile 300 Alaska Highway
1-800-663-5267 or 250-774-6961
www.bluebellinn.ca
57 air-conditioned rooms, kitchenettes. ATM, cable TV, self-service laundry, store, winter plug-ins. Restaurant, fuel station. Senior rates.

Fort Nelson Hotel
5110 50th Avenue North
1-800-663-5225 or 250-774-6971
www.fortnelsonhotel.com
134 air-conditioned rooms, kitchenettes. Cable TV, gift shop, indoor pool, saunas. Dining room, cocktail lounge, entertainment and dancing.

Fort Nelson Super 8
4503 50th Avenue South
888-888-5591 or 250-233-5025
142 units with microwaves and fridges; high-speed Internet, pool, hot tub, waterslide, gym. Fee for pets.

Kacee's Northern Suites
Main Street
1-866-769-6606 or 250-233-4800
22 air-conditioned rooms, suites, kitchenettes. Cable TV, in-room coffee, Internet access. Pets welcome.

Pioneer Motel
5207 50th Avenue South
250-774-5800
12 units; kitchenettes and cabins available. Cable TV, movie channel, laundry facilities. Senior rates. Pets welcome.

Ramada Limited Fort Nelson
5035 51st Avenue, Mile 300 Alaska Highway
1-866-774-2844 or 250-774-2844
41 units, some kitchenettes in central downtown location. Cable TV, coffee, irons and boards, free Internet access. Free continental breakfast, hot tubs. Winter plug-ins.

Thriftlodge Fort Nelson
4711 50th Avenue South
250-774-3911 / *www.travelodge.com*
More than 70 air-conditioned rooms, plus laundry service, office services, winter plug-ins. Sauna, whirlpool. Small pets welcome. Restaurant, dining room, lounge with TV and fireplace. Free airport shuttle.

Woodlands Inn
3995 50th Avenue South
1-866-966-3466 or 250-774-6669
www.woodlandsinn.bc.ca
131 spacious, air-conditioned rooms, suites, kitchenettes. Cable TV, high-speed Internet, coin-operated laundry, steam bath, hot tub, fitness room. Restaurant, sports lounge. Free shuttle.

CAMPGROUNDS

The BlueBell Inn
4203 50th Avenue South, Mile 300 Alaska Highway
1-800-663-5267 or 250-774-6961
42 full-service sites, laundry, fuel, store, ice, ATM. Sleeping rooms also available. Restaurant, Internet café.

Fort Nelson Truck Stop & RV Park
5 miles (8 km) south of downtown Fort Nelson on Alaska Highway
250-774-7270
44 RV sites with full hookups, some pull-throughs, 14 tent sites. Showers, laundry, store, fuel, restaurant. Cable TV, Internet access.

Pioneer Motel
5207 50th Avenue South
250-774-5800
RV spaces with full hookup, cable TV, showers, laundry facilities.

Westend RV Campground
On Alaska Highway, next to Heritage Museum
250-774-2340
170 sites with full and partial hookups, pull-throughs, grassy tent sites, free firewood, free wireless. Showers, laundry, cable TV, dump station. Gift shop, free car wash, RV supplies and wash. Walking distance to local attractions. Auto services, tours.

The province manages an easy–access park west of Fort Nelson. For more information on this and other provincial parks, contact the Parks District Office in Fort St. John at 250–787–3407.

Tetsa River Regional Park
48 miles (77 km) west of Fort Nelson, then south for 1 mile (1.5 km)
25 campsites, tenting area, firewood, outhouses, water, wheelchair access.

RESTAURANTS

Also stop by major local hotels, which feature full lunch and dinner menus in their dining rooms.

Backroads Sports Bar & Grill
4607 55th Street
250-774-2000
Full menu, licensed.

Coachhouse Restaurant
4711 50th Avenue North
250-774-3929
Full-menu dining room; licensed.

Dan's Neighborhood Pub
4204 50th Avenue North
250-774-3929
Full menu, daily lunch specials. Seating indoors or on the patio.

Dixie Lee Chicken
5011 50th Avenue South
250-774-6226
Hamburgers, chicken, fish and chips, ice cream.

Fort Pizza
5148 Liard Street
250-774-2405
Pizza, fast food, ice cream; eat in, take-out, or delivery.

Fort Restaurant
5100 50th Avenue North
250-774-7840
Full menu of dining choices; licensed.

Pantry Restaurant
3896 50th Avenue South
250-774-7060
Dining room seating; licensed.

P&T Restaurant
4103 50th Avenue South
250-774-6244
Family dining, full menu.

Pizzarama Pizzaria
12 Landmark Plaza
250-774-7100
Eat-in or take-out pizza.

Road Notes

Over the years, we've seen fewer mileposts and kilometerposts along the road, mainly because they aren't always replaced after road maintenance. Again, be aware that the mileposts won't necessarily jibe with mileage showing on your odometer.

Mileage and kilometer figures used in this text are based on the actual current number of road miles from Dawson Creek.

Thirty-four miles (54.5 km) past Fort Nelson, at the summit of 3,500-foot (1,067-km) Steamboat Mountain, you'll gain spectacular views of the Muskwa River Valley and the Rocky Mountains. Looking at the shape of Steamboat Mountain, you'll see how it got its name.

Another 8 miles (13 km) along, you'll catch the first views of a classic Indian profile in the high, craggy rocks. Stop for a photo at the turnout in another mile. Drive another couple of miles to Teetering Rock viewpoint, another turnout with litter barrel and trailheads.

The highest point on the Alaska Highway (4,250 feet) occurs at Summit, 90 miles (145 km) from Fort Nelson.

Again, while at times it may feel like you're alone in this unspoiled wilderness, you'll find rest stops along this long stretch. A few of the long-time businesses are no longer open, but Tetsa River Services (250-774-1005), about 75 miles west of Fort Nelson, has rooms, cabins, and RV parking as well as dining. Stick around and they'll take you fishing or on a trail ride.

One more note on wildlife, which seemed especially abundant on this early June trip of ours. Since early June is still spring in the Northland (after all, you may still find snow and ice at the river's edge), we were not surprised to see one or two dead moose at various spots along the road. They'd likely died during the snowy months and had only been revealed at breakup. I've already mentioned the four black bears we saw before Fort Nelson. In the miles

Two long-haul truckers enjoy breakfast at the Toad River Lodge before climbing back into their rigs. Longtime Fairbanks residents, they were reflecting on the changes they've seen on the Alaska Highway over the years. The men usually drive Alaska's Dalton Highway, also known as the Haul Road.

---

to come, we would see another five black bears, a dozen stone sheep, a red-tailed hawk, a gigantic bull bison, and what appeared to be a recently killed caribou, probably hit by a vehicle. All this without opening the door to the camper. The signs that advise watching out for wildlife are serious, and especially useful when animals such as stone sheep come right down to the shoulder of the road to sample the natural mineral licks, which is a common occurrence in the coming miles.

Heading toward Muncho Lake, you'll view several rivers, but the most beautiful must be the Toad River, which parallels the road for many miles. It's hard to keep your eyes on the road rather than watch its fast-moving and peculiarly beautiful blue-green water. The Toad River Lodge at Mile 422 is a favorite stopping place for pie and coffee when relatives of mine drive the road every summer. On their recommendation, we enjoyed a lakeside campsite this year, as we watched a moose browsing at the water's edge. Rooms and cabins are available, too. Inside the restaurant, owners keep a running tally on a whiteboard behind the cash register, tracking the ever-expanding baseball cap collection. Look up—they cover the ceiling in this room and the next, rows and rows of caps. Another attractive business is just a few more miles down the road: the Poplars Campground & Café, with cabins, RV sites, gifts, and plenty of baked goods to entice you (250-232-5465). And just one mile further, Stone Mountain Safaris offers adventure tours, housing, and meals, with four guest rooms. Call 250-232-5469 for reservations.

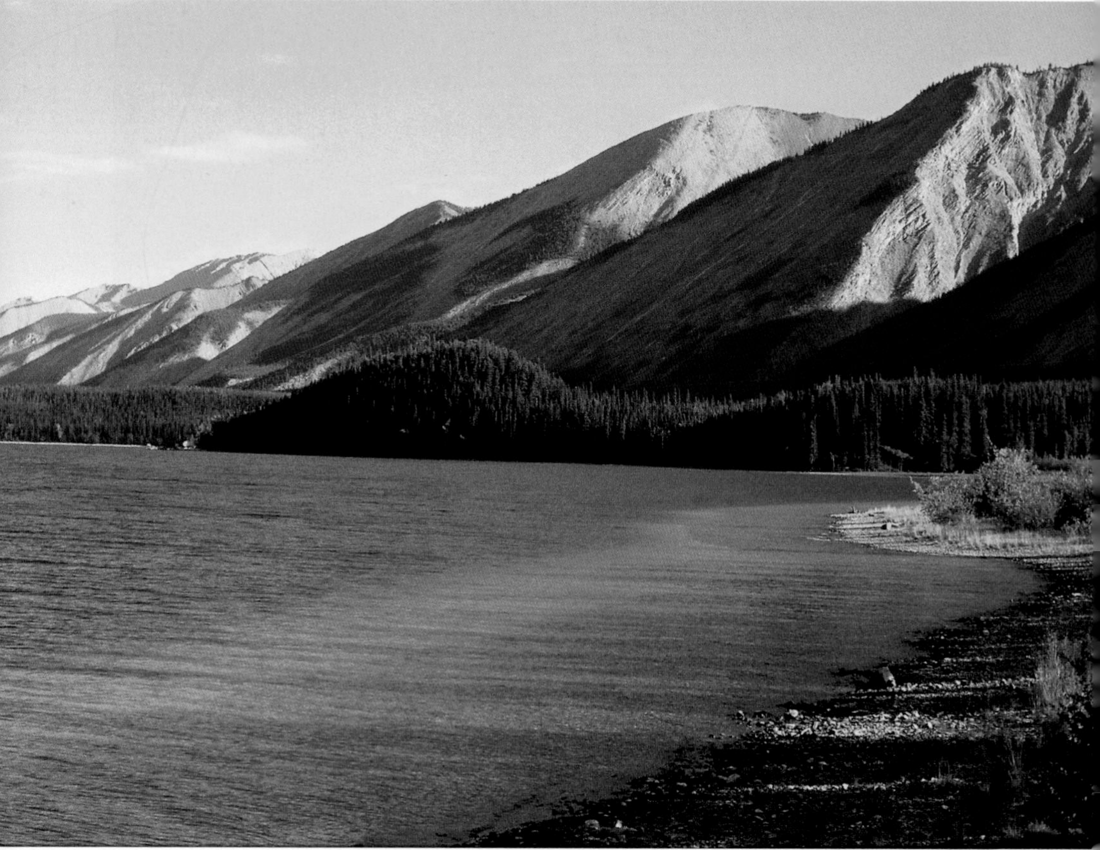

Muncho Lake is among the loveliest places on the Alaska Highway.

MUNCHO LAKE

From Fort Nelson: 153 miles (246 km)
To Watson Lake: 177 miles (285 km)

With the crown of the Rocky Mountains towering above, and the jewel-colored waters of Muncho Lake at roadside, the highway here lies at an elevation of 2,680 feet. The province has developed campgrounds right along the lake. What a wake-up view! Copper oxide leaching into the lake is what creates these dramatic deep greens and blues. Anglers pull in Dolly Varden, rainbows, whitefish, lake trout, and the occasional grayling.

Muncho means "big lake" in Tagish, the aboriginal language. At 7.5 miles (12 km) long, it is one of the largest natural lakes in the Canadian Rockies. To the west lies the Terminal Range. "Terminal" refers to the geographic position of the range—the northernmost section of the Rocky Mountains. Total length of the Rockies is almost 1,850 miles, from here to Santa Fe, New Mexico.

UP TO YOUR NECK IN HOT WATER

Try to make time to visit Liard River Hotsprings Provincial Park, some 42 miles beyond Muncho Lake. If you're planning to spend the night, check in early, as the camp-sites are on a first-come, first-served basis, and they fill up quickly. Interpretive programs about area wildlife and the Liard (pronounced LEE-ard) hot springs attract large numbers of campers each night.

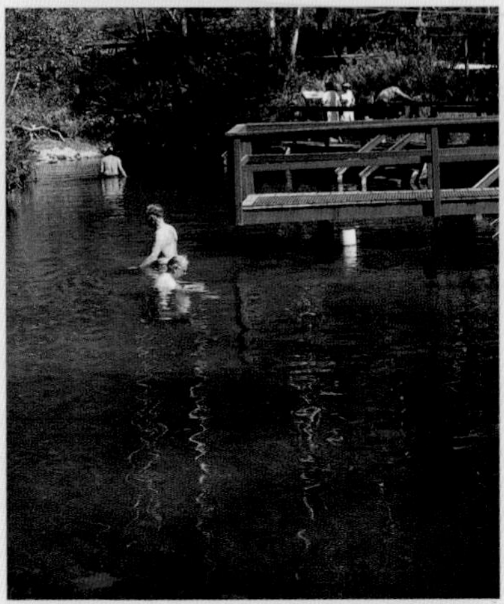

Liard Hotsprings is a favorite rest stop for road-weary travelers. Minimal improvements have been made to keep the springs a natural wonder.

The big draw here: the wondrous hot springs, which lie at the end of a boardwalk that crosses a superheated marsh. On either side of the walk, you can see the slow bubbling action of the mud beneath a clear layer of warm water. At the swimming hole, there are two simple changing rooms with wooden benches and hooks. Outside, more benches and a wooden deck overlook naturally heated pools. Take care on the slippery steps leading into the water. Depending on how hot you like it, you move around to different levels of the pool until you are sufficiently cooked. The experience was heavenly after a day on the road.

This is bear country, and the day we visited, another pool farther up the walkway was closed due to bear activity. A park ranger with a noisy popgun was headed in that direction to encourage the bears to move out. Bears that are regularly fed by humans lose their natural fear and, in fact, become demanding to the point of being dangerous. Many have to be shot simply because they've been "trained" to come to people for food. Signs at the campground read: "A fed bear is a dead bear."

After our wonderful soak, we crossed paths with a black bear—a little fellow that ran across the road at full tilt and headed into the woods on the other side. I remember thinking how awkward he looked, like a guy in a bear suit.

Nearly 175,000 people come through this campground each year, and while it used to be free, there's now a per-person charge for day use. However, no matter how popular it becomes, park ranger Stacy Wall told us, the government will not develop it further. The plan is to keep the boardwalk and campground in good shape, but the rustic facilities will not be enlarged or upgraded. There is no electricity, no running water.

"Trapper Ray's has showers," Stacy said, referring to a private lodge farther down the road. "I live on site and there's no electricity for us, either."

"I have a shower, though," she added, smiling, "because we have to deal with the public, after all."

LODGING/CAMPGROUNDS/MEALS

Muncho Lake is 437 miles (699 km) from Dawson Creek, but its Historical Milepost number is 456. For the locations of the following four businesses, we provide the actual distances from Dawson Creek. However, some of them prefer to use their Historical Milepost distances in advertising. Just be aware that all of these places lie along a 7-mile stretch of road on the eastern shore of the lake.

Double G Service
Mile 436.5 Alaska Highway
250-776-3411
Motel rooms, store, campsites, café. Narrated tours on the lake.

Muncho Lake Provincial Park
Strawberry Flats Campground
Mile 438 Alaska Highway
250-427-5452
15 sites with picnic tables on lakeshore amid spectacular natural beauty. Pit toilets. Swimming, boat launch. Pets on leash.

Northern Rockies Lodge Ltd.
Mile 462 Alaska Highway
1-800-663-5269 or 250-776-3481
www.northern-rockies-lodge.com
45 units in modern log lodge, some wilderness cabins. 35 lakeshore RV sites with full or partial hookups. Laundry, restaurant, bakery, service station. Guided fly-in fishing, photo safari, floatplane service, flightseeing.

Muncho Lake Provincial Park
MacDonald Campground
Mile 438 Alaska Highway
250-427-5452
15 campsites on the lake. Pit toilets, water pump. Swimming, boat launch. Pets on leash.

At Double G Service at the south end of Muncho Lake, you can book a guided, narrated tour on the lake aboard the M/V *Sandpiper*. They offer rooms, campsites, and home-style cooking. Call 250-776-3411 for information. Fishing, rafting, and flightseeing trips are available at various businesses in this stretch of the road, too. See below for details.

Road Notes

The Trout River follows the road beyond Muncho Lake, with swift, clear water that foams over the rapids. For several miles, this part of the highway seems to echo the old days: It's paved, but it's curvy. Left, right, left, right.

Watch for the suspension bridge over the Liard River, built in 1943—the last of its kind on the highway. All others have been replaced in the last six decades.

The must-stop on this section of the road is Liard River Hotsprings at Mile 478 (Historical Mile 469), where drivers can soak in naturally heated mineral waters, wash off a layer of dust, and ease that neck tension. It's an easy stroll from the parking lot along a boardwalk to the springs. Watch for signs of bear—park rangers are vigilant and will notify campers immediately. The Liard River Lodge is right across the highway from the park, if you're looking for a room and a hearty meal (250-776-7349). They're open all year.

The Coal River Lodge, Mile 519 (Km 823), clings to its old address on the early highway: Historical Mile 533. The lodge offers gas, lodging, camping, a laundry, and a pay phone. In the café, order a full breakfast or a buffalo steak or burger, and desserts. Later on down the road, a couple of pullouts provide good views of rapids along the Liard River and of surrounding vistas. In the miles that follow, note several sections of the old Alcan where the former roadbed is buckled, broken, and overgrown with weeds.

Stone sheep may be seen in the Muncho Lake area, where they are drawn to natural salt licks.

At Mile 566 (Km 911), or Historical Mile 588, is Contact Creek, with a plaque that remembers September 24, 1942, a key day in the construction of the Alaska Highway. On that day, soldiers from two regiments, one working from the north and one working from the south, met here. The southern segment of the highway was completed. In 1942, this place was 588 miles (946 km) from Dawson Creek; road improvements now put it 566 miles (911 km) from Dawson Creek. Evidence of the 1982 Eg Fire, which burned more than 400,000 acres, is still visible in the distant regrowth. It was the second-largest fire in the history of British Columbia.

Within a mile you'll enter the Yukon, the first of seven crossings. Just over the line, Contact Creek Lodge sells fuel, coffee, souvenirs, fishing licenses, and groceries; 867-536-2262. They have a wrecker here for 24-hour road help, too.

Construction work at the Hyland River Bridge is finished. There's parking at the north end of the bridge for access to the river. Locals say there's good fishing here for rainbow trout, Dolly Varden, and arctic grayling.

During several recent summers, motorists had to contend with extensive roadwork in these far-north reaches of British Columbia, as a large realignment project was underway. Fortunately, the project is completed and this section is in great shape. If you see large piles of brush alongside the road, that's where land has been cleared for more work.

And, to make things even more challenging for the motorist who pays close attention to kilometerposts, the British Columbia and Yukon governments are not on the same schedule for replacing their roadside signage. While B.C. has upgraded the posts in their reworked portion of the Alaska Highway, the territory is waiting until reconstruction work is finished in their section. So the kilometerposts on the Yukon side are, for now, incorrect. As of 2006, the distance between kilometerposts 967 and 1008, at the B.C.–Yukon border, was off by 40 km.

YUKON TERRITORY

Just before Contact Creek, the Alaska Highway begins a zigzag westerly route, crossing the British Columbia–Yukon border six times before it finally plunges fully into that immense northern territory—home to some 50,000 moose, 160,000 caribou, 10,000 black bears, 4,500 wolves, and 223 species of birds.

The Yukon was made famous by writers such as Jack London and Robert Service, each of whom had firsthand knowledge of this land's stark, gripping beauty in winter, and how its people, flora, and wildlife flourish under the midnight sun in summer. Tourism, mining, forestry, trapping, and fishing remain leading industries. The Yukon River, with its headwaters in British Columbia, flows through the territory for 3,185 km, the second-longest river in Canada.

At Mile 576 (922 km), you'll find Iron Creek Lodge. A motel, RV campground, and café are tucked away in these north woods. Call 867-536-2266. The trees are shorter, with pine and shrubby deciduous trees. Their uniform height suggests regrowth from a great fire some 40 years ago.

YUKON TERRITORY AT A GLANCE

Size: 186,661 square miles or 483,450 square km
Population: 32,212 (as of June 2007)
Capital: Whitehorse
Tourism and Lodging: Tourism Yukon and Culture, 1-800-661-0494 or *wwwtravelyukon.com*
Fishing and Hunting: Environment Yukon, 867-667-5721 or *www.environmentyukon.gov.yk.ca*. Hunters should consult *www.yukonoutfitters.net*.
Government Campgrounds: Parks Branch, Department of Environment, 867-667-5648 or *www.gov.yk.ca*. Stop by any Yukon visitor information center or see *www.travelyukon.com*.
Canada Border Information: 204-983-3500 (outside Canada) or *www.cbsa-asfc.gc.ca*
Road Report: 1-877-456-7623 (in Yukon) or *www.gov.yk.ca/roadreport*

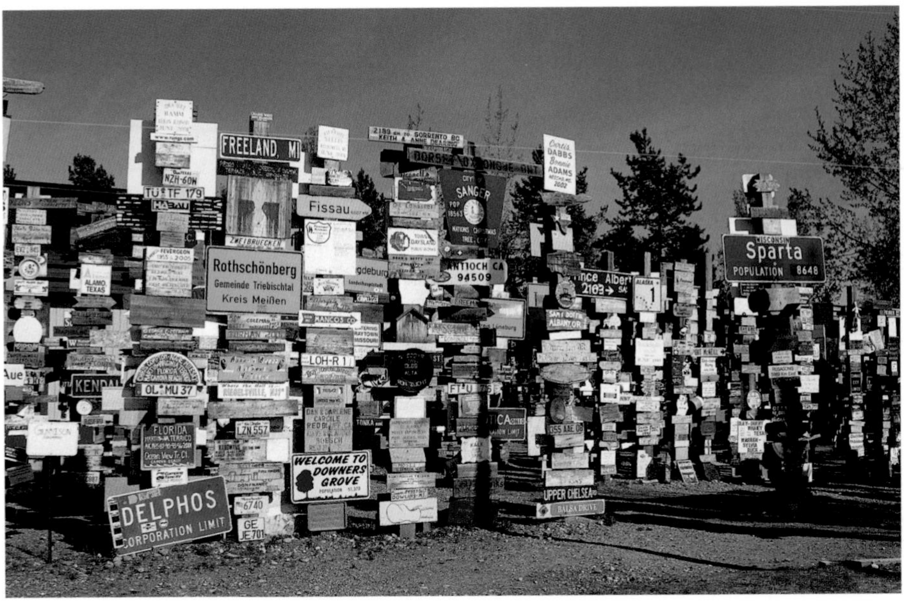

The Watson Lake Signpost Forest began with one sign and today sprawls over acres with signs from all over the world. At the close of the 2006 season, there were 61,398 signs.

WATSON LAKE, Yukon Territory

From Fort Nelson: 330 miles (531 km)
From Muncho Lake: 177 miles (285 km)
To Teslin: 163 miles (262 km)
To Whitehorse: 274 miles (441 km)

Welcome to Canada's Gateway to the Yukon. Driving through Watson Lake, you'll see the Stars and Stripes and the Maple Leaf paired on light-posts down the main drag. That may be a surprising sight to some, but it is reflective of the spirit of cooperation between Canada and the United States, not only in building the Alaska Highway, but also in using it for the last half-century. Watson Lake, population 1,800, also is the junction city for the Alaska Highway and Campbell Highway 4, a northbound unpaved highway.

When the Alcan was under construction, Watson Lake not much more than an air terminal on the Northwest Staging Route, a fueling and maintenance stop for American pilots of war planes on their way to Fairbanks. In the late 1940s, a small town began to grow as Watson Lake was linked to the outside by road and air. Its first residence, Dalziel House, built in 1948, is among a handful of log structures on a walking tour of historical buildings.

Stop by the Alaska Highway Interpretive Centre at the heart of the Watson Lake Signpost Forest (see sidebar) for information about the birth of the signpost forest and to see a small exhibit that details the building of the Alcan in pictures and artifacts. A film on the road's construction is worthwhile. You'll also enjoy a free cup of coffee, clean restrooms, and lots of printed material on towns and attractions still ahead. The centre's hosts are friendly and knowledgeable.

Across the highway, check out the Northern Lights Centre, decorated outside with banners that simulate the aurora borealis. Inside, learn about the myth and science behind the phenomenon. Electric sky theater shows six times daily until early September. Contact 403-536-7827 or *www.northernlightscentre.ca.*

The town's recreation department maintains 18 multiuse trails in and around Watson Lake. They are color-coded with green, for the beginner level, to blue for intermediate, and black for advanced. Call (867) 536-2246 with your questions.

Truck and RV service and repairs are available in Watson Lake. You can also arrange to go fishing, take a helicopter ride, or play nine holes of golf at Greenway's Greens, Yukon's first golf course to support grass greens. Full rentals are available, and a tee-time is not required. Call (867) 536-2477. Watson Lake's local shops sell art and jewelry pieces in gold, jade, and ivory.

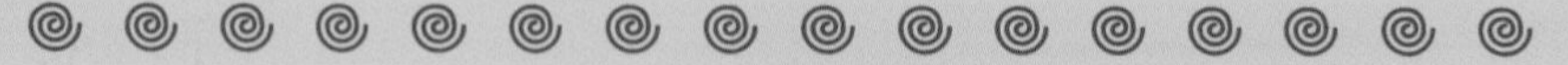

"I WAS HERE"

The Watson Lake Signpost Forest began with a single sign placed by Carl K. Lindley, an Illinois soldier, during construction of the Alaska Highway. By 1978, when I first came by this place, the addition of signs through the years had expanded to cover a row of telephone poles at a gravel pullout along the gravel road. (And we were covered in gravel dust!) Each pole was studded with signs from all corners of the world, placed there by passersby as the Signpost Forest had gained notoriety.

Today's forest is astonishing in its size, poles studding the grounds in all directions, in rows that make up walkways. By 2006, there were more than 61,398 signs, and the annual gain was accelerating. There is so much to see that it's hard to take in all of the colors, words, and messages that were meaningful to somebody, somewhere, at some time in this road's history.

If you're planning to drive the highway, be sure to bring along a sign—hopefully not ill-begotten from your hometown's city limits!—but something durable to show where you're from or who you are. The folks inside the Alaska Highway Interpretive Centre will direct you on where to add your sign, and you can view photos of that soldier Carl K. Lindley, who returned to Watson Lake for the Alaska Highway's 50th anniversary in 1992. Seeing what he'd started, he was nearly speechless.

The signpost forest, as garish as it is, has become a living testament to the road travelers, a guest book for people who want to tell the world: I WAS HERE.

LODGING

Please browse www.yukonbandb.com to locate a bed-and-breakfast.

Air Force Lodge
Adela Trail at south end of town
867-536-2890
Comfortable, quiet rooms in restored historic building.

Belvedere Motor Hotel
On the Alaska Highway
867-536-7712 / *www.watsonlakehotels.com*
48 rooms, suites, cable TV, whirlpools, in-room coffee. Cocktail lounge, coffee shop, dining room.

Big Horn Hotel
On Frank Trail, 1 block south of Alaska Highway in Watson Lake
867-536-2020
www.yukonweb.com/tourism/bighorn
29 rooms, wheelchair-accessible suite, kitchenettes, Jacuzzi rooms. Cable TV, phones, coffee.

Cedar Lodge Motel
Junction of Adela Trail and Stubenberg Boulevard
867-536-7406 / *www.cedarlodge.yk.net*
12 rooms, suites, kitchenettes, in-room coffee.

Gateway Motor Inn
Junction of Frank Trail and 8th Street South
867-536-7744 / *www.watsonlakehotels.com*
50 rooms, kitchenettes, in-room coffee. Restaurant.

Watson Lake Hotel
Next to Signpost Forest
867-536-7781 / *www.watsonlakehotels.com*
48 rooms, suites in historic building, nonsmoking available. Satellite TV, sauna. Coffee shop, dining room. Senior discount.

CAMPGROUNDS

Baby Nugget RV Park
Nugget City
Historic Mile 650, west of Watson Lake
867-536-2307
Pull-throughs, 15-, 30-, and 50-amp service. Room for big rigs. Modem access, laundry, RV wash. Restaurant, bakery, gift shop. Gold panning, hiking, fishing.

Campground Services
Mile 632 Alaska Highway
867-536-7448
140 full and partial hookups. Laundry, food mart, RV wash, RV repairs, fuel.

Downtown RV Park
Lakeview Avenue and 8th Street north, at center of town
867-536-2646
Full hookups, pull-throughs, showers, laundry, RV wash. Walking distance to shopping, restaurants, visitor information.

Junction 37 RV Park
Mile 659 Alaska Highway
867-536-2794
Full hookups, 30-amp service, some pull-throughs, showers, laundry. Restaurant, gift shop, store, saloon, gas, diesel, propane.

Watson Lake Recreation Park (Provincial Campground)
2.5 miles (4 km) west of town center via Alaska Highway
55 RV and tent campsites, 12 pull-throughs, hiking, kitchen shelter. Playground, trails, swimming, fishing.

RESTAURANTS

Bee Jay's Café
Adela Trail near 3rd Avenue
867-536-2335
Full menu, lunch and dinner specials. Pastries, bread, ice cream.

Belvedere Motor Hotel
On the Alaska Highway
867-536-7712
www.watsonlakehotels.com
Hotel restaurant with full service dining room and coffee shop.

Gateway Motor Inn
Junction of Frank Trail and 8th Street South
867-536-7744
www.watsonlakehotels.com
Pizza Palace take-out available; full-service restaurant and lounge.

Watson Lake Tags
Corner of Alaska and Campbell Highways
867-536-7422
Breakfast, lunch, dinner, baked goods. Dine in or take-out.

Wolf It Down Restaurant & Bakery
Nugget City
Historic Mile 650 Alaska Highway
867-536-2307
Breakfast, lunch, dinner, baked goods. Dine in or take-out.

Road Notes

West of Watson Lake on the Alaska Highway is the junction with Canada Highway 37, which leads southbound to Dease Lake and the Cassiar Highway. This is the way to the coastal communities of Stewart, B.C., and Hyder, Alaska. Travelers in early summer months of 2007 reported that a rainy spring in the western reaches of British Columbia had resulted in poor road conditions and some slide areas. Call ahead for road conditions to save yourself some time and frustration. Check *www.drivebc.ca* or call 900-451-4977 and, for a fee, you'll get a comprehensive, up-to-date report. (See the section on the Yellowhead-Cassiar Highways in Chapter 7, Western Canada's Northbound Byways.)

As you journey north, you'll see another form of the signpost forest idea on the slopes along the highway. For the past twenty years, "natural" graffiti artists have been writing messages using lines of small rocks.

Several day-use or recreation sites and viewpoints can be found in the beautiful miles between Watson Lake and Teslin. Rancheria Falls Recreation Site at Mile 695 (1,118.5 km) is a park-and-rest area with a boardwalk trail that leads to a waterfall.

About 3 miles farther along is the Continental Divide, and as you approach this point, the peaks become sharper and more crowded. At the crossing, a pullout includes signs with points of interest, maps, and outhouses. There are several lodges and visitor services through this section of the road. On the way to Teslin, the highway moves in gentle, winding curves through forest. Just before Teslin, you'll cross the longest bridge on the Alaska Highway, the Nisutlin Bay Bridge, which spans the Nisutlin River where it enters Teslin Lake. This is a gorgeous body of water—narrow, but long: 86 miles (138 km).

TESLIN

From Watson Lake: 163 miles (262 km)
To Whitehorse: 111 miles (179 km)

Teslin is an Inland Tlingit village of fewer than 500 people, many of whom are related to members of the Alaskan coastal Tlingit tribes. Although it is a small town, it offers much in the way of visitor services. You'll find a couple of major motels with in-house restaurants and lounges, groceries and general merchandise, RV parks, gift shops, and a trading post. Teslin's two cultural museums are good reasons to linger in this little town, and both have ample parking for RVs. At the Teslin Tlingit Heritage Center, you will come away knowing much more about the culture, traditions, and lifestyles of this unique people. Outstanding totem pole carvings are on display outside. Open May through September, the museum can be reached at 867-390-2526. And the George Johnston Museum & Heritage Park is named for an exceptionally resourceful Tlingit man who lived from 1884 to 1972. Learn more about Johnston, Teslin, and the area's natural and cultural history. It is operated by the Teslin Historical Museum Society. Call 867-390-2550 or see *www.gjmuseum.yk.net*.

Squanga Lake at sunset. We stayed at the government campground; like others throughout the Yukon, it presents less expensive, but more primitive camping.

LODGING/CAMPGROUNDS/MEALS

Dawson Peaks Resort & RV Park
Mile 770 Alaska Highway
1-866-402-2244 or 867-390-2310
www.yukonweb.com/tourism/dawsonpeaks
Lakefront cabins with private baths and decks. Campsites with pull-throughs, water, dump station, fire pits, showers. Tenting area. Free firewood. Restaurant, gift shop, fishing charters, boat rentals.

Teslin Lake Provincial Campground
Mile 783 Alaska Highway
27 RV and tent sites, 6 pull-throughs, hand-pump water, shelter, boat launch, fishing.

Yukon Motel and RV Park
Mile 804 Alaska Highway
867-390-2575
www.yukonmotel.com
Rooms with satellite TV. 40 pull-through RV sites with full hookups, RV wash, fuel. Restaurant, lounge, gift shop, liquor store. Fishing charters. Wildlife gallery of mounted animals.

Road Notes

A longtime landmark business 9 miles (14.5 km) north of Teslin, Mukluk Annie's Salmon Bake offers all-you-can-eat meals, motel rooms, cabins, free camping, and free RV wash. Call 867-390-2600.

A mile later, you'll cross the Teslin River Bridge, which is 1,770 feet (539.5 m) long and high enough to accommodate the steamers that once navigated the river between Whitehorse

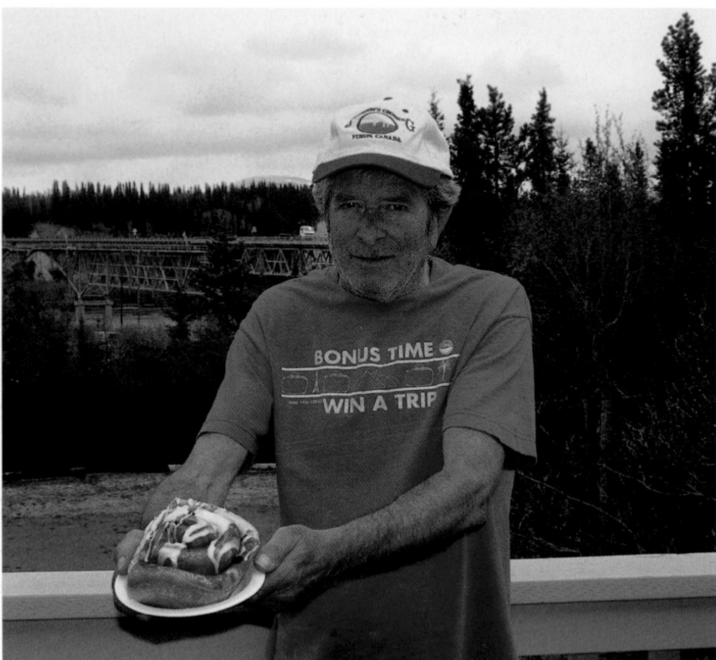

Johnson's Crossing, across from the Teslin River bridge claims its cinnamon buns are world famous.

and Teslin. At the north end of the bridge, Johnson's Crossing offers camping opportunities, as well as souvenir shopping, fishing, canoeing, and wildlife-watching. Johnson's Crossing Campground Services, across from the Teslin River bridge, claims that its cinnamon buns are world famous. They also offer deli items, camping, laundry, fuel, and fishing licenses. Foot-long grayling run in the river here from spring to late fall. Call 867-390-2607.

One year, we chose to camp at Squanga Lake, a Yukon government campground at Mile 821 (1,366 km). We'd heard there's good fishing for northern pike, grayling, burbot, rainbow trout, and whitefish (which are called *squanga* in the local Native language). The setting sun cast a brilliant pink across the sky and the lake's surface, silhouetting the spruce trees in black. That late-August night was dark, superbly quiet, and cool—a great combination for sleepy travelers. The next morning we saw (and heard) loons out on the lake in the rain. Another provincial campground, Marsh Lake, lies ahead about 40 miles (64 km). It offers 41 sites, including some pull-throughs, on a gravel loop road near the lake. Like other Yukon Government campgrounds, it's well-maintained and campers can build a nice fire for making s'mores. Not a whole lot of other amenities, but the $12 per night price tag can't be beat.

Farther up the highway comes an opportunity for an exciting side trip to the historic Alaska community of Skagway. To drive there, leave the Alaska Highway at Jake's Corner (Mile 874.5) and go west on Yukon Highway 8 for 34 miles (55 km) to Carcross and Klondike Highway 2. Skagway is then a scenic 66 miles (106 km) to the south. For details on the highway and on the history, attractions, lodging, and restaurants of Skagway, see the section on Klondike Highway 2 in Chapter 8, Alaska's State Highways.

WHITEHORSE

From Watson Lake, Yukon: 274 miles (441 km)
From Teslin, Yukon: 111 miles (179 km)
To Haines Junction, Yukon: 98 miles (158 km)
To Alaska–Yukon border: 303 miles (488 km)

The beautiful capital of the Yukon Territory is situated on the banks of the Yukon River, along the route of the stampeders who were headed for the goldfields more than a century ago. One of the city's landmarks is a lovely giant: the 210-foot SS *Klondike,* a restored paddle wheeler that is dry-docked on the west bank of the Yukon. Named a National Historic Site, the *Klondike* is a tangible reminder of this region's history—a retired workhorse left from a fleet of more than 250 riverboats that reigned in transportation until construction of the highway. Restored to its 1937–1940 appearance, the *Klondike* remains a figure of elegance and grace. Come aboard for a tour of the decks, cargo holds, and passenger accommodations; RV parking, a gift shop, and a visitor center are located nearby.

More than 24,000 people live in Whitehorse year-round, and it also serves as the economic base for outlying communities. This is an economy that was built on mining and transportation services, and those industries remain important, along with tourism and government. Major airlines connect Whitehorse to the rest of the world, and the Alaska Highway brings thousands of visitors to its doorstep, mostly during the summer.

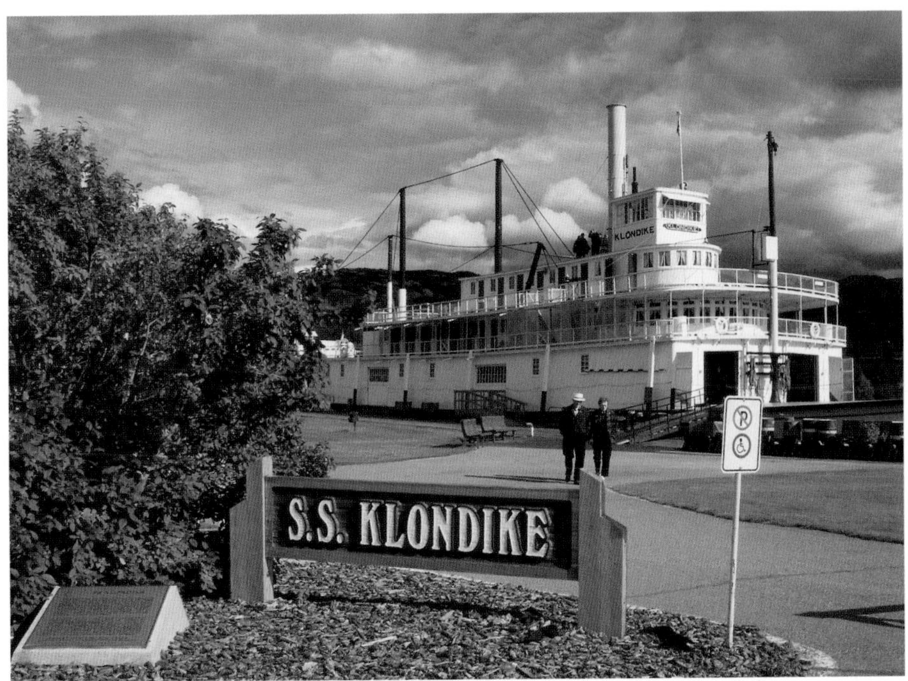

The Yukon River stern-wheeler *Klondike* in Whitehorse has been lovingly restored.

For the Klondike stampeders on the Trail of '98, Miles Canyon near Whitehorse represented one of the most treacherous passages on the Yukon River. A suspension footbridge over the river leads to the site of what was a gold-rush town.

As is the case in other far north cities, living in Whitehorse sometimes means sharing the streets with wildlife. As we drove through a Whitehorse neighborhood, we spotted a small family of coyotes trotting across mowed lawns. One of the local constables said he'd seen them often, that they were part of the urban landscape. Almost every morning, he said, they were out and about at the same early hour. You could almost set your clock by them.

The Visitor Information Centre, at 100 Hanson Street, offers films, advice, and printed materials on attractions throughout the area, as well as maps and displays. There's easy access for RV parking, and it's a good place to plan your day. For the active set, you'll find directions to golfing, fishing, nature hikes, trail rides, swimming, biking, canoeing, kayaking, and more. French and German speakers are on site. Call (867) 667-3084.

Downtown Whitehorse retains much of its old-time charm, with log structures and false-front buildings sharing city blocks with more modern stores and offices. Learn about local characters and the city's history, and view architectural marvels such as the Old Log Church at 3rd Avenue and Elliott Street, built in 1900, and now a museum housing artifacts from early Northern missionary and whaling history. Ask about the Bishop who ate his boots! For information, call 867-668-2555.

A hydroelectric dam built in 1958 created Schwatka Lake, which is now a floatplane base. Beneath this stretch of deep water, there still exists the boulder-strewn river bottom once known as Whitehorse Rapids. The town was named after those rapids—the plumes of foamy water were as white as the mane of a white horse. For gold seekers on the trail to the Klondike, this was the most perilous stretch of the Yukon River. Ill-prepared stampeders had to maneuver through the rapids, often aboard homemade boats that shattered against the rocks. Those who were successful were next met with the Devil's Punchbowl, a swirling mess of confused current, then the roaring water and hundred-foot sheer rock walls of Miles Canyon. After such a frightening river run, shaken and no doubt relieved, the miners often pulled ashore to dry out their goods and rest.

Entrepreneurs arrived with the miners, eager to find ways to make money without digging in the ground. In 1897 two men devised a way around the natural obstacles by building tramways on either side of the rapids and canyon. During a short-lived boom, a tent city called Canyon City sprang up, with businesses such as a saloon and roadhouse to further mine the pockets of the thousands who passed through. North-West Mounted Police arrived to maintain order as more than 20,000 stampeders used this gateway to the Klondike.

The historic site of Canyon City is accessible by walking trail, and interpretive signs mark the way. To get there, take Miles Canyon Road from Mile 910 (Km 1,465)

of the Alaska Highway. At the lookout, enjoy a spectacular view, then drive down to the suspended footbridge and walk over the bridge to the site where Canyon City once stood.

With completion of the White Pass & Yukon Route railway on July 29, 1900, miners could travel in comfort to a point beyond the rapids. However, by then all claims had been staked and the rush was in decline. The little railway was called into service during the construction of the Alaska Highway in 1942. The U.S. Army leased the railway and it became a main transportation corridor for supplies arriving by ship in Skagway en route to Whitehorse, the halfway mark between Dawson Creek and Fairbanks. Although the WP&YR no longer offers rail service between Skagway and Whitehorse, the communities are still connected by combination train/bus service between May and September. The historic depot stands on First Avenue near the river in downtown Whitehorse. The White Pass & Yukon Route remains the only operating narrow-gauge railroad in North America, and riding in the restored railcars is a rare treat. For tickets and reservations for daily departures in combination train and motor coach service to Skagway, call 1-800-343-7373 or 867-668-RAIL; see *www.wpyr.com.*

MacBride Museum, at 1st Avenue and Wood Street, provides mining displays, natural history, First Nations culture, artifacts from the gold rush, and geology of the area. Exhibits teach about different kinds of gold deposits, where they are found, and how they are taken from the ground. You can pan for gold here, too. Call 867-667-2709 or see *www.macbridemuseum.com.*

The Yukon Trappers Association operates a store in Whitehorse, offering snowshoes, moosehide slippers, and tanned furs.

Yukon Beringia Interpretive Centre, at Mile 915 (1,473 km) on the Alaska Highway, features prehistory displays that offer insight into a time when this land belonged to mastodons, saber-toothed cats, and lions. Call 867-667-8855 or see *www.beringia.com*. The Yukon Transportation Museum, next to the Beringia Centre, features displays on the various modes of transportation used on the Trail of '98, then and now, from snowshoes to dog-sleds and paddleboats and trains. Murals painted by Yukon artists serve as backdrops. Call 867-668-4792 or see *www.yukontransportationmuseum.com*

The Yukon First Nations Tourism Association invites visitors to learn more about the 14 ancient cultures of this region. Art, dancing, storytelling, and drumming are often part of important annual events such as the Moosehide Gathering, held every other year in Dawson City, and the International Storytelling Festival, held in Whitehorse each June. Visitors are always welcome. Many museums and interpretive centers share the stories and artifacts of the First Nations people. To gather more information on cultural tourism opportunities, visit YFNTA's Web site at *www.yfnta.org*.

The Frantic Follies has entertained audiences since 1970, so we expected a corny, tired stage show. Instead we discovered a first-class vaudeville show by talented performers. On the bill: ragtime piano, can-can girls, red-hot-mama singing, banjo extravaganzas, magic, family-oriented comedy—and some wild Robert Service poetry. You've never heard "The Cremation of Sam McGee" quite like this. The revue shows nightly from mid-May through mid-September. The box office is in the Westmark Whitehorse, 2nd Avenue and Steele Street. You also can make advance reservations through 867-668-2042, or see *www.francticfollies.com*.

The Whitehorse Fishway features the world's longest wooden fish ladder and three underwater viewing windows. Watch the migration of the Yukon River chinook salmon and other species, including trout and arctic grayling. The aquarium and fishway is open from June through August, and admission is free. Take 2nd Avenue from downtown, cross the bridge over the Yukon River to Lewes Boulevard, then follow the signs to Nisutlin Drive and the fish ladder. Call 867-633-5965.

One of the most popular river excursions is aboard the M/V *Schwatka*, which offers a 2-hour cruise that begins at Schwatka Lake. The dock is 5 minutes from the city center via Miles Canyon Road on the north side of town. Just follow the signs. The lake serves as a floatplane base, so you'll see lots of traffic in the air and on the water. The route takes you through Devil's Punchbowl and into Miles Canyon. You can wave to the foot traffic above you on the Robert Lowe Suspension Bridge. Points of interest include an old fox farm and the historic site of Canyon City. An evening dinner cruise is available as well. The trip is popular, so advance tickets are recommended. Call 867-668-4716.

Takhini Hot Springs, with its naturally heated outdoor swimming pool, is a star attraction any time of year, but it's especially popular when the temperature drops below freezing. To get there, drive several miles north of Whitehorse, turn right onto the North Klondike Highway (Highway 2), and follow it for about 4 miles to the turnoff to the hot springs; follow the 6-mile spur road to the west. Out of the ground, the source water is 117°F, so it is mixed with cool water to maintain a temperature around 100°F for the swimming pool. While it is rich in minerals such as calcium, magnesium, and iron, no sulfur is present to foul the air or your swimsuit. A café, campground, climbing wall, zip line, and horseback riding are also on the rounds. Call (867) 456-8000 or see *www.takhinihotsprings.yk.ca.*

Local shopping is an adventure unto itself. Customized gold-nugget jewelry is a regional specialty, and several shops will sell you raw nuggets or fashion a piece just for you. Check along Main Street as you prospect for your own gold.

Yukon Gallery is the showcase and shopping outlet for original art, prints, pottery, and crafts, as well as fine jewelry. The gallery is at the corner of Lambert and 2nd Avenue downtown, across from the Visitor Reception Centre (*www.yukongallery.ca*). Or stop by North End Gallery, at 1st Avenue and Steele Street (867-393-3590), for scrimshaw, Inuit sculpture, and other original art. Your art purchases may be shipped anywhere in the world. The Yukon Trappers Association operates a retail outlet at 4194A Fourth Avenue. Aside from trapping supplies and tanned furs, they offer finished items, such as beaded moosehide slippers, fur hats, old-style snowshoes and smaller gift items. Many of their items are handmade by First Nations people. Call 867-667-7091 or e-mail yukonfur@yknet.ca.

Whitehorse is either the starting or finish line every February during the annual running of the Yukon Quest International Sled Dog Race, one of two major long-distance races in the Far North that attract competitors from all over the world. At the other end of the race's grueling 1,000 miles is Fairbanks, Alaska. To learn more about the race, see *www.yukonquest.com* or to shop for memorabilia, visit *www.yukonqueststore.com.*

Services and parts for autos and RVs are available in Whitehorse. Twenty-four-hour cash machines may be found at banks all along Main Street. The Thomas Cook Foreign Exchange, 2101A 2nd Avenue, is open from 8 A.M. to 8 P.M., seven days a week during summer.

For information on city attractions and services, write the City of Whitehorse, 2121 2nd Avenue, Whitehorse, Yukon, Canada Y1A 1C2, or call 867-668-TOUR. Their Web site can be found at *www.city.whitehorse.yk.ca* or *www.travelyukon.com.*

LODGING

Please browse www.yukonbandb.com to locate a bed-and-breakfast.

98 Hotel
110 Wood Street
867-667-2641
Popular historic building dating from the 1940s, converted into a hotel and bar.

202 Motor Inn
206 Jarvis Street
867-668-4567
32 rooms, dining room, lounge with entertainment. Discount for miners.

Airline Inn Hotel
16 Burns Road (across from the airport)
867-668-4400
30 rooms, some kitchenettes, laundry, lounge, restaurant. Adjacent to convenience store and gas station.

Airport Chalet
91634 Alaska Highway
867-668-2166
29 units, offering gas, diesel, RV dump, and self-service laundry for guests. Restaurant and lounge.

Best Western Gold Rush Inn
411 Main Street
867-668-4500 / *www.goldrushinn.com*
106 deluxe rooms, suites, spas, barber shop, beauty salon, laundry and dry-cleaning services. Restaurant and lounge.

Bonanza Inn
4109 4th Avenue
867-668-4545 / *www.bonanzainn.com*
52 rooms, some kitchenettes, TV, wheelchair accessible. Dining facility.

Capital Hotel
103 Main Street
867-667-2565 / *www.capitalhotel–yukon.com*
17 rooms in historic downtown setting, restaurant, entertainment.

Casa Loma Motel
1802 Centennial, Mile 921 Alaska Highway
867-633-2266
28 rooms, some kitchenettes, phone, TV, wheelchair access. Dining.

Chilkoot Trail Inn
4190 4th Avenue
867-668-4190
32 rooms, some kitchenettes.

The Edgewater Hotel
101 Main Street
1-877-484-3334 or 867-667-2572
www.edgewaterhotel.yk.ca
30 deluxe rooms and suites, restaurant. Cable TV, Internet, coffee, hair dryers. Downtown location.

High Country Inn
4051 4th Avenue
1-800-554-4471 or 867-667-4471
www.highcountryinn.ca
Jacuzzi or executive suites and kitchenettes with view. Cable TV, free coffee, hair dryer, irons and boards, laundry. Downtown location.

Mountain Ridge Motel & RV Park
Mile 912 Alaska Highway
867-667-4202 / *www.mtnridge.ca*
Clean units with TV, wireless Internet. Close to downtown.

Pioneer Inn
2141 2nd Avenue
867-668-2828
Hotel in downtown location; restaurant on site.

River View Hotel
102 Wood Street
867-667-7801
www.riverviewhotel.ca
Comfortable rooms, cable TV, free coffee, hair dryers. Indoor parking for bicycles and motorcycles. English, German, French spoken. Walking distance to shopping, attractions.

Stop In Family Hotel
314 Ray Street
867-668-5558
44 air-conditioned rooms in full-service hotel. Laundry, hair salon, sauna, hot tub. Close to shopping and Yukon River.

Stratford Motel
401 Jarvis Street
867-667-4243
50 budget units, some kitchenettes, wheelchair access, laundry.

Town & Mountain Hotel
401 Main Street
1-800-661-0522 or 867-668-7644
www.townmountain.com
30 executive-style suites, fridges, microwaves, irons and boards. Cable TV, parking, restaurant.

Westmark Klondike Inn
2288 2nd Avenue
1-800-544-0970 or 867-668-4747
www.westmarkhotels.com
99 deluxe rooms, suites. Gift shop, restaurant, lounge.

Westmark Whitehorse Hotel & Conference Centre
201 Wood Street
1-800-544-0970 or 867-393-9700
www.westmarkhotels.com
180 deluxe rooms, suites. Gift shop, restaurant, lounge, box office of *The Frantic Follies.*

The Yukon Inn
4220 4th Avenue
1-800-661-0454 or 867-667-2527
www.yukoninn.yk.ca
98 luxury guest rooms, suites, kitchenettes. Laundry, dry cleaning, hair salon, office services, winter plug-ins. Gift shop, exercise facilities. Café, two lounges, big-screen TVs. Walking distance to local attractions. Handicap access.

AREA CAMPGROUNDS

WHITEHORSE:
Hi Country RV Park
91374 Alaska Highway
1-877-458-3806 or 867-667-7445
www.hicountryrvyukon.com
130 roomy, treed sites with power. Showers, self-service laundry, cable TV, store, gift shop. Close to downtown. French and German spoken.

Mountain Ridge Motel & RV Park
Mile 912 Alaska Highway
867-667-4202
Full and partial hookups, pull-throughs, store, Internet access, shower, sani-dump. French spoken.

Robert Service Campground
120 Robert Service Way
867-668-3721
www.robertservicecampground.com
68 treed sites along the Yukon River with showers, water, store, barbecue, playground. Close to downtown. French and German spoken.

NORTH OF WHITEHORSE:
Takhini Hot Springs
Mile 6 (Km 10) Hotsprings Road
(867) 456-8000
www.takhinihotsprings.yk.ca
88 treed sites, with 15- and 30-amp service, full and partial hookups. Sani-dump, showers, water, store, café. Horseback riding, swimming, hiking, sauna. Climbing wall and zip line.

OUTSIDE OF WHITEHORSE:
Caribou RV Park
Mile 904 Alaska Highway
14 miles (22.5 km) south of downtown Whitehorse
867-668-2961 / *www.caribou-rv-park.com*
47 treed sites with power, satellite TV, free wireless, car wash, sani-station, laundry, fire pits, tent camping available. Wolf's Den Restaurant on site.

MacKenzie's RV Park
18 Azure Road, junction of Alaska Highway and Azure
867-633-2337
79 spacious sites with full or partial hookups; 22 tent sites. Cable hookup, modem, showers, laundry, store. Playground, horseshoe pit, free gold panning. Wheelchair access. Vehicle wash. On city bus route.

Pioneer RV Park
Historic Mile 911 Alaska Highway
Actual: Mile 879 (Km 1,415)
1-866-626-7383 or 867-668-5944
www.pioneer-rv-park.com
150 sites, including full and partial hookup, some pull-throughs. Showers, laundry, restrooms, store, gift shop. Car and RV wash, some automotive services, windshield chip repairs. Tickets and reservations for local attractions.

Wolf Creek Government Campground and Recreation Site
Mile 875 (Km 1,408) Alaska Highway
40 RV and tent sites, 11 tent-only sites. Hand-pump water, shelters, playground, trails.

RESTAURANTS

The Cellar Steakhouse & Wine Bar
101 Main Street, in Edgewater Hotel
1-877-484-3334 or 867-667-2572
Fine dining, specializing in salmon, crab, halibut, arctic char, prime rib.

Cheechako's Sourdough Steakhouse
204B Main Street
867-393-2555
www.cheechakos.com
Steaks, seafood, salads, and more.

China Garden
301 Jarvis Street
867-668-2899
Chinese and Western menus; lunch buffet, dinners, take-out.

The Chocolate Claim
305 Strickland Street
867-667-2202
Soups, salads, sandwiches, coffee bar.

City's Steak and Pizza House
4092 Quartz Road
867-667-4963
Steaks, pizza, pasta, and more.

Cranberry Bistro
302 Wood Street
867-456-4898

G & P Steak House & Pizza
Mile 918 Alaska Highway
867-668-4708
Greek and Italian specialties, seafood, pasta.

Iron Horse Grill
151 Industrial Road, Unit 3
867-668-7871

Casual dining

Klondike Rib & Salmon BBQ
2116 2nd Avenue, across from Westmark Whitehorse
867-667-7554
Fresh local fish, Yukon-style BBQ ribs, caribou and musk ox Stroganoff.

La Gourmandise
4121 4th Avenue
867-456-4127
Fine dining, French and other world cuisines. Sunday brunch and dinner.

Legends Smokehouse & Grill
Inside the Yukon Inn
4220 4th Avenue
1-800-661-0454 or 867-667-2527
Dining in convenient downtown location.

Pandas European Dining
212 Main Street
867-667-2632
European fine dining, without the dress code. Northern seafood specialties, steaks, schnitzels, pasta.

Pasta Palace
201 Main Street
867-667-6888
Full selection of pastas and sauces.

Sam 'n' Andy's Tex Mex Bar & Grill
506 Main Street
867-668-6994
Mexican and Canadian food; outdoor patio.

Sourdough Clint's Pancake House
102 Wood Street
867-667-2292
Specializing in breakfast, with full lunch and dinner menu. Downtown.

Steele Street Restaurant and Lounge
201 Wood Street, in the Westmark Whitehorse
867-393-9747
Daily lunch and dinner specials. Arctic char, cedar plank salmon, locally brewed ales and beers.

Tim Hortons
Two locations:
2101B 2nd Avenue
2210 2nd Avenue
Eat in or take-out; soups and sandwiches; donuts and other pastries.

Tung Lock Chinese Restaurant
404 Wood Street
867-668-3298
Casual dining, specializing in seafood, daily lunch and weekend dinner buffets.

Yukon Meat & Sausage Deli
203 Hanson Street
867-667-7583
Homemade smoked sausages, homemade lunches from 11 A.M. to 3 P.M. Cheese and international grocery items.

Yukon Mining Company
4051 4th Avenue, in the High Country Inn
867-667-4471
Salmon, halibut, wild game. Barbecue on the deck, local beer specialties.

Road Notes

Just north of Whitehorse, the Alaska Highway connects with the North Klondike Highway (Highway 2), which heads north to Dawson City. (See the section on the North Klondike Highway in Chapter 7, Western Canada's Northbound Byways.)

It's 98 miles (158 km) between Whitehorse and Haines Junction. In 1958, more than 1.5 million acres of forest burned in this region, and even now you can still see evidence of that fire in the landscape around you.

More homes along the roadside are decorated with caribou antlers and moose horns. You'll see more log cabins, more outbuildings, and places where homeowners have something of a collection on their property. While some might call this "junk," people of the North call it "storage" that's defended with: "You never know when I might need this." The blue tarp—more essential here, it seems, than many points south—often covers broken appliances, or a woodpile, or inoperable equipment that truly is of value to its owner.

About halfway to Haines Junction, the road used to pass through the First Nations village of Champagne. The highway was rerouted in the last decade, and that surely brought traffic relief for this tiny community. A turnoff leads to the town now. Travelers are asked to be respectful of the villagers' private property and of their cemetery, which is not open to visitors. If you'd like to learn more about the Champagne-Aishihik Indian Band, see *www.cafn.ca* or call 867-634-4200. Dry camping is available for RV travelers who wish to overnight at Champagne.

Pay close attention to the junction at Haines Junction, at Mile 985 (1,585 km). To continue on the Alaska Highway, you must make a right turn, the first in many miles. Hundreds of wayward travelers have ignored the turn and ended up instead on Highway 3, heading south toward Haines, Alaska, instead of north toward Fairbanks. In the last decade, Canadian customs officials at the border before Haines reported more than 1,000 irate wrong-turners, even though signs at the intersection have gotten bigger. (See the section on the Haines Highway in Chapter 8, Alaska's State Highways.)

Historic Milepost 1061 is the site of Soldiers Summit, where the highway was officially opened during a ceremony on November 20, 1942. It was –35°F.

After Haines Junction, the Alaska Highway crosses Bear Creek Summit, elevation 3,294 feet (1,004 m), and Boutillier Summit, elevation 3,293 feet (1,003 m), en route to the picturesque Kluane Lake. The Alaska Highway skirts this vast and beautiful body of water for more than 60 miles (96.5 km), making this drive worthy of a few extra lines in your travel journal. Extensive road repairs were underway in 2006 and 2007 with pilot cars leading traffic through the busiest work sections.

On the way to the communities of Destruction Bay and Burwash Landing (where all services are available), take a few minutes to pull over at Mile 1,061 (1,707.5 km), the historical wayside for Soldiers Summit. A trail from the parking lot leads to the site of the Alaska Highway's official opening ceremonies, on November 20, 1942. Depending on whether road work is still in progress, signage may or may not be present. Try to imagine how, at this location, officers in full-dress uniforms (with inadequate footwear) endured deep cold and snow while officials made grand speeches and cut the ribbon. Another ceremony here in 1992 celebrated the highway's 50th anniversary.

Unlike the Alcan's early years, today it's easy to find motels, lodges, campgrounds, and restaurants from Haines Junction to Beaver Creek, which lies ahead. Gas and other services

The World's Largest Gold Pan resides outside the Kluane Museum of Natural History.

---

are available, too. While many miles through the Yukon may appear wild and unsettled, help is never far away. Small communities along these miles can meet most of your service and shopping needs.

A forest fire in 1999 blackened the landscape near Burwash Landing and beyond it for several miles. Stop by the Kluane Museum of Natural History, along the highway, and you'll see how close the fire came to burning down this structure and many others in the town. The fire line came within 30 feet of the museum's back door. For unexplained reasons, the winds changed direction and the town was spared. Get your picture by the "World's Largest Gold Pan" next to the museum.

The northernmost town on the Alaska Highway in the Yukon Territory is Beaver Creek, with a year-round population of 140. As at Contact Creek, this was a place where, in 1942, construction crews working from opposite directions met and completed a stretch of the Alaska Highway. U.S. Customs is just 20 miles (34 km) north from here. Last chance to mail a letter or postcard with a Yukon postmark!

ALASKA–YUKON BORDER

From Whitehorse: 303 miles (488 km)
From Haines Junction: 205 miles (330 km)
To Tok: 92 miles (148 km)
To Fairbanks: 298 miles (480 km)

Crossing into Alaska is an achievement, and you're due for another round of photos. There's a wonderful place to pull over and record this moment, right at the demarcation line that separates the United States and Canada. Alaska and the Yukon Territory have each erected impressive welcome signs, massive wooden affairs that are beautifully painted. Between them is a parking area with a gazebo-like structure over the international border marker. Stand here and look north, then south, and you'll see the border as a brushed-out band in the scrubby trees, signifying the 141st meridian. At this wayside, most people like to pose with a foot in each country or sit on the nearby bench that's divided by a carved line with the word Yukon on one side, Alaska on the other.

Just ahead is the U.S. Customs and Immigration station, which is open 24 hours a day. Turn your watch back an hour to reflect the Alaska Time Zone.

Gas, RV camping, and tire services are available at the border, and just beyond it.

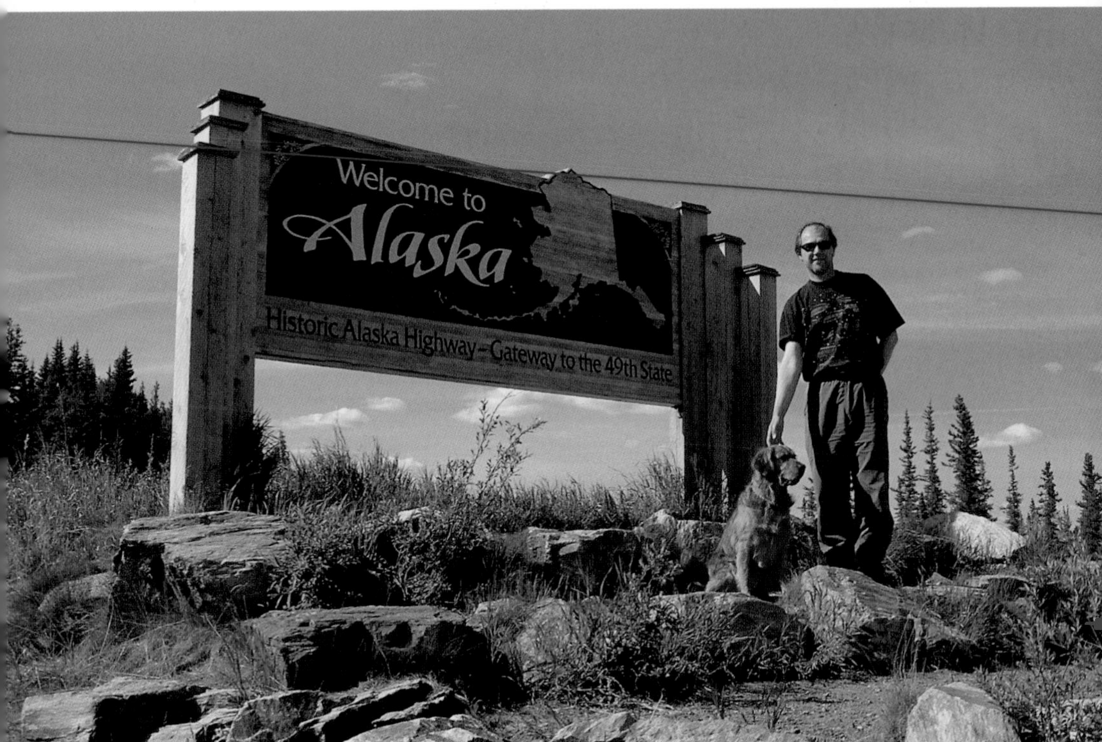

Crossing into Alaska usually involves a stop for picture taking at this magnificent sign.

Road Notes

For the first 65 miles (104.5 km) into Alaska, the highway follows the border of 730,000-acre Tetlin National Wildlife Refuge, a sparsely treed region of marshes and lakes that attract thousands of nesting waterfowl and migrating sandhill cranes. Watch for other birds, too, including ptarmigan, trumpeter swans, loons, and some species of raptors. Mammals include black and brown bears, moose, caribou, and smaller furbearers such as lynx, red foxes, and coyotes. The Forest Service maintains two campgrounds, Lakeview and Deadman Lake, along the Alaska Highway, both before Northway Junction. In the distance, view the Mentasta Mountains. For information on accessing the refuge, call 907-883-5312 or see *http://tetlin.fws.gov.*

Eighty miles (129 km) from the border, at Tetlin Junction (not to be confused with Tetlin, Yukon), you'll find the northbound turnoff to Alaska Highway 5 (the Taylor Highway), a road that's closed in winter. This route is paved to the Alaska village of Chicken, then turns to gravel (the village of Eagle lies at the end of a spur off the Taylor). Certain paved sections are severely disturbed by frost heaves and the effects of permafrost in the soil. This rustic road connects with the Yukon's Top of the World Highway, the northern route to Dawson City and another instance in which "highway" is used loosely. (See the section on the Taylor Highway in Chapter 8, Alaska's State Highways. Also see the section on the Top of the World Highway in Chapter 7, Western Canada's Northbound Byways.)

Twelve miles (19 km) beyond Tetlin Junction is Tok, which was a construction camp during the building of the Alaska Highway.

TOK

From Alaska/Yukon border: 92 miles (148 km)
To Delta Junction: 108 miles (174 km)
To Fairbanks: 206 miles (331 km)

Surrounded by stands of spruce trees, Tok (TOKE) is a junction city. Motorists can continue northwest on the Alaska Highway toward Fairbanks, or veer southwest onto the Glenn Highway (known by Alaskans as the Tok Cutoff). This panoramic shortcut for southbound drivers leads to Glennallen or Valdez on the Richardson Highway, or to Anchorage at the end of the Glenn Highway. In November 2002, the Tok Cutoff was temporarily closed when east-central Alaska was rocked by a magnitude 7.9 earthquake that damaged roads, homes, and businesses. Portions of the Richardson and Parks Highways also were shut down until repairs could be made.

With a population of about 1,400, Tok is geared toward travelers' services and stays, and is especially busy in the summer months. Alaska's Mainstreet Visitor Center is housed in a massive log structure at the junction of the two highways. Cultivated flower beds around the center and elsewhere in town flourish in the long, sunny days of Alaska's Interior. At the Center, you can learn about Tok's strategic role during the building of the Alaska Highway and about area wildlife, events, and attractions. Today it is known as Alaska's Dog Mushing Capital.

Take the kiddies to Mukluk Land at Mile 1317 of the Alaska Highway, just 2 miles (3 km) west of the highway junction. You'll find a lovely Alaska garden (mixing cabbages and flowers), videos on the trans-Alaska pipeline and the northern lights, golf, and a chance to do some gold panning (Mukluk Land guarantees the gold). Call 907-883-2571.

Tok is a great place to rest and restock. You'll find many choices here for comfortable accommodations, meals, gifts, groceries, and filling up the gas tank. Some campgrounds even offer a free breakfast for their guests.

LODGING

Golden Bear Hotel
Just south on the Tok Cutoff
907-883-2561
60 rooms, private baths. Cable TV, gift shop, coffee bar, Alaska displays, restaurant. Senior discount.

Snowshoe Motel
Mile 1314 Alaska Highway
907-883-4181
24 units, satellite TV, phones. Continental breakfast, picnic area. Pets welcome.

Westmark Tok
Junction of Alaska and Glenn Highways
1-800-544-0970 or 907-883-5174
92 deluxe rooms, nonsmoking available. Dining room, lounge. Adjacent to visitor center.

Young's Motel
Mile 1313 Alaska Highway
907-883-5023
43 rooms, private baths, nonsmoking available. Satellite TV, phones. Restaurant.

CAMPGROUNDS

Bull Shooter RV Park
Mile 1315 Alaska Highway
907-883-5625
Full and partial hookups, pull-throughs, sani-dump, clean restrooms. Walk to services and attractions. Next to sporting goods store for licenses, bait, tags, tackle.

Gateway Salmon Bake & RV Park
Mile 1313 Alaska Highway
907-883-5555
Space for big rigs to tenting campers. Water, electric, showers, restrooms. Lunch and dinner.

Golden Bear Motel & RV Park
Mile 123.5 Glenn Highway (Tok Cutoff)
907-883-2561
Full and partial hookups, pull-throughs, tent sites. Showers, laundry, restaurant, gift shop, phone.

Rita's Campground & RV Park
Mile 1316 Alaska Highway
907-883-4342
Hookups, dump station, drinking water, showers, tent camping.

Sourdough Campground
Mile 123 Glenn Highway (Tok Cutoff)
907-883-5543
Full hookups, shaded area, dump station, laundry, showers, car wash, vacuum. Sourdough pancakes and reindeer sausage breakfast. Live music nightly in the campground theater. Gift shop, outdoor museum. Sites available for winter campers.

Tok RV Village
Mile 1313.5 Alaska Highway
907-883-5877
95 sites, full and partial hookups, pull-throughs. Showers, laundry, dump station, vehicle wash. Connection to check e-mail. Fishing licenses.

Tundra Lodge & RV Park
Mile 1315 Alaska Highway
907-883-7875
78 sites with full or partial hookups, pull-throughs, tent sites, dump station, laundry, RV wash. E-mail access. Cocktail lounge.

RESTAURANTS

Fast Eddy's Restaurant
Mile 1313 Alaska Highway
Next to Young's Motel
907-883-4411
Steaks, seafood, pasta, burgers, pie.

Golden Bear Restaurant
Just south on the Tok Cutoff, adjacent to motel and RV park.
907-883-2561
Luncheon and dinner specials. Senior discount.

Tok Gateway Salmon Bake
Mile 1313 Alaska Highway
907-883-5555
King salmon, halibut, reindeer sausage, buffalo burgers. Shuttle pickup available.

Young's Café
At highway junction
907-883-2233
Breakfast all day. Lunch specials, dinner, beer and wine, baked goods.

Road Notes

From Tok to Delta Junction is 108 miles (174 km) of almost unpopulated wilderness. The road follows or crosses several streams, the biggest of which is the Tanana River. Many of these streams were formed by runoff from glaciers in the Alaska Range. That's why the water tends to be a cloudy gray; in it are particles of suspended rock, called rock flour, carried by glaciers. The forest here is largely of spruce. Watch for moose and caribou.

DELTA JUNCTION

From Dawson Creek: 1,422 miles (2,288.5 km)
From Alaska–Yukon border: 200 miles (322 km)
From Tok: 108 miles (174 km)
To North Pole: 83 miles (134 km)
To Fairbanks: 98 miles (158 km)

At Delta Junction, the Alaska Highway joins the Richardson Highway—marking the official end of the Alcan. Stop by the end-of-the-road milepost outside the Visitors Center at the junction of the two highways. (This may be the official end, but for most travelers, Fairbanks is still the destination that marks completion of their journey up the Alaska Highway.) A nearby log structure is the old Sullivan Roadhouse, which houses historical exhibits from the late 19th century, when the Richardson Highway was a crude route known as the Valdez-to-Fairbanks Trail and roadhouses were spaced about every 15–20 miles. Built in 1906, the Sullivan is the oldest of the roadhouses that are still standing.

Addresses for Delta Junction are Mile 1422 Alaska Highway or Mile 266 Richardson Highway. This crossroads town is an agricultural community of 5,760, where hardy strains of barley flourish in the short growing season and long hours of sunshine. More than 130,000 acres of land are in cultivation. Other crops include oats, wheat, grass seed, canola, and potatoes. Local farmers raise dairy cows, Tibetan yaks, elk, and reindeer. And Delta Junction is the site of a maintenance station for the trans-Alaska pipeline.

In Alaska, this little town is well known for its buffalo herd. Twenty-three plains bison, or buffalo, were transplanted to the area in 1928, and they flourished. A 90,000-acre bison range was established in 1978, with enough habitat to support between 400 and 500 animals. An annual hunt by permit keeps the population in line and helps feed families. New calves arrive in spring. In early summer you're most likely to see the free-ranging herd browsing on the west side of the Delta River, but they move back over to the bison range in

August. The Alaska Department of Fish and Game plants barley, oats, and hay on the range to keep the animals there and out of private fields. (Fences, as you can imagine, do not work when a headstrong herd wants to cross to the other side, especially if a meal is waiting.)

At Mile 275, a historic site along the Tanana River, Rika's Roadhouse, has been restored and put to good use as a favorite community gathering spot and visitor attraction. The grounds include museum displays, a barn, gift shop, restaurant, and bakery. The grounds and outbuildings are all part of Big Delta State Historical Park, managed by Alaska State Parks. A roomy parking area is perfect for turning around those big RVs, and 24-hour parking is available. Call 907-895-4201 or visit *www.rikas.com.*

Just a quarter-mile past the turn-off for Rika's Roadhouse, the Tanana River crossing is a fantastic photo-op for a picture of the trans-Alaska pipeline. Here, a suspension bridge supports the pipeline as it parallels the highway's Big Delta Bridge over the Tanana River. There's a pullout here for a quick photo.

Annual events in town include the Buffalo Wallow Square Dance in late May, the Buffalo Barbecue in July, and the Deltana Fair in late July and early August. A quirky mid-July event is the Mud Bog Races, when Alaskans pull out their snowmobiles in midsummer and race them through the mud.

Sample smoked reindeer, buffalo, elk, and yak sausage at Delta Meat & Sausage Co. at Mile 1413 Alaska Highway; 907-895-4006. See *www.deltameat.com.* Or try fishing in one of the more than 40 stocked lakes in the area. Local rivers hold trout and grayling, too. Outfitters are available to guide you on land and by air on your outdoor adventure.

Check in at the Delta Junction Visitor Information Center at the junction of the Alaska and Richardson Highways for more on what to see and do. While you're there, don't forget to ask for your end-of-the-road certificate. You can call the center at 1-877-895-5068 or 907-895-5068 or visit *www.deltachamber.org.*

LODGING

Alaska 7 Motel
Mile 270 Richardson Highway
907-895-4848
Rooms; kitchenettes available. TV, full baths. Daily and weekly rates.

Alaska Country Inn by Kelly's
1616 Richardson Highway
907-895-4667
Rooms with private bath, phone, TV, kitchenettes.

Alaskan Steak House & Motel
Mile 265 Richardson Highway
907-895-5175

Buffalo Lodge
1575 Richardson Highway
907-895-9913

Cherokee Two Lodge
Mile 1412 Alaska Highway
907-895-4814

Clearwater Lodge
7028 Remington Road
907-895-5152
Comfortable rooms. Restaurant, campground.

Tanana Loop Country Inn
2775 Tanana Loop Extension
907-895-4890

Trophy Lodge
1420 Alaska Highway
907-895-4685

CAMPGROUNDS

Clearwater Lodge
7028 Remington Road
907-895-5152
RV and tent camping, cabins, restaurant open for dinner 7 days a week.

Mountain House Lodge
Mile 1412.5 Alaska Highway
907-895-5160 / *www.mountainhouselodge.net*
Campsites, rooms, restaurant, lounge.

Smith's Green Acres RV Park & Campground
Mile 268 Richardson Highway
1-800-895-4369 or 907-895-4110
Full and partial hookups, pull-throughs, tent sites. Showers, self-service laundry, restrooms, phone, vehicle wash. Can arrange here for a pipeline pump station tour.

The Alaska State Parks system maintains five nearby campgrounds on the Richardson Highway. They are:

Delta State Recreation Site
1 mile (1.6 km) past visitor center, with 25 campsites, water, picnic tables, and toilets.

Clearwater State Campground
2 miles (3 km) past visitor center, turn right on Jack Warren Road for 10.5 miles (17 km). Offers 17 campsites, some along the river, on 46 acres. Picnic tables, toilets, water, fishing, and a boat launch.

Donnelly Creek State Recreation Site
Mile 238 Richardson Highway. 12 campsites, with picnic sites, toilets, picnic shelter, and trails.

Fielding Lake State Recreation Site
Mile 200.5 Richardson Highway. 17 campsites on 605 acres with picnic sites, water, toilets (including handicap accessible).

Quartz Lake Recreation Area
600-acre park that includes two campgrounds (Lost Lake and Quartz Lake) and a handicap-accessible fishing dock. 12 miles (19 km) past visitor center, turn right on Quartz Lake Road for 3 miles (5 km).

RESTAURANTS

Adam's Rib BBQ Restaurant
Mile 1412.5 Alaska Highway
907-895-5160
Ribs, chicken, brisket, seafood.

Alaskan Steak House & Motel
Mile 265 Richardson Highway
907-895-5175
Breakfast, lunch, dinner. Specializing in all-you-can-eat barbecue rib dinners.

Buffalo Center Drive-In
South of the Visitor Center
907-895-4383
Burgers, fries, and shakes.

Delta Petro-Wash
South of the Visitor Center at 4th Street
907-895-5053
Soups, sandwiches, hot breakfasts.

Leaphy's Restaurant
7028 Remington Road, in Clearwater Lodge
907-895-5152
Open for dinner 7 days a week; live music on weekends.

Mountain House Lodge
Mile 1412.5 Alaska Highway
907-895-5160
www.mountainhouselodge.net
Campsites, rooms, restaurant, lounge.

Packhouse Restaurant
Rika's Roadhouse & Landing
Big Delta State Historical Park
907-895-4938
Baked goods and meals.

Pizza Bella
Across from visitor center
907-895-4841
Pizza, pasta, sandwiches, salads.

Trophy Lodge
1420 Alaska Highway
907-895-4685
Fine dining, cocktails.

Road Notes

The Richardson Highway between Delta Junction and Fairbanks is a four-lane route, but it remains a challenging road because much of it was built over permafrost. With Interior Alaska's extreme seasonal cycles of hot and cold damaging the road, you've got a roller-coaster ride in places. About 10 miles (16 km) northwest of Delta Junction, you'll cross the

Tanana River where the Big Delta Bridge parallels the suspension bridge supporting the trans-Alaska pipeline at this crossing. The bridge was built to withstand an earthquake measuring up to a magnitude of 7.5 and temperatures as low as –60°F.

About 7 miles (11 km) before you reach the town of North Pole, you'll pass by Eielson Air Force Base, home to nearly 5,000 people in a major military installation named for Carl Ben Eielson, an early-day Fairbanks pilot. Eielson A.F.B. is the northernmost fighter wing in the United States.

A few miles later, note the eastbound turnoff for Chena Lakes Recreation Area at Mile 346 Richardson Highway. This popular park includes 82 campsites, without utility hookups, and dozens of picnic sites. Swimmers enjoy the sandy beach at Chena Lake; canoeists can navigate the lake or the Chena River, which flows through at one end. Boat rentals are available, and there's fishing, biking, hiking, and nature walks for outdoor fun. The Fairbanks North Star Borough charges a nominal use fee for first-come, first-served campers with a ten-night maximum.

NORTH POLE

From Delta Junction: 83 miles (134 km)
To Fairbanks: 12 miles (19 km)

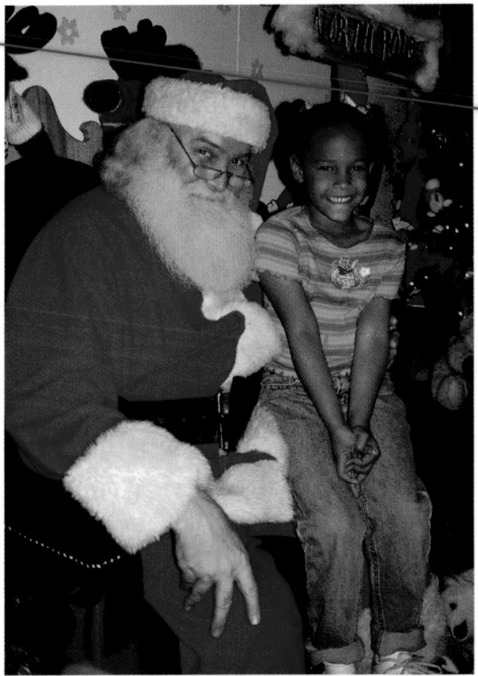

Santa's ready to receive little visitors year-round in North Pole, Alaska.

It's Christmas all year long in North Pole. That's because Santa doesn't disappear after Christmas Eve. On December 26, you can track him to his house and tell him what you want for next Christmas. This small community was founded in the 1950s, when several homesteading families sold their property for town lots. One far-thinking woman among them decided that a North Pole theme would likely help sell more lots, and maybe attract industry to their fledgling town.

The cheerful, candy-striped exterior of Santa Claus House is an invitation to any age, and the king-size likeness of Santa attracts photographers. Mail your letters from here for that impressive North Pole cancellation. Inside the gift shop is a kiddie toyland. You can buy Christmas ornaments and order up a personalized Christmas letter for your favorite little ones. Santa makes regular appearances (with Mondays and Tuesdays off!) and greets children in his throne room. To order a Christmas letter, mail $7.50 along with the child's address to Santa Claus House, 101 St. Nicholas Drive, North Pole, AK 99705. Call 907-488-2200. The jolly old elf is up-to-date on technology, too. He accepts e-mail. Write him at santa@santaclaushouse.com or browse his Web site at *www.santaclaushouse.com*. Visit Santa's reindeer next door at Santaland RV Park, a park with so many services, they even offer pet-sitting while you take a tour. Call 907-488-9132 or see *www.santalandrv.com*.

Several motels and campgrounds are nearby, and other North Pole businesses invite you to drive around town and enjoy all that this wonderful city of 1,600 people has to offer. Stop by the Visitor Center Log Cabin at 2550 Mistletoe Drive, or call 907-488-2242. See *www.northpolechamber.org*.

LODGING

Beaver Lake Resort Motel
2555 Mission Road, corner of Mission Road and Richardson Highway
907-488-9600
Quiet setting on a lake; close to Santa Claus House.

CAMPGROUNDS

Riverview RV Park
Between North Pole and Fairbanks
Exit 349 or 357 Richardson Highway to Badger Road
1-888-488-6392 or 907-488-6392
www.riverviewrvpark.net
160 RV sites with hookups, pull-throughs on the Chena River. Tent camping. Showers, laundry, water, dump station. Free car wash, good fishing. Gift shop, groceries, ATM, videos, gas and diesel. Shuttle service to local attractions.

Road's End RV Park
1463 Wescott Garden Lane
907-488-0295
65 campsites with full hookups and some tent sites. Showers, laundry, dump station.

Santaland RV Park & Campground
125 St. Nicholas Drive
1-888-488-9123 or 907-488-9123
www.santalandrvpark.com
85 RV sites with full hookups and pull-throughs, 9 tent sites. Shower, laundry, water, dump station. Tour arrangements.

RESTAURANTS

The Elf's Den
On Mistletoe Drive, next to visitor center
907-488-3268
Family dining, broasted chicken, Beef Wellington, pizza, lounge.

Mama C's Moose Creek Kitchen
3614 Old Richardson Highway, just outside the Eielson Air Force Base gate
907-490-0145
Family-operated café specializing in fried chicken, steaks, burgers.

Road Notes

It's a quick 12 miles (19 kms) from North Pole to Fairbanks, and the Richardson Highway is a four-lane route bordered by spruce, aspen, and birch trees as it heads toward town. Then it ends without fanfare, joining the Steese Highway near the entry to Fort Wainwright, which lies on the eastern edge of town. An army post today, Fort Wainwright was Ladd Air Field during World War II. Military spending has often stabilized or boosted the Fairbanks economy during the past 60-plus years.

FAIRBANKS

From Delta Junction: 98 miles (158 km)
From Alaska–Yukon border: 298 miles (480 km)
From Dawson Creek, British Columbia: 1,488 miles (2,395 km)

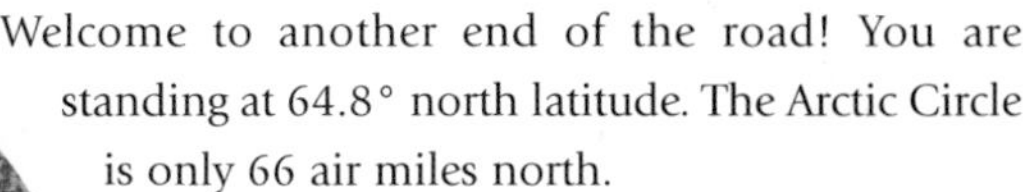

Welcome to another end of the road! You are standing at 64.8° north latitude. The Arctic Circle is only 66 air miles north.

Fairbanks was founded in 1901 by a trader named E. T. Barnette, who really didn't want to settle here. As a passenger aboard a sternwheel riverboat, he had intended to set up shop in a place that was more accessible to the gold miners in the area. But following the tip of a local Native, he directed the captain up the Chena River, which he thought was a shortcut to his destination. The Chena was too shallow, and the summer was ending. In a hurry to return without his argumentative passenger, the captain ordered Barnette and his party, and his trade goods, off the ship. They landed at a spot that's marked today with a low rock monument, by the Fairbanks Convention and Visitors Bureau log cabin on 1st Avenue near the Cushman Street Bridge.

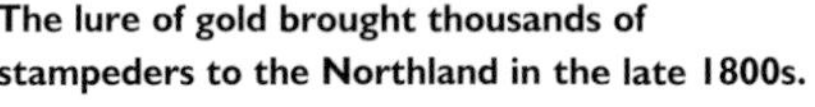

The lure of gold brought thousands of stampeders to the Northland in the late 1800s.

Luck was with Barnette. Within hours, he and his group had their first paying customers in the form of a couple of miners who had spotted the ship's plume of steam. One of the miners was Felix Pedro, an Italian immigrant who struck gold less than a year later. His find ignited a rush to Alaska's Interior, drawing miners from the goldfields of Fortymile country and the Klondike.

The long-term health of this fledgling community was cinched when Barnette struck a deal with federal district judge James Wickersham, who was stationed in Eagle, Alaska, a gold-mining town northeast of Fairbanks. Wickersham wanted to feed the ego of a political friend by naming a town after him. Charles W. Fairbanks was then a U.S. senator from Indiana; later he would be vice president under Theodore Roosevelt. In exchange for naming the town after Fairbanks, Wickersham promised Barnette that he would move the judicial seat from Eagle to Fairbanks—which he did, ensuring that the town was firmly rooted.

The 30,390 people of Fairbanks today commemorate Felix Pedro's gold discovery with a weeklong festival called Golden Days. Held in late July, the festival includes sourdough pancake feeds, gold-panning demonstrations and mining lectures, dances, historical exhibits, and an old-fashioned community parade. The winner of the Pedro look-alike contest leads the parade, and he walks the downtown route with his gold poke full of nuggets.

Gold nuggets are still in the barter system of Fairbanks. Just drop by Oxford Assaying at 29 College Road to pick out an Alaska nugget or a finished piece of jewelry (907-456-3967).

Or see Purdue's Jewelry, folks who've been doing business in gold-nugget jewelry since Kennedy was president. Their store is at the Shoppers Forum Mall on Airport Way (907-456-5105). Another resident-recommended favorite is Gold Rush Fine Jewelry at 531 2nd Avenue, downtown. And yet another option is to tour the El Dorado Gold Mine, pan for gold, then pick your favorite nugget and have it made into a ring, bracelet, or necklace (907-479-5573). Okay, the likelihood you get a big hunk of gold in your pan is low, but you are guaranteed to come away with a nice sprinkling of fine gold, which they can make into a necklace while you wait. And they do have a showcase of nuggets for sale, and a jewelry designer can make your custom piece.

Fairbanks has grown from the days of E. T. Barnette to a hub city for all of Alaska's Interior communities. It's also a major jumping-off point for flights into the bush. Overnight tours are available by air, and in fly/drive packages, to Barrow, the Arctic Circle, Nome, Kotzebue, and Anuktuvuk Pass. Another Alaska crossroads city, Fairbanks is the hub for the Elliott, Dalton (via Elliott), Steese, Richardson, and Parks Highways. Before you leave town for any of these highway trips, you can call or go online for road conditions, traffic hazards, closures, and so on, by dialing 5-1-1 or 1-866-282-7577. Also see *www.511.alaska.gov.*

Other annual events include a summer solstice celebration in late June with 10K fun run starting and ending in town. Another favorite each year is the late-night baseball game hosted by the Fairbanks semipro baseball team, the Goldpanners. The Midnight Sun Baseball Game begins at 10:30 P.M. under all-natural light. In July, the Midnight Sun International Powwow is held at the Tanana Valley State Fairgrounds, an intertribal event with dancing, drumming, Native art sales, and more. Call 907-456-2245 for information. Locals flock to the Tanana Valley State Fair, located on College Road, each August for agricultural displays, great fair food, rides, and entertainment. Call 907-452-3750 for dates. In February, mushing fans line the downtown streets for the start or finish of the Yukon Quest International Sled Dog Race, which follows a 1,000-mile route between Whitehorse, in the Yukon, and Fairbanks (*www.yukonquest.com*). Around town, you'll find movie theaters, shopping opportunities, bowling, golf, art galleries, and outdoor adventures.

The "end of the road" milepost, on the banks of the Chena River in Fairbanks, feels like the finish line for Alaska Highway travelers.

While you're in Fairbanks, visit some of these local attractions:

The University of Alaska Museum of the North. Newly expanded in 2006, this

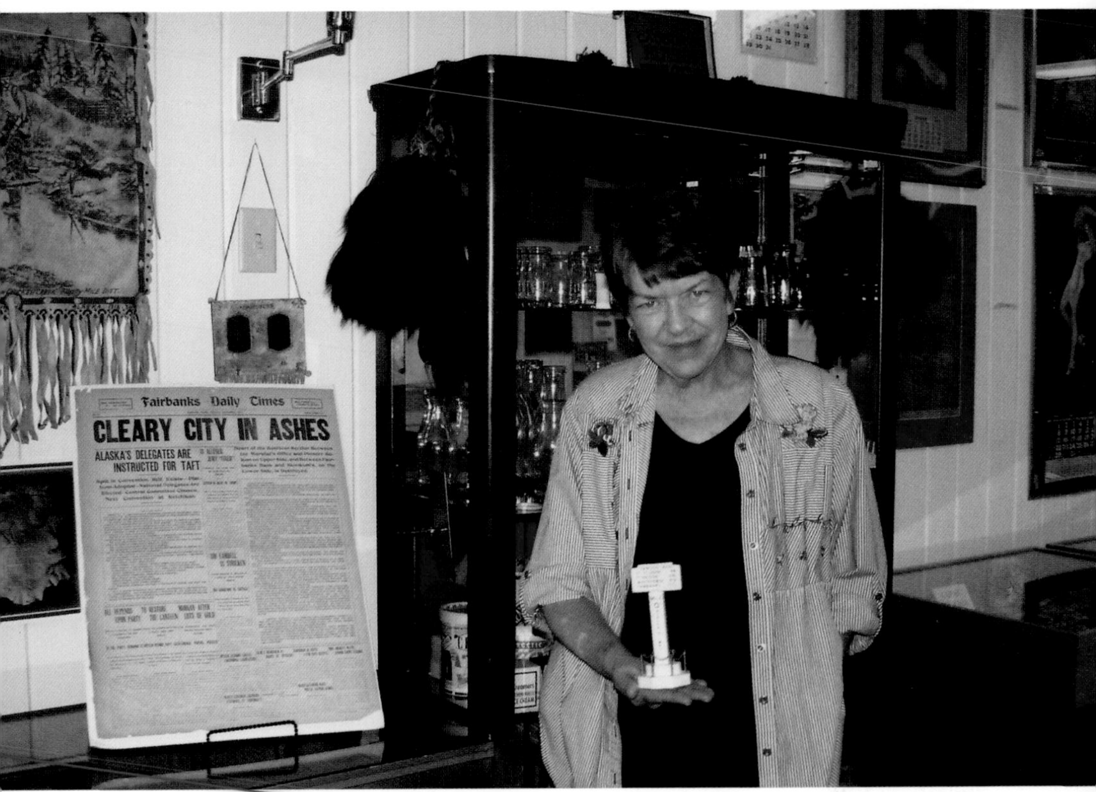

Renowned Alaskana collector Candace Waugaman displays a portion of her extensive archival collection at Historic Hall in downtown Fairbanks. The museum is free and within walking distance of the Fairbanks Convention and Visitors Bureau log cabin. Here, she holds a miniature of the famed Alaska Highway Mile 0 milepost.

---

museum is at once an architectural beauty and a rich depository of more than 1.4 million artifacts. Gallery exhibits include dinosaur fossils, ivory carvings, historical photos, totem poles, natural history dioramas, and lots of gold—the largest public display in Alaska. Be sure to visit Babe the Blue Bison, a 36,000-year-old bison mummy that was excavated by a Fairbanks scientist. Videos on the northern lights explain the scientific reason for the phenomenon. The museum store is a shopper's delight, with books, gifts, clothing, and Native art. The Museum of the North is on the University of Alaska Fairbanks campus, at College Road and University Avenue. Call 907-474-7505 for 24-hour information or see *www.uaf.edu/museum*.

Creamer's Field Waterfowl Refuge. What was once the northernmost dairy farm in the country was converted to a waterfowl refuge many years ago, but the old buildings remain. Anna and Charlie Creamer's farmhouse is now a visitor center, and signs along refuge trails describe the migratory birds that feed in great numbers here each spring and fall. Most are Canada geese and sandhill cranes. The Tanana Valley Sandhill Crane Festival is held the last week of August. See *www.arcticaudubon.org*.

Activity was high along the Chena River in the early 1900s, when the town was born of a gold-rush boom.

Historical walking tour. Meet at the Fairbanks Convention and Visitors Bureau log cabin on 1st Avenue near the Cushman Street Bridge. Guided or unguided walking tours of notable historic sites begin there. Call 907-456-5774 for information or visit *www.explorefairbanks.com.*

Historic Hall. A new don't-miss attraction is housed just a block away along the river in one of Fairbanks' oldest buildings at 825 1st Avenue. When Fairbanks was in its infancy, the building was the community bathhouse. It also served as the clubhouse for the Oddfellows, and in later years, was home to the Golden North Rebekah Lodge. Now owned by local historian Candace Waugaman, the Historic Hall is filled with a fraction of treasures from her collection—including artifacts, photographs, buttons, posters, brochures, and programs—that document the growth of a state and city. This mini-museum is a joy and it's absolutely free.

Golden Heart Park. Next door to the log cabin visitor center on 1st Avenue is Golden Heart Park, with its dramatic, 18-foot sculpture titled "The Unknown First Family." Plaques around the statue include names of people who helped build this town during its first century. This is a place for relaxing by the fountain or enjoying outdoor concerts on summer afternoons.

Alaska Public Lands Information Center. Just a block away from the Chena River, the center is located in the lower level of the old courthouse on 3rd and Cushman Streets. Operated by the National Park Service, and featuring films, books, gifts, and guest speakers, this is a terrific place to learn about Alaska's various cultures and ecosystems. Knowledgeable staffers are extremely helpful. Call 907-456-0527 or visit *www.nps.gov/aplic.*

World Ice Art Championships. Fairbanks in March is such a great place! This time of year, the sun has returned, yet it's still cold enough for clean, crisp snow and nice, clear ice. Sculptors from all over the world converge on Fairbanks to compete with monumental works. You can walk through the Ice Park, which is filled with giant ice statuary, all of it lit with colored lights that sparkle through the nearly clear ice. Call 907-451-8250 or see more at *www.icealaska.com.*

Pioneer Park. This 44-acre theme park, at Airport Way and Peger Road, was built in 1967 to commemorate the centennial of Alaska's purchase from Russia. The Centennial Exposition grounds were divided into themes that echoed Alaska history. In one section, replicas of Native villages were constructed. In another, a gold-rush town was created by relocating some of the oldest cabins and businesses of Fairbanks. The Palace Saloon is still operating as a bar and dance hall. Call the Palace to reserve a ticket to its popular "Golden Heart Revue," which shows at 8:15 P.M. nightly during summer months. Reserve your seat by calling 907-456-5960.

From the Palace, it's just a short walk to the Pioneer Air Museum, where antique aircraft from Alaska's early days, and stories to go with them, are yours to enjoy. In another part of the park, the Alaska Salmon Bake serves delicious northern fare from 5 P.M. to 9 P.M. nightly. Call 907-452-7274. The Salmon Bake is near the gold-mining "valley," which was created to demonstrate various ways that gold was extracted from the ground. And one of the region's hardworking stern-wheelers, the riverboat *Nenana,* was dry-docked here after retirement. It has since been beautifully restored. Come aboard for a tour. Pioneer Park admission is free.

Cruise the river on a modern stern-wheeler. The *Tanana Chief* and the riverboat *Discovery* are two popular tours for panoramic views and a dose of local history. Prime rib dinner and sightseeing cruises are available every evening on the *Tanana Chief*, an authentic stern-wheeler that plies these waters, a replica of a historic vessel. Call 907-452-8687. Browse *www.greatlandrivertours.com* for more information. The riverboat *Discovery* is operated by the Binkley family, whose members have been cruising Alaska rivers for five generations. The *Discovery* offers two tours daily and follows the Chena and Tanana Rivers on a narrated cruise that includes stops at a replica of an Athabascan Indian fish site and a sled-dog kennel. Reservations are a must for this popular attraction. Call 907-479-6673 or browse *www.riverboatdiscovery.com.*

The Bard. Since 1993, the Fairbanks Shakespeare Theatre players have gained popularity, so much that the troupe expanded its offerings and outreach, traveling nationally and internationally. Lucky Fairbanksans get to enjoy their productions year-round. A local favorite each winter is the annual nonstop performance of Shakespeare's entire poetry output in the "Bard-a-thon." Winter shows are held at the historic Empress Theatre, on Second Avenue. In mid-summer, visitors and residents in numbers bring their lawn chairs and blankets to enjoy outdoor performances of a Shakespeare play. For tickets and location, call 907-457-7638.

Anglers will find directions on how to line up a guided fishing trip, or a fly-in lodge experience, through the Fairbanks Convention and Visitors Bureau log cabin at 550 1st Avenue along the Chena River, not far from where founder E. T. Barnette built his first trading post. New to downtown Fairbanks in 2006 is a statue of Russian and American pilots, a salute to the flyers of the Lend-Lease Program during World War II, in which warplanes were ferried through Fairbanks and on to Russia and the frontlines.

For more information about local attractions and events, day trips, history, fishing, and hunting, contact the FCVB at 1-800-327-5774 or 907-456-5774. Visit their Web site at *www.explorefairbanks.com.*

LODGING

For bed-and-breakfast accommodations, contact the Fairbanks Association of Bed & Breakfasts at www.ptialaska.net/~fabb/.

Alaska Motel
1546 Cushman Street
907-456-6393
www.ak-motel.com
36 rooms, kitchenettes. Cable TV, laundry. Senior discount; weekly rates.

Alpine Lodge
1221 Gilmore Trail
907-455-4413
www.akalpinelodge.com
Luxury lodge with suites and kitchenettes, cable TV, business center, exercise facility, laundry. Near airport, shuttle service, continental breakfast.

Bear Lodge
212 Wedgewood Drive
1-800-528-4916 or 907-456-3642
www.fountainheadhotels.com
Well-appointed lobby and spacious rooms; adjacent to Creamer's Field Migratory Waterfowl Refuge.

Bridgewater Hotel
723 1st Avenue
1-800-528-4916 or 907-452-6661
www.fountainheadhotels.com
94 units, dining, cocktails. Downtown location. Airport/train shuttle.

Captain Bartlett Inn
1411 Airport Way
907-452-1888
www.captainbartlettinn.com
Log hotel with Alaskan décor near shopping, restaurants, movies. Restaurant, saloon, shuttle to train and airport.

Comfort Inn—Fairbanks
1908 Chena Landings Loop
1-800-4CHOICE or 907-479-8080
www.comfortinnfairbanks.com
Spacious rooms, indoor pool and spa, free continental breakfast.

Fairbanks Princess Riverside Lodge
4477 Pikes Landing Road
1-800-426-0500 or 907-455-4477
www.princesslodges.com
200 deluxe units on the Chena River. Gift shop, health club, restaurant, lounge. Airport/train shuttle. Tour tickets.

Fairbanks SpringHill Suites by Marriott
575 1st Ave
1-877-729-0197 or 907-451-6552
www.springhillsuites.com
Spacious studio accommodations with wireless and high-speed Internet, microwaves, fridges, coffeemakers. Business center, continental breakfast. Pool, workout room.

Golden North Motel of Fairbanks
4888 Old Airport Way
1-800-447-1910 or 907-479-6201
www.goldennorthmotel.com
62 units, free continental breakfast. Free high-speed and wireless Internet. Pets allowed. Shuttle service.

Pike's Waterfront Lodge
1850 Hoselton Rd
1-877-774-2400 or 907-456-4500
www.pikeslodge.com
Guest rooms and deluxe cabins along the Chena River, restaurant, saloon. Shuttle service, wireless Internet, sauna, exercise room, cable TV.

Regency Fairbanks Hotel
95 10th Avenue
1-800-348-1340 or 907-452-3200
www.regencyfairbankshotel.com
Rooms with kitchens and free wireless Internet. Suites. Business center, exercise room, lounge, shuttle, laundry. Full-service restaurant.

River's Edge Resort
4200 Boat Street
1-800-770-3343 or 907-474-0286
www.riversedge.net
Private cottages, each with two queen beds, along the Chena River in the heart of town. Restaurant, tours, shuttle.

Sophie Station Hotel
1717 University Avenue
1-800-528-4916 or 907-479-3650
www.fountainheadhotels.com
147 suites, kitchens, laundry. Dining, cocktails. Airport/train shuttle. Close to shopping.

Super 8 Motel
1909 Airport Way
1-800-800-8000 or 907-451-8888
www.super8.com
77 units, laundry, pets allowed. Free wireless Internet, continental breakfast, pet friendly. Walking distance to shopping.

Tamarac Inn Motel
252 Minnie Street
1-800-693-6406 or 907-456-4606
www.tamaracinnmotel.com
Rooms, some with kitchens. Laundry. Walking distance to city center.

Wedgewood Resort
212 Wedgewood Drive
1-800-528-4916 or 907-452-1442
www.fountainheadhotels.com
Elegant suites and guest rooms on beautifully landscaped grounds.

Westmark Hotel & Conference Center
813 Noble Street
1-800-544-0970 or 907-456-7722
www.westmarkhotels.com
244 well-appointed rooms, free wireless Internet, laundry. Restaurant, cocktails, coffee bar, gift shop. Airport/train shuttle.

CAMPGROUNDS

The American Legion Post 57 at 1634 Cushman Street wants visiting Legion members to know that they have a limited number of RV parking spaces available for free.

Chena Marina RV Park
1145 Shypoke Drive
907-479-4653
www.chenarvpark.com
40 grassy sites with hookups and pull-throughs on active Bush plane pond. Showers, water, dump station. Phone hookups, sleeping rooms, gift shop, store, free showers. Tour tickets, free RV wash. Reservations recommended.

Chena Wayside RV Park Campground
221 University Avenue
907-451-PARK
www.chenawayside.com
Roomy RV sites among the trees, hookups, restrooms, dump station. Picnic sites.

Ice Alaska Park and RV Campground
1925 Chena Landing Loop
907-451-8250
52 campsites; 15 with full hookups. Dump station and fresh water, Internet access, laundry, showers, restroom.

River's Edge RV Park & Campground
4140 Boat Street
1-800-770-3343 or 907-474-0286
www.riversedge.net
190 sites with hookups and pull-throughs, tent camping. Showers, water, laundry, dump station. Free shuttle to attractions. Close to shopping. Help with tours.

Tanana Valley Campground
1800 College Road, on Tanana Valley State Fairgrounds
907-456-7956
www.tananavalleyfair.org
32 RV units with hookups and pull-throughs, tent camping. Showers, laundry, fireplace/grills, dump station.

RESTAURANTS

Alaska Salmon Bake
3175 College Road, in Alaskaland's Mining Valley
1-800-354-7274 or 907-452-7274
www.akvisit.com
Salmon over an open fire, deep-fried halibut, roasted prime rib.

The Bakery Restaurant
69 College Road
907-456-8600
Pastries and other baked goods fill out breakfast anytime; lunch and dinner menus.

Bear 'n' Seal Grill & Bar
813 Noble Street
In Westmark Fairbanks
1-800-544-0970 or 907-456-7722
Pacific Rim cuisine, seafood specialties; open for breakfast, lunch, dinner.

Bushati's Pizzaria & Restaurant
511 Gaffney Rd
907-457-1317
Pizza, sandwiches, salads.

Café Alex Wine Bar
310 1st Avenue
907-452-2539
Dining and piano bar, eclectic wine list. Live music Tuesday through Saturday evenings.

Cookie Jar Restaurant
1006 Cadillac Court
907-479-8319
Breakfast, lunch, dinner, baked goods.

Co-Op Diner
535 2nd Avenue
907-474-3463
Fifties-style diner fare in historic Fairbanks building that once housed the Empress Theatre.

El Mariachi
541 3rd Avenue
907-457-2698
Mexican specialties. Salsa music on Friday evenings.

Gambardella's Pasta Bella
706 2nd Avenue
907-456-3417
www.gambardellas.com
Italian cuisine for lunch, dinner. Outdoor seating available.

Geraldo's Restaurant
701 College Rd
907-452-2299
American and Italian specialties, steaks, seafood. Hand-tossed pizza.

Home Town Restaurant
2223 S. Cushman
907-455-9113
Family-style restaurant, three meals a day.

Ivory Jack's
Mile 1.5 Goldstream Road
907-455-6666
Alaska dinner specialties: king crab, Nome reindeer.

Lavelle's Bistro
575 1st Avenue
907-450-0555
www.lavellesbistro.com
Fine dining; recipient of Wine Spectator Award.

Los Amigos
636 28th Avenue
907-452-3684
Authentic Mexican dishes.

Myong's Teriyaki
402 5th Avenue, downtown
907-452-5560
Japanese specialties. Homemade salad dressing and teriyaki sauces.

Pike's Landing Restaurant & Lounge
4438 Airport Way
907-479-7113
Brunch, lunch, dinner along the Chena River. Outdoor seating available.

The Pump House Restaurant and Saloon
796 Chena Pump Road
907-479-8452
www.pumphouse.com
Alaskan specialties, steak, seafood. Historic site with outdoor seating along Chena River.

Sourdough Sam's
3702 Cameron Street
907-479-0523
Popular diner among the locals, especially for breakfast. Indoor and outdoor seating.

Souvlaki
310 1st Avenue
907-452-5393
Souvlaki and other Greek and East Mediterranean dishes. Closed on Sunday.

The Turtle Club
10 Mile Old Steese Highway, in Fox
907-457-3883
Prime rib, prawns, lobster, ribs. Reservations recommended.

The Vallata
2190 Goldstream Road
907-455-6600
Italian-American cuisine; open for dinner. Reservations recommended.

CHAPTER 7

Western Canada's Northbound Byways

IN WESTERN CANADA, you have plenty of options for exploring even more backcountry than where the Alaska Highway roams. From the well-developed, high-speed trans-Canada route to the narrow gravel byways that reach into the Yukon's northernmost regions, choose which route suits your sense of adventure. Spur roads and loops lead through pastureland or tundra, across mountains, or down to the sea. Along them lie ghost towns, industrious small towns, farms, and glittering cities. Use this chapter to discover what lies along the bends of western Canada's beautiful byways.

NORTH KLONDIKE HIGHWAY

Part of the Klondike Loop
Alaska Highway (near Whitehorse) to Dawson City: 327 miles (526 km)
24-Hour Road Conditions:** 867-456-7623 or, from Yukon communities, call toll-free 1-877-456-7623. Also see **www.gov.yk.ca/roadreport.

The Alaska Highway skirts along the southern reaches of the Yukon Territory from Watson Lake to Whitehorse to Haines Junction, then crosses the international border and moves on to Tok, Alaska. But there's another way to reach Tok—a way that gives you more time in the Yukon.

From Whitehorse, you can drive north to Dawson City (via the North Klondike Highway), west to cross the Alaska border (via the Top of the World Highway), and then back south to Tok (via the Taylor Highway). Together, these three northerly highways are called the Klondike Loop.

If you have the yearning to see some of the Yukon Territory's most scenic vistas and experience even more gold-rush charm, take the Klondike Loop. Better yet, on the way to Alaska, take the Klondike Loop, and on the way back, take the Alaska Highway. You'll get the best of both.

Travelers will find the beginning of the Klondike Loop several miles north of Whitehorse, where the Alaska Highway (Highway 1) continues west and the North Klondike Highway (Highway 2) heads north. Highway 2 is paved for all of its 327 miles (526 km) to Dawson.

About 3 miles (5 km) north of the highway junction, watch for the left turn to Takhini Hot Springs, 6 miles (10 km) west on a spur road. There you can bask in a naturally heated outdoor pool, winter or summer. Hiking and trail rides are other summertime options. Unlike most hot springs, Takhini's water does not contain sulfur, so it doesn't have that lingering, unpleasant odor. Meals and overnight accommodations are available.

Continuing north on Highway 2, you'll soon spot Lake Laberge, made famous (and misspelled) in "The Cremation of Sam McGee," by Yukon poet Robert Service. The lake is among the bodies of water, big and small, that make up the headwaters of the Yukon River. On the west, the road soon begins paralleling long, narrow Fox Lake, its pristine waters sparkling in the long summer days. While it appears to be an autonomous body, the lake is connected to Lake Laberge by Fox Creek. Watch for signs that indicate where you can go fishing or find a campsite in one of the Yukon's government-operated campgrounds. They are clean and modestly priced.

The entire North Klondike Highway is a pleasure to drive, but one of the greatest pleasures may be found at Mile 55 (88.5 km) in the kitchen of the Braeburn Lodge: their world-famous giant cinnamon rolls. These folks even named their landing strip after the dinner plate–size delicacy: Cinnamon Bun Airstrip. And then there's the annual Cinnamon Bun Dog Sled Race, a 200-mile event held the first weekend in February. There are other items on the menu, believe it or not, and the lodge also offers necessities such as fuel, souvenirs, and tips on local fishing holes. Canoe rentals and campsites are available here, too. Braeburn Lodge is open year-round; its most famous winter guests are the mushers and the doggie athletes competing in the 1,000-mile (1,609-km) Yukon Quest International Sled Dog Race.

The remains of the historic Montague House, one of the earliest roadhouse stops on the

ON THE SILVER TRAIL

At Stewart Crossing, 45 miles (72 km) north of Pelly Crossing, you can begin a side trip along Yukon Highway II to visit the historic silver- and gold-mining towns of Mayo, Keno, and Elsa on the Silver Trail. In the early 20th century, Mayo was a major settlement and river port. You will also pass through the traditional territory of the Na-Cho Nyak Dun people.

The Silver Trail is partially paved and leads to areas for swimming, camping, and hiking, as well as stunning views of glaciated mountains. Government campgrounds, as well as privately owned motels, are available in Mayo and in Keno, which is 69 miles (111 km) east of Stewart Crossing. Take a walking tour of Mayo's historic sites, and later, visit the Keno Mining Museum, which documents an era through artifacts, photographs, and written histories. Call 867-995-2792.

old stagecoach line between Whitehorse and Dawson City, lies along this route, about 80 miles (128.5 km) north of the Alaska Highway junction.

You'll cross the famed Yukon River about a hundred miles from the junction, and enter the community of Carmacks, a historic stop for steamboats that needed to restock their wood supplies, and later, coal. There was once a telegraph line through here, and it was a stopping place for the Overland Stage route between Whitehorse and Dawson City. For fans of the Yukon Quest International Dog Sled Race, Carmacks is a well-known place name, as it hosts throngs of mushers and their dog teams that stop at this checkpoint along the trail. Each year, the race starts or finishes in Whitehorse, alternating with Fairbanks on the other end of the route. Fuel, groceries, and campsites are available in Carmacks.

Fifteen miles (23 km) north of Carmacks is an interpretive sign and viewing area for Five Finger Rapids—among the most treacherous places for stampeders to pass during the gold rush of 1898. There's a pullout here to get a photo of the killing stretch in the river.

The little town of Pelly Crossing lies ahead, about 176 miles (282 km) northwest of Whitehorse. Home of the Northern Tutchone people, this town of fewer than 500 people had its most significant growth spurt when workers were building the Klondike Highway. Like Carmacks, Pelly Crossing is an important stop on the Yukon Quest, and gains international media attention every year. Both communities also feature a First Nations interpretive center, where you can learn more about the area's archaeology and cultural history.

Pelly Crossing marks the halfway point of the North Klondike Highway—about equal in distance from Whitehorse and Dawson City. Basic services for your vehicle, as well as its occupants (bank, groceries, overnight accommodations) are all available here, and you are welcome to take a self-guided tour beginning at the Selkirk Heritage Centre, next to the Selkirk Gas Bar.

In the final 158 miles (253 km) to Dawson City, the road parallels or intersects numerous creeks and rivers, such as Crooked Creek, Moose River, McQuesten River, and Clear Creek. The streams of this gold-mining region continue to pique the interest of placer miners for their proximity to the great discovery by George Carmacks. His find on Bonanza Creek, just outside of Dawson City, incited the Klondike gold rush of 1898.

Apart from Stewart Crossing, you will find few settlements along the remainder of the road. A handful of businesses offer accommodations, sundries, and fuel. Rest areas and pullouts provide the basics of a level surface and a garbage can.

Dawson City

In 1897, when news of a great gold discovery in the Klondike reached the outside world, more than 100,000 people resolved to pack up and head north, the mayor of Seattle among them. Only about 40,000 actually made it to the Klondike, and of those, a mere fraction made it rich, but the get-rich-quick compulsion was too great to ignore (not unlike the impulse of lottery-ticket buyers when a growing jackpot makes the news). Tens of thousands made uninformed decisions, not realizing that the way was hazardous, the cold could break a person's body and spirit, and the work was murderously difficult. Some men literally worked themselves to death, never enjoying the fruits of their labor. What remained was the

Midnight Dome, above Dawson, is an excellent place to view the confluence of the Yukon and Klondike rivers.

romance—stories of men drinking champagne from ladies' slippers while gold nuggets spilled from their pockets. Most of it was bunk.

The gold rush still lingers in Dawson City, along with the refurbished and modernized historic buildings that are so attractive. But in little niches off the main streets are the derelict structures that have seen human dramas we can only imagine. Dawson was nearly falling down several decades ago when, in a drive to save historic buildings, city leaders began fund-raising in earnest. Today Dawson is an imaginative slice out of time. Begin your visit with a stop at the Yukon Visitor Information Centre, along the Yukon River at Front and King Streets, housed in a replica of the 1897 Alaska Commercial Co. store. If you want a preview of what's happening in Dawson, go to their Web site at *www.dawsoncity.ca* or phone 867-993-5566.

One of Dawson's favorite sons, Pierre Berton, is a trusted storyteller and historian who uses books and videos to share the true story of Dawson's riotous beginning, its years of quiet retirement, and its rebirth as a major visitor attraction. Berton's books and videos are available in gift stores throughout town, including the Dawson City Museum gift shop (or through your favorite online source).

Nearly 2,000 people live here year-round, with an influx of seasonal residents during the summer months. Gold is still king, and you can pan for some yourself. Or buy a hunk of the yellow metal at one of several jewelry stores. You can have your nuggets made into a special piece of jewelry at Gold Trail Jewelers, across from the paddlewheel *Keno* on Front Street; at Fortymile Gold, located at 3rd and York; or at the Klondike Nugget and Ivory Shop, at the corner of Front and Queen Streets, which has been in business since 1904. At the Nugget, gold samples from more than 70 creeks are on display.

Unlike refined gold, nuggets are slightly dull, dimpled, and irregular. They possess a compressed, raw beauty that still strikes a note of discovery in your chest. The metal and its shape remind you of the powerful forces that made it centuries ago under this very ground.

From the vantage point of Midnight Dome above the city, you can look out over this countryside that miners have tried to strip of its gold. Across the confluence of the Yukon and Klondike Rivers, the land below looks as if giant earthworms had burrowed beneath the surface. These peculiar marks are telltale signs of gold dredges, which operated like mechanical soil-eaters. These multistory gold-processing ships floated on small ponds and worked efficiently. Using a conveyor belt of steel buckets, a dredge would eat at the earth in front of it, sort out the gold from the useless rock and soil, then dump these tailings out the back. The dredges slowly moved forward, opening up the pond in front and filling it in behind the dredge. The machines followed the veins of gold, operating until the early 1960s and leaving behind these unique signs that are still visible today. Visit Gold Dredge No. 4 on Bonanza Creek for a tour of the largest wood-hull dredge in the world, built in 1912. Call 867-993-7200.

Mining remains the most important industry in the Yukon Territory, and tourists are invited to try their hand at gold panning, or digging with a shovel and pick ax, at Gold Claim No. 6 above Discovery Claim on Bonanza Creek. This venture is operated by the Klondike Visitors Association, and there is no charge. Bring your own gold pan or rent one in town. From Dawson Creek, take the North Klondike Highway 2 east to Bonanza Road for 13 miles (32 km). You'll drive past Dredge No. 4 and Discovery Claim. Signs will lead the way from there.

Other gold-panning adventures are offered in the area, possibly at your campground. Ask the folks at the Visitor Information Centre for details.

Many of Dawson's historic buildings saw their 100th birthday in 2001, among them the old Territorial Administration Building, the Commissioner's Residence, the Territorial Courthouse, and the Arctic Brotherhood Hall. And 2002 marked Dawson City's centennial, a formal designation, recognizing Dawson's incorporation as a Canadian city, even though it existed as a wild-and-woolly boomtown prior to that.

Dawson attractions include:

George Black Ferry. This ferry across the Yukon River is a free service offered by the Yukon government, at work 24 hours a day, except between 5 A.M. and 7 A.M. on Wednesday mornings, when the vessel is serviced. Commercial businesses hold special passes for priority boarding, so make sure you enter the correct lane for boarding your vehicle. Rush hours for tourists are as predictable as those for a big-city workforce. Between 7 A.M. and 11 A.M., most drivers are outbound tourists. Peak times for those headed into Dawson are between 2 P.M. and 8 P.M. Work around those rush hours and you'll have a shorter wait. Call 867-993-5441 for information.

Dawson City Museum. The features of this museum on 5th Avenue in the Old Territorial Administration Building include goldfield exhibits, a First Nations Collection, films, a

Klondike history library, and steam locomotives. A gift shop and coffee shop are on site. Open Victoria Day to Labour Day. Call 867-993-5291.

Robert Service Cabin. One block south of Mission Street and 8th Avenue is the site of the two-room Robert Service cabin, a Klondike National Historic Site, still standing on a hillside, its roof covered with sod. It was here that Service wrote such classics as *The Trail of Ninety-Eight* and his third and final book of verse, *Rhymes of a Rolling Stone.* He lived here from November 1909 to June 1912. Twice-daily recitals of Service's works are presented by Dawson actor Johnny Nunan on the front lawn. Afterward, interpretive guides invite visitors to peek inside the windows, but the cabin's condition cannot tolerate more than that. Just across the street is the boyhood home of a more contemporary Canadian author, Pierre Berton. For more Robert Service poetry, check with the Westmark Inn, which has hosted performances by Irish-born actor Tom Byren since 2004. Located at Fifth and Harper Streets, the Westmark can be reached at 867-993-5542.

Jack London Cabin. Just one block south of the Robert Service Cabin, you'll find the Jack London Cabin and Interpretive Centre. The former Dawson City bank teller who became a famous author lived in this cabin when he first made his way to the Yukon. (The cabin has been moved to this site from its original location in the backcountry.) Among London's most famous books are *White Fang* and *Call of the Wild.* Like other visitor offerings in Dawson, the Interpretive Centre is open from late spring to early fall. Call 867-993-5575.

Palace Grande Theatre. Another Klondike National Historic Site, the Palace Grande at King and Third Avenue continues to host top-flight entertainment such as the *Gaslight Follies.* Nightly family shows are performed throughout the summer. The theater opened in July 1899, built by Arizona Charlie Meadows, a showman from the Wild West who was not above performing shooting tricks if the party atmosphere needed a boost. It has been restored to its original splendor by Parks Canada.

The great motivator—gold—attracted thousands to the Northland in the last century. Only a fraction got rich.

Danoja Zho Cultural Centre. Located on Front and York Street, the center teaches visitors about the First Nations people who were so drastically affected by the gold rush. See exhibits on life at a traditional fish camp and enjoy contemporary dance, storytelling, and other special events. Call 867-993-6564 or see *www.trondek.com.*

Diamond Tooth Gerties Casino. The casino at 4th Avenue and Queen Street offers three different shows every night. A cover charge gets you in the door for can-can entertainment and gambling from

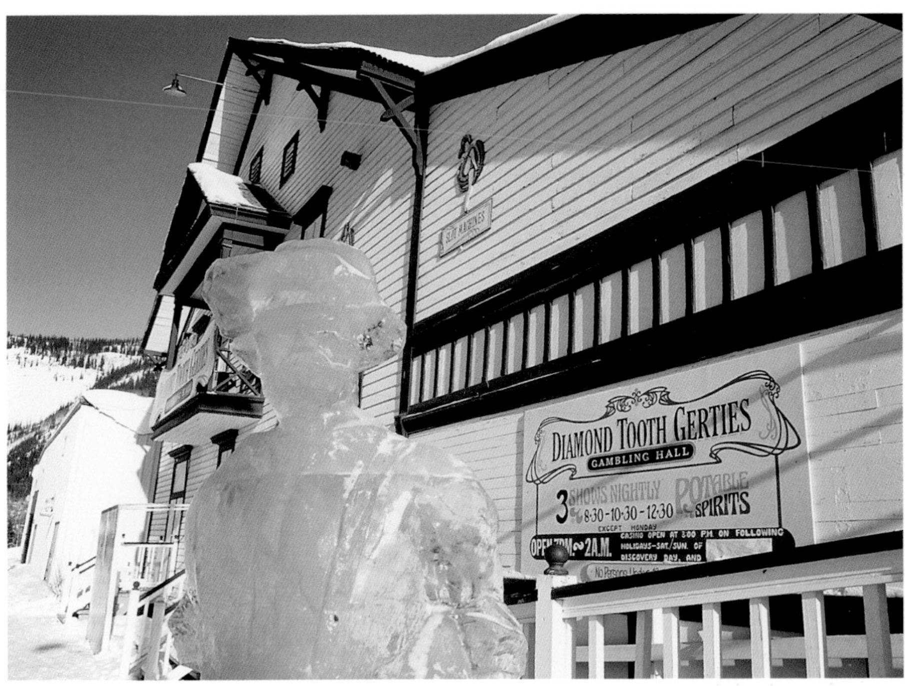

Ice sculptors created this statue at the door of Diamond Tooth Gertie's.

7 P.M. until 2 A.M. Open May through September; 19 and older only. Call 867-993-5575.

Top of the World Golf Course. This is Canada's northernmost golf course, with grass greens, 9 holes, a driving range, and a pro shop. Take the Top of the World Highway for 5 miles (8 km) out of Dawson City and follow the signs. No tee-times are required. Shuttle service from Dawson City is available; golfers arriving by RV are permitted to dry camp overnight. Call 867-993-5888 during the summer months or browse *www.topoftheworldgolf.com.*

Take a cruise. The newest attraction in Dawson is the paddle wheeler *Klondike Spirit*, which was launched in Eagle, Alaska, in July 2006 to make her maiden voyage of 109 miles (175 km) to Dawson City. After finishing the year in Alaska for certification, the vessel began Dawson tours in Spring 2007. Cruises on the Yukon River are filled with insider knowledge, as local people are there to interpret the area's natural and human history. Food and beverage service is available, too. Call 867-993-2628 or see *www.klondikespirit.com.*

Another favorite is a longer trip—follow the historic route of the old stern-wheelers on a cruise from Dawson City to Eagle, Alaska, aboard the M/V *Yukon Queen II*. Fare includes a meal. Call 1-800-478-6388.

For information on these and other things to do in Dawson, contact the Klondike Visitors Association at 867-993-5575 or see *www.dawsoncity.org.*

Two highways extend beyond Dawson: the Dempster Highway, which heads north, and the Top of the World Highway, which goes west to Alaska. See the sections on these two highways, in this chapter.

LODGING

Aurora Inn
5th Avenue and Harper Street
867-993-6860
www.aurorainn.ca
Clean and comfortable rooms, Jacuzzi suites. Senior discounts.

Bombay Peggy's
2nd Avenue and Princess Street
867-993-6969
Nonsmoking rooms in restored brothel. Downtown location. Lounge on site.

Bonanza Gold Motel
1 mile (1.5 km) from downtown, just past Bonanza Road
1-888-993-6789
www.bonanzagold.ca
45 air-conditioned rooms, suites, nonsmoking available, wheelchair-accessible suites. Cable TV, fax, high-speed Internet access, whirlpool. Restaurant.

Downtown Hotel
2nd Avenue and Queen Street
1-800-661-0514 or 867-993-5346
59 modernized rooms in a historic building. Cable TV, whirlpool, winter plug-ins. Gift shop, restaurant, saloon. Airport shuttle.

The El Dorado Hotel
3rd Avenue and Princess Street
1-800-764-3536 or 867-993-5451
www.eldoradohotel.ca
Modern rooms in a historic building, suites, kitchenettes. Laundry, winter plug-ins. Dining room, lounge. Open year-round.

Gold Nugget Motel
5th Avenue and Dugas Street
867-993-5445

Klondike Kate's Cabins, Rooms & Restaurant
1102 3rd Avenue
867-993-6527
www.klondikekates.ca
15 modern cabins with private baths, cable TV, phone, Internet hookup. Family restaurant, gift shop, wheelchair accessible.

Midnight Sun Hotel
3rd Avenue and Queen Street
867-993-5495
www.midnightsunhotel.com
Historic property in downtown Dawson City location. Restaurant, lounge.

Triple J Hotel
5th Avenue and Queen Street
1-800-764-3555 or 867-993-5323
Rooms, executive suite, kitchenette cabins. Laundry, restaurant, lounge. Free airport limo.

Westmark Inn
5th Avenue and Harper Street
1-800-544-0970 or 403-993-5542
www.westmarkhotels.com
177 nicely appointed rooms, restaurant, lounge. Gift shop, guest laundry, free parking.

Whitehouse Cabins
1626 Front Street, north end
867-993-5576
www.whitehousecabins.com
Units with kitchenettes, overlooking Yukon River. Cable TV, private bathrooms. Walking distance to town attractions.

CAMPGROUNDS

Bonanza Gold RV Park
1 mile (1.5 km) from downtown Dawson City
1-800-993-6789
Full hookups, cable TV, free wireless Internet, dry camping, tenting, laundry, showers, RV wash. Restaurant, gold panning.

Dawson City RV Park and Campground
1 mile (1.6 km) south of town, across Klondike River
867-993-5142
Full and partial hookups, tent campsites, showers, phone. Cable TV. Dining, gold panning, gift shop. Adjacent to gas and diesel station.

Gold Rush Campground / RV Park
5th Avenue and York Street
867-993-5247
www.goldrushcampground.com
Full hookups, downtown, close to most attractions.

GuggieVille RV and Gold Panning
Bonanza Road
1-888-993-6789 or 867-993-5008
Full hookups available along Bonanza Creek. Showers, free wireless Internet, self-service laundry, gift shop, car wash. Gold panning.

The Yukon Territory government operates two campgrounds near Dawson City:

Klondike River Territorial Campground
Near the airport, southeast of Dawson City
38 campsites for RV or tent camping. Partial hookups. Two pull-throughs. Nature trail.

Yukon River Territorial Campground
From downtown Dawson City, take the ferry across the Yukon River to reach this campground next to the ferry access road.
98 campsites for RV or tent camping. Partial hookups. Free firewood. Walk to steamboat graveyard.

RESTAURANTS

Aurora Inn Restaurant
Fifth and Harper Street, in Aurora Inn
867-993-6860
European, North American cuisine.

Belinda's Dining
Fifth and Harper Street, in Westmark Inn
867-993-5542
Dine in air-conditioning or on the deck.

Bonanza Dining Room and Sluice Box Lounge
3rd Avenue and Princess Street, in the El Dorado Hotel
867-993-5451
Steaks, ribs, chicken, northern specialties.

Jack London Grill and Sourdough Saloon
2nd Avenue and Queen Street, in the Downtown Hotel
867-993-5346
Barbecue, steaks, seafood.

Klondike Kate's Restaurant & Cabins
3rd Avenue and King Street
867-993-6527
www.klondikekates.ca
Breakfast, lunch, and dinner featuring Canadian and ethnic foods.

Mama Cita's Ristorante
2nd Avenue between Queen and Princess Street
867-993-2370
Lunch and dinner specials.

Midnight Sun Hotel
3rd Avenue and Queen Street
867-993-5495
Chinese and Western cuisine.

Riverwest Bistro Restaurant & Coffee Bar
Front Street
867-993-6339
Full-service coffee bar. Breakfast and lunch.

Sourdough Joe's Restaurant
Front and Princess Streets
867-993-6590
Fish and chips, berry desserts, bread pudding. Licensed.

The Sterndeck
2nd Avenue and Queen Street
867-993-5346
Covered outdoor dining.

Subsushi
Front Street
867-993-6453
Sub sandwiches, sushi.

TJ's Dining Room & Lounge
5th Avenue and Queen Street, inside Triple J Hotel
867-993-5323
Full menu restaurant and lounge.

TOP OF THE WORLD HIGHWAY

Part of the Klondike Loop
Dawson City to Alaska–Yukon border: 66 miles (106 km)
***24-Hour Road Conditions:** 867-456-7623 or, from Yukon communities, call toll-free 1-877-456-7623. Also see **www.gov.yk.ca/roadreport**.*

From Dawson to the Alaska–Yukon border, the Klondike Loop continues west on Highway 9 (the Top of the World Highway) for 66 miles (106 km). The Top of the World cuts into mountainsides and crosses peaks, dipping and rising hundreds of feet, while just beyond the edge of the road, a broad valley beckons. Above tree line, the view is so broad and inspiring that you suppress a loud "Wow!" (or maybe you don't). Seal-coated in some sections, dusty and gravelly in others, the road is less inspiring when you are traveling behind a truck or slow-moving RV. But take heart, the next pullout may offer a view that's too great to pass up.

This region is known as Fortymile country, for the Fortymile River that wends its way nearby. It was a place of uncertain possession when American miners thought they were mining U.S. soil. With the arrival of the North-West Mounted Police and officials who certified the international demarcation line, some of the miners left for more golden opportunities. Others settled in to live as Canadians.

This highway is not maintained in winter months, leaving it to snowmobilers and dog mushers who gladly use this major road as their trail. During three weekends in late February

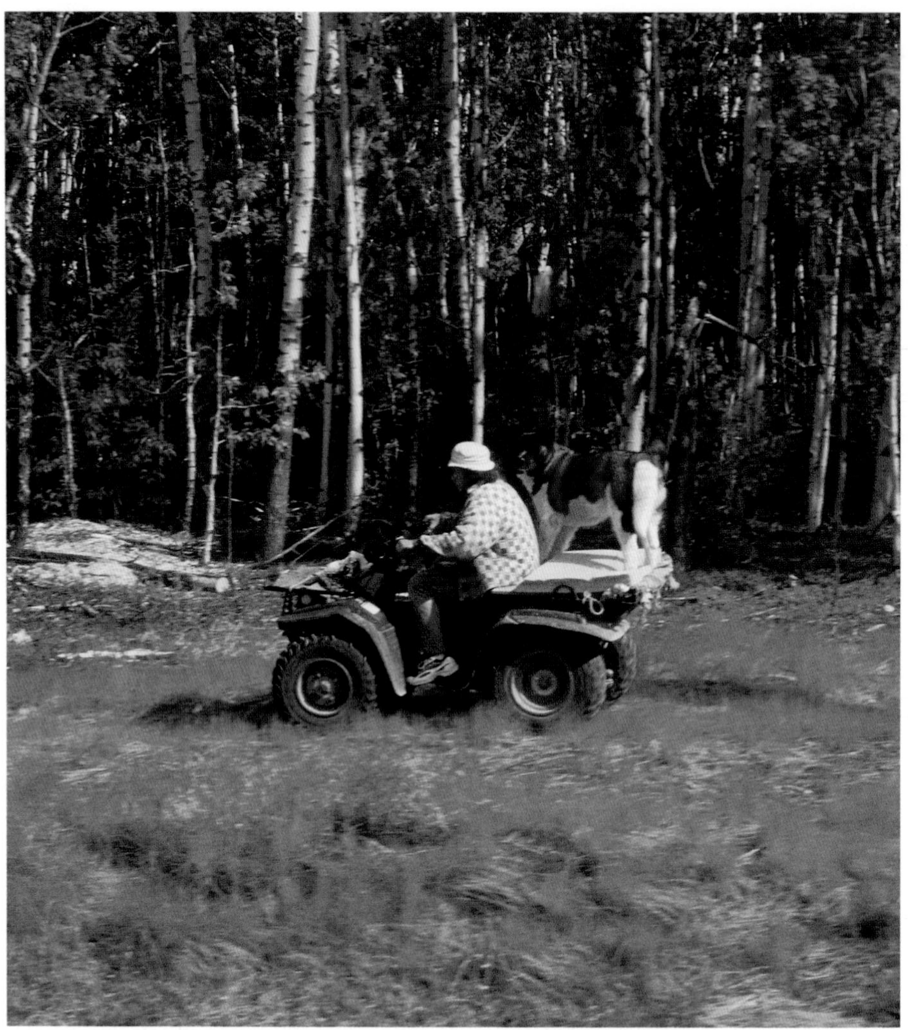

Throughout the Yukon and Alaska road systems, the broad swaths between the road and the forest edge provide a secondary highway for four-wheelers in summer and snowmachines in winter.

and early March, hundreds of snowmobilers travel this highway and Alaska's Taylor Highway for the Trek Over the Top event, a dash between Tok, Alaska, and Dawson City, Yukon.

The winter that I traveled in the pack of Trekkers, we were headed east from Alaska to the Yukon when, shortly after crossing the border, we spied a large hump in the deep snow. Mounties had placed sticks and pink flagging around the unusual rise on the side of the road. It was a car, completely snowed over, with only a few windows still slightly visible.

I remembered the story: Just a couple of months earlier, a man had tried to drive from Alaska to the Lower 48 via this closed road and had become stuck in the snow. He tried walking out for help. A few weeks later, snowmobilers found his body. The car would stay there until late spring, when the snow released its grip and the road reopened.

Between Dawson City and the border, there is little man-made clutter—just miles and miles of awe-striking scenery. The handful of buildings at the border are for customs officials only. There are no facilities, no restrooms, no currency exchange. And the customs station is open summers only, from 9 A.M. to 9 P.M. Yukon Time (or 8 A.M. to 8 P.M. Alaska Time).

From the border, the road continues into Alaska for a dozen miles before reaching the Taylor Highway.

TAYLOR HIGHWAY

Part of the Klondike Loop

For details on this section of the Klondike Loop, see the section on the Taylor Highway in Chapter 8, Alaska's State Highways.

DEMPSTER HIGHWAY

North Klondike Highway (near Dawson City) to Inuvik: 460 miles (740 km)

For only the most intrepid motorists, this undeveloped highway wends north from the Dawson City area to the upper reaches of the Yukon, across untamed wilderness and into the Northwest Territories. Completed in 1979, the route begins from the North Klondike Highway at a point 25 miles (40 km) east of Dawson and ends in the village of Inuvik, 460 miles (740 km) later.

This gravel road was named for Cpl. W. J. Dempster, a member of the North-West Mounted Police, who led the search for the famous Lost Patrol. The party had become lost near Fort McPherson in the winter of 1911 and froze to death.

This is wilderness at its finest, with humans few and far between as you drive over mountains and onto vast river floodplains. The only service stations are at Eagle Plains, Fort McPherson, and Inuvik. You'll cross the Arctic Circle at Mile 250 (402 km), at latitude 66° 33' N where you need to stop for a picture at the turnout. Free ferry service is available from 9 A.M. to 12:30 A.M., Northwest Territories time, at two crossings: the Peel River and the Mackenzie River.

Hotel accommodations, fuel, dining, camping, and other services are available at Eagle Plains Hotel, Mile 231 (371.5 km). Yukon government campgrounds may be found at Tombstone Mountain, Mile 45 (72.5 km); Engineer Creek, Mile 120.5 (194 km); and Rock River, Mile 278 (447 km). The Dempster Highway Interpretive Centre, at the Tombstone Mountain campground, is open from mid-June to early September. Explore area trails from here, too.

In the Northwest Territories, you can camp at Mile 340 (547.5 km) at the Nitainlaii Campground and Information Centre, operated by the territory government. Just a few miles later is Fort McPherson, home to fewer than 1,000 people, set on a hill overlooking the Peel River. Here, and at the end of the road in Inuvik, you realize how far you've come, so don't be in a hurry to leave. Soak in the wonder of these extreme north places. For Inuvik-area travel information, contact Inuvik's visitor center at 867-777-4727. For more on the Dempster Highway, visit *www.explorenwt.com.*

CAMPBELL HIGHWAY

Watson Lake to North Klondike Highway (near Carmacks): 362 miles (583 km)

Motorists on their way to Dawson City can shorten their drive by taking the alternate route around Whitehorse: the Campbell Highway (Highway 4). The road heads northwest from Watson Lake and, after 362 miles (583 km), connects with the North Klondike Highway (Highway 2) just north of Carmacks.

You accomplish three things by taking this route to Dawson City: You save 20 miles on your odometer; you miss out on all the fun that's waiting in Whitehorse; and you eat a lot of dust. On the other hand, you also see some beautiful land as you follow the route of early-day fur traders who worked for the Hudson's Bay Company. Robert Campbell himself was sent here in the 1840s to explore on behalf of the company.

Completed in 1968, the Campbell is mostly unpaved, and this road less traveled wends through the communities of Ross River and Faro, where you can buy gas, food, and groceries, as well as find a place to stay with or without an RV.

YELLOWHEAD-CASSIAR HIGHWAYS

Prince George to Alaska Highway (near Watson Lake): 744 miles (1,197 km)

Alaskabound travelers can shave some 100 miles (161 km) off the drive between Prince George and Watson Lake by taking westbound Yellowhead Highway 16 and then northbound Cassiar Highway 37. Some motorists are less concerned about time, but still take the Yellowhead-Cassiar route for a change of scenery through British Columbia's outstanding Skeena Mountains. Most portions of this route are paved, but drivers should stay alert for sections of washboard in gravel stretches of the Cassiar.

A rainy spring in 2007 created extra problems for motorists on this road, as certain sections were undermined by runoff. Some travelers reported numerous mudslides. Here's a perfect example of how checking ahead for a road report can help you determine which route to take. In British Columbia, check *www.drivebc.ca.*

Yellowhead Highway 16 is a trans-Canada route that extends from southern Manitoba and trends westward and north across Saskatchewan, Alberta, and British Columbia. In western Canada, it is a primary east-west route linking Edmonton with Prince George. Through mountain passes, along glacial lakes, and into canyons, the Yellowhead promises stunning vistas and plenty of wildlife-watching.

The Yellowhead continues west to the coastal city of Prince Rupert, B.C. From there, travelers may connect with the British Columbia ferry system and the Alaska Marine Highway System. (See Chapter 9, Alaska Marine Highway System.)

The junction of the Yellowhead and Cassiar Highways is 298 miles (480 km) west of Prince George near the village of Kitwanga. From here, the Cassiar trends north for 446 miles (718 km) to its junction with the Alaska Highway 13 miles (21 km) west of Watson Lake.

From the Cassiar Highway, motorists can access the coastal communities of Stewart, B.C., and Hyder, Alaska. The turnoff to these towns is at Mile 96 (155 km) on the Cassiar Highway, at Meziadin Junction. Stewart and Hyder straddle the international border 41 miles (66 km) west of the junction.

The Yellowhead Highway got its name from the story of an Iroquois-Caucasian trapper who was called Tête Jaune, or Yellowhead, for the blond cast to his hair. He led fur traders through the Rocky Mountains and opened the way for a trade route across western Canada.

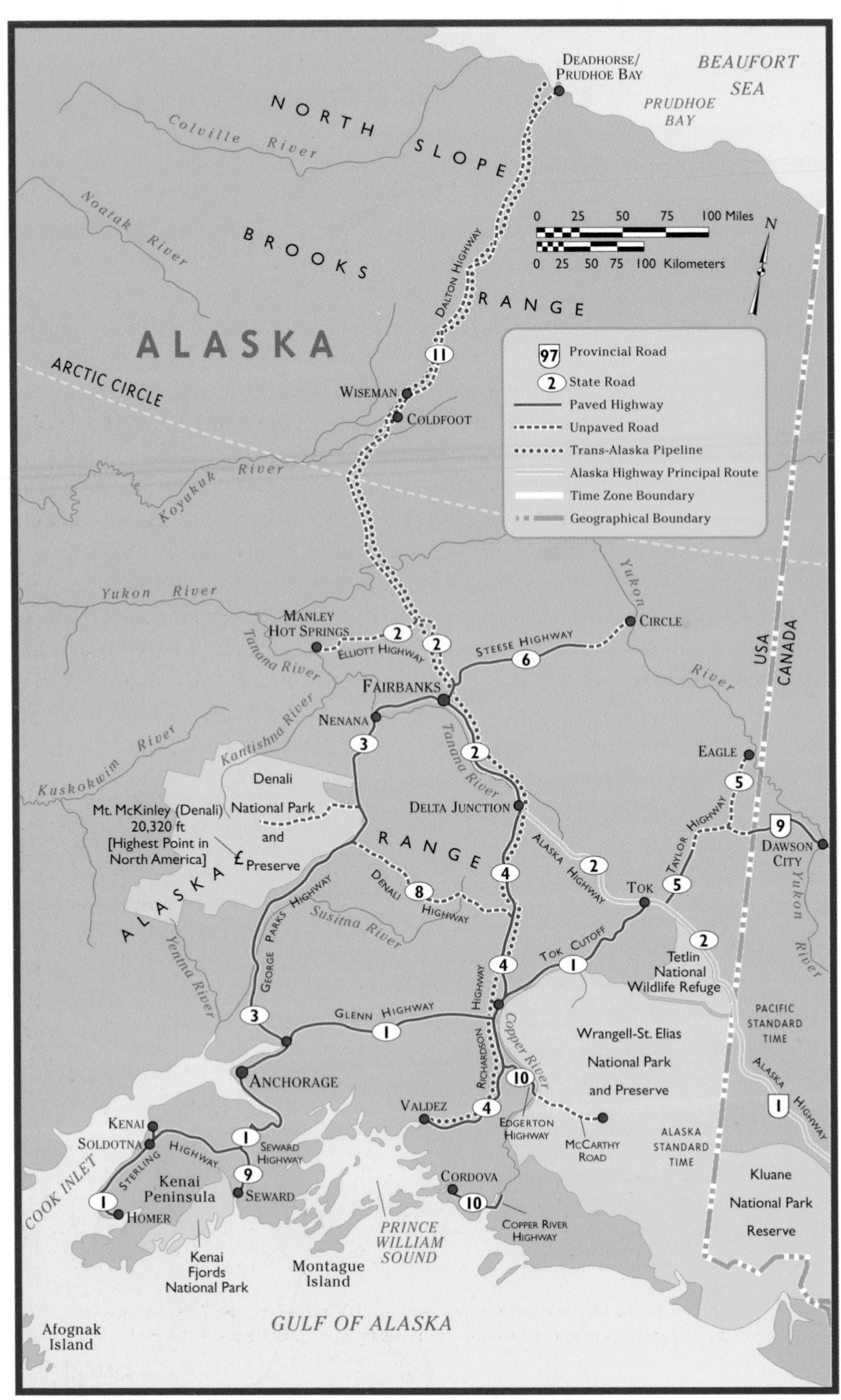

Deadhorse/ Prudhoe Bay
Beaufort Sea
Prudhoe Bay
North Slope
Colville River
Noatak River
Brooks Range
Dalton Highway
0 25 50 75 100 Miles
0 25 50 75 100 Kilometers
N
ALASKA
Arctic Circle
Wiseman
Coldfoot
97 Provincial Road
2 State Road
Paved Highway
Unpaved Road
Trans-Alaska Pipeline
Alaska Highway Principal Route
Time Zone Boundary
Geographical Boundary
Koyukuk River
Yukon River
Manley Hot Springs
Elliott Highway
Circle
Steese Highway
Tanana River
Fairbanks
Nenana
Kantishna River
Kuskokwim River
Denali National Park and Preserve
Mt. McKinley (Denali) 20,320 ft [Highest Point in North America]
Delta Junction
Alaska Range
Alaska Highway
Denali Highway
George Parks Highway
Susitna River
Yentna River
Eagle
Taylor Highway
Dawson City
Yukon River
USA
CANADA
Tok
Tok Cutoff
Tetlin National Wildlife Refuge
Glenn Highway
Richardson Highway
Copper River
Wrangell-St. Elias National Park and Preserve
Pacific Standard Time
Alaska Standard Time
Anchorage
Valdez
Edgerton Highway
McCarthy Road
Kenai
Soldotna
Sterling Highway
Seward Highway
Seward
Homer
Cook Inlet
Kenai Peninsula
Kenai Fjords National Park
Cordova
Copper River Highway
Prince William Sound
Montague Island
Kluane National Park Reserve
Gulf of Alaska
Afognak Island

CHAPTER 8

Alaska's State Highways

MOST VISITORS TO ALASKA are accustomed to choosing from a vast menu of roads, reading and following maps, and watching for their exits. When they ask directions, they commonly refer to route numbers. So when they arrive in Alaska, they might ask, "Where is the exit for Route 9?" The puzzled Alaskan will answer with another question, "Where do you want to go?" Choices are so few that decision-making is made easy. Name your destination and there's usually only one way to get there.

You may discover that the locals will answer in terms of time, rather than miles: Portage Lake is about 45 minutes south of Anchorage. Santa Claus House is about 15 minutes southwest of Fairbanks. Denali Park? A couple hours south of Fairbanks; about five hours

South of Anchorage, the Sterling and Seward highways of the Kenai Peninsula provide access to coastal communities, outstanding fishing, and unforgettable views.

Highway Name	*Length*	*Number*	*Route Description*
Copper River Highway	48 miles 77 km	10	Disconnected from highway system. Connects Cordova, on Prince William Sound, with the derelict Million Dollar Bridge to nowhere; mostly unpaved.
Dalton Highway	414 miles 666 km	11	Splits northbound from Elliott Highway (north of Fox) to Deadhorse, where it dead-ends at the Arctic Ocean; mostly unpaved; almost no services.
Denali Highway	136 miles 219 km	8	Road between Richardson Highway and Parks Highway; connects Paxson and Cantwell; unpaved; few services.
Edgerton Highway	33 miles 53 km	10	Connects Richardson Highway (south of Glennallen) to Chitina, 33 miles (53 km) east on paved road; from there, unpaved McCarthy Road travels east for 60 miles (96.5 km) almost to McCarthy; few services; not maintained in winter.
Elliott Highway	152 miles 245 km	2	From Fox (north of Fairbanks) to Manley Hot Springs, where it dead-ends at the Tanana River; partially paved; few services.
Glenn Highway	328 miles 528 km	1	Connects Anchorage with Glennallen and the Richardson Highway, and connects Gakona Junction with Tok via the Tok Cutoff; paved, sections often under repair; services at regular intervals. *(continued)*

north of Anchorage. Maps are optional when you drive in the country's biggest state, with fewer roads per square mile than Rhode Island.

A separate issue entirely is the Alaskan preference of calling highways by name, not route number: the Steese, the Parks, the Seward. You'll hear the names regularly, the route numbers rarely. Most of the highways dead-end at small towns along a major body of water. Consequently, the term "end of the road" applies to several communities around the state: Deadhorse, Circle City, Eagle, McCarthy, and Homer, to name a few.

If you want to drive northwest, west, or southwest from this narrow, north-south cluster of blacktop, you can forget it. Most of Alaska remains accessible only by air or, along Alaska's Panhandle (Southeast Alaska), by marine highway (see Chapter 9, Alaska Marine Highway System).

In 1942, when the Alaska Highway was built and attached to the existing Richardson Highway at Delta Junction, there were even fewer roads. Alaska's busiest highway, between Anchorage and Fairbanks—the Parks—didn't even exist. Travelers had to use the longer, roundabout way via the Richardson and Glenn Highways. The pipeline was still 30 years in

Highway Name	*Length*	*Number*	*Route Description*
Haines Highway (Via Yukon Route 3 and B.C. Route 4)	152 miles 245 km	7	Connects Alaska Highway at Haines Junction, Yukon, with Haines, Alaska, where it dead-ends on Lynn Canal; paved.
Klondike Highway 2 (Yukon road)	99 miles 159 km	2	Connects Alaska Highway just south of Whitehorse, Yukon, with Skagway, Alaska, where it dead-ends on Lynn Canal; paved.
Parks Highway	358 miles 576 km	3	Connects Anchorage with Fairbanks via the Glenn Highway. Completely paved; services at regular intervals.
Richardson Highway	364 miles 586 km	4 & 2	Connects Valdez with Fairbanks. Paved; services at regular intervals.
Seward Highway	127 miles 261 km	1 & 9	Connects Anchorage with Seward, where it dead-ends on Resurrection Bay off the Gulf of Alaska; paved; services at regular intervals.
Steese Highway	162 miles 261 km	6	Connects Fairbanks with Circle City, where it dead-ends on the Yukon River; mostly unpaved; few services.
Sterling Highway	143 miles 230 km	1	Branches off the Seward Highway for southbound travelers to Homer, where it dead-ends on Cook Inlet; paved; services at regular intervals.
Taylor Highway	160 miles 257 km	5	Connects Alaska Highway at Tetlin Junction (southeast of Tok) with Eagle, where it dead-ends on the Yukon River; unpaved; few services. Not maintained in winter.

the future, so the Dalton Highway (also known as the Haul Road for pipeline construction) hadn't been conceived. Nor had the Sterling Highway, which wends down the Kenai Peninsula. If you wanted to go to Homer, you took a ferry.

What are now considered major transportation routes (by Alaska standards) weren't much more than improved trails that had been used by early-day settlers, traders, and miners. A century ago and more, the pioneering Europeans simply traveled along the ancient trading routes of Alaska's first people, who were familiar with the passes through the mountains, and who graciously showed the newcomers the way.

Today, although Alaska's roads are called highways, a few remain rustic and unpaved; four of them (the Copper River, Edgerton, Taylor, and Denali Highways) are not maintained in winter months, so they are impassable and closed to vehicles. Snowmobilers, on the other hand, love these winter highways. Even if a road is regularly plowed, wise winter travelers will check the local phone book and call the Department of Transportation's recorded information line to obtain road conditions before setting out. (See the section on Driving in Winter in Chapter 1, Planning and Packing.)

Generally speaking, most of Alaska's major roads are in great shape. The paved roads are well-marked, two-lane routes (sometimes even four lanes) with ample shoulders. Unpaved sections are graded regularly, and sometimes serve better than the broken-down parts of paved roads. Small towns, gas stations, and other services appear at regular intervals, and restaurants and lodging aren't hard to find, either. That can't be said for all of Alaska's "highways," though, so read up on your route before you embark.

Road maintenance workers have a particular challenge in Alaska, considering what they have for a subsurface. In many parts of the state, they contend with an underground enemy called permafrost: permanently frozen sections of soil that are riddled with ice. When the insulating overgrowth is scraped away to create a road, the ground begins to melt and sink. Adding a layer of weighty, heat-conductive blacktop creates more subsurface problems. With the freeze and thaw of seasonal change, some roadbeds suffer, and an army of maintenance workers sets out to make repairs each year in the short summer construction season. As a motorist, plan for one or two delays, because flaggers, pilot cars, dust, and lumbering trucks are virtual guarantees. Please be patient. If they weren't out there doing their jobs, you wouldn't be willing (or able) to set out on these passageways into some of America's most magnificent places.

Of course, one must include gawking time in any Alaska road trip. When the evening light turns the sky pink-orange above a mountain range, the view can be distracting. Glacier-fed rivers merge and divide across a broad floodplain, and low clouds drag across the vivid, white mountain peaks. Wild animals step out onto the pavement ahead, or pause to feed along the shoulder, and your camera is at the ready. In the midst of such beauty, "making good time" loses its appeal.

Since 1993, the Alaska Department of Transportation and Public Facilities has named all or part of a dozen transportation corridors as Alaska Scenic Byways. To qualify for the state designation, a byway must possess some or all of these intrinsic qualities: scenic or natural beauty, cultural importance, recreational value, or archaeological or historic significance. Not all are paved roadways, however—the Alaska Railroad and the Alaska Marine Highway System are among the names on the list. The Marine Highway was "promoted" to a National Scenic Byway in September 2004. The others in the state list are the Dalton Highway, Haines Highway, Parks Highway (from Denali State Park to Healy), Richardson Highway (from Glennallen to Valdez), Seward Highway, Steese Highway, Sterling Highway (from Wye to Skilak, and Anchor Point to Homer), and the combination of the Taylor and Top of the World Highways. For more information and photos of Alaska's Scenic Byways, visit the following Web site: *www.dot.state.ak.us.*

This chapter features Alaska's highways, in alphabetical order, and includes the cities, services, access, recreational opportunities, and attractions that you'll find along this exceptionally scenic road system.

An innovative public service by the Alaska Department of Transportation and Public Facilities allows motorists to use any phone or the Internet to obtain the latest information about road conditions, traffic hazards, closures, and roadwork—even near times for state ferry arrivals—by dialing 5-1-1 or by visiting *www.511.alaska.gov.* If you're calling from out of state, dial toll-free 1-866-282-7577.

COPPER RIVER HIGHWAY

Cordova to Million Dollar Bridge: 48 miles (77 km)
Travel Opportunities: *Scenic fishing village; flightseeing over Wrangell–St. Elias National Park; Prince William Sound cruises; rafting on the Copper River; chartered fishing for salmon or halibut; Childs Glacier; Million Dollar Bridge; bird-watching.*

Among Alaska's unique roads, the Copper River Highway is a standout—a mere fragment of a highway that's disconnected from the rest of the highway system, but still official enough to merit a route number: Alaska Highway 10. To drive this road, you'll need to fly in and rent a car at Cordova on Prince William Sound—or bring your vehicle along on the Alaska Marine Highway System and disembark at Cordova (see Chapter 9, Alaska Marine Highway System). Pay heed to the return schedule if you choose to cruise, or you may stay longer than you had planned.

For centuries, Native Alaskans have lived in this region, moving with the seasons to fish and hunt as they drew life from the land. The ways of the early Native people are not just in museum displays today. In this area, you'll find many Athabascan, Eyak, and Alutiiq people who still follow the cultural practices of their ancestors in dance, song, and art, as well as through a subsistence lifestyle of hunting and fishing for food. Throughout the small Native villages of Southcentral Alaska, people live in log or wood-frame houses, drive cars, go to work, and follow the same television "soaps" as anybody else in the country. Some of them, however, have great-grandmas who remember the moment they saw a white person for the first time.

Explorers, gold seekers, and traders brought the stamp of the Western world to the Copper River Delta, especially during the 19th century. In 1902 geologists made the first major oil discovery in Alaska—at Katalla, southwest of Cordova. In 1907 entrepreneur Michael J. Heney began building the Copper River & Northwestern Railway to transport the ore mined from the Kennecott Copper Mine, to the north. The mine and railroad flourished for more than 20 years, closing in the late 1930s. In the mid-1940s, builders of the Copper River Highway chose to follow the railway's bed and planned to join Cordova with Chitina and the Richardson Highway. In 1964, a natural disaster thwarted the project, and the work stalled out. That year, the Good Friday Earthquake devastated Cordova and many Southcentral coastal communities. The earthquake originally was measured at a magnitude of 8.6 and later was upgraded to an unbelievable 9.2. One section of the Million-Dollar Bridge over the Copper River collapsed in the 1964 earthquake. And for the next forty years it remained in disrepair. It was added to the National Register of Historic Places in 2000. Finally, in 2005, after a year of work to repair the bridge, the Million Dollar Bridge reopened, once more allowing motorists from Cordova to cross the Copper River. Cordova remains disconnected from Chitina by road, however.

The first 12 miles (19 km) of the Copper River Highway are paved, followed by a gravel surface that threads for another 36 miles (58 km) through awesome beauty to the historic bridge. There are several USFS trailheads and recreational opportunities along this route.

Near the bridge, you'll get a panoramic view of Childs Glacier. Plan a picnic here amid unforgettable surroundings. A limited number of sites are available for RVers and tent campers who want to spend the night at Childs Glacier Recreation Area. A crude road extends another 10 miles (16 km) beyond the bridge, but only four-wheel-drive vehicles should give it a go.

In the course of its 48 miles (77 km), the highway crosses a number of glacially fed streams and the multifingered Copper River Delta. Magnificent glaciers are visible on the north side of the road as you drive east. And all around you, for miles and miles, is Chugach National Forest, close to 6 million acres of it. On this drive, you'll find viewpoint turnouts with informational plaques, numerous trailheads, and two developed recreation areas. Fishing, wildlife-watching, hiking, biking, and camping are popular activities around here, and the Copper River is famed for its annual runs of salmon. Freshwater and saltwater fishing takes place in an angler's paradise. Learn about local regulations and closures when you obtain your fishing license at any number of retail outlets in Cordova.

Cordova is a photogenic town with a population of about 2,300 people. Because its economy is largely based on fishing, commercial fishing vessels outnumber pleasure boats in the harbor, and a U.S. Coast Guard vessel is moored just outside the small-boat harbor. It's fun to walk the docks and read the names of the vessels and to watch the fishermen gear up or down from a trip. The catch may be salmon, halibut, or herring, depending on season. In town, nearly everything you need lies within walking distance. North of Cordova, the Alaska Marine Highway ferry terminal offers scheduled service aboard the M/V *Aurora* or the new fast ferry, the M/V *Chenega*, which connects travelers with Valdez and Whittier (see Chapter 9, Alaska Marine Highway System).

The region is a stopover on the largest shorebird migration in the world. Located on a major flyway for 2 million waterfowl and 5 million shorebirds, Cordova hosts the Copper River Delta Shorebird Festival in early May each year. Birders come from all over the world to view the millions of birds that nest and feed in the delta. So vital to the birds' survival, this portion of the Chugach National Forest gained added protection in 1978 when it was named a Critical Habitat Area.

The favorite party of the winter season is the Cordova Iceworm Festival, set each year on the first weekend of February. Events include a parade, entertainment, an arts and crafts show, skiing events, a best-beard contest, and selection of a king and queen. Call 907-424-5756 for more information.

Cordova Museum and Library on First Street offers exhibits on the rich Native cultures of this region, as well as its exploration in 1778 by Captain James Cook, the gold rush, and more recent copper-mining history. Also inside are art displays, a fishing diorama, gift shop, and a modest bookstore. Call 907-424-6655 or visit *www.cordovamuseum.org*.

At the U.S. Forest Service office, in a historic 1925 building at 612 2nd Street, you can learn about the Chugach National Forest and local natural history. The USFS offers 17 cabins in the area, available for a fee and by reservation. Call 1-877-444-6777 or see *www.reserveusa.com*.

Other options from Cordova include rafting the Copper River, a fly-in fishing trip, a cruise on Prince William Sound, or a flightseeing excursion above the fabulous Wrangell–St. Elias Range. For more information on what to see and do in Cordova, contact the Chamber of Commerce at 907-424-7260, or visit *www.cordovachamber.com*.

LODGING

Alaskan Hotel & Bar
600 1st Street
907-424-3288
Shared and private rooms, downtown location. Meet the locals in the bar.

Cordova Lighthouse Inn
212 Nicholoff Way
907-424-7080
www.cordovalighthouseinn.com
Comfortable guest rooms. Gift shop, café.

Cordova Rose Lodge
1315 Whitshed Road
907-424-7673
www.cordovarose.com
Historic setting of landlocked barge offers rooms with a view. Tour arrangements. Breakfast and dinner.

The Northern Nights Inn
P.O. Box 1564
907-424-5356
www.northernnightsinn.com
Rooms with a view of the inlet; kitchens, laundry, freezer for your fish.

Orca Adventure Lodge
2 miles north of Cordova
907-424-7249
www.orcaadventurelodge.com
1880s cannery town rebuilt for adventure clientele. Tours, hikes, kayaking, etc.

Prince William Motel
2nd and Council Streets
1-888-796-6835 or 907-424-3201
16 rooms and kitchenettes. TV, microwaves, refrigerators, laundry, store.

Reluctant Fisherman
407 Railroad Avenue
907-424-3272
www.reluctantfisherman.com
Nonsmoking rooms with cable TV, some with harbor views. Free local calls, data ports, wireless Internet. Laundry, free continental breakfast. Bar and grill on site.

CAMPGROUNDS

Alaska River Expeditions
800-776-1864
www.alaskarafters.com
Camping, raft adventures, tours.

Odiak Camper Park
Whitshed Road off Copper River Highway
907-424-6200
24 sites, tenting area, showers; operated by the city.

U.S. Forest Service
1-877-444-6777
www.reserveusa.com
17 cabins available in this district; most accessible only by boat or plane. Three are on the trail system.

RESTAURANTS

Ambrosia Restaurant
410 Main Street
907-424-7175
Comfortable setting, good selection of drinks and menu items.

Cordova Lighthouse Inn
212 Nicholoff Way
1-888-424-7080
www.cordovalighthouseinn.com
Café and bakery.

Cordova Rose Lodge
1315 Whitshed Road
907-424-7673
www.cordovarose.com
Sourdough pancakes, seafood specialties.

Killer Whale Café
Main Street
907-424-7733
Breakfasts and lunches, espresso, baked goods.

Powder House Bar and Restaurant
Mile 2 Copper River Highway
907-424-3529
Soups, sandwiches, seafood. Eat in or take-out.

Reluctant Fisherman
407 Railroad Avenue
907-424-3272
www.reluctantfisherman.com
Bar and grill on deck overlooking Orca Inlet.

The Dalton Highway is the northernmost state road in the country.

DALTON HIGHWAY (Haul Road)

From Elliott Highway to Deadhorse: 414 miles (666 km)
Travel Opportunities: *Trans-Alaska pipeline views; Yukon River; Coldfoot; Wiseman gold-mining village; Brooks Range continental divide; Arctic Circle crossing; guided tours to Prudhoe Bay oil operations.*

The Dalton Highway originally was called the Haul Road because it was built for one purpose: to haul goods and supplies for the building of the trans-Alaska pipeline. The road was named for James William Dalton, a principal player in North Slope oil development. Although experimental ice roads, seasonal at best, had been built in the Arctic, the Dalton was the first planned and engineered roadway into the farthest north reaches of the state. Even though the Dalton was finished in 1974, its entire length wasn't opened to the public until 1995.

You will share the road with mostly truckers headed to or from Deadhorse and Prudhoe Bay at the top of the state, a small number of hardy souls like yourself, and a handful of tourism operations. As far as services go, this route remains largely undeveloped. With a few exceptions—such as businesses at the Yukon River crossing, Coldfoot, Wiseman, Deadhorse, and a couple of wayside stops—you'll encounter long stretches of no towns, no gas stations, few outhouses, and few other travelers. The only ATM is at Deadhorse. Emergency medical services are not available. Officials suggest calling the Alaska State Troopers at 911 or by CB on Channel 19.

As you head north, the terrain changes in degrees of beauty: from sparsely treed rolling hills, to lofty mountains, to limitless undulating tundra. Your most constant companion is the nearby pipeline, visible only in the stretches where the permafrost in the soil was so bad that builders put it up on supports and ran it above ground. The 48-inch-diameter pipeline was built between 1974 and 1977. Its 800-mile (1,287.5-km) length stretches from Mile 0 at Prudhoe Bay to its terminus at Valdez on Prince William Sound. South of Fairbanks, most of the pipeline route parallels the Richardson Highway.

A mostly unpaved wilderness road, the Dalton extends from Mile 73 of the Elliott Highway, north of Fox, all the way to Deadhorse and the working oil fields of Prudhoe Bay. Don't expect to waltz in anywhere at will. Security precautions keep many places off-limits to the average traveler. In Deadhorse you'll find an airport, general store, filling station, and a couple of hotels, which are the best places to line up a guided tour of the area. With a guide, you may dip your toes in the frigid Arctic Ocean, view Mile 0 of the pipeline, and learn about how the vast oil reservoir beneath Alaska's North Slope was discovered and developed.

Most car rental companies prohibit taking their vehicles on the Dalton, and we don't recommend driving farther north than Coldfoot with your own vehicle, as there are no repair services between Coldfoot and Deadhorse. Consider the following option for less wear-and-tear on your vehicle and your sensibilities: take a fly-drive combo tour with a number of tour operators. I did this once and found the trip very worthwhile. For travel businesses that specialize in the Far North, contact the Fairbanks Convention and Visitors Bureau at 1-800-327-5774 or 907-456-5774 to talk to a travel expert. You can also visit their Web site at *www.explorefairbanks.com*. Also, the Bureau of Land Management annually updates its travel guide to the Dalton Highway. Look online at *www.blm.gov/ak/dalton* or call the BLM's Arctic Field Office in Fairbanks at 1-800-437-7021.

On a guided trip to the North Slope, you begin the trip with strangers, but make fast friends within hours. Pack an overnight bag, and a shuttle bus will pick you up from your Fairbanks campground or hotel. You'll be well fed throughout the trip.

After a 45-minute flight from Fairbanks to Deadhorse, we boarded an 18-passenger van and cruised around the oil fields, with permitted access to places where we would not have been allowed as independent visitors. Naturally this is a high-security area, and tourism is under development. The population of Deadhorse is officially 25—plus 3,500 to 5,000 transient workers. Most work a fluctuating schedule of two-weeks-on, two-weeks-off, or something similar. You won't see many people, actually. Most work indoors.

Around the low buildings and ground-level maze of pipes, the road meanders among the oil-company installations and enclosed drilling rigs. We saw numerous caribou, waterfowl, and wildflowers in what I considered unexpected places. In one spot, we saw a group of caribou resting under a raised part of the pipeline. Without trees to block the view, they were easy to spot. At the Arctic Ocean, I handed off my camera to a fellow traveler and asked him to take my picture standing ankle deep in the water. (I threw my arms in the air and said "Hurry!" through a clenched smile. The water was piercing cold in August.)

Our driver had packed lots of good food in coolers, and we had plenty of water, coffee, and soft drinks. Driving south that day, he told us all about the unique forces of nature here, the climate, the geology, and the wildlife. We learned how to pronounce "Sagavanirktok River," and understood instantly why everybody calls it the Sag.

Farther south we spied a hunter who had bagged a caribou with bow and arrow, and some of us tried walking out to him over the tundra. It was like trying to walk on and between underinflated basketballs that are covered with mossy, leafy growth.

We stopped again to share our drinking water with a British couple on a bicycle journey from Fairbanks to Prudhoe Bay, then visited the century-old mining town of Wiseman. A woman behind the counter in the general store told us that in the last couple of days, a local miner had uncovered a record-size gold nugget: flat and big enough to eclipse a saucer.

After an overnight at Coldfoot, in buildings that once housed pipeline construction workers, we continued our southbound trip and later came upon the only structure around for a hundred miles: the tour company's private, off-road outhouse, placed there just for our comfort. Next stop was the Arctic Circle, marked by a sturdy sign showing your place on the globe. Our driver asked us to wait a moment, then literally rolled out a red carpet and shook our hands, welcoming us across the invisible line. That evening, we pulled in to Fairbanks, tired but thrilled to have seen such rare sights.

My advice is to go with a tour guide if you want the best experience and the least worry. It was a privilege to have someone drive, especially when a good-size piece of gravel damaged the tour van's windshield (and not mine).

Places of note along the Dalton Highway, from south to north:

Yukon River Bridge. The highway crosses the bridge at Mile 56 (90 km), where many travelers are happy to find the services of Yukon River Camp, for lodging, food, and tours. Here at the crossing, you may launch your boat on the Yukon River, and there are good views of the pipeline from here. In summer months, the Bureau of Land Management staffs the Yukon Crossing Visitor Contact Station, a rest stop with outhouses, information, and viewing platform. Just a few miles ahead, the BLM maintains the Five Mile site for RV dumping and water fill-ups. Nearby, another popular business, the Hot Spot, offers food and lodging.

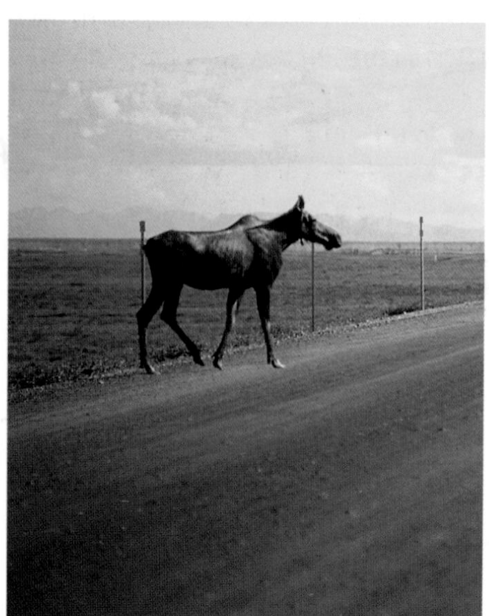

A cow moose crosses the Dalton north of the Brooks Range.

This area lies within the Yukon Flats National Wildlife Refuge, which supports moose, caribou, bears, millions of migrating birds, and small furbearers such as lynx, snowshoe hares, foxes, and beavers.

Arctic Circle. At Mile 115 (185 km), an expansive wayside with viewing platform, outhouses, and great signs is worth a stop

A tour driver literally rolled out the red carpet for his guests as he welcomed them across the Arctic Circle. Each was issued a certificate signifying this important event.

to record your momentous crossing of the Arctic Circle—that invisible boundary that encircles the globe at the southernmost latitude where the sun never sets on the day of the summer solstice (June 21 or 22). Likewise, at this latitude the sun does not rise on the day of the winter solstice (December 21 or 22). Nearby at Mile 115, the Bureau of Land Management offers undeveloped camping with tables, grills, and outhouses. No water is available.

Coldfoot. This former pipeline construction camp was given this name for obvious reasons. Winter temperatures plunge well below zero all along the Dalton Highway. The farther north you go, the deeper the plunge. I once visited Coldfoot with a television crew in January, and I still remember the heartbreaking sound of an expensive and important part of the camera when it went *crraack!* in the –50°F air. In summer, Coldfoot is pleasantly warm, but be advised that mosquitoes and other biting insects are a nuisance. There is no town here, but rather a welcome stop in the road at Mile 175 (282 km), where truckers and tourists refresh and refill at Coldfoot Camp. A post office, 24-hour fuel, tire repair, restaurant, and overnight accommodations in a former pipeline camp facility are available. Call 907-474-3500 or see *www.coldfootcamp.com*. Three government agencies jointly operate a visitor center in Coldfoot, with nightly slide presentations. Call 907-678-5209 for details.

In 2005, the Bureau of Land Management opened a developed campground at Mile 180. The Marion Creek Campground, five miles north of Coldfoot, has 27 sites, some for RVs, pit toilet, potable water, and trash containers. You can hike upstream to a 20-foot waterfall. This campground is wheelchair accessible.

Wiseman. Gold miners gather where there's gold to be found. Towns are created by the people who follow: the scores who offer services and supplies for those miners. That's how Wiseman came to be, nearly a century ago here in the Koyukuk Mining District. Disconnected from the rest of the world as it was, the town nearly died out before the Haul Road was built. Now located about 3 miles (5 km) off the Dalton Highway (at Mile 188) and populated by a scant 17 people, it has managed to cling to life as gold and tourism now feed the town. Pay mind to private property as you walk among the log homes—it's easy to imagine this as a Disney set, but people do live and work here! Visit the Wiseman Historical Museum to learn more about local and regional mining history. It's located in the historic

Carl Frank cabin in north Wiseman. On the south end of town, cross the river to reach the two log-cabin-and-breakfast businesses: Arctic Getaway (907-678-4456) and Boreal Lodging (907-678-4566). Ask permission and directions to the old cemetery on a beautiful hillside above town, where many area pioneers have gone to rest.

Continental Divide. Drive through the majestic Brooks Range and cross the northernmost Continental Divide in the United States, at Mile 245. Atigun Pass, at 4,739 feet, is the highest point on the 800-mile north-south route of the pipeline.

The North Slope. To oil company workers, this name—or its abbreviated version, the Slope—is synonymous with Prudhoe Bay. It is derived from a geographical feature. On the north side of the Brooks Range, this country takes its time returning to sea level. It is that slow, almost unrecognizable slope toward the Arctic Ocean that is referred to in "North Slope."

Deadhorse/Prudhoe Bay. End of the line. Stop at the Prudhoe Bay General Store (and U.S. post office) to send a postcard from the top of the world. The store features its own little museum, too, along with sales of souvenirs, sweatshirts, outdoor gear, hats, and more. Call 907-659-2412. Accommodations, meals, and fuel can be found in town.

The trans-Alaska pipeline parallels the Dalton Highway for the entire length of the route to Deadhorse.

LODGING/MEALS

AT OR NEAR YUKON RIVER BRIDGE:

Yukon River Camp
Mile 56 Dalton Highway
www.yukonrivercamp.com
907-474-3557
Salmon, burgers, homemade desserts. Lodging available.

The Hot Spot Café
Mile 60 Dalton Highway
907-451-7543
Rooms, burgers, pies, barbecue.

COLDFOOT:

Slate Creek Inn
Mile 175 Dalton Highway
907-474-3500
www.coldfootcamp.com
80 rooms, plus service station, post office, gift shop. Buffet-style dining at breakfast and dinner; some deli items, box lunches for the road. RV hookups for water and electric, and dump station. Tent sites available.

WISEMAN:

Arctic Getaway Cabin and Breakfast
Mile 189 Dalton Highway
907-678-4456
www.arcticgetaway.com
Located in a historic building: Pioneer Hall, Igloo No. 8.

Boreal Lodging
South end of Wiseman
907-678-4566
Cabins, rooms, showers, phone, TV. Aurora-viewing, sled-dog rides in winter.

DEADHORSE/PRUDHOE BAY:

Arctic Caribou Inn
Near the airport
1-877-659-2368 or 907-659-2368
75 rooms with private or shared baths. Near restaurant, gift shop, airport. Tours available: oil field; Mile 0 of the pipeline; Arctic Ocean walk.

Arctic Oilfield Hotel
Corner of Sag River Road and Spine Road
907-659-2614
Rooms, showers, laundry, buffet-style meals. Tire repair, towing, welding.

Prudhoe Bay Hotel
End of the Dalton Highway
907-659-2449
Rooms, showers, laundry, restaurant, gift shop, ATM, Internet access, car rental. Commercial tours of Prudhoe Bay oil field.

CAMPGROUNDS

COLDFOOT:

Coldfoot Camp
Mile 175 Dalton Highway
907-474-3500
www.coldfootcamp.com
RV hookups and dump station. Service station, post office, gift shop, café and saloon.

DEADHORSE:

Arctic Caribou Inn
Near the airport
1-877-659-2368 or 907-659-2368
RV parking is available adjacent to this hotel.

Arctic Oilfield Hotel
Corner of Sag River Road and Spine Road
907-659-2614
RV parking, showers, laundry, buffet-style meals. Tire repair, towing, welding.

The Bureau of Land Management oversees four camping areas along the Dalton Highway. For more information, contact the Northern Field Office in Fairbanks at 1-800-437-7021 or visit the bureau's Web site at www.aurora.ak.blm.gov. The camping areas are:

Sixty Mile Site
Mile 60 Dalton Highway
Undeveloped 5 acres with dump station, water, outhouse.

Arctic Circle Site
Mile 115 Dalton Highway
Undeveloped 5 acres above wayside, outhouse.

Marion Creek Campground
Mile 180 Dalton Highway
Developed 1.5 acres with 28 campsites, 11 pull-through sites, fire pits, water, toilets, campground hosts.

Galbraith Lake Site
Mile 275 Dalton Highway
Undeveloped 5 acres, outhouse.

DENALI HIGHWAY

From Richardson Highway to Parks Highway: 136 miles (219 km)
Travel Opportunities: *No towns, just fabulous mountain vistas; hiking, biking, berry picking; fishing at lakes and stream crossings; wildlife watching and bird watching.*

The Denali Highway opened in 1957 as the only road access to what was then called Mount McKinley National Park. The George Parks Highway, finished in 1972, made the park even more accessible. Using a grand scale, visualize the Richardson Highway and George Parks Highway as parallel uprights in the letter H. Then the Denali Highway is the crossbar that joins them. Connecting Paxson on the Richardson Highway to Cantwell on the Parks Highway, this mostly unpaved wilderness road is a 136-mile shortcut through an awesome landscape.

Three major peaks dominate the skyline in this section of the Alaska Range: Mount Deborah, at 12,339 feet; Mount Hess, at 11,940 feet; and Mount Hayes, at 13,892 feet.

In 1980 the national park's name was changed to reflect local use of the name for the highest peak in the continent: Denali. In the Athabascan language, the word means "the high one." The park became Denali National Park and Preserve, though the official name for the peak remains Mount McKinley.

The park attracts thousands of visitors who most often arrive via the Alaska Railroad or with major tour operators, such as Gray Line of Alaska and Princess Tours. But the road travelers are many as well. From June through mid-August, RV and tent campers often fill up every available spot in the park's camping areas. (See the section on the Parks Highway, in this chapter, for tips on securing a campsite reservation.)

The Tangle Lakes, Tangle River, and a dozen other lakes and streams along the Denali Highway are popular destinations for anglers. Typical in these waters are grayling, whitefish, burbot, and lake trout. Inquire in Paxson or Cantwell for licensing and tips on what is biting. Consider hiring a guide for a more fulfilling experience.

The Denali Highway is a wonderful drive, particularly during sunny days that offer boundless views of the Alaska Range. RV travelers take heed that while the road out of Paxson is paved and broad, after 20 miles (32 km) it is a gravel road that gradually narrows as it journeys west. The maximum recommended speed, even when no one is around, is 30 mph.

There are few services along its length, but plenty at each end. Milepost addresses are measured from Paxson, on the Richardson Highway. And, of course, keep your eye out for moose and caribou. This is their kind of country.

LODGING/MEALS

Tangle River Inn
Mile 20 Denali Highway
907-822-7304 or 907-822-3970
www.tangleriverinn.com
Rooms, cabins, liquor store, bar, restaurant overlooking Tangle Lakes. Canoe rentals.

Maclaren River Lodge
Mile 42 Denali Highway
907-822-5444
Cabins, campsites, full-service restaurant. Tire repair, gas, tours and guided fishing.

Gracious House Lodge & Flying Service
Mile 82 Denali Highway
907-333-3148 or 907-259-1111
www.alaskaone.com/gracious
Rooms, with or without private bath. Fuel, café, bar. RV parking and tent sites by the lake.

CAMPGROUNDS

The Bureau of Land Management overseas two campgrounds along the Denali Highway:

Tangle Lakes Compound
Mile 21.5 (from Paxson)
60 acres for RV or tent campsites with water, wheelchair-accessible toilets, boat launch, fishing.

Brushkana Campground
Mile 104.5 (from Paxson)
22 sites for RV or tent campsites with water, toilets, picket shelter.

EDGERTON HIGHWAY

From Richardson Highway to Chitina: 33 miles (53 km)
From Chitina to McCarthy (on McCarthy Road): 60 miles (97 km)
Travel Opportunities: *Athabascan Indian culture in Tonsina and Chitina; fishing or rafting the Copper River; salmon dip-netting in the Chitina River; McCarthy, historic copper-mining town; derelict Kennecott Copper Mine.*

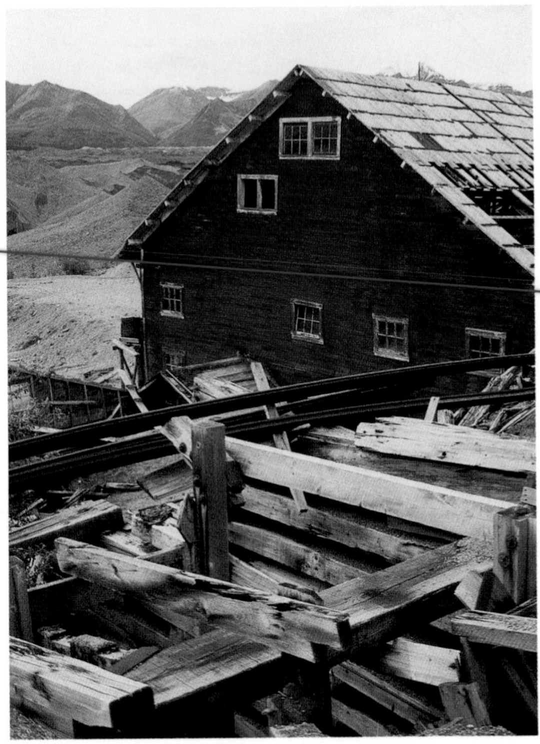

The derelict Kennecott Copper Mine saw its heyday in the early 20th century, and continues to be restored as a visitor attraction near McCarthy. In 1908, railroad builder Michael J. Heney began construction of the 196-mile Copper River Northwestern Railway. The road to McCarthy was built over a portion of the defunct rail bed.

Named for a former member of the Alaska Territorial Road Commission, U.S. Army Major Glenn Edgerton, the Edgerton Highway is an eastbound spur road off the Richardson Highway at a point 32 miles (51.5 km) south of Glennallen, or 83 miles (133.5 km) north of Valdez. You're on pavement for 35 miles (56 km)—to the village of Chitina—and there the Edgerton officially ends.

This village lies at the edge of Wrangell–St. Elias National Park and Preserve, 13.2 million acres of some of the most beautiful, glaciated mountain wilderness you've ever seen from ground level. From a plane, its mountain peaks and hanging valleys are even more incredible.

This region is the traditional homeland of the Athabascan Indians, and along the Edgerton Highway or in Chitina, take advantage of opportunities to purchase

A group of adventure tourists takes a backcountry trip on horseback in the Wrangell–St. Elias National Park and Preserve.

locally made Native art, as well as to visit with descendants of the first Alaskans. Roam around Chitina (CHIT-na) to view evidence of a boomtown grown old. A few buildings have been restored and placed on the National Register of Historic Sites.

In the early part of the 20th century, when the Kennecott Copper Mine was in its heyday, Chitina was a busy center of commerce, with hotels, restaurants, saloons, and even a movie theater. Today's Chitina, population 132, is no longer essential to the defunct copper mine, but neither is it a ghost town. As the gateway to Wrangell–St. Elias National Park, the village sees hundreds of visitors annually.

In summer, the tiny population really swells when the salmon are running in the Copper River and the Alaska Department of Fish and Game declares a "subsistence opener." This is a great time to come and watch the fishing action. Monitoring fish numbers throughout each run, the state opens the river to Alaska residents who depend on fish to feed themselves and their families. They hold a special permit for subsistence fishing. Dip-netting is the fast and preferred method of harvesting the fish. It's a partylike atmosphere as men and women don waders and walk into the river with billowy nets attached to a frame with a long handle. The fishing is as simple as dipping into the water and walking back to shore with the fish. It's that easy, or hard. These are weighty fish, ranging from 15 to 35 pounds or better.

You may see places along the river where local Athabascan Indians have set up a fish wheel to capture fish using the river current to turn the net-covered arms of the contraption. Beneath the surface, a fish is swept up and out of the water by the net and, as the wheel turns, the fish then drops into a holding box.

Stop at the Wrangell–St. Elias National Park and Preserve ranger station, housed in the historic Ed S. Orr cabin dating from 1910. Volunteers there share their knowledge of Chitina's colorful history and people, with publications, videos, and other resources for travelers. The office also is a good place to ask about weather and road conditions in the park, as well as questions on land ownership, as much of the land is privately owned. Call 907-823-2205.

From Chitina, the unpaved, 60-mile (96.5-km) McCarthy Road leads to the village of McCarthy within the park. At the end of the spur road, you'll park on one side of the Copper River, cross on a footbridge, and take a van or bus ride to visit the old Kennicott town site and the remains of a once-great copper operation: the Kennecott Mine. (The spelling of both place-names is correct. The mine and town names don't match due to a century-old spelling error!)

The McCarthy Road is so rugged, however, that big-rig RVs would be advised to think twice about making this adventure drive. Even family-car drivers have to stay under 25 mph to keep their hubcaps on! And flat tires are not unusual. Because the road follows the stripped railbed of the defunct Copper River & Northwestern Railway, drivers should watch out for old railroad spikes, along with potholes, washboard, or slippery sections in the rain. This isn't to say don't go—just know that it will be slow going.

So think about letting someone else do the driving. Backcountry Connection at 907-822-5292 offers scheduled one-way or round-trip van service between Glennallen and McCarthy, and on to Kennicott. Or you can arrange a fly-in day trip between Chitina and Kennicott with Wrangell Mountain Air, based in McCarthy. Call 1-800-478-1160 or visit their Web site at *www.wrangellmountainair.com.* Other charter air services may be arranged out of Gulkana, Glennallen, or Valdez.

The payoff for putting up with the McCarthy Road is getting to the village of McCarthy, population 70, in a striking, mountain-rimmed setting. But bear in mind that you can't just drive into the town itself. The McCarthy Road ends in a parking area on the west side of the Kennicott River. Overnight parking is permitted for RV travelers. To reach McCarthy, you still must cross the river via footbridge and travel another mile on land (shuttle service is available). The footbridge here is still a fairly new development, dating from 1997. For some, it's a most welcome replacement for the hand-operated cable tram that once spanned the river. Others believe that losing the tram was a blow to what makes McCarthy so charming. Pieces of the tram lie near the bridge. You decide.

This little village was founded in 1910 at the height of the copper rush. Several historic buildings are still standing and still doing business. In summer, the little community buzzes with activity as wilderness guides, bush pilots, anglers, photographers, mountain climbers, and tourists drift in and out of town.

Arrange for a rafting excursion on the Kennicott River; call Wrangell Mountain Air for a flightseeing expedition; book a shuttle ride to the ghost town of Kennicott and wander amid the ruins of a once-great copper mine. All businesses are within walking distance, and the locals will have answers to your questions.

LODGING/CAMPGROUNDS/MEALS

KENNY LAKE:

Kenny Lake RV & Mercantile
Mile 7 Edgerton Highway
907-822-3313
Rooms with shared baths. Store, fuel, fishing licenses, RV parking for dry or partial hookups. Tent sites, dump station, self-service laundry, showers, pay phone, café.

Liberty Falls State Recreation Site
Mile 23.5 Edgerton Highway
10 sites, picturesque camping near the falls, but the road is not recommended for large RVs. Toilets, no water.

Wrangell View RV Park
Mile 24 Edgerton Highway
907-823-2223
Full hookups, dump station, store.

CHITINA:

Gilpatrick's Hotel Chitina
In the heart of Chitina
907-823-2244 (summers)
www.hotelchitina.com
Restored 1914 building features rooms with private baths, restaurant, saloon.

Currant Ridge Cabins
Mile 57 McCarthy Road
907-554-4424
www.currantridgecabins.com
Rustic cabins, nicely appointed, family owned.

McCARTHY:

McCarthy Lodge
Ma Johnson's Hotel
Lancaster's Backpacker Hotel
Downtown McCarthy
907-554-4402
www.mccarthylodge.com
All-Alaskan decor in 1916 hotel with modern fixtures, lodge, saloon, dining room.

KENNICOTT:

Kennicott Glacier Lodge
Kennicott's main street
1-800-582-5128
www.kennicottlodge.com
25 rooms, dining room, spacious porch, overlooking Kennicott Glacier and Chugach Mountains.

ELLIOTT HIGHWAY

Fox to Manley Hot Springs: 152 miles (245 km)
Travel Opportunities: *Gold panning at Eldorado Gold Mine; viewing the pipeline; views of Minto Flats; hiking BLM trails; fishing the Tolovana River; wildlife watching; soaking in Manley Hot Springs.*

The Elliott Highway begins a short 11 miles (17.5 km) north of Fairbanks, at the town of Fox. At the only intersection in Fox, continue driving straight ahead and you'll be on the Elliott. Travelers who want to stay on the Steese Highway and head toward Chatanika, Central, or Circle have to take a hard right. About half of the Elliott is paved, and in these early miles, the surface is lumpy-bumpy from the damaging work of freeze-thaw action.

Just a mile from the intersection, on the left, is one of the most popular attractions in the Fairbanks area: the Eldorado Gold Mine. Featured on several national broadcasts, the two-hour Eldorado tour begins and ends with a ride on a narrow-gauge railroad, on tracks that were recycled from a railway that once operated among the gold-rich fields of this area. The train's engineer is a fiddler, too, and his entertainment and narration make for an enjoyable ride as you pass an old sourdough's cabin, enter a permafrost tunnel, and watch antique mining equipment at work once again. Round a bend to an expansive, old-time cookshack, where you are greeted by Yukon Yonda and Dexter Clark, a husband-and-wife mining team

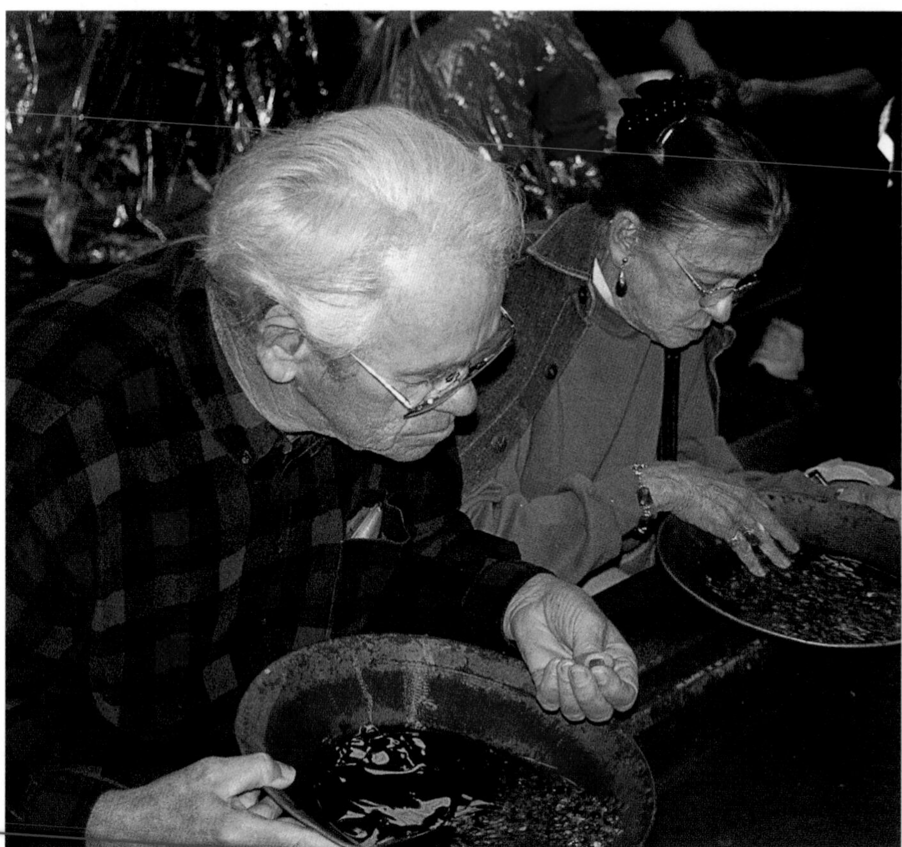

At the Eldorado Gold Mine, visitors learn about how gold is mined today, then get a chance to do some gold panning of their own. The family-owned business is a favorite stop on the Elliott Highway.

that has been extracting gold from Interior streams and valleys for more than 30 years. Through their demonstration and banter, you learn about modern mining practices. Next, everybody gets to pan, then have their gold weighed in the cookshack/gift shop. Call 1-866-479-6673 or 907-479-6673. See them online at *www.eldoradogoldmine.com.*

Mile 5.5 is a must-stop if pie is one of your major food groups. The Hilltop Truckstop feeds the truckers and fills their rigs, and visitors are welcome to dine and fuel up as well. There's an ATM, ice, groceries, propane, and showers, as well as a menu of hearty selections. The cream and fruit pies come to the table in slabs, not slices. Try the Fat Man pie.

For Fairbanks-area hikers, the 20-mile (32-km) trail up Wickersham Dome is a favorite. The trailhead is at Mile 28, providing access to Summit Trail and Wickersham Creek Trail, both in the White Mountains National Recreation Area.

The Arctic Circle Trading Post at Mile 49 is more than just a gift shop. They issue certificates to those who cross the circle and maintain the "Official Arctic Circle Registry," as well as sell Arctic Circle memorabilia. They also stay abreast of Dalton Highway road conditions, so go ahead and ask. Call 907-474-3507 or see *www.arcticcircletradingpost.com.*

At Mile 71 (113.5 km), the turnoff leads to the old mining camp known as Livengood. Although you may want to read that as "livin' GOOD," this place-name is actually pronounced "LIVE-en-good" for one of the two men who discovered gold near here in 1914. With a population of 28, there are no visitor services here. While the old town hints at the millions in gold that was taken out of the Livengood-Tolovana Mining District, large-scale gold-mining operations have ceased.

The Elliott Highway parallels the trans-Alaska pipeline for part of its path through the paper birch and spruce forests. You'll catch views of the above-ground stretches of the pipeline flashing silver through the trees. At Mile 73 (117.5 km), watch for the fork in the road. Here is Mile 0 of the Dalton Highway, which trends north while the Elliott veers west toward the Tanana River.

The Elliott's unpaved sections rise above tree line and grant vistas of grand valleys on either side of this ridge. Beyond them lay the White Mountains. At Mile 110 (177 km), a spur road leads to the Athabascan Indian village of Minto. Here you can refuel your car, and buy something to eat. This village is centrally located in Minto Flats, through which flows the Tolovana River. The area is exceptionally rich in fish, waterfowl, big game, and small furbearers. It is only natural that Alaska Natives would choose this location for its abundant resources. As were their ancestors, residents of Minto are dependent upon hunting and fishing to feed their families. Natives of contemporary times supplement their diets with store-bought groceries. You may be able to buy locally made Athabascan crafts, such as a birch-bark basket or beaded moosehide slippers.

Even though the Elliott is unpaved and dusty, up and down, the exceptional views and the prize at the end of the road make it all worthwhile. The highway dead-ends at Manley Hot Springs, a modest, mini–resort town that has offered comfort to miners and travelers for more than a century. It's even more historically significant if you consider that the Athabascans of the Interior knew and loved these springs long before the first non-Natives showed up on the scene.

Manley Hot Springs calls to visitors and Fairbanks residents, winter and summer. A quiet town along the Tanana River, its buildings include a trading post and a roadhouse dating from the early 1900s. Follow the road past the old Northern Commercial Co. store to reach the Tanana River and salmon fishing throughout the summer. Today there is no formal hot springs resort; however, the owner of the greenhouse, fed by the springs, allows visitors to soak in one of three concrete baths for a fee. At Mile 151, turn uphill, park on the road and walk up the boardwalk to the greenhouse, where posted instructions advise about reservations.

Winter travelers to Manley are rewarded with exceptional views of the northern lights, dogsled tours, and the opportunity to converse with local mining and dog-mushing folks. Gas and groceries are available at the Manley Trading Post. Roads are spare in town, so it's easy to find your way around.

LODGING/MEALS

MANLEY HOT SPRINGS:
Manley Roadhouse
152 Elliott Highway
907-672-3161
Rooms, cabins, dining room, bar. The roadhouse is a historic gem dating from 1906, with historical artifacts on display.

CAMPGROUNDS

RV travelers are permitted to dry camp in gravel pullouts along the Elliott Highway.

Olnes Pond Campground
Mile 10.5 Elliott Highway
Campsites, toilets, picnic areas, boat ramp, fishing. In the Lower Chatanika State Recreation Area.

Whitefish Campground
Mile 11 Elliott Highway
Campsites, toilets, picnic areas, boat ramp, fishing. Also in the Lower Chatanika State Recreation Area.

MANLEY HOT SPRINGS:
Manley Roadhouse
End of the road
Park with campground, playground, picnic area. Pay at the roadhouse, where showers are available.

GLENN HIGHWAY (including the Tok Cutoff)

Tok to Anchorage: 328 miles (528 km)

Travel Opportunities: *Glennallen; Matanuska Glacier and River; Musk Ox Farm; Independence Mine; Palmer Visitor Center and Garden; Eklutna; Anchorage-area attractions.*

The Glenn Highway is a well-traveled route because it connects the Anchorage area (where nearly half the state population lives) to the towns and wilderness areas along the Glenn and Richardson Highways. Further, this is the way to Tok, the Alaska Highway, and the most-used route to the Lower 48. Likewise, if you're headed into Alaska from Canada, and Anchorage is your destination, the Glenn is your highway. The Glenn is the single most important east-west road in the state highway grid.

The Glenn's official start is at Tok, at Mile 1314 (2114.5 km) Alaska Highway, where the Glenn branches south and west toward Anchorage, 328 miles (528 km) away. The first 125 miles (200 km) of the Glenn is widely known as the Tok Cutoff—a shortcut between the Alaska Highway and the Richardson Highway. In fact, it may come as a surprise to many Alaskans that this section actually is a part of the Glenn.

After leaving Tok, don't expect to find much development or services along this subtly beautiful stretch of road. An exception is the area of the Eagle Trail State Recreation Site, about 16 miles (26 km) from Tok, which offers a campground with picnic shelter, water, toilets, and trailhead access. A handful of B&Bs, lodges, and gas stations are tucked into the woods, so watch for their signs. This may seem like a lonely stretch of highway, but you're not alone.

The road crosses Mentasta Summit (2,434 feet/742 m) about 45 miles (72 km) from Tok. From here, most of the Tok Cutoff follows the boundary of Wrangell–St. Elias National Park and Preserve. These northern lowlands of the park are inhabited by caribou, moose, black and brown bears, coyotes, and numerous other creatures.

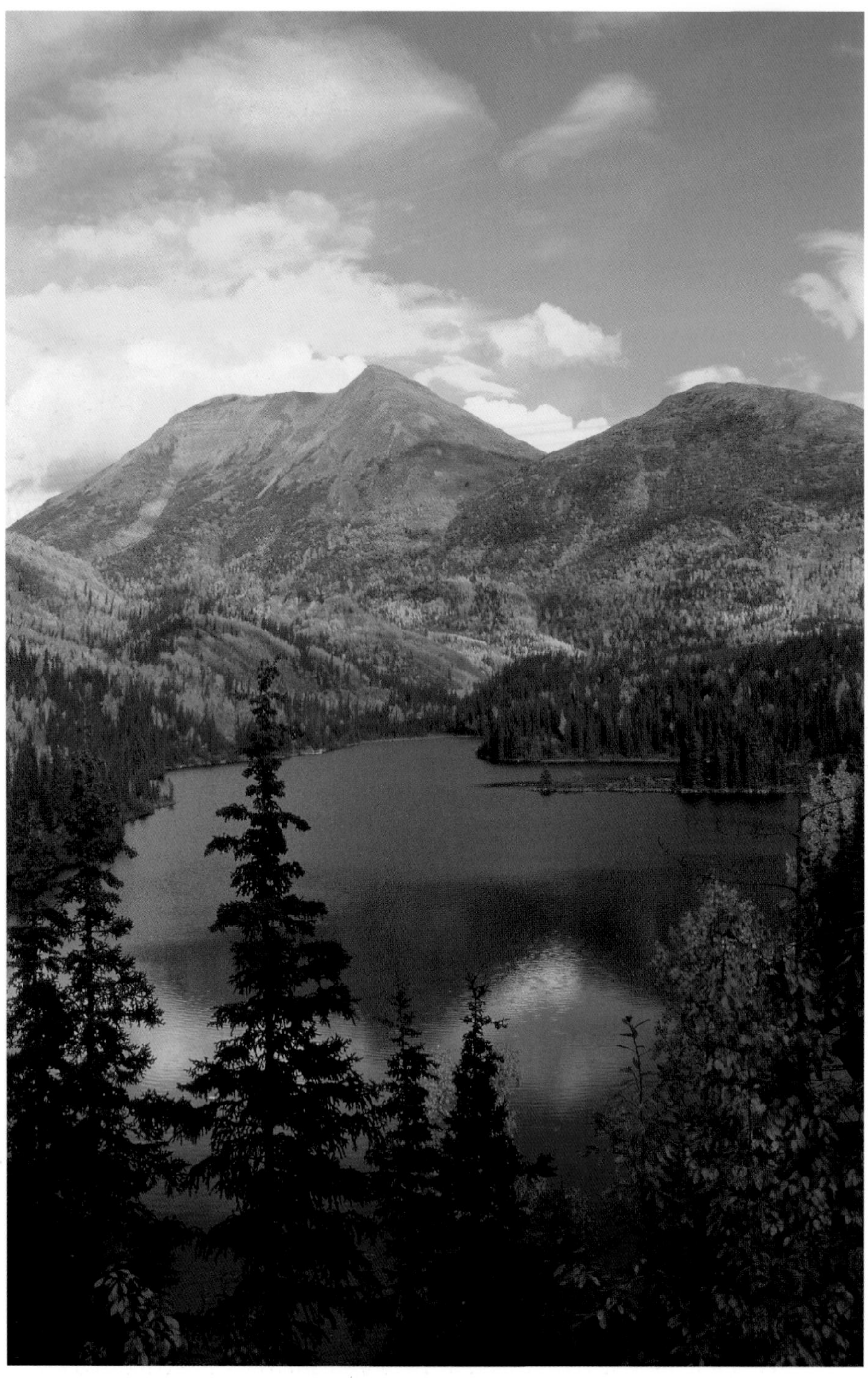

Index Lake in the Talkeetna Mountains lies about halfway between Glennallen and Anchorage on the Glenn Highway.

The Cutoff connects with the Richardson Highway near the village of Gulkana, about 15 miles (24 km) north of Glennallen. The most-traveled portion of the Glenn begins at Glennallen, 139 miles (223.5 km) from Tok at the busy junction of the east-west Glenn Highway and the north-south Richardson Highway. For decades, a gas station on this corner has called itself, in large letters, "The Hub of Alaska." It's an active intersection with more than just fuel and snacks for travelers on either road. A spacious visitor center at this intersection is staffed with informative people, along with the usual brochures and newsletters. For more information on local history, businesses, and attractions, call 907-822-5555 or see *www.traveltoalaska.com.*

Glennallen is the unofficial capital of this region, situated on the western edge of Wrangell–St. Elias Park and 189 miles (304 km) from Anchorage. This region is the traditional homeland of the Athabascan Indians, who have lived in the Copper River Basin for centuries. When a U.S. military party of explorers came through here in 1885, they were amazed at the accuracy of the hand-drawn maps they received from Native Alaskans who assisted them. (Glennallen is named for two of those explorers: Capt. Edwin F. Glenn and Lt. Henry T. Allen.)

Athabascans continue to fish and hunt for food (as do many other people groups who have arrived in the last 120 years). Some people trap for furs; others work at local businesses. Sales of locally made craft items such as birch-bark baskets and beaded combs, slippers, and earrings help support a small cottage industry. Watch for parking-lot craft fairs, where you can learn more about local culture as well as pick up some wonderful gifts.

The Copper River Basin is especially popular for winter recreation, such as snowmobiling, skiing, and snowshoeing. Flightseeing, mountaineering, hiking, biking, fishing, and rafting are favorite summertime activities. Numerous creeks and lakes are suitable for a fine day of fishing. For fishing regulations and openers, check with the Alaska Department of Fish and Game office in Glennallen, downtown at Mile 186 (299 km) Glenn Highway. Call 907-822-3309. Licenses are available at most retail outlets.

From Glennallen, the westward way begins flat and fairly straight, while to the east, the peaks of the Wrangell Mountains are standouts on clear days. On either side of the road, you'll see occasional boggy lowlands and sad, spindly-looking spruce trees that tell a story about survival against the odds. These "used pipe cleaners" are black spruce trees, tenaciously growing in poorly drained soil where permafrost is present. Their root systems are so shallow that they sometimes tip over into each other, hence the name Drunken Forest. Because of the seasonal freeze and thaw of permafrost, this road can be wavy or sunken in places. Watch for flagged signs that warn "Dip in Road." They really mean it.

The state maintains recreation sites with camping, water, and toilets in the stretch between Glennallen and Palmer. They include Little Nelchina, at Mile 137.5; Matanuska Glacier, at Mile 101 (162.5 km); Long Lake, at Mile 85 (136.5 km); and King Mountain, at Mile 76 (126.5 km). All distances are from Anchorage.

The land changes as you travel west through dry, treeless uplands and farther still into dazzling mountainous beauty. The road bends, rises, and falls as you follow the Matanuska River Valley, which flows between rocky mountains that turn purple in a certain light. This silty, braided river is a head-turner. You'll see it from various angles and elevations along the way, and its beauty is enhanced by the changes in light and weather.

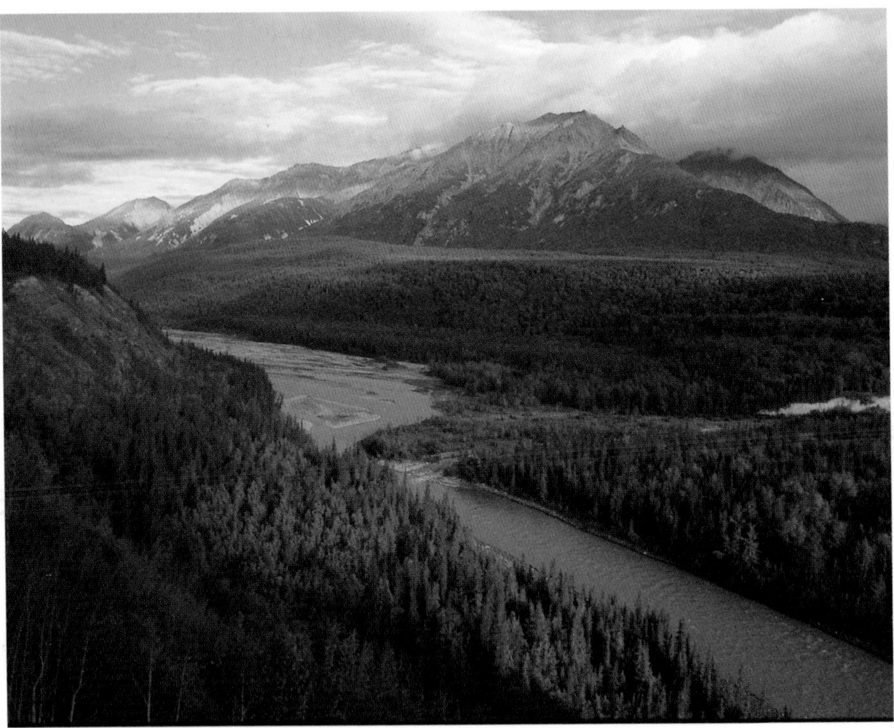

The Matanuska River is fed by glacial runoff from a massive glacier of the same name.

Views of the Matanuska Glacier only get better and better. Stop at the marked waysides that offer photo opportunities, or you'll always regret that you didn't. In broad daylight, the glacier is brilliant white with hints of blue, but overcast days are best, when the blue of the glacier seems to glow from within. The Matanuska River, which flows from beneath the glacier, is a milky gray color due to the ground "rock flour" that is suspended in its water. Float trips or whitewater adventures can be arranged at sites along the highway (watch for signs) or in Palmer, 42 miles (67.5 km) north of Anchorage.

About 74 miles from Anchorage, watch for a distinctive rock formation called Lion Head that at first looks like it's blocking the road. This striking feature is a glacial "erratic," a mini-mountain shaped by the Matanuska Glacier as it retreated from the area.

Between Glennallen and Palmer, you can stop at remote, family-operated roadhouses and restaurants—such as Tolsona Lake Resort (Mile 170.5 from Anchorage), Sheep Mountain Lodge (Mile 113.6) or Long Rifle Lodge (Mile 102)—to bring even more color to your trip. A classic old log place, King Mountain Lodge (Mile 76), boasts of a resident ghost.

As you approach Palmer from the east, you'll see signs and a right turnoff at Mile 50 (80.5 km) for the Musk Ox Farm, a don't-miss attraction with tour guides to explain the animals' natural history. A herd of musk oxen here are descended from animals transported to Alaska from Greenland in the 1930s. Musk oxen had roamed Alaska since prehistory, until about 1885, when the last of their kind was hunted. The Greenland emigrants were an experiment that flourished in Alaska. Wild herds have been restored, and two domesticated herds exist here and at the University of Alaska Fairbanks. Also, because of the animals, a cottage industry developed among Alaska Native women who knit garments from the spun underwool called *qiviut* (KIV-ee-oot). A gift shop here and in Anchorage features their handiwork. Tours introduce you to these unique animals and the wonderfully warm and soft garments made from their *qiviut*. For information, call 907-745-4151 or see *www.muskoxfarm.org* or *www.qiviut.com*.

Palmer is 42 miles (67.5 km) northeast of Anchorage, or 147 miles (236.5 km) west of Glennallen. During the Great Depression of the 1930s, the federal government offered Midwest farmers the opportunity to move to this valley for a fresh start in a new land, in a program known as the Matanuska-Susitna Colony Project. Whole families arrived to find that their free land first needed clearing of trees and rocks, and many spent their first cruel winter in a canvas tent with wood floors and a hungry woodstove. Through their hard work and perseverance, the community took root and thrived.

The colony project was the settlement seed for what is now the community of Palmer, with a population of about 5,500. Many descendants of those settlers still live in the Matanuska-Susitna (or Mat-Su) Valley. As you drive along the Glenn Highway, you'll see farmhouses and barns built in a style reminiscent of the Midwest. Wheat, hay, potatoes, lettuce, tomatoes, carrots, cabbages—the land keeps providing, and the abundance of grain and produce continues to support valley farmers.

Palmer is the seat of the Alaska State Fair, where the stiffest agricultural competition is seen in the giant-vegetables category. Under a blessed 22 hours of summer sunlight, Palmer farmers grow cabbages that balloon to between 40 and 60 pounds. Squash, carrots, and

OVER THE TOP ON THE HATCHER PASS ROAD

Scenic beauty and gold-mining history combine to make this side trip a memorable drive for the day or even an overnight. Turn north off the Glenn Highway at Mile 49.5 (79.5 km) and follow Hatcher Pass Road. This 49-mile road is paved for the first 17 miles and the last 10 miles, where it descends and meets the Parks Highway. From the Palmer side, the route follows the course of a boulder-strewn, fast-moving stream. Watch for pullouts to let faster drivers pass by, or stop for a picnic and stick your toes in these chilly waters.

Independence Mine Historical Park is just over 31 miles (50 km) up the road, at Hatcher Pass (elevation 3,886 feet). Getting there is slow driving for big-rig RVs at times. Where it isn't paved, it's dusty gravel with potholes and washboard that slows you down in a hurry. But it's still worth the effort. Walking trails lead throughout this extensive mine site, which includes restored buildings as well as others still in progress. The visitor center is a museum itself, the 1939-era home of the mine manager for the Alaska Pacific Consolidated Mine Co. Nearby, overnight accommodations and meals are available at Hatcher Pass Lodge. Call 907-745-5897 or visit the lodge's Web site at *www.hatcherpasslodge.com*.

other vegetables thrive in the cool soil and long doses of sunlight. If you're in Alaska in late August and early September, stop by the Palmer fairgrounds to see the giants for yourself, and enjoy the midway rides, food booths, and equestrian competitions. Although it's an Alaska state fair, it feels as cozy as a Kansas county fair, until you lift your eyes and take in the peaks of the Chugach Range, which seems to be just a field away.

Streams and lakes in this valley yield world-class fishing in picturesque settings. Anglers routinely land prized king salmon weighing an average of 20 to 30 pounds, but these fish can reach 70 pounds. Other salmon runs include reds, chums, pinks, and silvers. Trout, Dolly Varden, northern pike, arctic grayling, and other species also are found in local waters. Pick up your required license at any number of retail outlets, from grocery stores to sporting goods stores.

In Palmer, turn east off the Glenn Highway and drive four blocks to the railroad tracks. Across the tracks from the old railroad depot, you'll see the Palmer Visitor Center, a log building where a history of the colony can be found in photos and artifacts, and a gift shop is stocked with Alaska souvenirs. Ask about a walking tour of Palmer's historic buildings. Call 907-745-2880.

Next door to the visitor center is the Matanuska Valley Agricultural Showcase, where local gardeners have done a magnificent job of showing what happens when skilled hands sow seed under the midnight sun. Walk around the garden paths for a peaceful break from traveling.

Just a few miles south of Palmer, the Glenn Highway is joined by the Parks Highway, southbound from Fairbanks, in a recently constructed series of exits and on-ramps that are easy to negotiate and (happily for Alaskans) eliminated a time-consuming, three-way intersection. The Glenn is in excellent shape from here all the way to Anchorage, with four lanes of traffic and a legal speed of 65 mph. The lay of the land changes as you follow the Glenn around this side of the Chugach Range. The divided highway passes through a broad expanse of wild grasses dotted with tall trees that look like they died a long time ago—which they did. This is the Palmer Hay Flats State Game Refuge, which supports a diversity of wildlife, from big game to eagles to waterfowl and more. This entire region dropped several feet during the 1964 Good Friday Earthquake that damaged so much of the Anchorage coastline. Seawater flooded in, killing mature trees and creating wetlands where once there had been hayfields.

Up ahead, two four-lane bridges cross the Knik (kuh-NIK) River, a popular staging area for waterfowl hunters. Because Cook Inlet experiences such extreme tides (up to 30 feet), the tidal zone of the Knik River likewise fluctuates dramatically. Consequently, it's not a great place for recreational boating.

Twenty-six miles (42 km) from Anchorage, an exit leads to Eklutna Historical Park, which includes St. Nicholas Russian Orthodox Church, the Heritage Museum, and nearby graveyard. Developed by the Athabascan residents of Eklutna village (about 450 people), the park offers tours and cultural interpretation. A fee is charged. The tradition of placing brightly colored "houses" over the graves is neither completely Orthodox nor completely Athabascan. As in other areas of the state, Western religions have been integrated into the Native culture, and some practices reflect a unique third culture. Although the residents of

Eklutna live close to Alaska's biggest city, many continue in a largely subsistence-based life, hunting and fishing for much of their diet. Grocery stores supply the rest.

Inside the city limits of Anchorage, the Glenn Highway peters out, unmarked, somewhere along the small-plane airport called Merrill Field. Stay on the same road and it becomes 5th Avenue, which leads you into the downtown core.

Anchorage

Born of necessity, as many Alaska towns were, Anchorage was once a tent city along the muddy banks of Ship Creek. The people who gathered here in 1915 were builders of the Alaska Railroad, their families, hoteliers, restaurateurs, laundry operators, freight haulers, and others who supplied services.

When conditions at the tent city became dangerously overcrowded, threatening disease, officials took charge and cleared building lots on the bluff overlooking the creek. In July 1915, town-site lots were auctioned off, and building began immediately. Today, few original homes or businesses exist, mainly because they were wooden and therefore fairly expendable as the town matured. Notable survivors include two side-by-side buildings on the 5th Avenue and E Street corner of Town Square.

Anchorage is Alaska's biggest city, with 275,000 people, almost half of the state's population. It is an international crossroads in passenger and air cargo, as well as

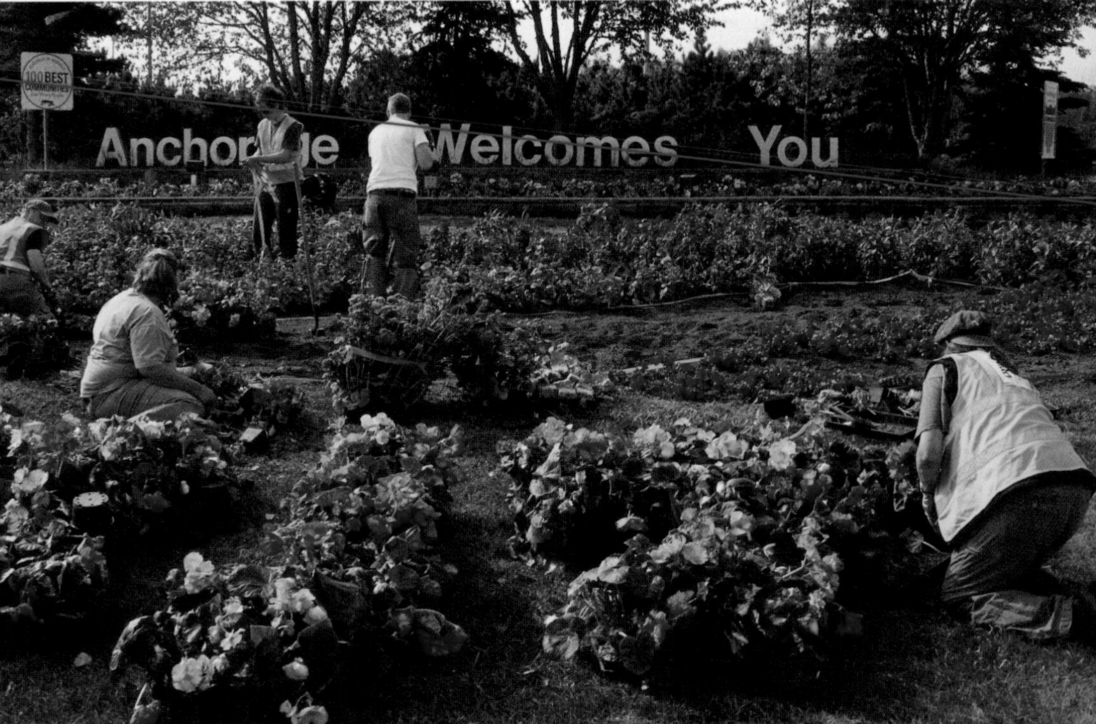

City workers roll out the welcome mat each spring with flowers grown in municipal greenhouses.

The annual "Wild Salmon on Parade" contest pits Alaska's wittiest artists against each other as they customize their works. "Sarah Salmon" takes a fun poke at the state's governor, Sarah Palin.

headquarters for the biggest names in the oil industry. This modern community is bordered on the north by military installations, on the east by the Chugach Range, on the south by Chugach National Forest, and on the west by Cook Inlet. Options for city sprawl are limited. Its proximity to wilderness means that moose often wander into the streets, making the "Anchorage bowl" a unique urban habitat. Car-moose encounters are causing city officials to ponder the question of what to do as moose numbers continue to multiply. In 2007, an unusually high number of bear sightings in urban areas kept residents on alert and especially careful about storing their garbage.

The Log Cabin Visitor Information Center on the corner of Fourth Avenue and F Street is operated by the Anchorage Convention and Visitor Bureau. Staffers can answer questions about local tours, restaurants, and best views, as well as direct you to a self-guided historical walking tour. Downtown, it's also fun to watch (or participate) in the Ship Creek fishery. Where else on the planet can a tourist walk a few blocks from a major downtown hotel, slip on a pair of waders, and fish for wild Pacific salmon? Check at your hotel's front desk for guidance, or contact the Anchorage Convention and Visitors Bureau. Call 907-276-4118 or see *www.anchorage.net.*

In summer, Anchorage is a tourism hub. Its downtown streets are filled with color and the contagious enthusiasm of people on vacation. Each summer, local artists contribute their take on a whimsical theme for the annual "Wild Salmon on Parade" challenge. Watch for the salmon statues sprinkled throughout the downtown area. Gift shops, restaurants, street vendors, and musicians lend a partylike atmosphere to every summer day. Dining experiences can range from a stop at a fast-food outlet, hot dog stand, grocery-store deli, or burger joint, to elegant dining above Cook Inlet. We suggest you steer away from eating at a chain restaurant and experience a locally owned establishment. If you get the chance, taste reindeer sausage, which is offered on many breakfast menus.

As Alaska's biggest city and hub of two major highways, this is an ideal spot to consider renting an RV if you didn't arrive in one. You may contact any number of local businesses for daily or weekly rentals (check the local phone listings). If you are traveling in your own RV, this is a good place to take care of any mechanical or windshield repairs or have your oil changed.

Walking 4th and 5th Avenues on foot, you can stop in and book a glacier day cruise on Prince William Sound or on Resurrection Bay, south of Anchorage. Tour operators usually offer rail or shuttle transportation to harbor cities. Down the street, you can book a flightseeing trip to fly over Mount McKinley and even land on a glacier to walk a bit. Large coaches provide day trips around town, north to the Matanuska-Susitna Valley, south to Portage Glacier, and beyond. Many adventure travelers book fly-in fishing or visits to remote, luxury lodges, such as those operated by celebrity chef Kirsten Dixon. See more at *www.withinthewild.com*.

If shopping for Alaska Native-made art is part of your plan—or a pure impulse—learn to read labels. A label with a silver hand indicates a guarantee that the item was made by a Native Alaskan artisan. A label with a mom-and-baby-bear silhouette is an official "Made in Alaska" indicator, but the maker may be an Alaskan company or a state resident, not necessarily a Native Alaskan.

Soak up local color as you stroll around downtown. Especially popular is 4th Avenue, where in summer every lamppost bears two huge flower baskets of lobelia and marigold, representing Alaska's state colors, blue and gold. In Anchorage's mild temperatures and prolonged light, the flowers are extraordinarily bright and fresh, here and in gardens throughout the city. Due to the low angle of the sun, there is little midday heat to wilt them. Each year, Anchorage recognizes its exceptional gardeners via the city's designation of "City of Flowers." If you can't get your fill of flowers, visit the Alaska Botanical Garden for a self-guided tour through their spectacular gardens. Call 907-770-3692 for more information.

All winter long, as dusk comes earlier and daybreak comes later, the Anchorage Chamber of Commerce calls for everybody to lighten up with the seasonal theme of "City of Lights." Millions of tiny white lights decorate trees, homes, and businesses, further illuminating the snow and creating a true winter wonderland.

Follow the crowds to the outdoor market in Anchorage, where about 400 vendors gather every weekend in the summer. This mini-fair includes entertainment, food booths, crafts, and sales of Mat-Su Valley vegetables. On Saturdays and Sundays, explore the Anchorage Market and Festival at the Third Avenue and E Street parking lot downtown (907-272-5634; *www.anchoragemarkets.com*).

Other attractions of the Anchorage area include:

Anchorage Fur Rendezvous. This is the country's biggest winter carnival, celebrated in Anchorage at the end of February. Events include snowshoe softball and a waiter/waitress competition in which contestants run an obstacle course while carrying a tray of drinks. Craft fairs, a fur auction, carnival rides, snow sculpture competitions, and an Eskimo blanket toss are other highlights. The World Championship Sled Dog Races are another main Rondy event, with dogs and drivers lining up to start the race on 4th Avenue.

Visitors to the Glenn Alps viewpoint can see nearly all of Anchorage and across Cook Inlet to Mount Susitna, more familiar to Alaskans as "The Sleeping Lady."

Iditarod Trail Sled Dog Race. Winter visitors can witness the excitement of the Iditarod starting line, set on Fourth Street in downtown Anchorage on the first Saturday of every March. Each year the men, women, and dogs of the 1,049-mile race are the stars as thousands jam the sidewalks to watch them set out for Nome. The Iditarod headquarters and museum is in Wasilla, north of Anchorage off the Parks Highway. Call 907-376-5155 or visit their Web site at *www.iditarod.com.*

Wild Ride Sled Dog Show. Iditarod Trail Sled Dog Race champion Mitch Seavey, along with other long-distance mushers, offer this family-oriented show that's all about the dogs. There are amazing stories from the trail, demonstrations of sled-dog athleticism, and photo ops with "Flapjack," a beautiful Malemute that starred in the Disney Film "Eight Below." Free shuttle service to the Ship Creek site is available from many downtown locations. Call 907-561-MUSH or check the showtimes, fees, and shuttle schedules on *www.iditarodexperience.com.*

Alaska Experience Center, located on the corner of Sixth Avenue and G Street in downtown Anchorage. Hourly Omnimax showings of "Alaska, the Great Land," along with the excellent exhibit on the Good Friday Earthquake of 1964, makes this place one of the must-see attractions in Anchorage. Call 907-276-3739 or go to *www.alaskaexperiencetheatre.com.*

Alaska Railroad. Daily north-south rail service between Anchorage, Denali National Park and Preserve, and Fairbanks is available through the Alaska Railroad or through tourism companies that operate specialty railcars on the train. Southbound passengers between Anchorage and Whittier or Anchorage and Seward can do the same: book a seat with the Alaska Railroad or travel in a luxury railcar operated by a tour operator. The luxury railcars offer a great way to take in the scenery, enjoy bar service and an excellent meal, and stretch your legs regularly while crossing the state in style. In 2007, the railroad also offered day trips from Anchorage to Spencer Glacier. Contact the Alaska Railroad at 907-265-2494 or toll-free at 1-800-544-0552. Online, see *www.alaskarailroad.com.* For special railcar travel information, call Gray Line of Alaska at 1-800-452-1737, browse *www.graylinealaska.com,* or contact Princess Tours Rail Operations at 1-800-426-0500.

Chugach State Park. Serving as a spectacular backdrop for Alaska's biggest city, the Chugach (CHOO-gatch) Range lies along the eastern edge of Anchorage. Here too is Chugach State Park, nearly a half-million acres, an extremely popular getaway for hikers, bikers, picnickers, or those who simply want to drive uphill and get a great view of the city and the twin bodies of water around it, Knik Arm and Turnagain Arm.

A hike up the sawed-off mountain known as Flattop is invigorating, yet suitable for a family outing. Groomed trails lead the way from the Glenn Alps parking area. On clear days, you can see Mount McKinley from here. Park headquarters is in the Potter Section House, just south of Anchorage on the Seward Highway, but the park is accessible from Anchorage's Hillside area as well as from Eagle River. For directions and information, call park headquarters at 907-345-5014. See *www.anchorage.net/hike* for details on other hikes.

Alaska Wild Berry Park. Meet a reindeer, pose by a giant rock man, and watch the experts make the candy you'll want to take home with you. This place has something for everybody, including the chocoholic in the family who will want to dive into the chocolate waterfall. Hourly showings on widescreen theater of "Alaska: The Land Beyond." Bring the family to 5225 Juneau Street. For free shuttle service from downtown hotels, call 907-563-2272. See *www.alaskawildberryproducts.com.*

Alaska Native Heritage Center. One of Anchorage's most popular attractions focuses on the wonders and diversity of Alaska's Native cultures. Located near the intersection of the Glenn Highway and Muldoon Road, the Heritage Center features art, music, photography, films, and a variety of exhibits. The spacious Welcome House at the center offers programs of dancing and singing in the theater, photography and artifact exhibits, and a chance to watch an artist at work. From there, paths lead to five village settings that show traditional home-building methods and tools. Interpreters from each culture are on site too. Free shuttle service from several downtown locations. Call 907-330-8000 or browse *www.alaskanative.net.*

Anchorage Museum at Rasmuson Center. The museum, at 121 West 7th Avenue, is an architectural beauty that shows Alaska art treasures as well as visiting exhibits. It is currently in an expansion phase which, when finished in 2010, will include art, history, and science treasures and exhibits. The Alaska Gallery currently includes exquisite displays from Alaska's Native, Russian, and U.S. history. Other features include a children's gallery, gift shop, café, and special programs in a theater that entertain visitors and residents year-round. For more information, call 907-343-4326 or browse *www.anchoragemuseum.org.*

Other popular museums include the wonderful Alaska Aviation Heritage Museum, near the airport (907-248-5325; *www.alaskaairmuseum.org*), the Alaska Law Enforcement Museum, downtown at 245 W. 5th Ave. (907-279-5050; *www.alaskatroopermuseum.com*), and the Alaska Heritage Library and Museum, housed in the Wells Fargo Building, 301 W. Northern Lights Blvd. (907-265-2834). The collection includes Alaska Native artifacts, Alaska fine art, and a 2,600-volume Alaska reference book library.

Town Square Park. An army of gardeners takes exquisite care of this floral showcase. Split by curving paths, with a simple fountain at the center, Town Square Park is frequented by businesspeople, travelers, walkers, and people-watchers. In places, inscribed sidewalk bricks pay homage to people and businesses that have helped make Anchorage great. The adjoining Alaska Center for the Performing Arts is a venue for national and international talent, further evidence that Anchorage has come a long way since its days as a tent city.

LODGING

The Mat–Su Bed and Breakfast Association has information on rooms, apartments, and cabins from Glennallen to Anchorage to Denali. Visit the association's Web site at www.alaskabnbhosts.com.

TOK: *See listings in the section on Tok in Chapter 6, The Alaska Highway.*

Caribou Hotel
Mile 187 Glenn Highway, Glennallen
907-822-3302
www.caribouhotel.com
55 rooms, suites, kitchenettes, wheelchair access. Satellite TV, whirlpool. Caribou Café family restaurant, gift shop, fuel, propane, tires.

Gakona Lodge & Trading Post
Mile 2 Tok Cut-Off (Glenn Highway)
907-822-3482
Warm accommodations in log-cabin lodge.

Lake Louise Lodge
Mile 160 Glenn Highway turn-off
to Mile 16 Lake Louise Road
1-877-878-3311 or 907-822-3311
www.lakelouiselodge.com
Rooms and cabins with free breakfast and use of canoe. Fuel, propane, oil. Restaurant. Swimming, fishing, boating. Open year-round.

PALMER:

Alaska Choice Inn Motel
Mile 41 Glenn Highway
Across from Alaska State Fairgrounds
1-800-745-1505 or 907-745-1505
Clean rooms, plenty of parking, satellite television.

Colony Inn
325 Elmwood Street
907-745-3330
Located in historic Teachers' Dorm from the Mat-Su Colony.

Gold Miner's Hotel
918 South Colony Way
1-800-7ALASKA or 907-745-6160
Large rooms, all with fridges and microwaves. Restaurant, lounge. Downtown location. Pets upon approval.

Pioneer Motel
124 West Arctic Avenue
907-745-3425 / *www.thepioneermotel.com*
28 units with cable TV. Daily or weekly rentals.

Valley Hotel
606 South Alaska Street
1-800-478-7666 or 907-745-3330
www.valleyhotelsalaska.com
Rooms with private bath, cable TV. 24-hour coffee shop. Lounge, liquor store.

ANCHORAGE:

For B&B accommodations, call the Anchorage Alaska Bed & Breakfast Association at 1–888–584–5147 or 907–272–5909, or browse www.anchorage–bnb.com.

America's Best Inns & Suites
4110 Spenard Road
1-866-344-6835 or 907-243-3433
www.alaskabestinn.com
35 rooms, near airport. Free continental breakfast, shuttle.

Anchorage Grand Hotel
505 West 2nd Avenue
1-888-800-0640 or 907-929-8888
www.anchoragegrandhotel.com
31 luxury suites, kitchen, cable TV, high-speed Internet, free continental breakfast. Downtown location.

Anchorage Mariott Downtown
820 West 7th Avenue
1-800-228-9290 or 907-279-8000
392 rooms in full-service hotel. Pool, exercise facility.

Best Western Barratt Inn
4616 Spenard Road
1-800-221-7550 or 907-243-3131
www.barrattinn.com
Deluxe rooms, restaurant, lounge, freezer, free Internet access. Shuttle service.

Best Western Golden Lion Hotel
1000 East 36th Avenue
1-800-528-1234 or 907-561-1522
www.bestwesterngoldenlion.com
83 large rooms with microwaves, fridges, exercise room, restaurant.

Chandler Inn
4400 Spenard Road
1-800-478-3346 or 907-243-4044
www.puffininn.net
Boutique hotel near airport, free wireless Internet, continental breakfast, shuttle. Close to airport.

Clarion Suites
325 West 8th Avenue
1-888-389-6575 or 907-274-1000
Suites with fridges, microwaves, phones, two TVs. Free continental breakfast. Pool, spa. Free 24-hour airport and train shuttle.

Coast International Inn
3450 Aviation Avenue
1-800-544-0986 or 907-243-2233
www.intlinnanchorage.com
141 rooms with coffeemakers, hair dryers. Sauna, fitness center, restaurant, lounge. Free airport shuttle.

Comfort Inn
111 West Ship Creek
1-800-4CHOICE or 907-277-6887
100 rooms and suites, free continental breakfast. Indoor pool, spa. Along Ship Creek, downtown. Airport shuttle.

Courtyard by Marriott
4901 Spenard Road
800-729-0197 or 907-245-0322
Rooms, pool, restaurant, lounge.

Creekwood Inn
2150 Seward Highway
1-800-478-6008 or 907-258-6006
www.creekwoodinn–alaska.com
Rooms with private bath, kitchenettes. Coffee, cable TV, data ports, bicycle rentals.

Days Inn Downtown
321 East Fifth Avenue
1-800-DAYSINN or 907-276-7226
www.daysinnalaska.com
130 rooms, high-speed Internet, near shopping and restaurants.

Dimond Center Hotel
700 East Dimond Boulevard
866-770-5002 or 907-770-5000
www.dimondcenterhotel.com
Boutique hotel next to major shopping mall. Free breakfast, wireless Internet, free shuttle.

Fairfield Inns & Suites
5060 A Street
1-888-236-2427 or 907-222-9000
www.fairfieldinnanchorage.com
Spacious units in full-service facility. Midtown location.

Hampton Inn
4301 Credit Union Drive
1-800-HAMPTON or 907-550-7000
www.hamptoninn.com
Rooms with deluxe breakfast. Indoor pool, fitness facility. Midtown location. Free shuttle.

Hawthorn Suites
1110 West Eighth Avenue
1-888-469-6575 or 907-222-5005
Suites with fridge and microwave. Free breakfast buffet, parking, wireless Internet, pool, shuttle. Downtown location.

Hilton Anchorage
500 West 3rd Avenue
1-800-245-2527 or 907-272-7411
www.hiltonanchorage.com
Deluxe accommodations, fitness room, gift shops, three restaurants. Walking distance to downtown attractions.

Hilton Garden Inn
100 West Tudor Road
1-800-HILTONS or 907-729-7000
www.anchoragegardeninn.com
Rooms include free high-speed Internet access. Pool, fitness facility. Free shuttle.

Historic Anchorage Hotel
330 E Street
1-800-544-0988 or 907-272-4553
www.historicanchoragehotel.com
Boutique hotel in central downtown location. Free breakfast, newspaper, high-speed Internet. On National Register of Historic Places.

Holiday Inn Express
4411 Spenard Road
1-800-HOLIDAY or 907-248-8848
www.hieanchorage.come
Rooms with pool, spa, fitness facility, free continental breakfast, shuttle. Near airport.

Homewood Suites by Hilton
140 West Tudor Road
1-800-225-5466 or 907-762-7000
www.anchorage.homewoodsuites.com
Studios, 1- and 2-bedroom suites, in Midtown.

Hotel Captain Cook
4th Avenue and K Street
1-800-843-1950 or 907-276-6000
www.captaincook.com
Rooms and suites, plus health club, travel agency, gift stores, café, lounge. Penthouse-level restaurant with view. Central downtown location.

Howard Johnson Plaza Hotel
239 West Fourth Avenue
1-800-446-4656 or 907-793-5500
www.hjplazaanachorage.com
Downtown location, close to attractions, shopping, dining. Indoor pool.

Inlet Tower Hotel & Suites
1200 L Street
1-800-544-0786 or 907-276-0110
www.inlettower.com
Boutique hotel offers free parking, free airport shuttle. Restaurant.

Lake Hood Inn
4702 Spenard Road
1-866-663-9322 or 907-258-9321
www.lakehoodinn.com/acvb
Rooms with private decks overlooking floatplane lake. Near airport. Free continental breakfast, airport shuttle.

Lakeshore Motor Inn
3009 Lakeshore Drive
800-770-3000 or 907-248-3485
www.lakeshoremotorinn.com
45 rooms and suites close to airport and Lake Hood.

Long House Alaskan Hotel
4335 Wisconsin Street
1-888-243-2133 or 907-243-2133
www.longhousehotel.com
54 rooms, free continental breakfast. Close to airport; shuttle service.

Microtel Inn & Suites
5205 Northwood Drive
1-888-771-7171 or 907-245-5002
www.microtelanchorage.com
Rooms, suites, free continental breakfast, laundry facility. Close to airport; shuttle service.

Millennium Alaskan Hotel
4800 Spenard Road
1-800-544-0553 or 907-243-2300
www.millenniumhotels.com/anchorage
248 deluxe guest rooms, some lakeside rooms with views of floatplanes. Wildlife displays, historical photos decorate lobby. Gift shop, restaurant, lounge.

Motel 6
5000 A Street
1-800-4MOTEL6 or 907-249-2503
www.motel6anchorage.com
Midtown location, shuttle service, near restaurants.

Ramada Anchorage Downtown
115 East 3rd Avenue
866-RAMADA-7 or 907-272-7561
www.alaskaramada.com
Full-service hotel with business center. Microwave, fridge, safe in each room. Downtown location.

Red Roof Inn
1104 East Fifth Avenue
1-800-733-7663 or 907-274-1650
www.redroof.com
Rooms and suites close to downtown. Free high-speed Internet.

Residence Inn by Marriott
1025 East 35th Avenue
1-877-729-0197 or 907-563-9844
www.residenceinn.com
Studio, one-, and two-bedroom suites in Midtown. Kitchens, fireplaces, pool, sauna, wireless.

Sheraton Anchorage Hotel
401 East 6th Avenue
1-800-478-8700 or 907-276-8700
www.sheraton.com/anchorage
Well-appointed rooms and suites, cable TV, room and laundry service, fitness room. Gift store, lounge, penthouse restaurant with view.

Sourdough Lodge
801 Erickson Street
800-777-3716 or 907-279-4148
www.alaskasourdoughlodge.com
32 suites with kitchens. Close to dining, recreation.

Springhill Suites by Marriott
3401 A Street
877-729-0197 or 907-562-3247
www.springhillsuites.com
Spacious suites near shopping, entertainment in Midtown. Free continental breakfast, wireless.

Super 8 Motel of Anchorage
3501 Minnesota Drive
1-800-800-8000 or 907-276-8884
Rooms with cable TV, 24-hour shuttle.

Travelodge Anchorage
720 Gambell Street
1-800-478-1511 or 907-277-1511
www.travelodge.com
Downtown location. Breakfast, shuttle service.

The Voyager Hotel
501 K Street
800-247-9070 or 907-277-9501
www.voyagerhotel.com
40 well-appointed rooms in downtown location. Close to shopping, dining, entertainment.

Westmark Anchorage Hotel
720 West Fifth Avenue
1-800-544-0970 or 907-276-7676
www.westmarkhotels.com
Deluxe accommodations in one of Anchorage's few high-rise buildings. Views, restaurant, fitness center.

CAMPGROUNDS

TOK: *See listings in the section on Tok in Chapter 6, The Alaska Highway.*

GLENNALLEN:
Lake Louise Lodge
Mile 160 Glenn Highway turn-off
to Mile 16 Lake Louise Road
1-877-878-3311 or 907-822-3311
www.lakelouiselodge.com
RV parking with electric, satellite television. Fuel, propane, oil. Restaurant. Swimming, fishing, boating. Open year-round.

Moose Horn RV Park
Mile 187.5 Glenn Highway
907-822-3953 / *www.mhrvp.com*
12 RV sites, some full hookups, wireless, dump station, potable water hose.

Northern Nights Campground & RV Park
Mile 189 Glenn Highway
907-822-3199 / *www.northern-nights-rv.com*
Campsites with partial hookups, pull-throughs, tent sites. restrooms, hot showers, phone, wooded setting, close to visitor center and shopping. Open May–September.

Tolsona Wilderness Campground
Mile 173 Glenn Highway
907-822-3865
80 campsites with full or partial hookups, tenting, creekside location. Showers, laundry, dump station, Internet access, store.

MIDWAY, GLENNALLEN TO PALMER:
Grand View RV Park & Lodge
Mile 110 Glenn Highway
907-746-4480
24 sites including pull-throughs; some with full hookups; 10 for slide-outs. Café, espresso, views of glacier and mountains.

PALMER:
Fox Run RV Park & Campground
Mile 36 Glenn Highway, on Matanuska Lake
1-877-745-6120 or 907-745-6120
www.foxrun.freeservers.com
Full hookups, restrooms, showers, tables, playground, e-mail access. Tenting area, boat rental, tackle.

The Homestead RV Park
Mile 36 Glenn Highway
.5 mile east of Glenn and Parks junction
1-800-478-3570 or 907-745-6005
Campsites with a view. Partial hookups, tent sites, dump station, showers, laundry, walking trails, wireless Internet. Square dancing on Thursdays.

Mountain View RV Park
Off Old Glenn Highway on Smith Road
1-800-264-4582 or 907-745-5747
83 sites with full hookups, most pull-throughs, laundry, restrooms, pay phone.

Town & Country RV Park
Mile 39.5 Glenn Highway
907-746-6642
Full hookups, pull-throughs, laundry, showers, dump station. Close to golf, stocked lakes, fairgrounds.

ANCHORAGE:
Anchorage Ship Creek Landings RV Park
Ingra Street north to East First Avenue
1-800-778-7700
Full hookups, pull-throughs, dry sites. Showers, wireless Internet, laundry, gift shop. Handicap access. Blocks from downtown.

Creekwood Inn
2150 Seward Highway
1-800-478-6008 or 907-258-6006
www.creekwoodinn-alaska.com
RV hookups, cabin rentals with fridges, coffeemakers, hair dryers, cable TV. Walking distance to restaurants, shopping.

Golden Nugget Camper Park
4100 Debarr Road
1-800-449-2012 or 907-333-2012
www.goldennuggetcamperpark.com
Full and partial RV hookups.

John's Motel & RV Park
3543 Mountain View Drive
907-277-4332
Full hookups, rooms, cabins, cable TV. Close to downtown.

RESTAURANTS

TOK: *See listings in the section on Tok in Chapter 6, The Alaska Highway.*

GLENNALLEN:
Caribou Café Family Restaurant
Downtown Glennallen
907-822-3656
Open daily; homemade soups, pies, baked goods.

Lake Louise Lodge
Mile 160 Glenn Highway turn-off
to Mile 16 Lake Louise Road
1-877-878-3311 or 907-822-3311
www.lakelouiselodge.com
Full-service restaurant specializing in steaks and seafood.

Park's Place
Mile 187.5 Glenn Highway
907-822-3334
Hot foods, espresso, sandwiches.

PALMER:
Butte Café
3655 North Old Glenn Highway
907-746-3688

Colony Kitchen
Mile 40.5 Glenn Highway
Across from fairgrounds
907-746-4600
Breakfast all day; steaks, burgers, salad, pie.

Gold Miner's Restaurant
918 South Colony Way, in Gold Miner's Hotel
1-800-7ALASKA or 907-745-6160
Steaks, seafood, burgers, sandwiches, salad bar.

The Inn Café
325 Elmwood Avenue
907-746-6118
Fine dining in historic Colony Inn.

La Fiesta Mexican Restaurant
132 West Evergreen Avenue
907-745-3335
Mexican fare.

Open Café
606 South Alaska Street, in Valley Hotel
907-745-3330
Gourmet pizza, full menu, take-out available. Open 24 hours.

Palmer Bar
828 S. Colony Way, downtown
907-745-3041
Bar food and special grill-your-own-steak nights.

Peking Garden
775 West Evergreen Avenue
907-746-5757
Chinese specialties.

Pioneer Pizza
Mile 3.2 Palmer-Wasilla Highway
907-745-5400
Pizza, sandwiches.

Pizzaria Delphi
Old Glenn Highway
907-745-2929
Pizza, Italian and Greek specialties.

Vagabond Blues
Downtown Palmer
907-745-2233
Homemade soups, wraps, quiche, pastries. Coffee and live music.

ANCHORAGE:
Alaska Salmon Chowder House
443 West 4th Avenue
907-278-6901
Casual dining featuring crab, halibut, salmon.

Arctic Roadrunner
5300 Old Seward Highway
907-561-4016
Burgers, fries, shakes.

The Bridge Restaurant
221 W. Ship Creek Avenue
907-667-6771
Fine dining in covered bridge over Ship Creek.

Club Paris
417 West 5th Avenue
907-277-6332
Popular downtown steakhouse since 1957.

Corsair Restaurant
944 West 5th Avenue
907-278-4502
Fine dining, Alaska seafood specialties.

Country Kitchen
346 East 5th Avenue
907-677-2122
Family restaurant in downtown core.

Crow's Nest
939 West 5th Avenue, in Hotel Captain Cook
907-276-6000
Fine dining with panoramic views from atop hotel.

Dianne's Restaurant
550 West 7th Avenue, in Atwood Building
907-279-7243
Soups, salads, sandwiches, lunch specials.

Downtown Deli & Café
525 West 4th Avenue
907-276-7116
From sourdough pancakes to reindeer stew, and more.

Fancy Moose
4800 Spenard Road, in Millennium Alaskan Hotel
907-226-2249
Light meals, sandwiches; overlooking floatplane lake.

Glacier Brewhouse
Corner of 5th Avenue and H Street
907-274-2739 / *www.glacierbrewhouse.com*
Brew pub featuring wood-grilled seafood, pizzas, grilled meats.

Gwennie's Old Alaska Restaurant
4333 Spenard Road
907-243-2909
Alaska decor, Alaska-size meals.

Hogg Brothers Café
1049 West Northern Lights Boulevard
907-276-9649
Inventive breakfasts, "hogg-size" meals.

Humpy's Great Alaskan Alehouse
610 West 6th Avenue
907-276-2337
43 brews on tap, live music nightly. Downtown.

Jens' Restaurant
701 West 36th Avenue
907-561-5367
Fine dining, featuring pepper steak, seafood, lamb, veal.

Josephine's
401 East 6th Avenue, in Sheraton Anchorage Hotel
907-343-3160
Fine dining on the 15th floor. Dinner and Sunday brunch, excellent views.

Kincaid Grill
6700 Jewel Lake Road
907-243-0507 / *www.kincaidgrill.com*
Fine dining specializing in seafood, quality meats.

La Hacienda Mexican Restaurant
6307 DeBarr Avenue
907-338-0109
Hearty meals, margaritas.

Lucky Wishbone
1033 East 5th Avenue
907-272-3454
A local favorite for chicken and burgers; eat in, take-out.

Marx Brothers Café
627 West 3rd Avenue
907-278-2133
www.marxcafe.com
Fine dining, award-winning wines, memorable desserts.

Moose's Tooth Pub & Pizzaria
3300 Old Seward Highway
907-258-2537
Ales, sodas, gourmet hand-tossed pizzas.

ORSO
737 West 5th Avenue
907-222-3232
www.orsoalaska.com
Alaska seafood, wood-grilled meats, pasta, desserts, cocktails.

Phyllis's Café and Salmon Bake
Corner of 5th Avenue and D Street
907-274-6576
Specializing in seafood. Downtown location.

Ptarmigan Bar and Grill
401 East 6th Avenue, in Sheraton Anchorage Hotel
907-276-8700
Alaska cuisine, casual dining.

Roscoe's Catfish & Bar-B-Que
3001 Penland Parkway
907-276-5879
Catfish, ribs, Southern cuisine.

Sack's Café & Restaurant
328 G Street
907-276-3546
Fine dining, downtown location.

Simon & Seafort's Saloon & Grill
420 L Street, Suite 202
907-274-3502
Seafood, prime rib, desserts; great view of Cook Inlet.

Snow City Café
1034 W. Fourth Avenue
907-272-3235
www.snowcitycafe.com
Local favorite for breakfast.

Snow Goose Restaurant & Sleeping Lady Brewing Co.
3401 Denali Street
907-277-7727
www.alaskabeers.com
Brew, burgers, pizza, views, live music.

Sourdough Mining Company
5200 Juneau Street
907-563-2272
Seafood, ribs, sourdough bread. Family dining. Free evening show.

Sullivan's Steakhouse
Anchorage Fifth Avenue Mall
907-258-2882
Steaks, martinis, fine dining.

The Winter Thyme
930 W. Fifth Avenue
907-677-3843
Fine dining, downtown location.

HAINES HIGHWAY

Haines Junction, Yukon, to Haines, Alaska: 152 miles (245 km)
Travel Opportunities: *Chilkat Bald Eagle Preserve; Tlingit culture; Fort Seward.*

Haines is an all-Alaska town, but it's disconnected from the rest of the state highway system by miles and miles of water on one side, and miles and miles of Canada on the other. Alaskans on the highway system literally have to leave the country for the roundabout drive to this Alaska town. And international cooperation makes it possible. Built in 1943, just after principal construction of the Alaska Highway, this single spur road crosses land belonging to a state and two provinces.

The paved 152-mile Haines Highway is a southbound road off the Alaska Highway at Haines Junction (985 miles, or 1,635 km, north of Dawson Creek). The highway cuts through the Canadian and Alaska wilderness as Yukon Route 3, B.C. Route 4, and Alaska Route 7. It borders sparkling lakes and rivers, and crosses mountain passes, portions of a historic trade route used by First Nations people for centuries.

Haines also is accessible via the Alaska Marine Highway System, which connects the town of little more than 1,500 with other Southeast and Southcentral Alaska coastal communities by ferry. Some travelers choose the mostly water route to get to Alaska, boarding their vehicles onto the ferry system at Bellingham, Washington, the southernmost port, and disembarking at Haines, thus skipping the 1,000 miles-plus of driving through Canada. (See Chapter 9, Alaska Marine Highway System.) You can also book a day trip to Skagway on Chilkat Cruises' M/V *Fairweather Express,* which operates daily in summers (907-766-2100) or board an Alaska Fjordlines vessel for transportation to Juneau (907-766-3395).

Set beneath an alpine range that includes impressive peaks, such as 3,610-foot Mount Rapinsky and 1,760-foot Mount Riley, Haines was settled in the early 1900s and incorporated in 1910. Presbyterian missionaries arrived, hoping to convert, serve, and educate the Native population. Like other towns on the route to the goldfields, Haines grew wild in the atmosphere of greed and hurry.

Evidence of Alaska's first permanent military post is still present at Fort Seward, which has long since been decommissioned. Still, its clean-cut parade grounds are encircled by former officer's quarters, now private homes and businesses.

Long before the arrival of any military or gold miners, this beautiful coastal region supported people for thousands of years. Nearly all of today's Southeast Alaska was traditional land for the Tlingit Indian people. In the Haines area, local tribes include the Chilkat and Chilkoot, which may be best known for intricately woven blankets and raven's tail robes, as well as carvings in totems and masks.

Salmon and the small, greasy fish known as hooligan have traditionally been important to the Native diet, as have goat, sheep, and deer, which are hunted for meat and hide. And centuries-old stories are still passed from one generation to the next. In Haines, you can be part of the hearing. A workshop in the old hospital of Fort Seward is home to the Alaska Indian Arts carvers and weavers. Drop by to watch them at work, and visit their Web site at *www.alaskaindianarts.com*. You're also invited to watch dance demonstrations, or enjoy the salmon dinner held on Wednesday and Thursday nights at the Tribal House on the Fort Seward parade grounds. For reservations, call 907-766-2540.

The Sheldon Museum and Cultural Center, at 11 Main Street near Beach Road, exhibits typical offices and living quarters from early-day Haines. You can also learn there about the valley's natural history, the Tlingit people and their traditions, the founding of Fort Seward, and the influences of early missionaries and gold miners. Call 907-766-2366 or visit *www.sheldonmuseum.org*.

Just outside town, at the Southeast Alaska Fairgrounds, visit the set used in the filming of the Disney movie *White Fang*, based on the Jack London novel. Many locals were enlisted for the production. These days, shops, a restaurant, and a microbrewery have taken up residence.

Along the Haines Highway, the 48,000-acre Chilkat Bald Eagle Preserve attracts thousands of visitors each year who arrive in late fall to observe the great numbers of eagles. Their rendezvous is determined by the salmon—a late-season run of chum makes the Chilkat River one of the last places where the eagles can easily feed before the water freezes. So they congregate here—sometimes 3,500 and more—and roost in the cottonwood trees along the riverbank. The birds engage in unique social behavior, fighting for a single scrap of fish when thousands more fish are within reach.

Depending on when you visit the preserve, the highest concentration of eagles usually is found between 18 and 22 miles (29–35.5 km) northwest of Haines on the Haines Highway. Make sure your camera batteries don't fail you now. Don't expect to see large groups of eagles in spring or summer, but you should see some individuals or pairs because the preserve is the year-round home to several hundred birds. Learn all about the birds, their behavior, and their favorite habitat at the American Bald Eagle Foundation interpretive center in Haines, at 2nd Avenue and the Haines Highway. A fee is charged. Knowledgeable staffers can answer your questions, and they offer videos, books, and other printed materials. Call 907-766-3094 or see *www.baldeagles.org*.

If you've come to fish, you'll find plenty in these rich waters. Book a charter for halibut or salmon fishing. Lakes and streams also support hooligan, trout, and Dolly Varden. Keep your license current, and check in with the Alaska Department of Fish and Game for regulations at 907-766-2625. Other recreation includes flightseeing, biking, rafting, canoeing, and hiking. There are several tour operators and guiding businesses in town. Contact the Haines Chamber of Commerce at 907-766-2202 or see *www.haineschamber.org*.

A must-stop is the visitor center at 2nd Avenue and Willard Street. Call the Haines Convention & Visitors Bureau at 1-800-458-3579 or 907-766-2234, or visit their Web site at *www.hainesak.us*.

LODGING

Bear Creek Cabins
Mile 1.5 Small Tracts Road
907-766-2259
www.bearcreekcabinsalaska.com
Cabins for the family; bunks for solo travelers. Kitchen and bath facilities. Camping, laundry.

Cabin Fever
Mile 8 Mud Bay Road
907-766-2390
Cabins on the beach. Private baths, kitchenettes.

Captain's Choice Motel
108 2nd Avenue North
907-766-3332 / *www.capchoice.com*
39 rooms with view of Lynn Canal. Room service, tour booking, car rentals. Walking distance to restaurants. Shuttle service.

Eagle's Nest Motel
Mile 1 Haines Highway
907-766-2891
13 rooms, kitchenettes, free continental breakfast. Tours, car rentals, courtesy van.

Hotel Halsingland
On Fort Seward grounds
1-800-478-5556 or 907-766-2000
www.hotelhalsingland.com
60 rooms, private bath, cable TV, phones, car rental. Seafood restaurant, lounge. Historic building with canal views.

Mountain View Motel
2nd Avenue and Mud Bay Road, near Fort Seward grounds
1-800-478-2902 or 907-766-2900
9 rooms, kitchenettes, views. Walking distance to restaurants.

Thunderbird Motel
2nd Avenue and Dalton Street
1-800-327-2556 or 907-766-2131
www.thunderbird–motel.com
20 rooms, kitchenettes. Walking distance to restaurants, shops.

CAMPGROUNDS

HAINES:

Haines Hitch-up RV Park
Haines Highway and Main Street
907-766-2882
www.hitchuprv.com
92 sites with full and partial hookups, dry camping. Wireless Internet, laundry, gift shop. Tour tickets available.

Oceanside RV Park
Front and Main Streets
907-766-2437
Full hookups overlooking Lynn Canal. Walking distance to showers, shopping, laundry, dining.

Port Chilkoot Camper Park
Next to Fort Seward
1-800-542-6363 or 907-766-2000
Full and partial hookups, showers, laundry, dump station. Close to town. Property was up for sale in October 2007.

Salmon Run RV Campground and Cabins
Almost 2 miles (3 km) north of ferry on Lutak Road
907-766-3240 or 907-723-4229
Forested campsites with fire rings, tables, showers, trails, boat launch. Inlet and mountain views.

NORTHEAST OF HAINES:

Swan's Rest RV Park
On Mosquito Lake Road, off Mile 27 Haines Highway
907-767-5662
12 sites with full hookups, cabin available. Borders the Chilkat Bald Eagle Preserve. Showers, laundry, restrooms, fishing and boat rental.

Chilkat Charlie's RV & Tent Park
Mile 33 Haines Highway
907-767-5510
8 sites with full and partial hookups, some pull-throughs, dry camping, showers. Next to 33 Mile Roadhouse.

The state maintains four campgrounds near Haines, offered on a first-come, first-served basis:

Chilkat State Park
8 miles (13 km) south of Haines on Mud Bay Road
32 pull-through sites, 3 beachfront tent sites. Water, toilets, fishing, boat launch, hiking, log cabin interpretive center.

Chilkoot Lake State Recreation Area
10 miles (16 km) north of Haines, off Lutak Road
32 spaces, lake views, water, toilets, fishing, boat launch, log cabin interpretive center.

Mosquito Lake State Recreation Site
Mile 27.3 Haines Highway
13 sites next to the lake in Sitka spruce and Western hemlock forest. Dock and boat launch, picnic shelter.

Portage Cove State Recreation Site
About 1 mile (1.5 km) south of Haines on Beach Road
Tent camping for backpackers and bicyclists, no overnight parking. Water pump, tables, fire rings, toilets.

RESTAURANTS

33 Mile Roadhouse
Mile 33 Haines Highway
907-767-5510
Breakfast, lunch, dinner. Boasts of "best burger" around. Homemade pie.

Bamboo Room Restaurant
2nd Avenue and Dalton Street
907-766-2800
Breakfast, lunch, dinner; espresso, halibut fish and chips. Seniors' and children's menus. Sports bar.

Chilkat Restaurant & Bakery
5th Avenue and Dalton Street
907-766-2920
Breakfast, lunch, dinner; pastries.

Hotel Halsingland Restaurant
On Fort Seward grounds
907-766-2000
Seafood and other Alaska specialties; historic building. Property was for sale in October 2007.

Klondike Restaurant
Dalton City
On the grounds of Southeast Alaska State Fair
907-766-2477
Open summers only.

Lighthouse Restaurant & Harbor Bar
Main and Beach Streets, by Small Boat Harbor
907-766-2442
Open for breakfast, lunch, and dinner; view of harbor.

KLONDIKE HIGHWAY 2

From Alaska Highway to Skagway: 99 miles (159 km)
Travel Opportunities: *White Pass & Yukon Route railway; Skagway; Gold Rush Cemetery; Slide Cemetery; Arctic Brotherhood Hall; Dyea and trailhead to Chilkoot Pass.*

Klondike Highway 2 is a fairly new road (built in 1978) that covers very old ground. This route over White Pass is an ancient one used by the coastal Tlingit who traveled to trade with inland tribes. During the 1898 Klondike gold rush, White Pass and nearby Chilkoot Pass were the two major overland routes to the goldfields.

Klondike Highway 2 heads south to Skagway from the Alaska Highway at Mile 874 (1,407 km), about a dozen miles south of Whitehorse. The high-elevation lakes and rocky cliffs along this highway rank it among the most impressive topographically. At White Pass, the wind is fast and chilly, even in the middle of summer.

You will cross from the Yukon into Alaska at the international border about 7 miles (11 km) before you reach Skagway, so be prepared for U.S. Customs and Immigration. Remember to turn your watch back an hour—you'll be in the Alaska Time Zone.

Skagway

Skagway is one of two Alaska communities on the northern end of the Inside Passage that are served by the Alaska Marine Highway System; Haines is the other. It's possible to board your vehicle in Bellingham, Washington, and take the ferry all the way along the protected waters of Southeast Alaska, then rejoin the road system at Haines or Skagway. (See Chapter 9, Alaska Marine Highway System.)

Walking through Skagway is like stepping into a colorized postcard from 1898, when businesses like these also lined the streets and served the gold seekers who were headed to Dyea and over Chilkoot Pass. This northernmost town on the Inside Passage was the gateway to the Klondike, and in the two years between 1897 and 1899, the primary reason to be here was to get rich quick—by either mining the ground or mining the pockets of the miners. Skagway boomed into a city of 20,000 in a few months' time.

The Chilkoot Trail was a steep and treacherous route over Chilkoot Pass to the goldfields. Photos often depict a dark line of men (and a few women) hiking an arm's length from each other as they climbed the snowy steps to the pass. Today the 33-mile (53-km) route remains a challenge, even to hikers dressed in the latest outdoor gear. If you're planning to try the Chilkoot, check first with the Klondike Gold Rush National Historical Park visitor center at 2nd and Broadway in Skagway. The center is housed in

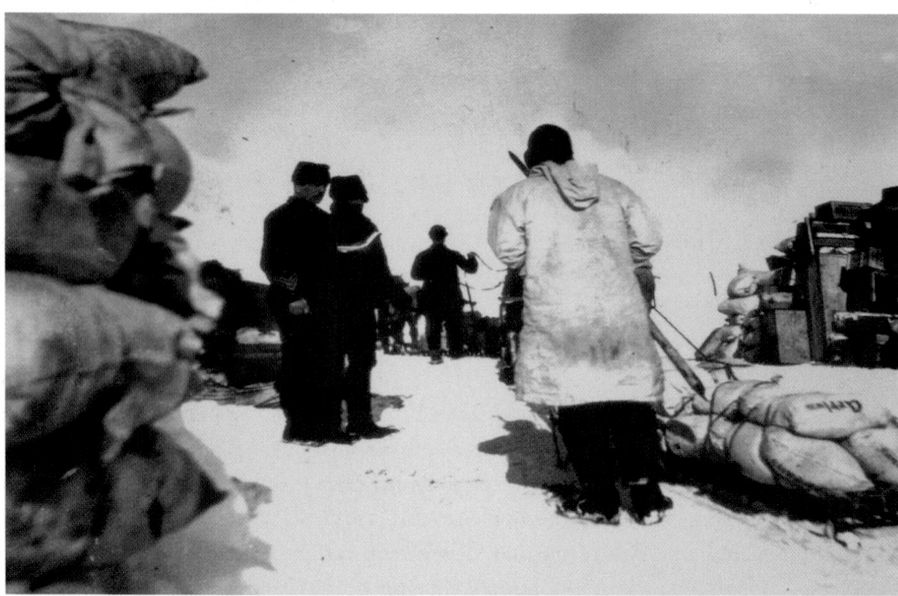

A historical photo depicts the summit of White Pass during the Gold Rush of 1898. Stampeders were not allowed to cross without a year's worth of supplies.

the restored White Pass & Yukon Route railway depot. Ask about guided tours of the historic downtown, or programs in the auditorium. Call 907-983-9200.

The White Pass & Yukon Route narrow-gauge (36-inch) railway offers trips in railcars pulled by a steam locomotive, letting full- and half-day-trippers retrace the steps of gold-rush stampeders. Call 1-800-343-7373 or 907-983-2217 to arrange a ride.

The Arctic Brotherhood Hall on Broadway between 2nd and 3rd, its false front decorated with 10,000 pieces of driftwood, looks the same today as it did a century ago. The Visitor Center is inside. 1-888-786-1898 or 907-983-2854, or browse *www.skagway.com.* They can help set you up with an adventure of a lifetime, rafting, hiking, chartering a fishing trip, flightseeing, you name it.

Having scaled the Chilkoot Pass, these hikers were ready to celebrate in Skagway. (Note the duct tape on the righthand man's boots!)

The Skagway Museum and Archives, loaded with gold-rush artifacts, records, and photos, can be found at 7th Avenue and Spring Street. The collection also includes personal artifacts from the late 1800s, donated by local people since 1961. Call 907-983-2420.

The saloons, restaurants, gift shops, and soda fountains of Skagway are all wrapped in historical storefronts. A horse-and-buggy tour operator is dressed in the garb of old. The storefront windows along Main Street are trimmed with the hats, gloves, and doodads that would have pleased your grandma. The big difference between then and now, besides the plumbing and telephone lines, lies in the harbor: Enormous cruise ships bring their passengers to Skagway to soak up a little atmosphere of the Days of '98.

A century ago, outlaw Soapy Smith reigned here, along with his gang of con artists and thugs who took advantage of the weak, the innocent, and even the dead. One story tells of the terrible avalanche that killed dozens of men on the Chilkoot Trail. Soapy set up a "morgue" near the site, and he and his men dug up bodies, took them into his morgue, and stripped them of their valuables before the real authorities arrived. His reign ended when he was confronted by a man named Frank Reid, who shot Soapy several times and was mortally wounded himself.

The graves of both men, in the Gold Rush Cemetery, are visited by thousands of people every year. To get to the cemetery, go north on State Street, then follow the signs. Reid's

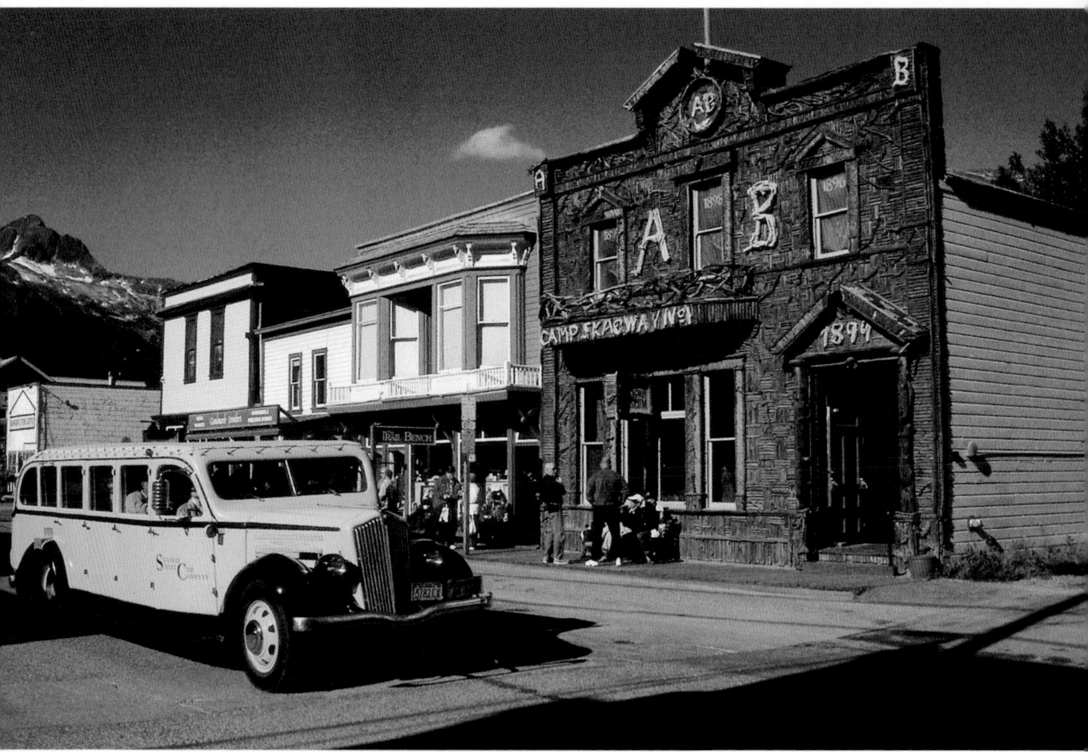

Many thousands of pieces of driftwood adorn the exterior of the Arctic Brotherhood Hall, a Skagway original still standing from the Gold Rush.

---

grave bears these words: "He gave his life for the honor of Skagway." Every July 4, the city remembers those days with an event called Soapy Smith's Wake. Another cemetery holds the remains of victims from that Chilkoot avalanche.

You can drive to what used to be Dyea, a town of thousands, where nothing but a derelict dock remains. From the parking area, you can walk to the Chilkoot Pass trailhead.

LODGING

4th Street Hotel
444 4th Street, above the Pizza Station
907-983-3200
10 rooms, some with bath.

At the White House
8th and Main Streets, near downtown
907-983-9000
www.atthewhitehouse.com
Rooms with private baths in 1902 family-run inn. Complimentary breakfast.

Chilkoot Trail Outpost
Dyea Valley
907-983-3799 / *www.chilkoottrailoutpost.com*
Modern luxury log cabins nestled in the woods, free breakfast.

Sgt. Preston's Lodge
6th Avenue and State Street
907-983-2521
30 rooms on street level. Cable TV and phones. Courtesy van. Close to bank and post office.

Skagway Bungalows
Near town
907-983-3986
Log cabins furnished with microwaves, fridges, king- or queen-sized beds.

Skagway Inn
7th Avenue and Broadway Street
1-800-752-4929 or 907-983-2289
12 rooms in historic district. Breakfast, van service. Reservations for White Pass & Yukon Route, shows, tours.

Westmark Inn Skagway
3rd Avenue and Spring Street
1-800-544-0970 or 907-983-6000
www.westmarkhotels.com
195 deluxe rooms, nonsmoking available. Cable TV, dining room, lounge. Close to shopping and entertainment.

CAMPGROUNDS

Garden City RV Park
State Street between 15th and 17th Avenues
907-983-2378
Level sites with full and partial hookups, pull-throughs. Laundry, restrooms, coin-operated showers.

Pullen Creek RV Park
2nd Avenue near Alaska State Ferry dock
1-800-936-3731
Partial hookups. Showers, dump station. Walking distance to shopping and attractions.

Skagway Mountain View RV Park
12th Avenue and Broadway Street
1-888-778-7700
Wooded sites with partial hookups, pull-throughs, cable TV access. Picnic tables, firewood. Showers, laundry, restrooms, dump station. RV wash facilities. Tour reservations. Near downtown historic district.

National Park Service Ranger Station & Dyea Campground
9 miles from Skagway in Dyea
907-983-2921
22 campsites, not recommended for RVs. Bring your own water. Vault toilets, picnic tables, bear-proof food storage containers, fire rings. Self-registration.

RESTAURANTS

Alaska Gourmet
5th Avenue between Broadway and State
907-983-2448
Home-cooking from local seafood and produce.

Bonanza Bar & Grill
Broadway, between 3rd and 4th Avenues
907-983-6214
Seafood, pizza, drink specials, entertainment.

Chilkoot Dining Room
242 3rd Avenue
907-983-6000
Meat, pasta, salads, crab legs.

The Corner Café
4th Avenue and State Street
907-983-2155
Three meals a day, specializing in pizza. Free delivery.

Excelsior Café
270 2nd Avenue
907-8983-2908
Espresso, bakery, deli.

Haven Café Espresso & Light Fare
870 State Street
907-983-353
Breakfast, soups, sandwiches, salads, desserts, espresso.

Ofelia's Restaurant
230 4th Street
907-983-3324
Chinese and American, seafood, crab, halibut. Breakfast, lunch, dinner.

Olivia's Restaurant
7th and Broadway, in Skagway Inn
907-983-2289
Alaskan tapas menu, with full bar and select wine list. Wild salmon, organic kitchen garden.

The Red Onion Saloon
2nd Avenue & Broadway Street
907-983-2222
Food and libations in 1898 saloon, entertainment, brothel museum.

Skagway's Pizza Station
444 4th Avenue
907-983-2200
Dine in or take-out. Delivery.

Sweet Tooth Café
315 Broadway Street
907-983-2405
Breakfast, lunch, dinner. Homemade donuts, soups, bread, fries. Take-out available.

PARKS HIGHWAY

Anchorage to Fairbanks: 358 miles (576 km)
Travel Opportunities: *Iditarod Trail Sled Dog Race Headquarters, Wasilla; Independence Mine; Talkeetna; Denali State Park; Denali National Park and Preserve; Fairbanks.*

The (George) Parks Highway connects the state's two largest cities, Anchorage and Fairbanks, in a 358-mile south-to-north trek from the Southcentral coast into Alaska's great Interior. It is among the newest of the highways (completed in 1972) and sees heavy summer use, often by motorists on their way to Denali National Park and Preserve.

To reach the Parks Highway from Anchorage, take the Glenn Highway north for 35 miles (56 km). At a major interchange near Wasilla, the Glenn continues east, while the northbound Parks is marked with clear roadside signs directing drivers toward Denali Park and Fairbanks. Even though this place is the official start of the Parks Highway, roadside mileposts will reflect total mileage from Anchorage. (For details on Anchorage-area attractions, lodging, campgrounds, and restaurants, see the section on the Glenn Highway, in this chapter.)

Just north of the Glenn Highway and Parks Highway junction is Wasilla. Once a sleepy little stop along a two-lane road, Wasilla has experienced a population boom in the past two decades; every lane of the four-lane Parks Highway is busy as the road passes through town. Wasilla is a good last-chance, full-service shopping stop before you begin your lengthy road trip north. Although many small, family-operated stores and service stations lie ahead, Wasilla offers a variety of goods, services, fast-food restaurants, grocery stores, and so forth. Almost the entire shopping district lies at roadside.

To learn more about local history, visit the Dorothy Page Museum & Historic Townsite, 323 Main Street, in Wasilla. Exhibits focus on the development of the Iditarod Trail Sled Dog Race, area homesteading, and settlement in the Mat-Su Valley. Admission is charged. For information, call 907-373-9071.

At the Knik–Goose Bay Road traffic light in Wasilla, you can turn west and follow the road for a little more than 2 miles (3 km) to the impressive log building that is the Iditarod Trail Sled Dog Race Headquarters. Inside are the administrative offices of the famous 1,000-mile race across Alaska, as well as a museum, video theater, and gift shop. Admission is free. A mount of a champion sled dog named Andy is on display here, too. A leader for five-time Iditarod champion Rick Swenson, Andy is a testimonial to the athletic ability of Alaska sled dogs. For a nominal fee, you can take a dogsled ride in summer with a member of the Redington family, descendents of "Father of the Iditarod," Joe Redington, Sr. The teams pull wheeled carts instead of sleds. At a replica of a checkpoint cabin, learn more about this phenomenal race. Call 907-376-5155 or visit the Iditarod Web site at *www.iditarod.com.*

Transportation buffs will enjoy a visit to a special museum north of Wasilla off the Parks Highway at Mile 47 (75.5 km). Follow the signs for another mile to the Museum of Alaska Transportation & Industry at 3800 Museum Drive. Here you'll see early-day snowmobiles, vehicles, airplanes, trains, buildings, and more. Open seasonally, May through September. Call 907-376-1211 or see *www.museumofalaska.org.*

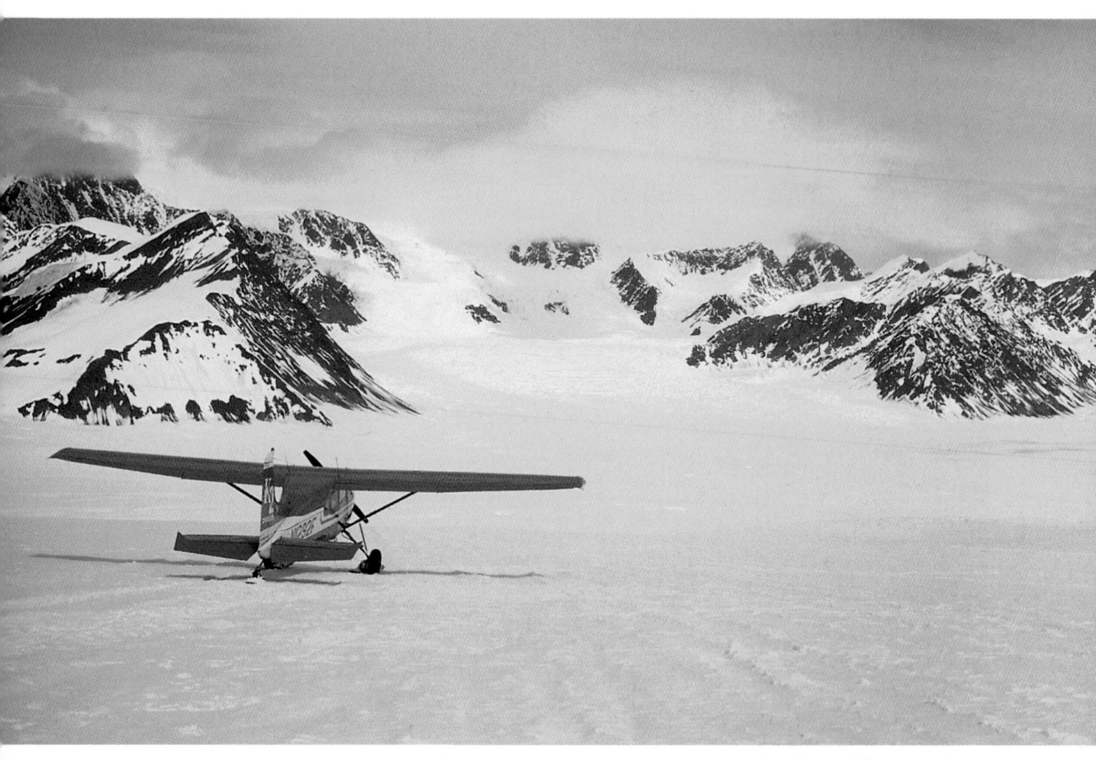

Bush pilots out of Talkeetna land on Ruth Glacier daily, allowing visitors to step out of the plane and onto a glacier.

As you drive the Parks Highway, you'll occasionally pass through little enclaves where people choose to live far away from big cities. Willow is such a town. It has its own post office, library, convenience store, gas station, café, lodge, and dozens of little homes sprinkled throughout the surrounding forests and around lakes. Roadside fishing opportunities exist all along this stretch of the Parks Highway. Even if you don't fish, it's fun to pull over and watch the anglers.

A popular attraction for campers and fishers is Nancy Lake State Recreation Area, at Mile 67.5 (107 km) Parks Highway, developed with two separate campgrounds, both with water and toilets. The Nancy Lake State Recreation Site, on the northeast shore, has 30 campsites, water, toilets, a trail, and a boat launch. The South Rolly Lake Campground has 99 sites, and is accessed at the end of Nancy Lake Parkway.

Just past Willow at Mile 71 (114.5 km) is the westbound turn for Willow Creek State Recreation Area, located at the end of the Willow Creek Parkway, about 5 miles (8 km) from the highway. The area is nicely developed with RV parking, water, outhouses, tent camping, trails, and river access.

Just north of the entrance to Willow Creek Parkway is the eastbound turnoff for Hatcher Pass Road and access to Independence Mine. (See details in the section on the Glenn Highway, in this chapter.)

The Alaska Railroad wends through the Alaska Range, traveling daily in summers between Anchorage and Fairbanks.

Take a side trip to Talkeetna for a taste of old Alaska. Almost 99 miles (159 km) north of Anchorage, make the right turn onto a spur road that leads to Talkeetna. This is an excellent drive along a paved 14-mile (22.5-km) road that dead-ends in a historic gold-mining town. On clear days, views of Mount McKinley practically fill up the windshield. And at certain times of the year, Talkeetna is overrun with mountain climbers who have journeyed here from all over the world. Local Bush pilots fly the climbers and their gear to the base camp of Mount McKinley for ascents up North America's tallest peak. And tourists flocks here to sign on for a flightseeing trip over the mountain, sometimes landing for a walk on a glacier.

Park on Main Street and poke around Talkeetna on foot. A car only gets in the way. At one end of the street, you'll find tent camping or RV sites for dry camping. Outhouses are nearby. Several of Talkeetna's buildings are on the National Register of Historic Places. Although it's small, the town features museums, two roadhouses, a modern National Park Service ranger station, a post office, motels, a country store, and several gift shops.

Each summer, Talkeetna hosts the Mountain Mama Contest, where women can prove their mettle by chopping wood and hauling water while packing a baby doll in a carrier on their backs. The town also hosts the infamous Moose Dropping Festival on the second weekend of July. Come for the parade, the food, the entertainment, and games with moose droppings. (Yes, droppings, as in scat.)

Here you can arrange a jet-boating adventure, a flightseeing trip, a float trip, a day or more on the water fishing for big salmon. In Talkeetna, you'll find a number of outfitters, some of them with storefronts along Main Street. Ask for directions at the visitor information cabin by the sign that says "Welcome to Beautiful Downtown Talkeetna." The Talkeetna Chamber of Commerce can be reached at 907-732-2330 or browse *www.talkeetnachamber.org.*

On clear days, a crowd gathers at the Mile 135 (237 km) wayside on the Parks Highway. From here, you'll gain the best roadside view of 20,320-foot Mount McKinley and the lesser surrounding mountains, which would receive more notice were they not flanking McKinley. Neighboring peaks include Mount Foraker, rising to 13,395 feet (4,082 m); Mount Hunter, at 14,580 feet (4,444 m); and Mount Silverthrone, at 13,220 feet (4,029 m); plus three others with summits that exceed 12,000 feet (3,658 m). Interpretive signs name the mountains and more about this terrain. Other stops along the Highway are at Mile 158, 162, and 174. There's no way to make the mountain visible when the clouds are out, though, so be prepared. You may never see it, even though it's right in front of you.

The boundary of Denali State Park lies about 132 miles (213 km) north of Anchorage. This park straddles the highway and offers 325,240 acres filled with recreational opportunities: fishing, hiking, biking, camping, canoeing, floating. Three state-operated campgrounds are in the park: Byers Lake, Lower Troublesome Creek, and Denali View North. Thirty-seven miles (59 km) of developed trails thread above and below tree line in a panoramic landscape. For more information, call the Alaska State Parks office in Wasilla at 907-745-3975, or visit the Web site at *www.dnr.state.ak.us/parks.*

A popular landmark at Mile 188.5 (303 km) is a private business that has long been a curiosity as well as a milepost: a three-story igloo. The giant geodesic structure originally was built as a hotel but never served that purpose. The igloo marks roughly the halfway point between Anchorage and Fairbanks.

At Mile 210 (338 km), near Cantwell, an eastbound turnoff leads to the Denali Highway, which connects the Parks Highway with the Richardson Highway. (See the section on the Denali Highway, in this chapter.)

The crown jewel of North America, Mount McKinley rises within the 6-million-acre Denali National Park and Preserve. And while views of "The Mountain" tease motorists during their northbound drive, the park entrance doesn't arrive until Mile 237 Parks Highway (382 km), about 4.5 hours north of Anchorage.

An extended visit to Denali National Park takes some advance planning, because reservations are necessary for campsites, for hotel rooms, and for seats on the shuttle buses that travel on the only road that penetrates the park. You can easily drop in and check out the visitor center, walk around the local trails, enjoy a picnic, and take off. But overnight stays are more complicated. The nationwide reservation phone number is 1-800-622-7275; in Anchorage, call 907-272-7275. See *www.reservedenali.com.*

Most visitors to the park stay in hotels along the Parks Highway just a few miles farther north, where development of restaurants, gas stations, hotels, gift shops, and tour operators has clustered outside the park's boundaries. In the park, a modern visitor center serves as the operation center as people come and go on hikes, catch rides to sled-dog demonstrations, head out on guided nature walks, or leave for the bus ride to the end of the 87-mile

Four-time Iditarod champion Jeff King poses with Joe and Margaret Stenson, who were visiting from Ireland. King and his family live in Denali Park, where he trains his dogs. Tours of his kennel, the Husky Homestead, are among the many choices for visitors to Denali National Park and Preserve.

(140-km) park road. Private vehicles are not allowed beyond Mile 30 (48 km) on that road, so if you want the best chance to see wildlife, you have to take the shuttle bus. Wildlife watching (and mountain watching) remain the top draw. Chances are you might see a bear, caribou, moose, ptarmigan, fox, Dall sheep, or snowshoe hare.

The Eielson Visitor Center closed for several seasons while construction crews worked on the new facility, set to open in 2008.

The Alaska Railroad depot lies within the park, too, and shuttle buses transport passengers to their waiting hotels. The place is abuzz with activity—and the scenery, close and far away, is awesome. Out on the Parks Highway, the Nenana River races below the road's edge. Look for whitewater rafters down there any time of day. Overhead, small airplanes and helicopters engage in viewing Denali from the top down.

About a half-hour farther north on the Parks Highway, the coal-mining town of Healy lies in the northern foothills of the Alaska Range. This is the next place along the road to find a meal, accommodations, and fuel. A small community, Healy is growing as more visitors to Denali National Park want to leave the crowds behind when they find a hotel room.

From here, the Parks Highway continues north through the boreal forests of Alaska's Interior. Set between the Alaska Range and the Brooks Range, this vast region charts the coldest colds and the hottest hots in the state. From Healy to Nenana, you'll find occasional services, gift shops, and gas stations, but little other development.

The section of the Parks between Nenana and Fairbanks wends through the Tanana uplands, round-topped tall hills (they would be called mountains elsewhere) that border the Tanana Valley. As you cross these hills, passing lanes are available for faster traffic. Be sure to stay to the right if your vehicle pulls hills slowly. Every few miles, pullouts offer clear views, from the top down, of the braided Tanana River and its tributaries. Local forests are mostly spruce, birch, and aspen.

About 5 miles (8 km) before entering Fairbanks on the Parks Highway, you'll note signs that lead west to Ester Gold Camp. Ester was once a vibrant gold-mining community; today it's a historic site where a handful of people live.

For information on Fairbanks history, attractions, events, lodging, campgrounds, and restaurants, see the section on Fairbanks in Chapter 6, The Alaska Highway.

LODGING

The Mat–Su Bed & Breakfast Association has information on rooms, apartments, and cabins from Glennallen to Anchorage to Denali. Visit the association's Web site at www.alaskabnbhosts.com.

WASILLA:

Agate Inn
4725 Begich Circle
907-373-2290
Country-style inn located just north of Anchorage. Open year-round.

Alaska Kozey Cabins
351 East Spruce
907-376-3190

Alaskan View Motel
2650 East Parks Highway
907-376-6787
26 rooms, Alaska décor in log building. Cable TV, mountain and inlet views.

Best Western Lake Lucille Inn
1300 West Lake Lucille Drive
907-373-1776
54 deluxe rooms, suites, high-speed Internet. Athletic facility, whirlpool, gift shop. Floatplane and boat docks, boat rentals.

Grand View Inn & Suites
2900 East Parks Highway
907-357-7666
79 rooms, new in 2004, with views of Chugach Mountains and Cook Inlet. Fishing and shopping nearby.

The Windbreak
2201 East Parks Highway
907-376-4484 / *www.windbreakalaska.com*
Rooms, plus café serving breakfast, lunch, dinner. Lounge.

DENALI PARK:

Denali Backcountry Lodge
Kantishna, end of 95-mile Park Road
1-800-841-0692 or 907-783-1342
www.denalilodge.com
30 units, dining, cocktails. Inside the park. Private wildlife-viewing bus. Train shuttle service.

Denali Bluffs Hotel
Mile 238.5 Parks Highway
866-683-8500 or 907-683-8500
www.denaliparkresorts.com
112 rooms with views, private baths, coffee service, fridges, phone. Restaurant, tour desk, gift shop. Shuttle service.

Denali Cedars Lodge
Mile 231 Parks Highway
800-208-0200
www.alaskatravel.com
48 hotel-style rooms in two-story cedar buildings. Deck, sauna, courtesy shuttle, activities desk. Free deluxe continental breakfast. Borders the Nenana River.

Denali Crow's Nest Log Cabins
Mile 238.5 Parks highway
1-888-917-8130 or 907-683-2723
www.denalicrowsnest.com
39 deluxe cabins with private baths, close to park entrance. Views, hot tub, tour desk, shuttle. Bar and grill.

Denali Grizzly Bear Resort
Mile 231 Parks Highway
907-683-2696
54-room cedar hotel with private decks on the Nenana River; kitchenette units, laundry. Pets allowed. Campsites.

Denali Princess Wilderness Lodge
Mile 238.5 Parks Highway
1-800-426-0500
www.princesslodges.com
Deluxe accommodations, outdoor hot tubs, tour desk, shuttle service. Free train transfers from the depot. Pizza pub, espresso, full-service restaurant. Health and tanning spa.

Denali River Cabins
Mile 229 Parks Highway
1-800-450-2489 or 907-683-2642
www.denalirivercabins.com
43 cedar cabins with private bath. Hot tubs, dining. South of park entrance, train shuttle service.

Denali Sourdough Cabins
Mile 238.8 Parks Highway
1-800-544-0970 or 907-683-2773
www.westmarkhotels.com
Comfortable, well-appointed cabins, close to park entrance.

Grande Denali Lodge
Mile 238 Parks Highway
1-866-683-8500 or 907-683-8500
www.denaliparkresorts.com
159 roomy guest rooms, deluxe cabins, amenities in the wilderness. Lounge, gift shop, tour desk, laundry, courtesy shuttle. Alpenglow Restaurant.

McKinley Chalet Resort
Mile 238 Parks Highway
1-800-276-7234 or 907-279-2653
www.denaliparkresorts.com
Beautifully appointed lobby, café, gift shop. 345 units, restaurant, cocktails. Train shuttle service. Wildly popular theatrical production, "Alaska Cabin Nite Dinner Theater."

McKinley Creekside Cabins
Mile 224 Parks Highway
1-888-5DENALI or 907-683-2277
www.mckinleycabins.com
Lodge, cabins, café on Carlo Creek near the Park.

McKinley Princess Wilderness Lodge
Mile 133 Parks Highway, in Denali State Park on Chulitna River
1-800-426-0500
www.princesslodges.com
Luxury accommodations with views of the mountain. TV, phones, hot tub, tour desk, theater, gift shop. Restaurants, lounges. Shuttle service.

McKinley Village Lodge
Mile 231 Parks Highway
1-800-276-7234 or 907-276-7234
www.denaliparkresorts.com
150 luxury units, dining, cocktails. Rafting adventures. Overlooks Nenana River. Train shuttle service.

HEALY:

Denali North Star Inn
Mile 249 Parks Highway
907-683-1560
100 rooms in buildings originally constructed in Prudhoe Bay. Gift shop, salon services, sauna, exercise room, tour desk, lounge. Train shuttle service.

Denali Park Hotel
Mile 247 Parks Highway
1-866-683-1800 or 907-683-1800
www.denaliparkhotel.com
Lobby is refurbished Alaska Railroad train car. King or two full beds. Satellite TV, phone.

Denali Suites
15 minutes north of Park entrance on Healy Spur Road
907-683-2848
www.denalisuites.com
Units include 2- or 3-bedroom suites, kitchens, TV, VCR, private bath, laundry facility.

Motel Nord Haven
15 minutes north of Park entrance on Parks Highway
1-800-683-4501
www.motelnordhaven.com
28 rooms with queen beds, RVs, phones, private baths.

Park's Edge
Off Mile 247 Parks Highway on Hilltop Road
907-683-4343
www.parks–edge.com
Log cabins in quiet, convenient location. Adjacent to golf course and restaurant.

Totem Inn
Mile 249 Parks Highway
1-800-478-2384 or 907-683-2420
50 units, plus laundry, dining, cocktails. Train shuttle service.

FAIRBANKS:
See listings in the section on Fairbanks in Chapter 6, The Alaska Highway.

CAMPGROUNDS

WASILLA:
Alaska R & R Laundry & RV Park
Mile 49.5 Parks Highway
907-373-7286
16 RV sites with full hookups, 4 pull-throughs. Dump station, restrooms.

Best View RV Park
Mile 35.5 Parks Highway
1-800-478-6600 or 907-745-7400
101 sites with full hookups, pull-throughs, tenting area. Mountain views. Free showers; laundry, dump station.

Big Bear RV Park
Mile 37 Parks Highway
907-373-4049
43 campsites with pull-throughs.

Lake Lucille Park
Operated by Matanuska-Susitna Borough
Follow signs from Mile 2.5 Knik–Goose Bay Road
907-745-9690
64 sites in treed area, covered picnic area, firewood, restrooms. Walking distance to lake and fishing. On-site host.

DENALI PARK:
Denali Grizzly Bear Cabins and Campground
Mile 231 Parks Highway
907-683-2696
40 RV sites with full hookups and pull-throughs, tent sites. Showers, laundry, water, dump station.

Denali Rainbow Village RV Park
1 mile north of Denali Park entrance
907-683-7777 / *www.denalirv.com*
77 sites with full or partial hookups, satellite TV, close to park and activities.

Denali Riverside RV Park
Mile 240 Parks Highway
907-388-1748
Sites with hookups, dump station, drinking water, showers, toilets, laundry, store. Tent camping. Pets allowed.

McKinley RV and Campground
Mile 248.5 Parks Highway
1-800-478-2562 or 907-683-2379
77 RV sites with full hookups and pull-throughs, tent sites. Fireplace/grills. Showers, water, dump station.

FAIRBANKS:
See listings in the section on Fairbanks in Chapter 6, The Alaska Highway.

RESTAURANTS

WASILLA:
Great Bear Brewing Co.
238 North Boundary Street
907-373-4782
www.greatbearbrewing.com
Brews, sandwiches, soups, salads.

Mat-Su Resort
1850 Bogard Road
907-376-3228
American cuisine, seafood, steaks. Weekend breakfasts. Reservations suggested.

The Windbreak Café
2201 East Parks Highway, Windbreak Hotel
907-376-4484
www.windbreakalaska.com
Breakfast, lunch, dinner.

DENALI PARK:
Coffee shops, pizza places, salmon bakes, and sit-down restaurants can be found on both sides of the Parks Highway jut outside of Denali National Park & Preserve.

Check the Denali Park lodging listings, above. Nearly every hotel has one or more restaurants for every level of dining experience, from sandwiches to fine dining.

FAIRBANKS:
See listings in the section on Fairbanks in Chapter 6, The Alaska Highway.

The Worthington Glacier is accessible for those who wish to hike alongside its path. A visitor information wayside instructs readers about glaciers and local history.

RICHARDSON HIGHWAY

Valdez to Fairbanks: 364 miles (587 km)

Travel Opportunities: *Valdez; glacier cruises, pipeline terminus on Prince William Sound; Thompson Pass; Worthington Glacier; pipeline pump stations; Delta Junction; North Pole; Fairbanks.*

The original name for this historic route was the Valdez-Fairbanks Trail. Work on the road began in 1903, after the Tanana Valley gold strike near Fairbanks. In 1904 the government pushed development along by requiring every man along the length of the road to work two days per year on the project or pay a tax of $8.

You are forgiven if you pronounce Valdez as val-DEZ, because everywhere else in the world, that's how you'd say it. But in Alaska, a mispronunciation has stuck and it's called val-DEEZ. The massive 1964 earthquake virtually destroyed the original townsite, and the current location was chosen when the townspeople rebuilt. This is an ice-free, deepwater port on an arm of Prince William Sound in an area that's also known as Alaska's "Little

Switzerland," as it is surrounded by the Chugach Mountains, the tallest coastal range in North America. Here, too, is the terminus of the 800-mile (1,280-km) trans-Alaska pipeline. From town, you can see the terminal and massive tanker ships coming and going.

With a population of about 4,450, Valdez lies along the Alaska Marine Highway System (see Chapter 9), with the ferry terminal located near Hazelet Avenue and Fidalgo Drive. Valdez is the place for outdoor adventures. You can arrange for a fishing charter, rent a kayak, book a glacier-viewing cruise, go whale-watching, or sign up for a whitewater rafting trip. There's hiking, tours of the salmon hatchery, gold panning, or taking in all that the Museum has to offer. The best place to begin is with the Valdez Convention & Visitors Bureau at 200 Fairbanks Street. Phone 907-835-4636 or browse their Web site at *www.valdezalaska.org.*

This little city gets more snow than any other in Alaska. In the winter of 1999–2000, some 380 inches of snow fell on the town. A paralyzing 596.9 inches fell in the winter of 1994–1995. That's almost 50 feet of snow—enough to bury a house, or at least cave in its roof during many months when there is rare chance of any snow melting. Snow, and what to do with it, is the reason Valdez is laid out as it is. Side streets end in cul-de-sacs with rights-of-way for snowplows to push snow out of the streets and into a dump area behind the homes. Note that most roofs are metal, and angled so that snow slides off into yards, not onto walkways or driveways.

You'll find lots of opportunity to view wildlife in and around Valdez, so keep your telephoto lens or field glasses handy. Make noise while hiking or biking so you don't surprise the bears. It's common to see eagles, sea otters, harbor seals, humpback whales, and orcas. Shorebirds and waterfowl move through seasonally.

The Valdez Museum, at 217 Egan Drive, features rotating exhibits as well as displays and photos on town history, the gold rush, cultural history, and the Exxon Valdez oil spill that tainted Prince William Sound in 1989. Call 907-835-2764 or see *www.valdezmuseum.org.* A host of restaurants and gift shops and a couple of grocery stores are easy to find on the simple street grid of Valdez.

Each year Valdez hosts the Last Frontier Theater Conference, which attracts top writers and actors, debuts new works by developing playwrights, and continues to gain in national prominence.

Traveling north from Valdez on the Richardson Highway, you'll encounter awe-inspiring canyons and waterfalls, and the looming Worthington Glacier, named a National Natural Landmark. A visitor information wayside at Thompson Pass, elevation 2,678 feet (816 m), provides information about the nearby glacier. The deepest single snowfall in recorded history occurred at Thompson Pass on December 5, 1955, when 62 inches fell. The route to Thompson Pass remains a daunting climb, even in modern vehicles, but a century ago and more, the trail included numerous switchbacks to make it easier for the horse-drawn double-ender sleighs that traveled in winter and the wagons that crossed the pass in summer.

Record snowfall on the pass in the winter of 1952–1953 measured 974.5 inches. And yet Thompson Pass is not the highest on the Richardson Highway. That honor goes to Isabel Pass, at 3,000 feet. It was named for the wife of Fairbanks founder E. T. Barnette, who traveled with his wife, Isabelle (yes, it's spelled differently than the pass), over this route several times, summer and winter, in a horse-drawn sleigh or stage.

Occasionally the trans-Alaska pipeline is visible from the Richardson on its route from Prudhoe Bay to Valdez.

Eighty-three miles (134 km) north of Valdez, the Edgerton Highway splits off to the east, leading to Chitina. From Chitina, the McCarthy Road continues to the town of McCarthy, and access to the former mining town of Kennicott. (See the section on the Edgerton Highway, in this chapter.)

Watch for views of the trans-Alaska pipeline along the Richardson Highway, and pullouts for pump stations with signs that explain the operation of these sites.

Plan to stop farther north, about 106 miles (170 km) north of Valdez, where the staff at Wrangell-St. Elias Visitor Center can answer questions, direct you to nearby campgrounds and attractions, and name the mountains you've been admiring. Informational displays, restrooms, and a gift shop can be found here, too.

Some 115 miles (185 km) from Valdez, Glennallen marks the junction of the Richardson and Glenn Highways. (See the section on the Glenn Highway, in this chapter.) For 14 miles, the Richardson and Glenn Highways now share the same route—until Mile 129 (207.5 km) on the Richardson, at Gakona Junction, where the Glenn veers northeast toward Tok. (This section of the Glenn is widely referred to as the Tok Cutoff.)

From Gulkana to Paxson, you'll be driving on the Richardson toward the Alaska Range and great picture-taking possibilities. The Gulkana River near Sourdough, Mile 147.5 (237 km), is popular with anglers, canoeists, and river rafters. Gulkana River paddlers usually put in at Paxson, almost 30 road-miles ahead, and then float the 50 river-miles down to

Sourdough Creek for takeout. Managed by the Bureau of Land Management, the Gulkana was designated a Wild and Scenic River in 1980. A BLM campground at Sourdough Creek offers 60 campsites near the boat launch.

Farther north at Paxson is the turn onto the Denali Highway, which travels west to meet the Parks Highway near Denali National Park (see the section on the Denali Highway, in this chapter). Here in the foothills of the Alaska Range, the views are broad and mountainous, and plenty of camping opportunities exist, either in developed campgrounds or simply along a broad road wayside, where it is permissible to dry camp overnight. Paxson is home to 40 people. Services include lodging, meals, fuel, and fishing guides.

At Delta Junction—266 miles (428 km) north of Valdez and 98 miles (157 km) south of Fairbanks—the Alaska Highway joins the Richardson Highway at the community that marks the official end of the Alaska Highway. The Richardson gets the credit for finishing the ride into Fairbanks, passing by the community of North Pole on the way. For details on attractions, lodging, and restaurants in Delta Junction, North Pole, and Fairbanks, see the last portion of Chapter 6, The Alaska Highway.

LODGING

VALDEZ:

Numerous bed-and-breakfast businesses operate in Valdez. For more information, call the Valdez Convention & Visitors Bureau at 907-835-4636 or browse www.valdezalaska.org.

Aspen Hotel
100 Meals Avenue
1-800-478-4445 or 907-835-4445
www.aspenhotelsak.com
104 rooms in newer, downtown hotel. Cable TV, modems, microwaves, coffeemakers. Pool, spa, exercise room, free continental breakfast.

Best Western—Valdez Harbor Inn
100 Fidalgo
1-888-222-3440 or 907-835-3434
www.valdezharborinn.com
Renovated hotel on harbor with view of the port and small boat harbor. Barbershop, airport and ferry shuttle.

Downtown Inn
113 Galena Drive
1-800-478-2791 or 907-835-2791
31 rooms with private or shared baths, free continental breakfast.

Glacier Sound Inn
210 Egan Drive
1-888-835-4485 or 907-835-4485
www.glaciersoundinn.com
40 rooms, microwaves, fridges, coffeemakers. Restaurant, lounge, free continental breakfast. Downtown location.

Keystone Hotel
401 West Egan Drive
1-888-835-0665 or 907-835-3851
www.keystonehotel.com
107 rooms with free continental breakfast. Close to ferry.

Pipeline Inn
112 Egan Drive
907-835-4444
15 rooms, cable TV, restaurant, lounge.

Totem Inn
144 East Egan Drive
1-888-808-4431 or 907-835-4443
www.toteminn.com
70 units including suites, standard rooms, cottages. Restaurant, gift shop. Central location.

DELTA JUNCTION, NORTH POLE, AND FAIRBANKS:

See listings under the respective town names in Chapter 6, The Alaska Highway.

CAMPGROUNDS

VALDEZ:

Bayside RV Park
230 Richardson Highway
1-888-835-4425 or 907-835-4425
www.baysidervpark.com
95 RV sites with full and partial hookups, cable TV. Bookings for cruises and charter fishing trips.

Bear Paw Camper Park
101 N. Harbor Drive
907-835-2530
150 sites with power, water, sewer. Cable TV, modems, showers, laundry, dump station.

Captain Jim's Campgrounds
Allison Point & Glacier Campgrounds
907-835-2282
www.valdezcampgrounds.com
Allison Point features 75 oceanfront sites and three access ramps to the water. Pink and silver salmon fishing. Glacier Campground has 101 wooded private sites, each with a fire pit and picnic table.

Eagle's Rest RV Park & Cabins
131 East Pioneer Drive
1-800-553-7275 or 907-835-2373
www.eaglesrestrv.com
Campsites with full or partial hookups, pull-throughs, tent camping. Showers, laundry, dump station. Freezer space and fish-cleaning table. Tickets for local tours. Private cabins available.

Sea Otter RV Park
South Harbor Drive
907-835-2787
Full service RV park on the water. Fishing, wildlife watching.

DELTA JUNCTION, NORTH POLE, AND FAIRBANKS:
See listings under the respective town names in Chapter 6, The Alaska Highway.

RESTAURANTS

VALDEZ:
Alaska Halibut House
208 Meals Avenue
907-835-2788
Three meals a day, fast service, affordable menu choices.

Alaskan Restaurant
144 East Egan Drive, in the Totem Inn
907-835-4443
Family dining. Hearty breakfast, lunch, and dinner, Alaskan seafood, steaks.

Alaska's Bistro
100 Fidalgo Drive, in Best Western
907-835-5688
Fine dining, seafood, steaks, extensive wine list. View of the water.

Fu Kung Chinese Restaurant
207 Kobuk Street
907-835-5255
Chinese food, sushi; beer and wine. Lunch and dinner.

Mike's Palace
201 North Harbor Drive
907-835-2365
Greek, Italian, Mexican, and American.

Old Town Burgers
Eagle's Rest RV Park, East Pioneer Road
907-831-1434
Handmade patties for good burgers.

Pipeline Club
112 Egan Drive, in Pipeline Inn
907-835-4332
Steaks, Alaska seafood. Lounge, entertainment.

DELTA JUNCTION, NORTH POLE, AND FAIRBANKS:
See listings under the respective town names in Chapter 6, The Alaska Highway.

SEWARD HIGHWAY

Anchorage to Seward: 127 miles (204 km)
Travel Opportunities: *Potter Marsh; Turnagain Arm; Alyeska Ski Resort at Girdwood; Portage Glacier and Exit Glacier; Seward and Resurrection Bay.*

The Seward Highway was named for former Secretary of State Henry Seward, a key figure in the purchase of Alaska from Russia in 1867. Looking at a map of Alaska, you'll see that the Seward name gets around. The Seward Highway is on the Kenai Peninsula; the Seward Peninsula is in Northwest Alaska; and then there's Fort Seward in Southeast Alaska.

The Seward Highway, wending south from Anchorage to the ice-free port of Seward, is on the list of National Scenic Byways.

The views along this highway are so stunning that the road has been designated a National Scenic Byway. From Anchorage heading south, it cuts into the foot of the mountains along the edge of Cook Inlet's Turnagain Arm. Wending between the mountains and the water, motorists may see Dall sheep, whales, eagles, and running salmon. Rest stops and recreation areas are abundant. Most of what you're driving through is public land, either Chugach State Park or Chugach National Forest. Only a handful of small communities existed before development of the parks.

Just south of Anchorage, the road borders Potter Marsh, a portion of the Anchorage Coastal Waterfowl Refuge. A boardwalk trail winds above the wetlands, with interpretive signs. Here, and in other places along the Seward Highway, you'll see some unusual areas of sunken land where the ground dropped by several feet during the huge 1964 earthquake. In these coastal areas, still-standing dead trees were killed when their roots were flooded with saltwater from Turnagain Arm.

Continuing south on the Seward, Turnagain Arm flanks the right side of the road. The water is not the cerulean blue that one might imagine at oceanside, but rather a flat gray from the many tons of glacial silt that is carried in streams pouring from the mountains. Over the centuries, the silt buildup has created a mudflat all around Anchorage's coastal areas, and the extreme tide at this point (sometimes surpassing 30 feet) means that for part of every day, the view is of gray mudflats. At other times, it's a vision—especially when the returning water creates a bore tide, sometimes a foot high or more, which floods the twin arms of Cook Inlet on either side of Anchorage. In Turnagain Arm, sightings of the bore tide often cause motorists to pull over and watch in awe. In a bore tide, the volume of returning water is so great that a low wall of water forms the leading edge of the incoming tide. Signs warn about the dangers of walking on the mudflats. Even though the surface looks firm, it's possible to become trapped in the silty mud—a perilous spot when the tide is about to turn.

Turnagain Arm was given its name by Captain James Cook. In his search for the Northwest Passage, Cook ventured down this body of water, mistakenly believing it was a river. When Cook saw the retreating tide taking the water out from beneath his ship, he realized his error and advised his men to hurriedly "turn again." Take your time and stop at the waysides for photos.

Most drivers slow down at bridges to check on the progress of salmon fishermen. Keep your eye out for Indian Creek, Bird Creek, and Twentymile Creek. Hiking trails are well marked, too, with parking at trailheads.

Thirty-seven miles (59.5 km) south of Anchorage, turn left at the spur road into Girdwood for world-class skiing at Alyeska Ski Resort. This picturesque little town beneath 3,939-foot (1,200.5-m) Mount Alyeska has been on the map since a minor gold rush in the early part of the 20th century. It was only in the last half of the century that Girdwood discovered its economic potential as a ski resort.

Although known internationally, Girdwood and Alyeska Resort retain a small-town feel. Among the area's amenities is luxurious Alyeska Prince Resort, as well as an enclosed tram that travels up the mountain to the Seven Glaciers Restaurant. The views are spectacular. At ground level, take Crow Creek Road to Crow Creek Mine, where you can pan for gold or enjoy a picnic among the old buildings and artifacts. Crow Creek Mine is a national historic site. Dry camping is available here. See *www.crowcreekgoldmine.com*.

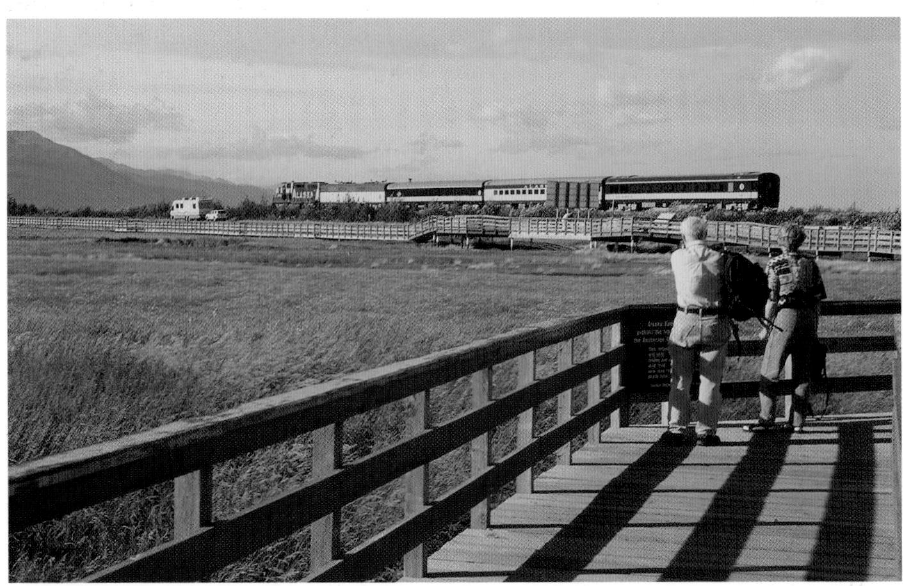

The Alaska Railroad train is headed south from Anchorage as visitors walk the Potter Marsh boardwalk, which is marked with interpretive signs about the birds and fish that inhabit this protected wetland.

Further down the Seward Highway, view the remains of Portage, a small town that was ravaged in the 1964 earthquake. You can still see remnants of homes and business structures in the abundant fireweed along the road. Dead trees in this area are a testament to that terrible event, too.

Near Portage, 50 miles (80 km) south of Anchorage, the Portage Glacier Highway connects the Seward Highway with Whittier, a port on Prince William Sound, via the Anton Anderson Memorial Tunnel. A toll is charged to pass through the 2.5-mile-long tunnel for eastbound travelers; there is no fee for westbound drivers. The travel direction in the tunnel alternates every 15 minutes, as it is a one-lane road. Check online at *www.tunnel.alaska.gov.* The Alaska Railroad also offers passage from Portage to Whittier.

Whittier is a port on the Alaska Marine Highway System, connected with Valdez and Cordova by ferry. Whittier was originally a military post, valued for its ice-free, deepwater location on Prince William Sound. Today the harbor is home port for dozens of pleasure vessels and several cruise operations. If you book your cruise in Anchorage, operators often make the arrangements for travel by bus to Whittier for a Prince William Sound cruise, or to Seward, for cruises on Resurrection Bay.

Travelers wishing to see Portage Glacier should veer right on the Portage Glacier Highway when the road forks, leading to Portage Lake, within Chugach National Forest. At lakeside you'll find cafeteria-style food and gift shopping at Portage Glacier Lodge, and natural history information and displays nearby at the Begich, Boggs Visitor Center. Kids will have fun touching fur samples and bones from various animals and learning more about them. Photos tell the story of a gold rush that boomed here a century ago.

Because Portage Glacier has been in retreat for decades, it's difficult to see it from the visitor center. But you can travel near the face of the glacier on a one-hour cruise aboard the M/V *Ptarmigan*, operated by Gray Line of Alaska; call 1-888-452-1737.

Back on the Seward Highway, at Mile 79, look for the Alaska Wildlife Conservation Center, where you can view bison, elk, eagles, moose, caribou, and musk oxen in a natural setting. This drive-through park is open 7 days a week. Call 907-783-2025 or brouse their Web site at *www.alaskawildlife.org.*

The Seward Highway rounds the end of Turnagain Arm, which is fed here by the Placer River. Sometimes, especially during late winter and early spring, a dozen or more moose may be seen resting here among the sparse trees. It's a rare sight, as moose are usually solitary travelers.

A "Welcome" sign greets drivers at the gateway to the Kenai Peninsula, and the road now rises and falls as it wends its way through the pristine Kenai Mountains above and below tree line. There are no exit ramps on this highway, but there is one fork in the road about 89 miles (143 km) south of Anchorage. All you have to do is drive straight ahead. The town of Seward lies another 38 miles (61 km) away. (A right turn at the fork marks the start of the Sterling Highway, which leads to Soldotna, Kenai, and Homer. See the section on the Sterling Highway, in this chapter.)

About 4 miles (6.5 km) north of Seward, you can follow the signs for several miles to reach Exit Glacier. Trails lead the way to this very accessible glacier. You can even walk up to its face, but be wary—multiple signs warn of the danger.

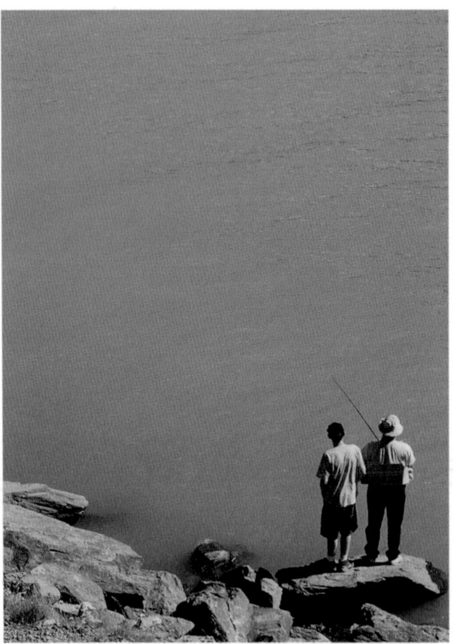

Bird Creek's jadelike color is caused by the suspended sediment in the water, often a sign that the water is fed by glacial runoff.

The oceanside community of Seward lies at the end of the Seward Highway, 2.5 hours south of Anchorage. Settled in 1903, Seward was founded as a shipping port and in 1915 became the southernmost terminal on the Alaska Railroad. Seward is a port along the Alaska Marine Highway System.

At the edge of Resurrection Bay, protected waters off the Gulf of Alaska, Seward is the home of the Alaska SeaLife Center. Educational exhibits bring viewers close to seabirds and to marine mammals such as sea lions, seals, and otters. The center also serves as a research lab and a rehabiltation facility, designed so marine biologists can work as visitors look on. Call 907-224-7908 for ticket information, or visit *www.alaskasealife.org*.

As the gateway to Kenai Fjords National Park, Seward has a small-boat harbor that is filled with pleasure craft as well as commercial fishing vessels and tour boats. The Kenai Fjords National Park Visitor Center at the harbor has information on the birds and animals that inhabit the park; call 907-224-3175. Cruise operators offer full-day or half-day tours for wildlife watching or glacier viewing or both. Usually a meal is served on board. At the harbor, you can also find fishing charters. Seward's Silver Salmon Derby and Jackpot Halibut Tournament are hot competitions sponsored by the local Chamber of Commerce. The Silver Salmon Derby alone offers more than $150,000 in prizes.

Seward's visitor information center is at Mile 2 Seward Highway. Stop by and learn more about how to make the most of your time here. Call 907-224-8051 or see *www.sewardak.org*. Staffers can also direct you on a 1- or 2-hour walking tour of the town's historic area. Seward was among the coastal communities severely damaged in the 1964 earthquake. See the Seward Museum at Jefferson Street and 3rd Avenue. The collection includes historical and cultural artifacts, photos from the 1964 earthquake, World War II, and other pieces of local history. The Community Library, at 5th Avenue and Adams Street, presents a movie and slide show about the devastating 9.2 earthquake at 2 P.M. daily, except Sundays, throughout the summer.

Each July 4, scores of runners and walkers assault Mount Marathon, the peak just at the town's back. It's a grueling race to the top and back down, and city streets are choked with spectators. The walkers' trailhead is at First Avenue and Monroe Street. Runners begin their trek at First Avenue and Jefferson Street.

Check at the Chugach National Forest district office at 334 4th Avenue for information on hiking and biking. Call 907-224-3374.

LODGING

ANCHORAGE:

See information at the end of the section on the Glenn Highway, in this chapter.

INDIAN:

Bird Ridge Motel
Mile 101 Seward Highway
907-653-0100
Rooms near excellent fishing. RV parking, café and bakery.

Brown Bear Saloon-Hotel
Mile 103 Seward Highway
907-653-7000 / *www.brownbearmotel.com*
Rooms and cabins with private baths, kitchens. Near salmon fishing, hiking, wildlife watching.

GIRDWOOD:

You may book Girdwood accommodations through Alyeska/Girdwood Accommodations Association at 907–222–3226 or www.agaa.biz.

Alyeska Prince Resort
1000 Arlberg Avenue
1-800-880-3880 or 907-754-1111
www.alyeskaresort.com
307 deluxe rooms, suites in AAA Four-Diamond hotel. Fitness center, shops, tour desk, tramway sightseeing. Lounges, cafés.

MOOSE PASS:

Summit Lake Lodge
Mile 46 Seward Highway
907-244-2031
www.summitlakelodge.com
Rooms, plus gift shop, restaurant, lounge in beautiful setting.

SEWARD:

Alaska Saltwater Lodge
Beach Drive
907-224-5271 / *www.alaskasaltwaterlodge.com*
Rooms with gorgeous views, fishing, kayaking, sightseeing.

Breeze Inn
At Small Boat Harbor
1-888-224-5237 or 907-224-5238
86 rooms, nonsmoking available. Gift shop, coffee and espresso bar, restaurant, lounge.

Harborview Inn
804 3rd Avenue
1-888-324-3217 or 907-224-3217
Rooms with view, wheelchair access. Cable TV, phone/data ports. Walking distance to tours, train, downtown.

Holiday Inn Express Seward Harbor
1412 4th Avenue
1-888-400-9714
Rooms on the harbor, with all the amenities. Walk to attractions.

Hotel Edgewater
200 5th Avenue
1-888-793-6800 or 907-224-2700
Well-appointed rooms with cable TV, nonsmoking available. Overlooks Resurrection Bay.

Hotel Seward
221 5th Avenue
1-800-656-2723 or 907-224-2378
Rooms and executive suites, nonsmoking available, cable TV, movies. Half-block to Alaska SeaLife Center.

Marina Motel
Near Train Station
907-224-5518
www.sewardmotel.com
Two double beds, private baths, fridges, coffeemakers, cable TV, free movies.

Miller's Landing
On Resurrection Bay
1-866-541-5739 or 907-224-5739
Oceanfront cabins. Laundry, showers, toilets. Tours, fishing, kayaking, transportation. Country store.

Murphy's Motel
911 4th Avenue
907-224-8090
Rooms with a view.

Seward Military Resort
205 Diamond Blvd.
1-800-770-1858 or 907-224-5559
www.sewardresort.com
Motel rooms, cabins, RV sites. Fishing charters. Exclusive use by current and retired military personnel, their guests, and families, as well as federal employees, their guests, and families.

Taroka Inn
235 3rd Avenue
907-224-8975
Rooms and kitchenettes, cable TV close to downtown, Alaska SeaLife Center. Pet friendly.

Windsong Lodges
31772 Herman Leirer Road
907-224-7116
www.sewardwindsong.com
Comfortable, newer rooms with cable TV, VCRs, phones. Forested setting. Dining, lounge. Info on local tours and attractions.

The Van Gilder Hotel
308 Adams Street
1-800-204-6835 or 907-224-3079
Immaculate accommodations in a National Historic Site.

CAMPGROUNDS

ANCHORAGE:

See information at the end of the section on the Glenn Highway, in this chapter.

BIRD CREEK:
Bird Creek State Recreation Site
26 miles (42 km) south of Anchorage
28 campsites, picnic tables, water, toilets. Close to salmon fishing, bike trails.

GIRDWOOD:
Crow Creek Mine
3 miles (5 km) up Crow Creek Road
907-278-8060
Historic gold mine offers sites for dry camping and tenting.

PORTAGE:
Portage Valley Cabins & RV Park
Mile 1.7 Portage Glacier Road
907-783-3111
www.portagevalleycabins.com
Cabins, RV park, campground. Hiking trails, stocked fishing ponds.

Williwaw Creek Campground
Mile 4 Portage Glacier Road
1-877-444-6777 for reservations
60 campsites, picnic tables, water, toilets. Deck for viewing spawning salmon, late July to mid-September. Nature trails. Campground operated by U.S. Forest Service.

SEWARD:
Bear Creek RV Park
6.5 miles (10.5 km) north of Seward on Bear Lake Road
907-224-5724
www.bearcreekrv.com
Full and partial hookups. Showers, laundry, restrooms, dump station, store. Fishing and glacier tours, courtesy van.

Miller's Landing
On Resurrection Bay
1-866-541-5739 or 907-224-5739
Oceanfront cabins, RV and tent camping. Laundry, showers, toilets. Tours, fishing, kayaking, transportation. Country store.

Stony Creek RV Park
From Mile 6.3 Seward Highway, off Stoney Creek Avenue
907-224-6465
www.stonycreekrvpark.com
81 creekside campsites, full and partial hookup, some pull-throughs. Satellite TV, showers, laundry.

RESTAURANTS

ANCHORAGE:

See information at the end of the section on the Glenn Highway, in this chapter.

INDIAN:
Bird Ridge Café & Bakery
26 miles (42 km) south of Anchorage
907-653-7302
Home-style cooking, pastries, beer, wine.

GIRDWOOD:
Alyeska Prince Resort
1000 Arlberg Avenue
1-800-880-3880 or 907-754-1111
www.alyeskaresort.com
Choose from several restaurants for the dining experience of your choice; casual to fine dining.

The Bake Shop
At Alyeska Ski Resort
907-783-2831
www.thebakeshop.com
Homemade soups, sourdough pancakes, breads, pizza.

Chair 5 Restaurant
5 Linblad Avenue, off Hightower Road
907-783-2500
www.chair5.com
Seafood, pizza, microbrews.

Double Musky Inn
On Crow Creek Road
907-783-2822
Cajun specialties, Alaska seafood; funky Alaska decor.

PORTAGE:
Portage Glacier Lodge
Across from visitor center
907-783-3117
Soups, sandwiches, cafeteria-style. Eat in or take-out.

MOOSE PASS:
Summit Lake Lodge
Mile 46 Seward Highway
907-244-2031
Restaurant, lodge, lounge, gift shop.

SEWARD:

Apollo Restaurant
229 4th Avenue
907-224-3092
Mediterranean, Italian.

Breeze Inn
At small boat harbor, adjacent to motel
1-888-224-5237 or 907-224-5238
Family friendly dining with a view; seafood specialties.

Christo's Palace
133 4th Avenue
907-224-5255
Pizza, steak, seafood, Mexican, cocktails.

Exit Glacier Salmon Bake
Mile .25, Exit Glacier Road
907-224-2204
Full-service restaurant. Salmon, halibut, steaks, burgers.

Harbor Dinner Club
220 5th Avenue
907-224-3012
Steaks, seafood, lounge, outdoor seating.

Peking Restaurant
338 4th Avenue
907-224-5444
Chinese cuisine.

Ray's Waterfront
Overlooking Seward Boat Harbor
907-224-5606
Seafood specialties.

Resurrection Roadhouse
Mile 0.5, Exit Glacier Road
1-800-208-0200
Good food, casual atmosphere with a view, microbrews.

STEESE HIGHWAY

Fairbanks to Circle City: 162 miles (261 km)
Travel Opportunities: *Chena Hot Springs; Gold Dredge No. 8; Fox; Eagle Summit; Central, Circle Hot Springs, and Circle City.*

If the Steese Highway were ever renamed, it should be the Gold Road, for this is the historic transportation corridor between some of the state's richest goldfields near Central and Circle City, and Fairbanks, the boomtown that was built on the discovery of gold. In fact, the road edges Pedro Creek, near the very place where Italian immigrant Felix Pedro discovered gold in 1902, launching yet another gold rush. By 1910, nearly $2 million in gold had moved through Fairbanks.

The Steese Highway begins at the intersection of Airport Way and Gaffney Boulevard in Fairbanks. Quickly, it splits into the Old Steese and, a block away, the New Steese. The older road has been absorbed into a district of malls, gas stations, and businesses. But the New Steese is a four-lane highway that skirts Fairbanks then heads north. Drive carefully on this section, as the pavement rocks and rolls for several miles on your way to Fox. Insidious permafrost works against the road builders' best efforts.

These early miles of the Steese are heavily used by Fairbanks residents who live in the surrounding hills or along Chena Hot Springs Road. Take this 57-mile paved spur road east to its dead end and you'll land at Chena Hot Springs Resort. Winter or summer, you can soak in 100-degree pools of mineral water that seem to suck the tension out of every pore. The resort offers nicely appointed rooms or rustic cabins. Swim in an enclosed pool area, or soak in outdoor hot tubs. You can go horseback riding, camp, hike, pick blueberries, and in

A pullout north of Fairbanks brings you up close and personal to the trans-Alaska pipeline. Informational signs tell more about this monumental building project as well as critters of the Interior.

winter, view the aurora. Visit the year-round ice museum and ice bar, where you can have your drink served in a piece of ice that's ground into a glass as you watch. Call 907-451-8104 or visit *www.chenahotsprings.com.*

Back on the Steese Highway, press on past Chena Hot Springs Road to experience some of the area's best tourism sites, as well as unparalleled views of the Tanana Valley and beyond.

Ahead on the Steese, portions of the trans-Alaska pipeline will be visible on your right. At Mile 8.5 (13.5 km), a spacious parking area with interpretive signs allows visitors to roam around and walk up to the pipeline. A visitor information center there is usually staffed, and free brochures are available. A sign cautions, "Please do not climb on the pipeline." Near here, the Steese Highway reduces from four lanes to two, but remains paved for many more miles.

A mile later, turn left to access Gold Dredge No. 8, a piece of mining history that has been restored for visitors. Operated by Gray Line of Alaska, the attraction includes tours aboard this floating gold-processing ship. You can pan for gold yourself, and eat hearty at a miners' buffet lunch. For tour information, call 907-457-6058 or see *www.golddredgeno8.com.*

If you plan to stay on the Steese Highway, the upcoming intersection, at Mile 11 (18 km), may be confusing. The Old Steese joins Steese here, so a right turn is necessary to continue north. If you go straight, you'll be on the Elliott Highway and bound for the Brooks

Range. The Fox General Store and gas station on this intersection is the last place to fuel up, buy propane, or stock up on snacks for many miles, so top off here if you haven't done so in Fairbanks.

One other option is well worth your time, particularly if you're hungry or thirsty. Turn left onto the Old Steese, and you'll be driving through the "main street" of beautiful downtown Fox, where few people live, but many come to eat and drink. Notable businesses include The Howling Dog Saloon, your classic funky Alaska bar. Pizza and other bar grub are available, as well as a full bar selection of beverages. There's live music on the fare, too. Across the road is the Silver Gulch Brewing & Bottling Co., home of the historic Fox Roadhouse. This is America's most northern brewery and offers lunch and dinner, with locally produced beers on tap. Tours are available, too. A few miles farther down the road, The Turtle Club is a Fairbanks-area favorite for prime rib and seafood. Dinner reservations are suggested.

Fox welcomed a new attraction in 2008: Yukon Yonda's at Gilmore Station, where small groups enjoy Robert Service poetry, first-person survival stories, and the "Ask an Alaskan" segment, finished with coffee and dessert. Presented on Friday and Saturday evenings only throughout the summer. Call 907-457-1884 for reservations.

Back on the Steese Highway, 20 miles (32 km) from Fairbanks at the Cleary Summit Scenic Viewpoint, outstanding valley views were marred by wildfires in summer 2004. Regrowth is visible today.

At about Mile 28 (45 km), watch for the turn-off to the old Fairbanks Exploration Gold Camp, which is on the National Register of Historic Places. The company's bunk house, built between 1922 and 1925, is part of a complex that includes original miners' cabins, and the old Chatanika Schoolhouse. The F.E. Gold Camp is now a restaurant and lodge. Chatanika was the site of an old gold-mining town. Miners here pulled about $70 million in gold out of the ground between 1926 and 1957. During those years, more than 10,000 people lived here, making it larger than Fairbanks.

Another half-mile down the road is another remnant of Chatanika's boom days, Gold Dredge No. 3, which operated until 1962. Although the old dredge may be barely visible from the road, it lies on private property and trespassing is not permitted. You can learn more about it and the boomtown, and enjoy a home-style meal across the highway from the dredge at the Chatanika Lodge.

Just a few miles ahead is the entrance to Poker Flat Research Range, a 5,132-acre site where the University of Alaska Fairbanks Geophysical Institute, in conjunction with the National Aeronautics and Atmospheric Administration, has conducted studies on the aurora borealis, arctic atmosphere, and ionosphere since 1979. For more on the university's work in space science, see *www.pfrr.alaska.edu.* Call 907-474-7558 for information on public tours.

Up ahead, a series of summits and interesting switchbacks makes driving the Steese an on-your-toes proposition. For one, you run out of pavement. However, the gravel surface is well graded in summer, and the snowy surface is plowed often in winter. Views of the river valleys from above are panoramic, and as you drive over the mountain range, above tree line, with few guardrails along the road, you can experience something like vertigo.

The road leads over Cleary Summit and Twelve-Mile Summit with access to the Pinnell Mountain National Recreation Trail, managed by the Bureau of Land Management. For maps

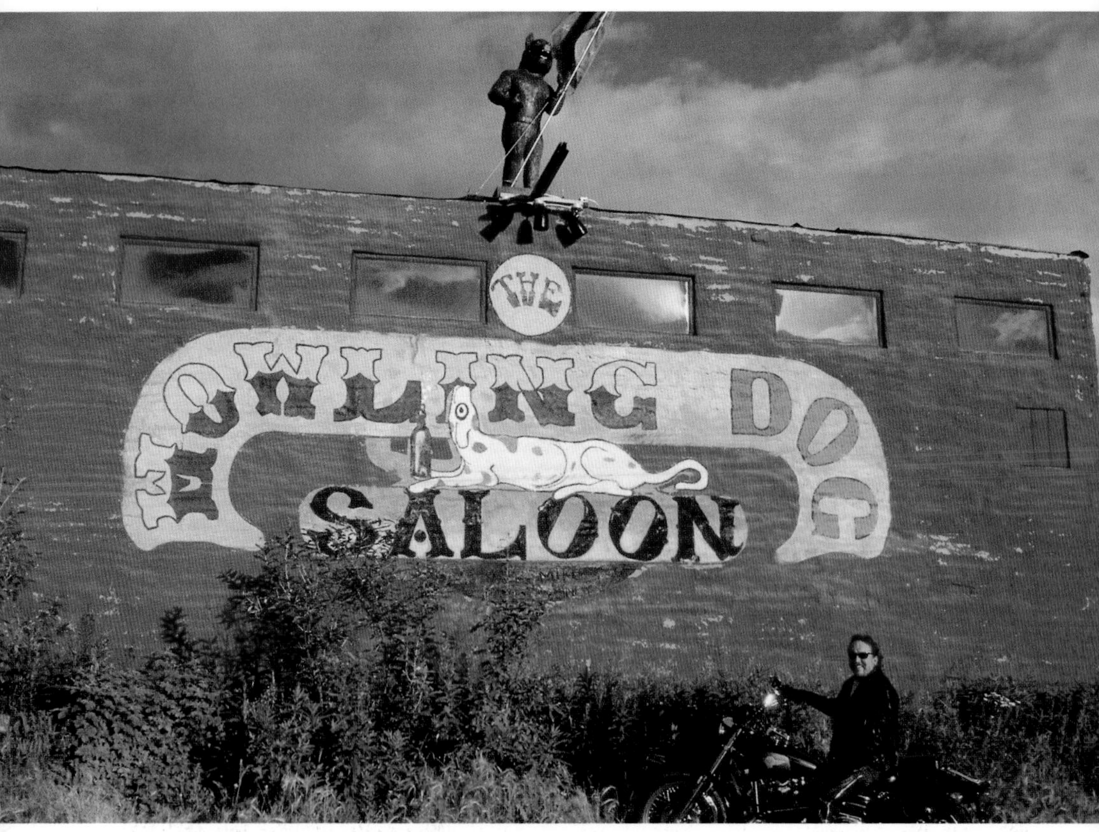

The Howling Dog Saloon in Fox isn't a tourist attraction in the classic sense, but it's a good place to meet local folks.

---

of this trail and others in the area, contact the BLM's Fairbanks District Office at 1-800-437-7021 or visit *www.ak.blm.gov.*

At Mile 107.5 (173 km), you'll cross Eagle Summit, the tallest of them all at 3,685 feet (1,123 m) above sea level. For those accustomed to trees and roadside businesses, the trek up and over Eagle Summit will come as a surprise in its nakedness. The road threads over rolling mountains and above tree line with nothing between you and the distant valley floor except fresh air. At the top, the view is nearly dizzying, with nothing but undulating country on all sides. Here is where dozens of people drive on June 20 or 21, summer solstice, to observe and photograph an unobstructed view of the midnight sun. Their photographs, taken over several hours with timed exposures, will show an orange orb gently touching down to the horizon line before beginning its slow ascent.

In the village of Central, 127 miles (203 km) northeast of Fairbanks, most of the residents are gold miners, or have been miners, or are related to a miner. Members of the Circle Mining District hold their annual picnic here each summer. This little town of log cabins includes a school, a small grocery and gift shop, a couple of cafés, and some roadside lodging. The people of Central raised money to open the town's mining museum, which is open noon to 5 P.M. during summer months. It's well worth a nice, long browse.

From Central, an 8-mile (13-km), unpaved spur road leads southeast to Circle Hot Springs, and a three-story wooden building that served as a resort for nearly a century. The business is currently closed. The natural springs drew Athabascan Indians long before gold miners discovered the natural wonder in the late 1800s. A century ago, pioneers Frank and Emma Leach ran the hotel, worked this ground, and watered their superb gardens with hot-springs water. Their graves are on a nearby hill, and it is said that they still haunt the place.

Beyond Central, the Steese Highway consists of nearly 34 unpaved miles (54 km) of winding road through the boreal forest. At the end of the road, you'll find Circle City and a sign welcoming you to the banks of the Yukon River, a braided stream in this section, and one of only three places in Alaska where motorists can drive to the river. The Yukon is a 2,000-mile (3,219-km) waterway that flows westward from its headwaters in Canada to Alaska's Bering Sea. Several boomtowns seem to have claimed the title "Paris of the North" during the gold rushes of the late 1800s. Such was true for Dawson City, Yukon, but Circle City came up with it even earlier. Founded in 1893 and misnamed by early miners who thought they were on the Arctic Circle (they were 50 miles off), the city was home to more than 10,000 at its peak, attracting the usual rabble, along with others who brought with them the cultural refinements of home, including theater productions, teas, readings, and book exchanges.

Looking at this little community of fewer than 100 people today, it's hard to believe what once stood here. A smattering of cabins makes up the town. The H.C. Company Store at the end of the road serves the community year round with groceries and gas. If you're interested, ask here for directions to the Pioneer Cemetery. Camping is available near the river, as boaters frequently access the river here.

LODGING/CAMPGROUNDS/MEALS

FOX:

Howling Dog Saloon, Motel & Café
Mile 11 Old Steese Highway
907-456-HOWL
www.howlingdogsaloon.com

Silver Gulch Brewing & Bottling Co.
2195 Old Steese Highway
907-452-2739

The Turtle Club
Old Steese Highway
907-457-3883
Prime rib, seafood, salad bar, lounge. A local favorite.

CHATANIKA TO CENTRAL:

F.E. Gold Camp
Mile 27.5 Steese Highway
www.fegoldcamp.com
907-389-2414

Chatanika Lodge
Mile 28.5 Steese Highway
907-389-2164

Long Creek Trading Post
Mile 45 Steese Highway
907-389-5287

CENTRAL:

Mills Junction
Mile 127.5 Steese Highway
907-520-5599
Motel rooms, laundry facility. Café, bar, gas, diesel, propane, store.

CIRCLE CITY:

H.C. Company Store
End of the Steese Highway
907-773-1222
Gas, groceries, snacks, phone, tire repair.

Russian Orthodox missionaries were among the earliest outsiders to influence the Native cultures on the Kenai Peninsula, and Russian place-names linger on. This church overlooks Cook Inlet at Ninilchik.

STERLING HIGHWAY

From Seward Highway to Homer: 143 miles (230 km)

Travel Opportunities: *Kenai Lake at Cooper Landing; fishing the Kenai and Russian Rivers; deep-sea charter fishing at Anchor Point or Homer; day trips to Seldovia and Halibut Cove.*

The Sterling Highway leaves the Seward Highway at a fork 90 miles (145 km) south of Anchorage. It wends west and south through a sparsely populated wilderness area and passes through a handful of small towns on the way to its dead end in another small town, Homer. Lofty mountains shoulder the two paved lanes, and nearby lakes and streams run clean and cold. Most of the land is included in the 1.9-million-acre Kenai National Wildlife Refuge. Moose and bear numbers are strong, and you might see Dall sheep, caribou, loons, eagles, and trumpeter swans. Offshore, watch for sea otters, seals, puffins, and numerous birds.

Flightseeing operations offer bird's-eye views of unbelievable beauty. Hiking, canoeing, and rafting are other recreation offerings on the Kenai Peninsula. Nature photography ranks high on the list as well. Beautifully adorned subjects lie all around you. Distant glaciers flow from the Harding Ice Field, and along the road the gem-green Kenai Lake flows into a magnificent river of the same color and name.

The biggest towns along the Sterling Highway are Cooper Landing, Mile 11 (17.5 km); Sterling Highway, 101 miles (162.5 km) south of Anchorage; Sterling, at Mile 44 (71 km); Soldotna, at Mile 58 (93 km); and the end of the road at Homer, Mile 142.5 (229 km). In each town, you'll find gas, food, campgrounds, services, fishing licenses, hotels, and opportunities to line up a guide or gather some local knowledge.

What the Kenai Peninsula may be best known for worldwide is its prime fishing. Sportfishers travel great distances to fish the Kenai River, to wade into turquoise-colored waters in the hope of wrestling with a king, the salmon that can grow into the size and weight of a 7-year-old child. (The world-record king salmon of 97.4 pounds was taken from the Kenai River in 1985.) Equally attractive is another world-class, roadside sportfishing stream, the Russian River. On this river, the prized fish is the red salmon.

Every day of every summer, campgrounds near these rivers are jammed with RVs and cars as anglers head for the water. This is a camping experience like none other. Don't expect peace and solitude when the salmon are running. Anglers stand shoulder to shoulder and work in cooperation to flip out their lines to drift with the current without tangling with those of their neighbors. The cry "Fish on!" is the signal to reel in your line and get out of the way until a lucky angler nets his or her fish.

Charter fishing operations at Anchor Point, Deep Creek, Ninilchik, and Homer lead clients to unforgettable deep-sea halibut fishing. Getting a 100-pound lunker off the bottom and over the side of the boat takes more than finesse. It's just sheer muscle-fishing. The biggest halibut caught in Cook Inlet weighed about 465 pounds.

Six peninsula towns offer prizes for the biggest salmon or halibut in annual fishing derbies (combined, the prizes equal about $100,000). The Soldotna Visitor Information Center is across the bridge in Soldotna, and offers information on wildlife viewing, fishing, and other outdoor recreation. Call 907-262-9814 or visit *www.soldotnachamber.com.*

Fishing in a new region always carries with it a hefty learning curve, so consider whether you want to devote the time necessary to learning how these fish behave. Hiring a guide is often the best option. They know the best holes, the best time of day, and the regulations. It's likely, too, that a guide will haul you away from the crowds in a boat or floatplane. Most places can arrange to have your fish smoked or frozen and shipped home when you're ready to receive it.

The biggest town on the Kenai Peninsula lies on the shores of Cook Inlet and shares the same name as the peninsula: Kenai. Located on the Kenai Spur Highway, westbound from Soldotna, the city is home to fishing and oil industry workers, tourism operators, and other people in support services.

A visitor information log cabin is at the corner of Kenai Spur Highway and Main Street Loop. Pick up a walking map for Old Town Kenai, and learn about its early Kenaitze Indian and Russian residents. The Holy Assumption of the Virgin Mary Russian Orthodox Church has stood here since 1894. The Dena'ina Athabascans have lived and hunted in this region for thousands of years. Get information about the area at 907-283-1991 or see *www.visitkenai.com.*

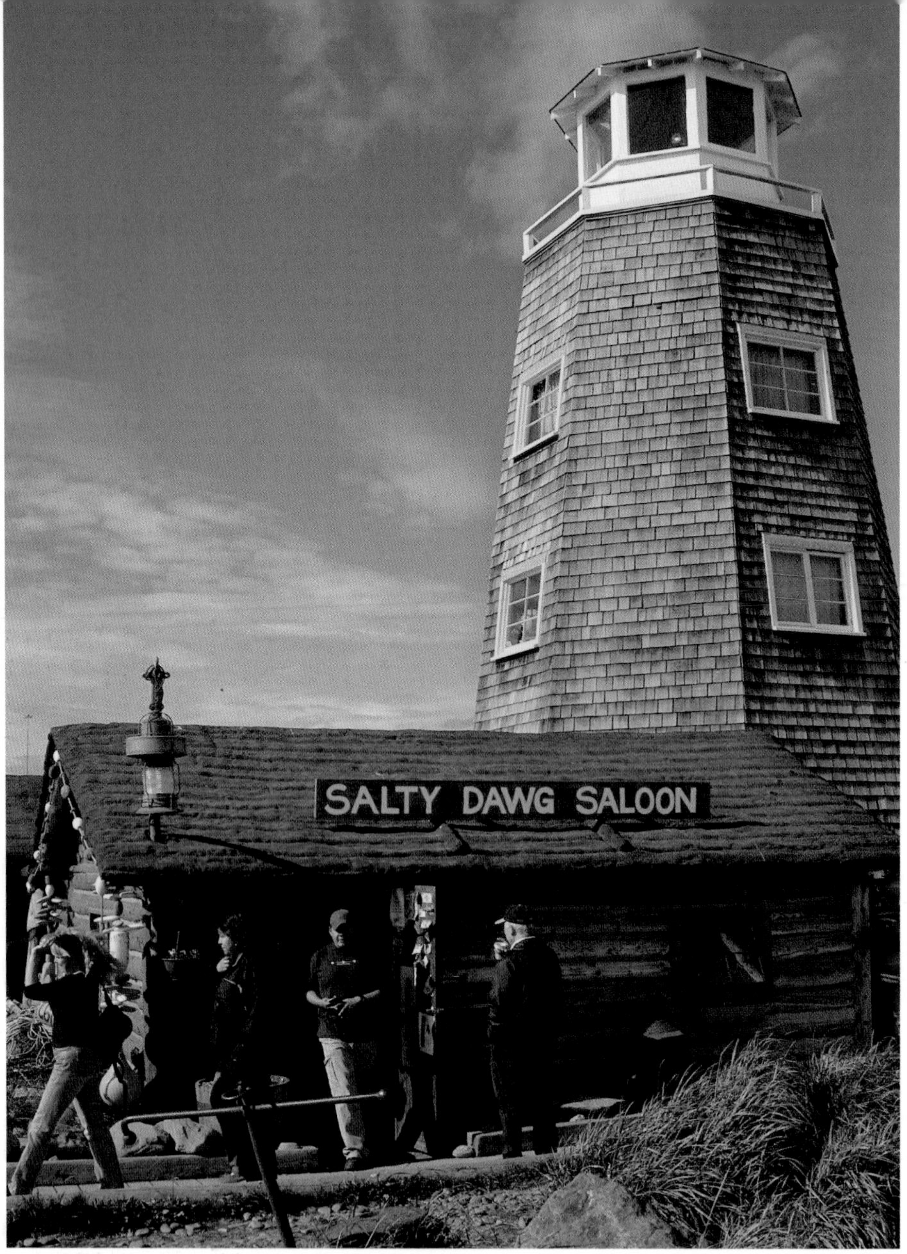

The Salty Dawg on the Homer Spit is a favorite watering hole for residents and visitors alike.

From Kenai and its neighboring town, Nikiski, the view across Cook Inlet is panoramic: Mount Spur, Mount Redoubt, and Mount Iliamna are the cone-shaped volcanoes on the horizon—and they are not dormant. There have been several eruptions in the last 20 years, as Mount Kiska, Mount Redoubt, and Mount Spur each rumbled to life, spewing fine ash that rained down on Southcentral Alaska for hundreds of miles.

Private campgrounds may be found near or in the towns that dot the length of the Sterling Highway and the Kenai Spur Highway. The state maintains several recreation areas and sites along these roads, too, and campsites are plentiful at Clam Gulch, Deep Creek, Ninilchik, Kenai, Nikiski, and Johnson Lake, and in Homer at Kachemak Bay State Park. Another dozen less-developed grounds also offer campsites, restrooms, and water. For full details, call the Division of Parks and Outdoor Recreation's Soldotna office at 907-262-5581.

The Kenai is steeped in the ancient Kenaitze Indian culture and in that of the Russians, whose two centuries of influence are still visible in the blue-domed churches at Kenai and Ninilchik. Native surnames often possess an echo of Russia, as do place-names such as Kalifornsky, Nikiski, Kasilof, and Ninilchik. At the village of Ninilchik, the Russian Orthodox church majestically overlooks Cook Inlet from atop a bluff. Visitors are welcome to photograph the church, but remember that this is a place of worship. The local people ask that you do not enter the cemetery. Throughout the Kenai, shops offer handmade Native crafts and Russian gift items, as well as the more typical Alaska souvenirs.

The Sterling Highway ends at the sea at Homer, a town that's a wonderful mix of artist colony, commercial fishing seaport, small-town Alaska, and tourist destination. Homer is a port of call on the Alaska Marine Highway System; for information, call 1-800-642-0066 or visit *www.ferryalaska.com.* See Chapter 9, Alaska Marine Highway System.

The Alaska Islands and Oceans Visitors Center, headquarters for the Alaska Maritime National Wildlife Refuge Visitor Center, is right at the entrance to town at 50 Sterling Highway. The 4.4-million-acre refuge extends along much of the Alaska coastline. Allow lots of time to explore this beautiful building and the free exhibits. Call 907-235-6961. Visit their Web site at *www.islandsandocean.org.*

More than 100,000 shorebirds migrate through this part of the state annually. Each May the city hosts the Kachemak Bay Shorebird Festival, drawing hundreds of birders to witness thousands of sandpipers, turnstones, dowitchers, and dunlins. Eagles are year-round residents.

You can learn more about the natural and cultural history of this area at the Pratt Museum in Homer, on Bartlett Street off Pioneer Avenue. Artifacts from prehistory to homesteaders, information on marine mammals, and guided ecology tours are among the offerings. The items for sale at the art gallery and gift shop include Alaska-made crafts and collectibles. Call 907-235-8635 or see *www.prattmuseum.org.*

Fine art galleries featuring the work of local and guest artists may be found through-out town and on the Homer Spit, a 4.5-mile finger of land that extends into Kachemak Bay. Homer is a creative place, so take a gallery trek. Along the Homer Spit, you can walk along an elevated boardwalk and watch happy anglers posing with the day's catch of halibut. You can book a salmon or halibut charter, or arrange a day boat trip across the bay to visit the tiny villages of Seldovia and Halibut Cove. Look into the options at the Homer Chamber of Commerce at 907-235-7740 or *www.homeralaska.org.*

On the spit are RV and tent camping, hotel rooms, gift shops, art galleries, pleasure boats, and commercial fishing vessels. Have a cold drink at the Salty Dog Saloon; enjoy a meal with an amazing view at Land's End; walk the beach with your kids and examine what high tide has delivered. The spit, with its festival-like atmosphere, is a gathering place for revving up or winding down. Rest your eyes on the horizon. You've reached the end of the road.

LODGING

COOPER LANDING:

Gwin's Lodge
Mile 52 Sterling Highway
907-595-1266
Cabins, rooms, full RV hookups, restaurant, bar. Tours, charters, outdoor clothing, licenses, souvenirs. Fish processing and shipping drop site.

Kenai Princess Wilderness Lodge
Mile 48 Sterling Highway
1-800-426-0500
Beautiful log hotel overlooking Kenai River. Adventure tours, luxury accommodations. Dining, elegant or casual.

STERLING:

Naptowne Inn & Café
Mile 84.5 Sterling Highway
907-260-2005
www.naptowneinn.com
15 rooms with queen-sized beds, restaurant serving three meals a day.

SOLDOTNA:

Alicia's Eagle Rock Lodge
286 Arlington Court
907-283-1951
Single and double rooms, plus suites with full kitchens. All with cable TV, coffee, etc. Close to The Pillars and Eagle Rock boat launch.

Aspen Hotel
326 Binkley Circle
907-260-7736
63 rooms and suites. Pool, spa, exercise room, free deluxe continental breakfast. Open year-round.

Best Western King Salmon Motel, RV Park & Restaurant
Downtown Soldotna
1-888-262-5857 or 907-262-5857
www.bestwestern.com
Large rooms, kitchenettes, cable TV, coffee. Restaurant. 39 RV sites, most pull-throughs. Full hookups, restrooms, showers, laundry.

Eagle's Roost Lodge
35555 Spur Highway
907-262-8444
Log cabins, RV and tent camping. Sauna, tackle and gift shop, salmon bake, smokehouse. Fishing charters, boat rentals.

Hooligan's Lodging & Saloon
44715 Sterling Highway
907-262-9951
www.hooliganslodge.com

The Riverside House
44611 Sterling Highway
1-877-262-0500 or 907-262-0500
www.riverside-house.com
Rooms, RV parking, restaurant, lounge, nightclub.

Soldotna B&B Lodge
399 Lovers Lane
1-877-262-4779 or 907-262-4779
www.soldotnalodge.com
16-unit European-style lodge on banks of Kenai River. Multilingual hosts. Full breakfast, fishing packages, guides, private bank fishing, and other charters.

Soldotna Inn
35041 Kenai Spur Highway
907-262-9169
Comfortable rooms and good meals. Mykel's Restaurant inside.

KENAI:

Beluga Lookout Lodge & RV Park
929 Mission Avenue, in historic Old Town
907-283-4939
www.belugalookout.com
Lodge rooms. 75 full-hookup spaces, pull-throughs, grills, picnic tables, restrooms, showers, laundry, Internet. Gift shop, bike rentals.

Kenai Merit Inn
260 South Willow Street
907-283-6131
Rooms with cable TV, phones, free continental breakfast. Fishing packages. Downtown location.

HOMER:

To learn more about Homer-area cabins, cottages, vacation rentals, and bed-and-breakfasts, call 1-877-296-1114 or 907-226-1114, or see www.homerbedbreakfast.com.

Anchor River Inn
Just north of Homer at Anchor Point
1-800-435-8531 or 907-235-8531
20 rooms, fitness facility, pool tables, dance floor, store, gift shop, restaurant, lounge.

Bay View Inn
Overlooking Kachemak Bay
1-877-235-8485 or 235-8485
www.bayviewalaska.com
Rooms, kitchenettes, and cottages with a view, free TV, wireless Internet, local calls. Free continental breakfast.

Best Western Bidarka Inn
575 Sterling Highway
1-866-685-5000 or 907-235-8148
www.bidarkainn.com
Full-service hotel, restaurant, sports bar, charters. Pet friendly.

Driftwood Inn & Lodge
135 West Bunnell Avenue
1-800-478-8019 or 907-235-8019
www.thedriftwoodinn.com.
Beachfront rooms and kitchenettes with freezers. Cable TV, Internet, barbecue.

Heritage Hotel
147 E. Pioneer Avenue
1-800-380-7787 or 907-235-7787
www.alaskaheritagehotel.com
37 rooms and suites in log hotel near shopping and restaurants. Laundry, wireless Internet. Pet friendly.

Land's End Resort
4789 Homer Spit Road
1-800-478-4800 or 907-235-0400
www.lands–end–resort.com
Beachfront rooms, mountain and bay vistas, wireless Internet, assistance with charters. Chart Room Restaurant.

Ocean Shores
3500 Crittenden Drive
1-800-770-7775 or 907-235-7775
www.oceanshoresalaska.com
Seaside rooms, kitchenettes, laundry, freezer, private beach, walking distance to town.

CAMPGROUNDS

COOPER LANDING:

Kenai Princess RV Park
Turn at Mile 47.5 (Km 76.5) Sterling Highway, then drive 2 miles (3 km) on Bear Creek Road.
907-595-1425
35 sites, power, tables. Shower, laundry, water, dump station. Groceries. Next to Kenai Princess Lodge.

Kenai Riverside Campground & RV Park
Mile 50 Sterling Highway
1-888-536-2478
25 partial hookups, dump station, restrooms, showers. Fishing and licenses on site.

The U.S. Forest Service manages the following campgrounds near Cooper Landing:

Quartz Creek Recreation Area
Turn off at Mile 45 Sterling Highway and follow Quartz Creek Road
45 RV parking and tent sites. Water, toilets, fishing.

Cooper Creek Campground
Mile 50.5 Sterling Highway
23 RV parking and tent sites. Water, toilets. On south bank of upper Kenai River.

Russian River Campground
Mile 52.5 Sterling Highway
84 RV parking and tent sites. Water, toilets, dump station. Excellent salmon fishing in season. Fish-cleaning stations. Popular place, so arrive early.

The Kenaitze Indian Tribe operates a traditional/cultural campground within the Seward Ranger District of the Chugach National Forest:

K'Beq Footprints
Mile 52.5 Sterling Highway
907-398-0598
Camping, guided tours, traditional plant lore, legends, stories. Gift shop.

The U.S. Fish and Wildlife Service has developed several campgrounds between Cooper Landing and Sterling:

Skilak Lake
21 miles (33.5 km) west from the junction of Sterling and Seward Highways is the first turnoff for Skilak Lake Road, a loop along which there are three campgrounds. Two developed campgrounds are on Skilak Lake; a third lies nearby on Hidden Lake. All three have fire pits, toilets, water, and boat ramps. Hidden Lake campers enjoy campfire programs on Friday and Saturday evenings in an outdoor theater. Campground hosts.

STERLING:

Alaska State Parks manages the following recreation sites and campgrounds near Sterling:

Bing's Landing, Mile 79 (Km 127), 36 sites
Izaak Walton, Mile 81 (Km 130), 25 sites
Morgan's Landing, Mile 85 (Km 136.5), 42 sites

Alaska Canoe & RV Park
Mile 84 Sterling Highway
907-262-2331
RV sites, laundry, showers. Canoe and mountain bike rentals. Shuttle service. Fishing licenses and gear.

Bing Brown's RV Park & Motel
Mile 81 Sterling Highway
907-262-4780
www.bingbrowns.com
Full RV hookups, dump station, showers, laundry. Kitchenettes. Book guided fishing and tours, tackle, licenses, liquor, snacks.

Mike's Moose River Resort & Hot Tub
Overlooking river at Sterling
907-262-9777
www.mooseriverresort.com
Riverfront chalet & RV park.

Moose River RV Park
Mile 81.5 Sterling Highway
907-260-7829
www.stayalaska.com
Full hookups; some pull-throughs. Visitor center, restrooms, high-speed Internet, satellite TV, showers, laundry. Café. Local fishing.

Real Alaskan Cabins and RV Park
Mile 80 near Bing's Landing
907-262-6077
www.realalaskan.com
33 sites with full hookups, cabins, wooded setting, showers, laundry. Park/fishing packages. Boat rentals.

SOLDOTNA:

Best Western King Salmon Motel, RV Park & Restaurant
Downtown Soldotna
1-888-262-5857 or 907-262-5857
www.bestwestern.com
Large rooms, kitchenettes, cable TV, coffee. Restaurant. 39 RV sites, most pull-throughs. Full hookups, restrooms, showers, laundry.

Centennial Park Municipal Campground
On Funny River Road near Mile 96 Sterling Highway
126 campsites, some along river, tables, fire pits, firewood, water, dump station. Boat launch and on-site fishing.

Discovery Campground
(Part of the Captain Cook State Recreation Area)
Near intersection Kenai Spur and Sterling Highways
53 campsites, hiking trail, water, fireside programs.

Edgewater RV Park
44770 Funny River Road
907-262-7733
www.sunriseresorts.com
40 full hookups and pull-through sites, 20 partial hookups, showers, laundry. Bank fishing on the river, guide services, fish-cleaning station.

The Riverside House
44611 Sterling Highway
1-877-262-0500 or 907-262-0500
www.riverside–house.com
RV park, hotel, riverview dining, lounge, nightclub.

Swiftwater Park Municipal Campground
Turn south onto Redoubt at Mile 94 Sterling Highway; just past Fred Meyer
42 sites above Kenai River, some pull-throughs. Tables, fire pits, water, dump station, firewood, boat launch.

KENAI:

Beluga Lookout Lodge & RV Park
929 Mission Avenue, in historic Old Town
907-283-4939
www.belugalookout.com
Lodge rooms. 75 full-hookup spaces, pull-throughs, grills, picnic tables, restrooms, showers, laundry, Internet. Gift shop, bike rentals.

Captain Cook State Recreation Area
Miles 36–29 Kenai Spur Highway
Campsites, fishing, hiking, picnic shelter, boating.

Diamond M Ranch RV Park, Cabins & B&B
Mile 6 K-Beach Road
907-283-9424
www.diamondranch.com
RV sites, pull-throughs, laundry, shower, fish-cleaning station, wireless Internet. Family owned, working ranch.

Kenai Riverfront RV Park
Mile 2 Big Eddy Road
907-262-1717
www.kenairiverfront.com
10 RV sites with electric, gravel sites, riverfront views. Boat launch, bank fishing.

Kenai RV Park
Corner of Highland and Upland Streets
907-398-3382
18 sites with hookups, tent camping, showers, laundry, restrooms. One block from Kenai visitor center.

ANCHOR RIVER:
Kyllonen RV Park
Mile 1 Anchor River Beach Road
1-888-848-2589
www.kyllonenrvpark.com
Full and partial hookups, fish-cleaning station, free firewood, showers, restrooms, laundry. Gift shop, espresso bar. Licenses and charters. Close to Cook Inlet and Anchor River.

HOMER:
Driftwood Inn & RV Park
135 West Bunnell Avenue
1-800-478-8019 or 907-235-8019
www.thedriftwoodinn.com
Full hookups on beachfront sites. Open year-round.

Heritage RV Park
3550 Homer Spit Road, by the Fishing Hole
1-800-380-7787 of 907-226-4500
www.alaskaheritagervpark.com
Bayview sites with 20-, 30-, or 50-amp power, sewer, water, satellite TV. On-site gift shop, coffee shop, showers, restrooms, laundry. Walking distance to fishing, beach, shopping, restaurants.

Homer Spit Campground
At the end of the road
907-235-8206
www.homerspitcampground.com
Oceanfront camping for RVs, with partial hookups, tent camping, showers, dump station. Gift shop, charter bookings, trailer rentals.

Oceanview RV Park
173 Sterling Highway
907-235-3951
Full and partial hookups, pull-throughs, tent camping. Panoramic views. Showers, restrooms, gift shop. Special charter rates.

Alaska State Parks manages the following campgrounds between Ninilchik and Homer; for more information, call the Kenai Area Office at 907–262–5581.

Ninilchik River Campground
North end of Ninilchik
Mile 134.5 Sterling Highway
RV parking and tent sites. Water, toilets, dump station. Fishing.

Ninilchik Beach Campground
Beach access road, Mile 135 Sterling Highway
35 campsites, toilets, water.

Ninilchik View Campground
Mile 135.7 Sterling Highway, east side of highway
12 campsites, water, toilets, fishing.

Deep Creek State Recreation Area
Mile 137 Sterling Highway
164 sites near excellent halibut and king salmon fishing.

Stariski State Recreation Site
Mile 152 Sterling Highway
Partial hookups, tent camping. Water, picnic shelter, wheelchair-accessible toilets.

Anchor River State Recreation Area
Mile 157.5 turnoff to Anchor River Beach Road
5 campgrounds with more than 150 campsites.

RESTAURANTS

COOPER LANDING:
Gwin's Lodge
Mile 52 Sterling Highway
907-595-1266
Restaurant, bar, cabins, rooms, RV hookups.

SOLDOTNA:
Acapulco Mexican Restaurant
44758 Sterling Highway
907-260-4999
Authentic Mexican cooking.

China Sea Buffet Restaurant
Soldotna Mall, half a mile north of the bridge
907-262-5033
All-you-can-eat buffet, salad bar.

Coffee Concepts
35041 Kenai Spur Highway
907-260-3255
Sandwiches, soups, gourmet coffees, muffins.

Golden Dragon Restaurant
36100 Kenai Spur Road
907-262-6366
Chinese cuisine.

Grand Burrito Restaurant
44096 Sterling Highway
907-262-2228
Mexican fare.

Jersey Subs
44224 Sterling Highway
907-260-3393
Hot and cold submarine sandwiches.

King Salmon Restaurant
35545 Kenai Spur Highway in Best Western Hotel
907-260-8292
Breakfast, lunch and dinner; sack lunches for fishermen.

Mykel's Restaurant & Lounge
35041 Spur Road
907-262-4305
Beef, seafood, especially salmon and halibut.

The Riverside House
44611 Sterling Highway
1-877-262-0500 or 907-262-0500
Riverview dining, lunch and dinner; lounge, nightclub.

Sal's Klondike Diner
Mile 95.5 Sterling Highway
907-262-2220
Alaskan and Yukon burgers, breakfast anytime. Sack lunches to go.

Wild King Grill Restaurant
Mile 101.5 Sterling Highway
907-262-4606
Steaks, halibut, cedar-plank salmon, special desserts.

KENAI:

Burger Bus
Corner of Highland and Upland Streets
Next to Kenai RV Park
907-283-9611
Burgers, hot dogs, fries, and more. Call for pickup.

Charlotte's Restaurant
115 South Willow
907-283-2777
Home cooking and baking. Soups, desserts, and more.

Don Jose's
205 Willow Street
907-283-8181
Authentic Mexican food.

Louie's Steak & Seafood
Mile 47 Spur View Drive
Adjacent to Uptown Motel
907-283-3660
Fine Alaska seafood.

Kenaitze Indian Tribe Salmon Bake
On Mission and Cook
907-283-3612
All-you-can-eat salmon, with cultural stories of Old Kenai.

Veronica's Coffee House
604 Peterson Way
907-283-2725
Food, coffee, live music on weekends, in historic building in Old Town.

HOMER:

Boardwalk Fish & Chips
4287 Homer Spit Road
907-235-7749
Chowder, fresh halibut, and the works.

Captain Patties Fish House
4241 Homer Spit Road
907-235-5135
Lunches and dinners; sack lunches for anglers.

Caribou Family Restaurant
672 East End Road
907-299-1013
Fine dining with a view.

Crabbie's Seafood & Steak House
639 East Pioneer Road
907-235-7300
Steaks, seafood, specials.

Fresh Sourdough Express Bakery & Café
1316 Ocean Drive
907-235-7571
Breakfast, lunch, dinner; box lunches, desserts, espresso, bakery.

Hole in the Wall BBQ & Rib Shack
Homer Spit Road Boardwalk
907-235-8022
Ribs, sandwiches.

Homestead Restaurant
Mile 8 East End Road
907-235-8723
Fine dining, lunches and dinners; views of Kachemak Bay.

Two Sisters Bakery
233 E. Bunnell Street
907-235-2280
Soups, sandwiches, baked goods.

TAYLOR HIGHWAY

Part of the Klondike Loop

From Alaska Highway to Eagle: 160 miles (257 km)

Travel Opportunities: *Town of Chicken; Fortymile gold-mining country; Jack Wade No. 1 Gold Dredge; Eagle; Fort Egbert; Yukon River; riverboat Yukon Queen II.*

The Taylor is the highway for stouthearted drivers who promise to pay close attention to the road; let your navigator take the pictures for you to enjoy later. Partially paved and narrow, the Taylor climbs and descends, turns and doubles back, changing its mind multiple times in a matter of miles as it wends through and above some of the most spectacular country in east-central Alaska. For those who want a taste of what the Alaska Highway used to be like, this is the road.

The Taylor Highway takes off northward from Tetlin Junction on the Alaska Highway, about a dozen miles east of Tok. The Taylor is part of the Klondike Loop, the route over a series of three highways that connects Tok and Whitehorse via Dawson City. (See the sections on the North Klondike Highway and the Top of the World Highway in Chapter 7, Western Canada's Northbound Byways.)

The Taylor provides access to two distinctive Alaska towns, Chicken and Eagle, both of which are steeped in gold-mining history. The towns are inaccessible by road in winter, however. The Taylor is one of the few Alaska highways that is not maintained throughout the winter, meaning that the state does not plow it, making it good for dog-mushing and snowmobile traffic, but not much more.

Chicken is the town that the late author Ann Purdy made famous in *Tisha,* her novel based on her own life. The book details the adventures of a young teacher who moves to Chicken, falls in love with the place and her Athabascan Indian students, and settles down to make it home. She learns that Chicken got its name in 1902 when founding miners couldn't correctly spell the name of the local chickenlike bird, the ptarmigan.

It's easy to pass by the best parts of Chicken if your eyes look dead ahead. At about Mile 66 (106 km) from Tetlin Junction, follow the Airport Road turnoff to the historic Chicken business district. The two dozen or so year-round residents are not on the state's power grid, but generators supply any necessary electricity. Neither have they phones nor plumbing. They get their mail twice a week when the mail plane lands. Nonetheless, the locals operate several gift shops, a couple of restaurants, a saloon, gas station, and salmon bake. The Goldpanner at the Chicken Center hosts RV parking and daily tours of Chicken, including a stop at Tisha's Schoolhouse. The ruins of a locally famous gold dredge, the Jack Wade No. 1, have been a roadside fixture at Mile 86 (138 km); however, in an agreement between the BLM, the state, and the Fortymile Mining Association, plans were made to salvage parts of the dredge and relocate them outside the Chicken post office with interpretive signs explaining the dredge's history.

At Mile 96 (154 km) is the only fork in the highway. At this point, you may choose to continue north on the Taylor Highway to its dead end at the town of Eagle on the Yukon River. Or you may turn east and connect with the Top of the World Highway to continue along the Klondike Loop.

If you turn east, 12 miles (19 km) of travel will take you to the Alaska–Yukon border—and after another 66 miles (105 km) of driving adventure on a winding, unpaved road, you'll land in Dawson City, Yukon. Along the way, you'll catch a glimpse of why they named it the Top of the World Highway. At Dawson City, you can connect with the North Klondike Highway as you proceed along the Klondike Loop.

Each late February and early March, over the course of three weekends, more than a thousand snowmobilers dominate the Taylor and Top of the World Highways during a fun run between Tok and Dawson City that's called the Trek Over the Top. Trekkers travel 200 miles (322 km) one way in a day, stopping to refuel in Chicken. They spend a couple of days seeing Dawson and visiting Diamond Tooth Gerties for entertainment and one-armed bandit fun, then jump back on their machines for the return trip. Since all of the traffic is headed in one direction, and there's no concern of meeting a car or RV on a nasty bend, the snowmobilers pull out all the stops and enjoy the ride.

The Fortymile caribou herd migrates across the Taylor Highway twice a year: from east to west during March and April, and from west to east during October and November. Watch for moose and bears, too.

At the end of the Taylor Highway is Eagle. Imagine this sleepy little town as the hustle-bustle community it was in 1897. The city was crawling with gold miners, traders, merchants, and soldiers; commerce often was conducted with gold. This was a regular stop for the fleet of steam paddleboats that traveled the Yukon, delivering passengers and supplies. Here, too, was Fort Egbert, a military installation that brought order to the gold boomtown.

A mature community when Fairbanks was still merely a forested bend on the Chena River, Eagle was then the seat of the Third Judicial District, with Judge James Wickersham on the bench. The judge would play a major role in Eagle's decline, however, when he made a deal with the founder of Fairbanks, E. T. Barnette, to move the judicial seat from Eagle to Fairbanks. The old courthouse has been restored to its days of yore, as have the old customs building and the adjacent Fort Egbert. From the waterfront, the catamaran *Yukon Queen II* offers daily trips between Eagle and Dawson City.

At the river, you may see rafters preparing for a float trip from Eagle to Circle City, several days away by raft. Planning for this trip takes some extraordinary effort in shuttling vehicles and rafts, as Circle is hundreds of miles away by road at the end of the Steese Highway. But most say it's worth it for the experience of floating through this stretch of the Yukon-Charley Rivers National Preserve. The National Park Service offers informational talks, videos, publications, and books, along the river near historic Fort Egbert. Other rafters or canoeists may be arriving from a Dawson City-to-Eagle excursion. (Having crossed an international border on the water, they need to check in with U.S. Customs at Eagle.)

Eagle is still a part of the active Fortymile Mining District, and gold-mining operations continue in this region. You may meet a gold miner or support crew member during your stay here, as the town is the nearest point of civilization for many of these folks. They'll come into town for mail, gossip, and a change of menu, as well as to stock up on supplies.

For more information on what Eagle has to offer, contact the Eagle Historical Society and Museums at 907-547-2325.

LODGING/MEALS

Eagle Trading Co. Motel
Along the Yukon River, in Eagle
907-547-2220
Rooms, laundry, public showers. Store, fuel, café. Hunting and fishing licenses.

Falcon Inn
220 Front Street, Eagle
907-547-2254
Rooms with private baths, hot breakfast. Walking distance to museums. Along the Yukon River.

CAMPGROUNDS

The Original Chicken Gold Camp
Mile 66.4 Taylor Highway
907-235-6396
24 RV sites, four pull-throughs, some partial hookup. Laundromat, sani-dump, Internet, showers. Summers only.

Chicken Center RV Park
Mile 66.8 Taylor Highway
480-951-5371
24 sites, some with electric, restrooms, sani-dump.

The Bureau of Land Management oversees three camping areas along the Taylor Highway. They are open seasonally, mid–April to October, based on road openings. For more information, contact the Fairbanks District Office at 907–474–2280.

West Fork Campground
Mile 48.5 Taylor Highway
Developed campsites on 20 acres, with 7 pull-throughs, wheelchair-accessible toilets. Fishing.

Walker Fork Campground
Mile 82 Taylor Highway
21 developed campsites on 60 acres. Water, toilets, hiking trails, fishing, gold panning.

Eagle Campground
Mile 160 Taylor Highway
16 developed campsites on 80 acres, with toilets.

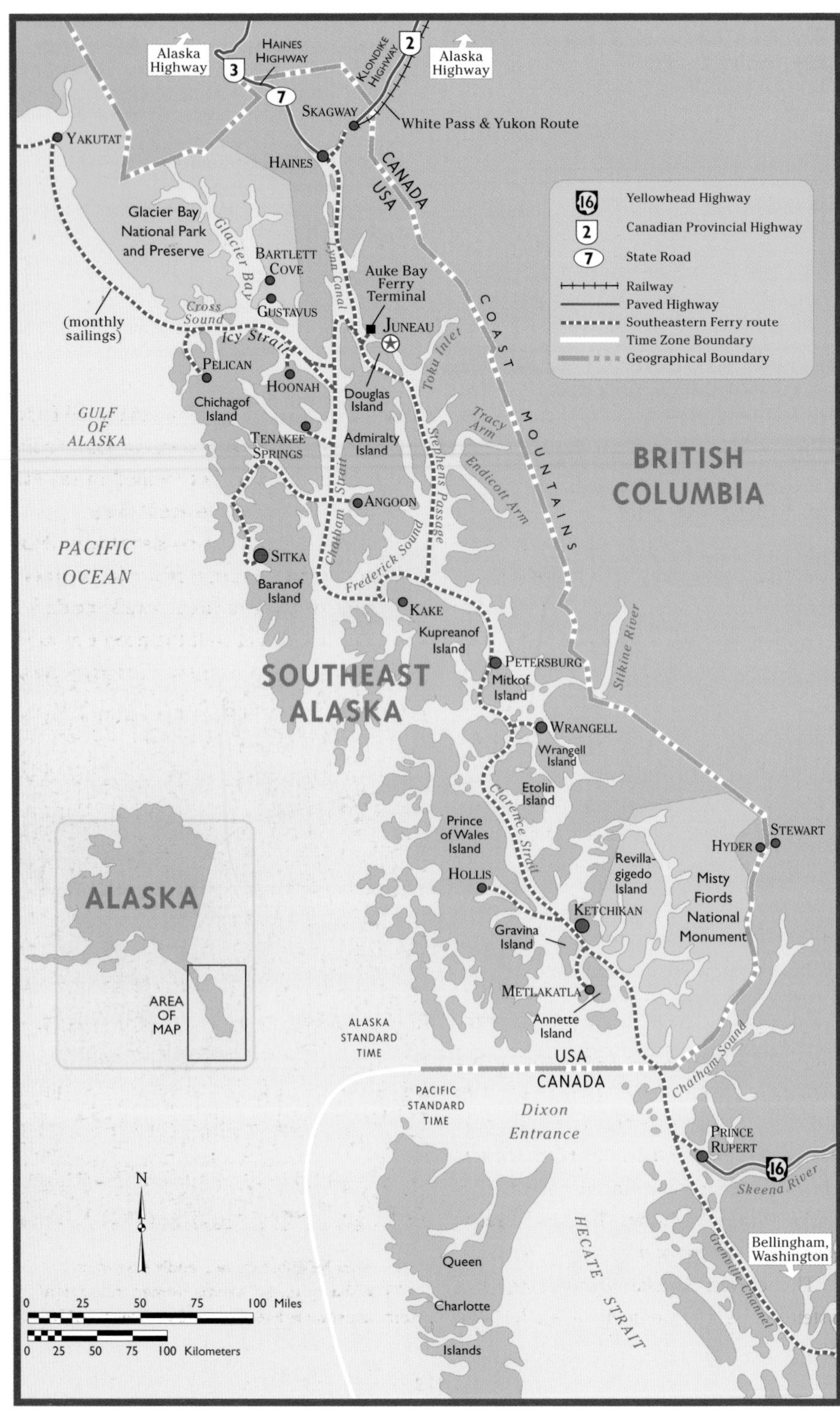
Alaska Highway
Haines Highway
Klondike Highway
Alaska Highway
Skagway
White Pass & Yukon Route
Yakutat
Haines
Canada
USA
Glacier Bay National Park and Preserve
Glacier Bay
Bartlett Cove
Gustavus
Lynn Canal
Auke Bay Ferry Terminal
Juneau
Cross Sound
Icy Strait
(monthly sailings)
Pelican
Hoonah
Douglas Island
Toku Inlet
Coast Mountains
Chichagof Island
Gulf of Alaska
Tenakee Springs
Admiralty Island
Tracy Arm
Stephens Passage
Endicott Arm
British Columbia
Angoon
Chatham Strait
Pacific Ocean
Sitka
Frederick Sound
Baranof Island
Kake
Kupreanof Island
Stikine River
Petersburg
Mitkof Island
Southeast Alaska
Wrangell
Wrangell Island
Etolin Island
Prince of Wales Island
Clarence Strait
Stewart
Hyder
Revillagigedo Island
Misty Fiords National Monument
Hollis
Ketchikan
Alaska
Gravina Island
Metlakatla
Annette Island
Area of Map
Alaska Standard Time
USA
Canada
Chatham Sound
Pacific Standard Time
Dixon Entrance
Prince Rupert
Skeena River
Hecate Strait
Bellingham, Washington
Grenville Channel
Queen Charlotte Islands
N
0 25 50 75 100 Miles
0 25 50 75 100 Kilometers
Yellowhead Highway
Canadian Provincial Highway
State Road
Railway
Paved Highway
Southeastern Ferry route
Time Zone Boundary
Geographical Boundary

CHAPTER 9

Alaska Marine Highway System

THE INSIDE PASSAGE marine route from Washington to Alaska gained international fame in the late 1890s when Klondike miners and their gold arrived in Seattle and ignited a gold rush. The news spread quickly, and people came to believe that riches awaited in the Far North—and that all it took was to jump on a steamer headed up the Inside Passage.

The thrill of traveling by ship on the Inside Passage has taken on a new slant today. Even occasional dreary weather cannot suppress the extraordinary beauty of a trip on these protected waters between mainland and islands. As you travel, you are free to walk the decks, sleep when you're tired, buy a meal when you're hungry, and visit with the people around you. There's nothing else to do but enjoy the incredible vistas as they slowly slide by.

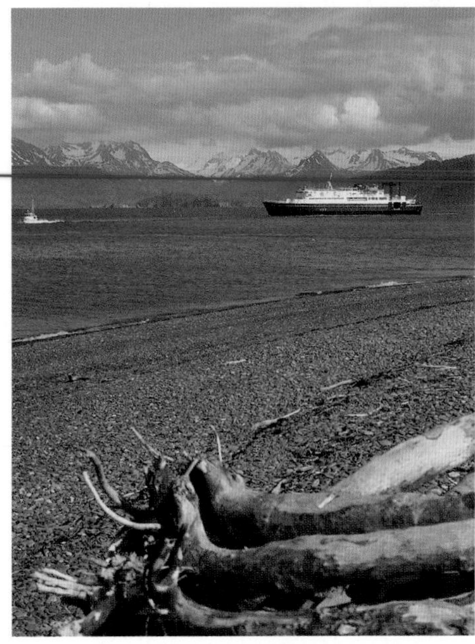

The M/V *Tustamena*, fondly known as "The Trusty Tusty," serves Homer and several other coastal communities in Southcentral Alaska.

Three ferry systems operate in these waters. BC Ferries, an arm of British Columbia's transportation system, owns a fleet of 36 vessels of all sizes, which cruise among the islands and mainland ports of the province. From Victoria to Prince Rupert, with many stops between, BC Ferries connects with the Alaska Marine Highway System at Prince Rupert. The Inter-Island Ferry Authority operates in the southernmost part of the Alaska Panhandle, linking the communities of Coffman Cove and South Mitkof with Wrangell, and Hollis with Ketchikan. In both routes, schedules allow for connections with the Alaska Marine Highway. Their Web site is *www.interislandferry.com*

The eleven Alaska Marine Highway System ferries, affectionately called the "blue canoes," stick to a routine schedule for picking up and dropping off passengers at coastal communities, almost like a vast city bus system. The vessels of the fleet also vary in size and in their specialized routes. In 2005, the M/V *Chenega* joined the fleet, a high-speed ferry operating between Cordova, Valdez, and Whittier in the Southcentral region. Two other newer vessels, inaugurated in 2004, include the M/V *Fairweather* and the M/V *Lituya*.

The southeastern portion of the Alaska system offers scheduled service from Bellingham, Washington, on the southern end, to Prince Rupert, B.C., then farther northward to the cities of Alaska's Inside Passage, up to Skagway.

The southwestern portion of the Alaska system serves the towns and villages of Chenega Bay, Cordova, Homer, Kodiak, Port Lions, Seldovia, Tatitlek, Whittier, and Valdez. And the M/V *Tustamena* sails among the communities of the Aleutian Islands and the Alaska Peninsula: Akutan, Chignik, Cold Bay, False Pass, King Cove, Sand Point, and Unalaska/Dutch Harbor. The M/V *Kennicott*, the largest vessel in the fleet, crosses the Gulf of Alaska every couple of weeks from May to September.

People come aboard the Alaska state ferries on foot, sometimes for a day trip to a nearby town. Or they arrive in campers, ready to drive their rigs into the hold and then head upstairs to a stateroom and a warm bed. Others carry their belongings on their backs. Travelers without a stateroom are welcome to bunk under the stars on the vessel's top deck. This is freedom at its finest—come one, come all—and presents plenty of opportunity to make friends with someone from a local village or someone from the other side of the planet.

Major ports of call in Southeast Alaska are Ketchikan, Wrangell, Petersburg, Sitka, Juneau, Haines, and Skagway. Between them, shorter trips link larger towns with the villages of Kake, Angoon, Tenakee Springs, Hoonah, Metlakatla, and Pelican.

These major Inside Passage ports each claim a unique personality: Petersburg, the fishing town with Norwegian roots; Sitka, the former capital of Russian America, as Alaska was known before its 1867 purchase by the United States; Native villages that welcome visitors eager to know more about Tlingit, Haida, and Tsimshian culture; Juneau, Alaska's capital—and, like most Southeast Alaska towns, inaccessible by road. Skagway and Haines, the northernmost ports in Southeast Alaska, are connected to the Alaska Highway by spur roads. (See the sections on the Haines Highway and Klondike Highway 2 in Chapter 8, Alaska's State Highways.) Consider a southbound trip on the marine highway as a way to return home after your northbound drive up the Alaska Highway.

The cost for passage depends on distance between ports, whether a stateroom is reserved, length of your vehicle, and other factors. You can customize your trip so that you can disembark and tour the towns of your choice before continuing on your journey.

Here are some contacts for more information on marine travel in Alaska and along the Inside Passage:

Alaska Marine Highway System
1-800-642-0066 or 907-465-3941
www.ferryalaska.com

BC Ferries
1-888-223-3779 from anywhere in North America
250-386-3431 from outside North America
www.bcferries.com

Inter-Island Ferry Authority
1-866-308-4848 or 907-826-4848
www.interislandferry.com

Further Reading

Canada

Berton, Pierre. *The Klondike Fever.* New York: Carroll & Graf, 1985.

———. *The Klondike Quest: A Photographic Essay 1897–1899.* North York, Ontario: Stoddart Publishing, 1997.

Bruhn, Karl. *Best of B.C.: Lake Fishing.* Vancouver, B.C.: Whitecap Books, 1998.

Coull, Cheryl. *A Traveller's Guide to Aboriginal B.C.* Vancouver, B.C.: Whitecap Books, 1996.

Madsen, Ken, and Graham Wilson. *Rivers of the Yukon: A Paddling Guide.* Whitehorse, Yukon: Primrose Publishing, 1990.

Neering, Rosemary. *A Traveller's Guide to Historic B.C.* Vancouver, B.C.: Whitecap Books, 1993.

Schofield, Janice J. *Discovering Wild Plants: Alaska, Western Canada, the Northwest.* Portland, Oregon: Alaska Northwest Books, 1989.

Short, Steve, and Bernie Palmer. *Best of B.C.: Exploring Canyons, Glaciers, Hotsprings, and Other Natural Highs.* Vancouver, B.C.: Whitecap Books, 1992.

Wolf Creek. *The Klondike Gold Rush: Photographs from 1896–1899.* Whitehorse, Yukon: Wolf Creek, 1997.

Zuehlke, Mark. *The Alberta Fact Book.* Vancouver, B.C.: Whitecap Books, 1997.

———. *The B.C. Fact Book.* Vancouver, B.C.: Whitecap Books, 1995.

———. *The Yukon Fact Book.* Vancouver, B.C.: Whitecap Books, 1998.

Alaska

Alaska Geographic. *Denali.* Anchorage: Alaska Geographic Society, 1995.

———. *Kenai Peninsula.* Anchorage: Alaska Geographic Society, 1997.

———. *Southeast Panhandle.* Anchorage: Alaska Geographic Society, 1997.

Alaska Northwest Books. *The Alaska Almanac: Facts About Alaska, 31st ed.* Portland, Oregon: Alaska Northwest Books, 2007.

———. *The Alaska–Yukon Wild Flowers Guide.* Portland, Oregon: Alaska Northwest Books, 1990.

Armstrong, Robert. *Guide to the Birds of Alaska, 5th ed.* Portland, Oregon: Alaska Northwest Books, updated 2008.

Brown, Tricia, ed. *Alaskan Wilderness* (Discovery Travel Adventures). London: Discovery Channel Inc., 1999.

———. *Fairbanks: Alaska's Heart of Gold.* Portland, Oregon: Alaska Northwest Books, 2000.

Ewing, Susan. *The Great Alaska Nature Factbook.* Portland, Oregon: Alaska Northwest Books, 1996.

Hunt, William R. *North of 53°: The Wild Days of the Alaska–Yukon Mining Frontier, 1870–1914.* New York: Macmillan, 1974.

Jettmar, Karen. *The Alaska River Guide: Canoeing, Kayaking, and Rafting in the Last Frontier, 2nd ed.* Portland, Oregon: Alaska Northwest Books, 1998.

Kelley, Mark, and Sherry Simpson. *Alaska's Ocean Highways: A Travel Adventure Aboard Northern Ferries.* Seattle: Epicenter Press, 1995.

Littlepage, Dean. *Hiking Alaska.* Helena, Montana: Falcon Publishing Co., 1997.

Maschmeyer, Gloria (text), and Alissa Crandall (photography). *Along the Alaska Highway.* Portland, Oregon: Alaska Northwest Books, 1992.

Morgan, Lael. *Good Time Girls of the Alaska–Yukon Gold Rush.* Seattle: Epicenter Press, 1998.

Murie, Margaret E. *Two in the Far North, 2nd ed.* Portland, Oregon: Alaska Northwest Books, 1997.

Murphy, Claire Rudolf, and Jane G. Haigh. *Gold Rush Women.* Portland, Oregon: Alaska Northwest Books, 1997.

Piper, Ernie. *Alaska Sportfishing.* Anchorage: Alaska Geographic Guides, 1997.

Ritter, Harry. *Alaska's History: The People, Land, and Events of the North Country.* Portland, Oregon: Alaska Northwest Books, 1993.

Satterfield, Archie. *Chilkoot Pass: A Hiker's Historical Guide.* Portland, Oregon: Alaska Northwest Books, updated 2004.

Sherwonit, Bill. *Alaska's Bears: Grizzlies, Black Bears, and Polar Bears.* Portland, Oregon: Alaska Northwest Books, 1998.

Simmerman, Nancy (photography), Helen Nienhueser, and Johnson Wolfe. *55 Ways to the Wilderness of Southcentral Alaska, 4th ed.* Seattle: The Mountaineers Books, 1994.

——— and Tricia Brown. *Wild Alaska: The Complete Guide to Parks, Preserves, Wildlife Refuges, & Other Public Lands, 2nd ed.* Seattle: The Mountaineers Books, 1999.

Smith, Dave. *Backcountry Bear Basics: The Definitive Guide to Avoiding Unpleasant Encounters.* Seattle: The Mountaineers, 1997.

———. *Alaska's Mammals.* Portland, Oregon: Alaska Northwest Books, 1995.

Distance Charts

Distances in Western Canada and the U.S.

In **Miles** *and* Kilometers

	Cache Creek, BC	Calgary, AB	Dawson City, YT	Dawson Creek, BC	Edmonton, AB	Fairbanks, AK	Fort Nelson, BC	Great Falls, MT	Prince George, BC	Seattle, WA	Watson Lake, YT	Whitehorse, YT
Anchorage, AK	**2135**	**2160**	**515**	**1608**	**1975**	**363**	**1281**	**2473**	**1678**	**2435**	**967**	**724**
	3416	3456	824	2573	3160	581	2136	3960	2685	3896	1611	1158
Cache Creek, BC		**438**	**1722**	**527**	**545**	**2013**	**800**	**753**	**277**	**294**	**1139**	**1411**
		701	2755	843	872	3221	1280	1205	443	470	1822	2258
Calgary, AB			**1747**	**549**	**108**	**2037**	**835**	**315**	**635**	**738**	**1164**	**1436**
			2795	878	291	3259	1336	504	1016	1181	1862	2298
Dawson City, YT				**1195**	**1562**	**393**	**900**	**2078**	**1390**	**2022**	**586**	**327**
				1912	2499	629	1501	3325	2318	3235	976	523
Dawson Creek, BC					**367**	**1488**	**282**	**867**	**250**	**821**	**612**	**886**
					587	2395	451	1387	400	1314	979	1418
Edmonton, AB						**1855**	**630**	**500**	**442**	**790**	**979**	**1253**
						2968	1050	800	737	1264	1566	2005
Fairbanks, AK							**1206**	**2353**	**1728**	**2313**	**875**	**601**
							1930	3765	2781	3701	1400	962
Fort Nelson, BC								**1335**	**532**	**1027**	**330**	**604**
								2225	851	1712	528	966
Great Falls, MT									**790**	**681**	**1615**	**1731**
									1317	1090	2692	2731
Prince George, BC										**571**	**737**	**983**
										914	1228	1639
Seattle, WA											**1272**	**1707**
											2120	2781
Watson Lake, YT												**274**
												438
Whitehorse, YT												

To read, choose a place-name at the bottom of a column and scan upward to meet the corresponding horizontal line.

Distances within Alaska

In **Miles** *and* Kilometers

	Circle	Delta Junction	Eagle	Fairbanks	Glennallen	Haines	Homer	Prudhoe Bay	Seward	Skagway	Tok	Valdez
Anchorage	**520**	**338**	**501**	**363**	**187**	**775**	**226**	**847**	**127**	**832**	**328**	**304**
	832	541	802	581	299	1240	362	1355	204	1331	525	486
Circle		**260**	**541**	**162**	**411**	**815**	**746**	**1972**	**646**	**872**	**368**	**526**
		416	866	259	658	1304	1194	3155	1034	1395	589	842
Delta Junction			**281**	**98**	**151**	**805**	**564**	**587**	**464**	**603**	**108**	**266**
			450	157	242	1288	902	939	742	965	173	426
Eagle				**379**	**324**	**620**	**727**	**868**	**627**	**579**	**173**	**427**
				606	518	992	1163	1389	1003	926	277	683
Fairbanks					**249**	**653**	**584**	**489**	**487**	**710**	**206**	**364**
					398	1045	934	783	779	1136	330	582
Glennallen						**589**	**413**	**738**	**313**	**636**	**141**	**115**
						942	661	1181	501	1018	226	184
Haines							**1001**	**1142**	**901**	**359**	**447**	**701**
							1602	1827	1442	574	715	1122
Homer								**1073**	**173**	**1058**	**554**	**530**
								1717	277	1693	886	848
Prudhoe Bay									**973**	**1199**	**695**	**853**
									1557	1918	1112	1365
Seward										**958**	**454**	**430**
										1533	726	688
Skagway											**504**	**758**
											806	1213
Tok												**254**
												406
												Valdez

To read, choose a place-name at the bottom of a column and scan upward to meet the corresponding horizontal line.

Index

Page numbers in *bold italic* indicate maps.
Towns are identified with their province or state: AB–Alberta, AK–Alaska, BC–British Columbia, MT–Montana, NT–Northwest Territories, WA–Washington, YT–Yukon Territory

N

O

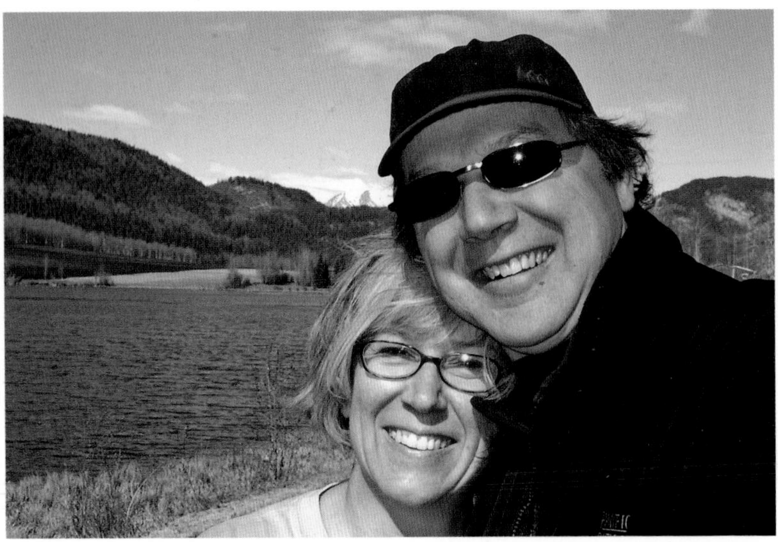

Tricia and Perry Brown pause for a photo at the Toad River Lodge and Campground in northern British Columbia.

About the Author

TRICIA BROWN is the author of numerous books on Alaska subjects, for adults as well as for the younger readers in the house. Look for these other titles at your favorite bookstore:

For Children:

Children of the Midnight Sun
Groucho's Eyebrows
The Itchy Little Musk Ox
The Alaskan Night Before Christmas

For Adults:

The Iditarod Fact Book
Sled Dog Wisdom
Wild Alaska
Fairbanks: Alaska's Heart of Gold